Care-Based Methodologies

Also Available from Bloomsbury

Children's Transitions in Everyday Life and Institutions,
edited by Mariane Hedegaard and Marilyn Fleer
Ethics and Research with Young Children: New Perspectives,
edited by Christopher M. Schulte
Feminist Research for 21st-century Childhoods, edited by B. Denise Hodgins
Feminists Researching Gendered Childhoods: Generative Entanglements,
edited by Jayne Osgood and Kerry H. Robinson
Friedrich Froebel: A Critical Introduction to Key Themes and Debates, by Tina Bruce
Give Children the Vote: On Democratizing Democracy, by John Wall
Post-Qualitative Research and Innovative Methodologies,
edited by Matthew K E Thomas and Robin Bellingham
Promoting Children's Rights in European Schools: Intercultural Dialogue and Facilitative Pedagogy, by Claudio Baraldi, Erica Joslyn, Federico Farini, Chiara Ballestri, Luisa Conti, Vittorio Iervese and Angela Scollan
Qualitative Studies of Exploration in Childhood Education: Cultures of Play and Learning in Transition, edited by Marilyn Fleer, Mariane Hedegaard,
Elin Eriksen Ødegaard and Hanne Værum Sørensen
Research Methods for Early Childhood Education, by Rosie Flewitt and Lynn Ang
Rethinking Philosophy for Children: Agamben and Education as Pure Means,
by Tyson E. Lewis and Igor Jasinski
Supporting Difficult Transitions: Children, Young People and Their Carers,
edited by Mariane Hedegaard and Anne Edwards
The Bloomsbury Handbook of Culture and Identity from Early Childhood to Early Adulthood: Perceptions and Implications, edited by Ruth Wills, Marian de Souza,
Jennifer Mata-McMahon, Mukhlis Abu Bakar and Cornelia Roux
Transition and Continuity in School Literacy Development, edited by Pauline Jones,
Erika Matruglio and Christine Edwards-Groves
Why Do Teachers Need to Know About Child Development?: Strengthening Professional Identity and Well-Being, edited by Daryl Maisey and Verity Campbell-Barr

Care-Based Methodologies

Reimagining Qualitative Research with Youth in US Schools

Edited by Veena Vasudevan, Nora Gross,
Pavithra Nagarajan, and Katherine Clonan-Roy

BLOOMSBURY ACADEMIC
LONDON · NEW YORK · OXFORD · NEW DELHI · SYDNEY

BLOOMSBURY ACADEMIC
Bloomsbury Publishing Plc
50 Bedford Square, London, WC1B 3DP, UK
1385 Broadway, New York, NY 10018, USA
29 Earlsfort Terrace, Dublin 2, Ireland

BLOOMSBURY, BLOOMSBURY ACADEMIC and the Diana logo
are trademarks of Bloomsbury Publishing Plc

First published in Great Britain 2022
This paperback edition published in 2023

Copyright © Veena Vasudevan, Nora Gross, Pavithra Nagarajan,
Katherine Clonan-Roy and Bloomsbury,

Veena Vasudevan, Nora Gross, Pavithra Nagarajan, Katherine Clonan-Roy and
Bloomsbury have asserted their right under the Copyright, Designs and
Patents Act, 1988, to be identified as Author of this work.

For legal purposes the Acknowledgments on p. xiv constitute
an extension of this copyright page.

Cover design: Charlotte James
Cover image © XiXinXing/ iStock

All rights reserved. No part of this publication may be reproduced or transmitted
in any form or by any means, electronic or mechanical, including photocopying,
recording, or any information storage or retrieval system, without prior
permission in writing from the publishers.

Bloomsbury Publishing Plc does not have any control over, or responsibility for,
any third-party websites referred to or in this book. All internet addresses given
in this book were correct at the time of going to press. The author and publisher
regret any inconvenience caused if addresses have changed or sites have
ceased to exist, but can accept no responsibility for any such changes.

A catalogue record for this book is available from the British Library.

Library of Congress Cataloging-in-Publication Data
Names: Vasudevan, Veena, editor. | Gross, Nora, editor. | Nagarajan,
Pavithra, editor. | Clonan-Roy, Katherine, editor.
Title: Care-based methodologies: reimagining qualitative research with
youth in US schools / Edited by Veena Vasudevan, Nora Gross, Pavithra
Nagarajan, and Katherine Clonan-Roy.
Description: London; New York: Bloomsbury Academic, 2022. |
Includes bibliographical references and index.
Identifiers: LCCN 2021035399 (print) | LCCN 2021035400 (ebook) |
ISBN 9781350215597 (hardback) | ISBN 9781350215603 (pdf) |
ISBN 9781350215610 (ebook)
Subjects: LCSH: Youth with social disabilities–Education–United States. |
Education–Research–United States–Methodology. | Critical pedagogy–United States.
Classification: LCC LC4069.3 .C37 2022 (print) |
LCC LC4069.3 (ebook) | DDC 371.826/94–dc23
LC record available at https://lccn.loc.gov/2021035399
LC ebook record available at https://lccn.loc.gov/2021035400

ISBN: HB: 978-1-3502-1559-7
PB: 978-1-3502-1563-4
ePDF: 978-1-3502-1560-3
eBook: 978-1-3502-1561-0

Typeset by Integra Software Services Pvt. Ltd.

To find out more about our authors and books visit www.bloomsbury.com
and sign up for our newsletters.

Contents

List of Figures	vii
List of Contributors	viii
Acknowledgments	xiv
Foreword	
Yolanda Sealey-Ruiz	xv
Introduction: Caring in Research with Youth in Schools *Veena Vasudevan, Nora Gross, Pavithra Nagarajan, and Katherine Clonan-Roy*	1

Part I Re/Unlearning Our Orientation to Research: Critical Frameworks for Research in Schools

1. *All or Nothing*: Demystifying the "What," "When," and "How" of Participant Observation in School-Based Research with Black Youth *Natalie R. Davis and Alaina Neal-Jackson* — 19
2. *Platicando entre Compañeras*: The Use of *Pláticas* to Navigate Ethical Dilemmas in Ethnographic Research with and for Latina High School Students *Bianca N. Haro* — 31
3. Care as Resistance and Epistemological Necessity in YPAR *Meagan Call-Cummings and Melissa Hauber-Özer* — 45

Part II Collaborating and Co-Creating with Youth: Caring through Sharing Ownership of the Research

4. From Hallway Conversations to Making Together: How Care Can Shift Relationships with Young People in Schools *Veena Vasudevan* — 59
5. "The Life of Julio Good": The Black Ratchet Imagination and Messy Methods as Caring Ethics *Ariana Brazier* — 73
6. The Reception and Reward of Relationship-Building and Enacting Care with Black Boys *Pavithra Nagarajan* — 89
7. Developing Sustainable Partnerships between Researchers and Youth Participants: Fostering Shared Learning across Time and Difference *Matthew R. Deroo and Ilhan Mohamud* — 103

Part III Negotiating Emergent Tensions: Developing and Sustaining Caring Relationships with Youth

8   Intervening through Intimate Inquiry with Youth *Katherine Clonan-Roy* 119
9   A "Friend" or an "Experiment"?: The Paradox of Ethnographic Relationships with Youth *Nora Gross* 133
10 Unraveling a Researcher's Practices of Care with One Disabled Youth *Katie Scott Newhouse* 147
11 Culturally Responsive Caring and Emergent Tensions in a Bilingual Mentoring Program in a Diverse School *James S. Chisholm, Melanie Jones Gast, and Ashley L. Shelton* 159

Part IV Collaborating with Universities, Communities, and Schools: Navigating the Challenges of Caring Research Partnerships

12 Conceptions of Care and Graduate Student Researcher Positionality: Struggling to Reconcile "Researcher" Care with Personal Moral Commitments *Van Anh Tran, Errol C. Saunders II, Shamari Reid, and Lum Fube* 175
13 Pedagogical Reflections: Teaching Care in Qualitative Research Classrooms *Stephanie Masta and Ophélie Allyssa Desmet* 187
14 Establishing, Executing, and Extending Caring Community-Based Research Partnerships *Charity Lisko, Katie Woolford, and Rand Quinn* 197
15 *Just* Inquiry Rooted in Critical Care: Participatory, Intergenerational Research Tracing the Legacy of School in the Square *Samuel Finesurrey, Camille Lester, Sherry King, Michelle Fine, and the Intergenerational S2 Research Collective* 211

Conclusion: Caring in Contentious Times *Veena Vasudevan, Nora Gross, Pavithra Nagarajan, and Katherine Clonan-Roy* 225

Notes 229
References 233
Index 256

Figures

5.1	Katelyn's writing and drawings in my notebook	85
6.1	David Sanchez's photograph in response to the prompt: "Take a photo of a place where you feel comfortable or that you belong"	98
6.2	Isaiah Edwards' photograph in response to the prompt: "Take a photo of something that represents 'Manhood'"	100
8.1	Conceptual framework for care-based research	121
10.1	School cafeteria	154
14.1	Caring community-based research partnerships	200
15.1	Student drawing	212
15.2	Student drawing	213
15.3	Student drawing	213
15.4	Our research collective	215
15.5	Just inquiry: Commitments, enactments, and citations	218
15.6	Word cloud	222

Contributors

Ariana Brazier is a play-driven community-organizer and educator. She has a PhD in English, Critical and Cultural Studies from the University of Pittsburgh, USA. Her research centers Black children living in poverty and their play as an intergenerational community-building practice. Brazier is also the cofounder of ATL Parent Like A Boss, Inc., which is a 501(c)(3) nonprofit whose mission is to enhance generational literacies through play in underserved African American communities. She is also the vice president of Products & Storytelling at Daymaker, which helps organizational partners connect deeper with their community, their team, and themselves through intentional acts of giving and service.

Meagan Call-Cummings is Assistant Professor of Qualitative Research Methods in the College of Education and Human Development at George Mason University, USA. Call-Cummings teaches courses in qualitative inquiry, narrative inquiry, and participatory action research. Her research takes youth participatory action research forms and, most recently, she has been working with high school students and teachers on a project called Courageous Conversations, which uses critical arts-based inquiry to help students express themselves on social issues including racial injustice, global warming, immigration policy, and LGBTQ rights. She holds a PhD from Indiana University, Bloomington, USA.

James S. Chisholm is Associate Professor in the College of Education & Human Development, University of Louisville, USA. He studies inquiry-based literature discussions and adolescents' multimodal literacy practices in high school English classrooms. In his current research projects, he examines the roles of young adult literature and the arts in promoting social transformation and the affordances of digital tools in supporting English teachers' response to writing. His research has appeared in journals such as *Research in the Teaching of English*, *Journal of Literacy Research*, *Journal of Adolescent & Adult Literacy*, and the *60th Yearbook of the Literacy Research Association*.

Katherine Clonan-Roy is Assistant Professor in the College of Education and Human Services' Department of Curriculum and Foundations at Cleveland State University, USA. Her research focuses on the intersections of education, adolescent development, and gender and sexuality studies. Her current work takes on intersectional and critical perspectives in examining the experiences of nondominant youth in all-girls schools, inequities in school-based sexuality education for sexual and gender diverse youth, and the preparation and education of justice-focused teachers.

Natalie R. Davis is Assistant Professor in the Department of Early Childhood and Elementary Education and for the MA program in Creative and Innovative Education at Georgia State University, USA. Broadly, her research explores the relationship between teaching and learning, cultural ecologies, and the sociopolitical development of children from nondominant communities with emphasis on the educational experiences and "freedom dreams" of urban-based Black children. Her work also considers the challenges and possibilities of political education in elementary classrooms and the extent to which learning environments nourish children's imaginative spirits. She holds a PhD from the University of Michigan, USA.

Matthew R. Deroo is Assistant Professor in the Department of Teaching and Learning in the School of Education and Human Development at the University of Miami, USA. His research interests include the social and cultural contexts of transnational immigrant youth, critical, digital media literacies, language education, and community-engaged scholarship. Deroo's work draws upon his ten years of experience as a language teacher and teacher-educator in China.

Ophélie Allyssa Desmet is Assistant Professor in the Dewar College of Education and Human Services at Valdosta State University, USA. Her research focuses on underachievement, achievement motivation, and talent development among historically underrepresented student populations. She started her career as a K-16 educator and founded and cochairs the Underachievement Resource Institute in Belgium.

Michelle Fine is Distinguished Professor of Critical Psychology and Urban Education at the Graduate Center, City University of New York, USA, and Professor Extraordinarius at the University of South Africa. Her primary research interest is the study of social injustice: when injustice appears as fair or deserved, when it is resisted, and how it is negotiated by those who pay the most serious price for social inequities. She studies these issues in public high schools, prisons, and with youth in urban communities, using both qualitative and quantitative methods. Her recent work includes the book, *Just Research: Widening the Methodological Imagination* (2017).

Samuel Finesurrey is Assistant Adjunct Professor in the Urban Studies Department at Guttman Community College, USA. With his students, Finesurrey founded Voices from the Heart of Gotham: The Undergraduate Scholars Oral History Collection at Guttman Community College, which has gathered hundreds of oral histories—as pedagogy and historic method—to cultivate in his students a sense of themselves as knowledge producers and to build an archive for the college. He earned a PhD in Cuban History with specializations in IS foreign policy and oral history at University of North Carolina, Chapel Hill, USA, in 2018.

Lum Fube is a doctoral student in the Department of Curriculum and Teaching at Teachers College, Columbia University, USA. Her background is in early childhood education and working with preservice teachers. Her research interests include ecologies and the roles of individuals and pedagogies enacted within ecologies, policies, and its impact on varying ecologies, and how conceptions of social and emotional well-being are enacted by individuals within the ecologies.

Melanie Jones Gast is Associate Professor in the Department of Sociology at the University of Louisville, USA. Her research focuses on contemporary racism, mechanisms of inclusion/exclusion, and support opportunities in schools and community programs serving diverse racial and ethnic groups. In one project, she analyzes counseling norms and racial and class stratification in a diverse high school. Other projects examine intersections of race, citizenship, and language statuses and the inclusion of immigrant youth and parents. She has published in journals such as the *Du Bois Review, Ethnic and Racial Studies, Journal of Adolescent Research, Teachers College Record,* and *Urban Education.*

Nora Gross is Core Fellow and Visiting Assistant Professor in Sociology at Boston College, USA. She received her PhD in sociology and education from the University of Pennsylvania, USA, in 2020, where she was a Harry Frank Guggenheim Dissertation Fellow. Her research examines educational inequality with a focus on race, gender, and emotion in secondary school contexts. She is currently working on a book manuscript from her dissertation research: an ethnographic study of the role of grief in the school lives of Black adolescent boys who lose friends to neighborhood gun violence and the school practices and policies that shape their emotional and educational recovery. A secondary project explores the way white students in elite private high schools experience their schools' diversity and inclusion effort. Prior to doctoral studies, Gross earned an MA in sociology of education at New York University, USA, and directed a Chicago high school writing center. She is also a documentary filmmaker, often collaborating with youth on film projects.

Bianca N. Haro is a feminista-educator-activist and a first-generation college graduate and daughter of immigrant parents from Guadalajara, Jalisco, Mexico. Currently, she is Visiting Assistant Professor of Sociology at Pitzer College, USA. Using a Critical Race Feminista Praxis, her research examines the factors that push Latina students out of school. Her commitment to research is paired with a dedication to organizing with Communities of Color. She is currently collaborating with Gente Organizada, a predominantly Latinx community-led social action nonprofit organization based in Pomona, California, USA, which focuses on educational, economic, and social justice. In partnership with the ACLU of Southern California, USA, Haro supported the analysis of Pomona Police Department's arrest data recorded between 2016 and 2020, which led to the publication of a report titled *Pomona Police Department's Crusade against Black and Latinx Youth.* Her research agenda is a lifelong commitment to centering the voices of youth who are often overlooked in research, policy, practice, and social justice efforts.

Melissa Hauber-Özer is Adjunct Faculty in the College of Education and Human Development at George Mason University, USA, where she instructs teacher education and research methods courses. Her research focuses on language and literacy education in migration contexts and employs critical participatory methodology to examine issues of equity and access for linguistically and culturally diverse learners. Prior to completing her PhD in International Education at George Mason University, USA, Hauber-Özer taught adult literacy, English as a second language, and German in several community-based and university programs in Philadelphia and Northern Virginia in the USA.

Sherry King has been a high school English teacher, high school assistant principal, principal, and superintendent of schools. After over thirty years based in New York, USA, she led Field Services for America's Choice, a comprehensive school improvement organization that grew out of the National Center on Education and the Economy. Today, King spends much of her time supporting School in the Square Public Charter School as well as other educational consulting. She has a BA from University of Pennsylvania, USA; MAT from Manhattanville College, USA; and EdD from Teachers College, Columbia University, USA.

Camille Lester is a doctoral student in Developmental Psychology at the Graduate Center, City University of New York, USA.

Charity Lisko is an independent education consultant who designs and supports the implementation of elementary STEM curricula in the United States and abroad. Throughout her career, Lisko has advocated for increasing access and inclusion in STEM education efforts at national, district, school, and classroom levels. Two questions encountered in her graduate studies at the University of Pennsylvania, USA, continue to shape her work today: how can academic research better serve and support the participating individuals and communities and how can teachers, administrators, and other practitioners better access and effectively apply research in their practice?

Stephanie Masta is Associate Professor in Curriculum Studies at Purdue University, USA. She is also a member of the Sault Ste. Marie tribe of Chippewa Indians. In her role, Masta teaches multiple courses on qualitative research methods, including several classes on the use of Indigenous and critical methodologies in educational research. Masta is particularly interested in the intersections of race and colonialism in the academy and how underrepresented students make meaning of their sense of place within academic spaces.

Ilhan Mohamud is a student at a research-based university in the Midwest studying for a career in the medical field. Her engagement with social media and her interests in global politics developed in response to individuals who posted disparaging things about Islam in online spaces but appeared to know little about her lived experiences.

Pavithra Nagarajan is Senior Research Associate at the Institute for State and Local Governance at City University of New York, USA. Nagarajan earned her PhD in sociology and education in the Department of Education Policy and Social Analysis at Teachers College, Columbia University, USA. Her research interests include urban education, school culture and discipline, school socialization, race, gender, masculinity, identity, and boyhood. Her doctoral dissertation and related publications examine how adolescent boys of color in a single-sex school experience, negotiate, and reconcile school (re)definitions of and messaging about masculinity. Nagarajan began her career in education as a founding teacher in a single-sex public school for boys, teaching 6th grade mathematics, social studies, and art.

Alaina Neal-Jackson is Postdoctoral Fellow in the School of Education at the University of Michigan, USA, where she earned her PhD in educational foundations and policy. Her research is centered on race and gender in schooling as per a larger interest in the health and welfare of Black students, particularly, but not singularly, in underserved contexts. More specifically, drawing upon sociological frames and critical race and gender theories, Neal-Jackson examines how schools, as social institutions, structure Black girls' and women's experiences and opportunities and in what ways this structuring reproduces social inequalities along raced, gendered, and classed lines.

Katie Scott Newhouse is Postdoctoral Fellow in the Media and Social Change Lab (MASCLab) at Teachers College, Columbia University, USA. Her fields of study include disability studies in education, disability justice, and critical spatial theory. Her research focuses on the experiences of youth mandated to attend specialized restricted programs (such as special education and juvenile justice) and the spatial implications of enrollment in these programs. She uses qualitative ethnographic multimodal methods alongside narrative inquiry to theorize about restricted educational programs from the lived experiences of people within them.

Rand Quinn is Associate Professor of Education at the University of Pennsylvania, USA. He studies the origins and consequences of education organizing and activism, the politics of race and class in urban school reform, and the impact of private and voluntary sector engagement in public education.

Shamari Reid is Assistant Professor of Critical Studies in Education at the University of Oklahoma, USA. His specific research interests include Black youth agency, the role of critical love in education, and transformative teacher education.

Errol C. Saunders II is a doctoral student in the Department of Curriculum and Teaching at Teachers College, Columbia University, USA, as well as an experienced middle- and high school humanities teacher. His research interests include public pedagogies, how students are socialized into schooling, and how crossing geographic boundaries affects students' school transitions.

Yolanda Sealey-Ruiz is an award-winning Associate Professor at Teachers College, Columbia University, USA. Her research focuses on racial literacy in teacher education, Black girl literacies, and Black and Latinx male high school students. Sealey-Ruiz works with K-12 and higher education school communities to increase their racial literacy knowledge and move toward more equitable school experiences for their Black and Latinx students. Sealey-Ruiz appeared in Spike Lee's "2 Fists Up: We Gon' Be Alright," a documentary about the Black Lives Matter movement and the campus protests at Mizzou. Her coauthored book, *Advancing Racial Literacies in Teacher Education: Toward Activism for Equity in Digital Spaces*, was published in 2021; her first full-length collection of poetry, *Love from the Vortex & Other Poems*, was published in 2020; and her sophomore book of poetry, *The Peace Chronicles*, was also published in 2021.

Ashley L. Shelton is Clinical Assistant Professor in the College of Education & Human Development at the University of Louisville, Kentucky, USA. She researches the ways in which discussion practices in the classroom shape identities, circulate power, and foster agency. In one project, she analyzes how critical talk on political topics can encourage the development of perspective taking as teachers learn to navigate disagreement in the classroom. Her research has appeared in the *Journal of Adolescent and Adult Literacy*, *The ALAN Review*, and *English Journal*.

Van Anh Tran is a doctoral candidate in the Department of Social Studies Education at Teachers College, Columbia University, USA. Formerly a high school history teacher, Tran works with pre-service and in-service teachers in curriculum development and instruction. Moreover, she finds joy in collaborating with grassroots community organizations as a facilitator and curriculum developer. Her research interests include refugee narratives, collective memory, community organizing and action, healing justice, and notions of belonging.

Veena Vasudevan is Assistant Professor of Digital Media and Learning in the School of Education at University of Pittsburgh, USA. Her research agenda explores STEM learning, educational equity, and urban education with an emphasis on understanding the lives of children and youth through the lenses of identity, learning, and literacies. She draws on multimodal ethnographic and qualitative methods in her research work. She holds a Master of Public Administration (MPA) from the School of International and Public Affairs at Columbia University, USA, and a PhD from the Graduate School of Education at the University of Pennsylvania, USA.

Katie Woolford is a data analytics officer at the City of Philadelphia's Office of Children and Families, Philadelphia, USA. She is responsible for managing reporting portfolios tied to education support, early childhood, and child welfare. Prior to working in child welfare, Woolford conducted mixed methods research and evaluations for educational systems and out-of-school time programs. She also taught 2nd grade in Baltimore, Maryland, USA, and received her master's in education policy from the University of Pennsylvania, USA.

Acknowledgments

This book is the product of a multitude of caring relationships and would not have been possible without them.

We are thankful to the students who were part of our respective research studies from whom we learned a great deal about the importance of care and love. It was our relationships with young people and their willingness to share with us, to let us spend time with them, and to express and receive care that ultimately inspired this work and kept us committed to it. We also want to acknowledge the educators and staff members at our various school sites who were supportive of our presence and our projects.

We are so grateful to each of our chapter authors for sharing their important work and going with us on this journey; their work deepened our understanding of care in research. Throughout an incredibly challenging period of time, they inspired us, pushed our thinking, and received our care, and we will forever be grateful.

We want to thank Yolanda Sealey-Ruiz for her thoughtful foreword and for seeing the value in our early conceptualizations of care-based research. We feel fortunate to have benefitted from her wisdom, love, and commitment to developing the next generation of justice-oriented scholars.

We want to express our gratitude to the many colleagues and mentors who nurtured our nascent ideas about care-based research and helped us push forward. Many thanks to Lalitha Vasudevan for her enduring support and at-the-ready advice throughout this process and to Kathy Hall who encouraged us to think bigger. We are thankful for venues like Ethnography in Education Research Forum, American Educational Research Association's Qualitative Research SIG, and the Eastern Sociological Society for creating space for us to share our early thinking and receive feedback from our peers.

Big thanks to Mark Richardson for believing in the vision for this book and the team at Bloomsbury Publishing for their support.

Finally, we are endlessly appreciative of our families, partners, and friends for affirming our ideas, offering love and moral support, and sharing their own expertise to make this book a reality.

Foreword

Complicating the Status Quo: Daring to Care in Educational Research with Youth

Yolanda Sealey-Ruiz

This book could not have come at a better time. If this recent pandemic has taught us anything, it is that we need to move through the world with care—care for ourselves and for others. COVID-19 reminds us of the fragility of human life, the unpredictability that can hit and change our lives in an instant. In the world of education, when we research alongside other humans, we actually have time to plan for the care our participants deserve. It is important that we think about how we will enter and exit "the field" when we conduct research, especially with young people. This book, *Care-Based Methodologies: Reimagining Qualitative Research with Youth in US Schools*, is a blueprint for how to do this. This book affirms the words of thirteenth-century poet Rumi in his poem *The Guest House* as he reminds us of the fragility, beauty, and caretaking required to live our lives. He writes:

> This being human is a guest house. Every morning is a new arrival. A joy, a depression, a meanness, some momentary awareness comes as an unexpected visitor ... Welcome and entertain them all. Treat each guest honorably. The dark thought, the shame, the malice, meet them at the door laughing, and invite them in. Be grateful for whoever comes, because each has been sent as a guide from beyond.

Regarding research, Rumi's words can be a poetic representation of what could happen when studies are conducted in culturally relevant and humanizing ways. The editors of this book, Veena Vasudevan, Nora Gross, Pavithra Nagarajan, and Katherine Clonan-Roy, centered the humanity of the youth participants in their research and ask that we do the same.

Unfortunately, in much of the research conducted with young people in schools, and young people of color specifically, the idea of caring for youth participants is not the central focus. The field of education has an abundance of qualitative and quantitative studies that name participants as "subjects" and whose sole purpose is to advance the research agenda of the researcher. The editors of this volume noted that, in particular, "youth from nondominant communities are the subjects of countless social scientific and educational studies, but the processes through which researchers come to make meaning of youth's lives and their well-being during and after a study often go unquestioned and unexamined" (p. 1–2). This status quo approach to educational research desperately needs to be interrupted. Even when research is conducted in the spirit of "helping" those who are the focus of research, the "help" and, therefore, the care shown by the researchers are subjective and often depend on the researcher's generosity. In other words, as Vasudevan, Gross, Nagarajan, and Clonan-Roy remind us, there are no existing *standards of care* to guide researchers, and particularly there is "little training in graduate schools or within professional organizations on how to navigate complex interpersonal dynamics and relationships with youth" (p. 2) when designing and conducting research. That is, of course, *until now*, with the publication of this book.

Through her work, scholar and feminist bell hooks (2001) suggested that the beginning of truth is love. hooks also told us, "[T]here can be no love without justice … abuse and neglect negate love. Care and affirmation, the opposite of abuse and humiliation, are the foundation of love" (p. 19, 21). In the chapters of *Care-Based Methodologies: Reimagining Qualitative Research with Youth in US Schools*, there is a clear connection between care, love, and social justice when conducting qualitative research with youth and more specifically BIPOC (Black, Indigenous, People of Color) young people. Researchers often take their cue on how to work with BIPOC youth in their research studies by how schools in society treat them. School for many BIPOC students has been void of a loving, affirming, academically rich learning environment that recognizes their individuality and genius. Schools are often absent of care—but that does not mean our research should be. It is evident in all of the examples in this book, and echoed through the words of their research participants, that care in research requires vulnerability on the part of researcher *and* participant; care for participants often becomes/is love for participants. The chapters in this book give vivid examples of the importance of centering honesty and truth as *acts of care* when working with youth participants. I, too, view truth as an act of love and care and have always sought for a reciprocal love to exist—between teacher and student as well as researcher and participant in my teaching and my research.

For more than a decade, I have written about love and care in my work (Jackson et al., 2014; Ohito et al., 2019; Sealey-Ruiz, 2007, 2020; Watson et al., 2016). I see the two as interrelated. Much of my research probes the role of love in educational settings. For example, in the articles "Reciprocal Love: Mentoring Black and Latino Males through an Ethos of Caring" (Jackson et al., 2014) and "Daring to Care: The Role of Culturally Relevant Care in Mentoring Black and Latino Male High School Students" (Watson et al., 2016), my colleagues and I focused on a group of Black and Latinx male students who were part of an in-school mentoring program: UMOJA Network for Young Men. The mentoring program centered love and care as a practice of being with one another while in school. The mentor of the program was explicit about the care he offered the young men, to whom he referred as his "little brothers." As Black feminist researchers, we entered and left "the field" guided by an ethic of care (Greene, 1988; Noddings, 2005b). We were deliberate about how we cared for the youth participants while researching *with* them, as we studied the ways in which they cared for each other as members of the mentoring group.

For me, care in teaching and research is fundamental. If I do not care deeply about my students or those youth with whom I am researching, it is difficult for me to bring my full self to the classroom or research project. I was *not* taught this in graduate school. Caring for my participants just felt right to me. It is perhaps what I learned from being a Black woman in a society that is care-less with me and was care-less and reckless with my ancestors. The lack of care that BIPOC children face in school and society is a principal driving force behind how and why I approach them with care whenever I am in their presence. This book has taught me lessons I wish I had as a graduate student and beginning researcher. It is scholarship that resonates with me and the work I have been thinking about and inviting others to think about since I entered the academy. What is also significant about this book is how it offers a lens on care from multiple epistemological stances. The chapters collectively draw on feminist, Indigenous, critical, decolonial, and humanizing approaches that critique, speak back to, and oppose status quo research norms.

Care-Based Methodologies: Reimagining Qualitative Research with Youth in US Schools generously offers a framework for how to begin and sustain care in our research with youth in US schools—schools that are inherently unequal because of the social construction of race and heavily influenced by capitalism and neoliberalism. The editors write: "Care-based research methodologies recognize the youth who participate in research not as *subjects*, but as *people* first—whose full selves must be considered, taken seriously, and prioritized at each stage of the research process" (p. 2). It is imperative that researchers who work with the youth who are experiencing these unequal and unjust systems learn about how to care for them as they invite them into their research agenda. It is crucial for researchers to understand how these systems impact the lives of youth (and our own lives, for that matter) so that they are able to provide care without over-essentializing youth's positionality or romanticizing the struggles they navigate daily. The youth are more than the marginalization they are experiencing at the hands of society, and the editors of this book remind us of this with every chapter, sharing "we have witnessed youth experiencing the joy, promise, and possibilities of schools as well the sadness, humiliation, and sense of impossibility that sometimes fill school buildings" (p. 3).

The book presents the power of care in research that is based in critical love—a love that I define as a profound and ethical commitment to caring for the communities in which we work and whom we serve. If we are to heed some of the lessons we learned during the COVID-19 pandemic and succeed in creating research practices and policies that center the humanity of our participants, especially our youth participants, then our approaches to research—from design to implementation—must be created and executed with care in mind.

This book shows us the way.
In response to Ferlazzo's (2014) blog post "How does caring relate to standards?" on Classroom Q&A, British-Australian feminist scholar Sara Ahmed asked and answered an important question: "As educators, where are our standards for caring and empathy? They are inherent. They exist in our hearts and minds. However, they do not exist in the document that drives the work in our classrooms." As I relate Ahmed's quote to

researchers, I am drawn to what the scholars in this volume say about the reality of our role: "Researchers also bring their own subjectivities and past experiences into the work; our work is 'unavoidably subjective'" (Laura, 2016, p. 219). In other words, in cultivating relationships and connecting with research participants, "we make space for our own vulnerability—and as a result, we have something on the line too" (p. 9). Given that schools can be such dehumanizing spaces, when working with youth in schools, a critical question arises: Are we researchers in the moment or humans in the moment? Given the marginalization experienced by youth of color in schools and society, approaching our work in a humanizing way—by, for example, encouraging our youth participants to tell their personal stories—can bring forth racial healing (Bell, 2010; Hardy, 2013). This edited volume reminds us why care must be a central part of the research we do with young people. By building meaningful relationships through an ethic of care, researchers and their youth participants can work together to learn and exercise the power of resistance and effectively push for justice in schools and society where dehumanizing inequities persist.

All of the chapters in this volume put forth a clear and compelling rationale for why researchers who work with youth must engage care-based methodologies as essential to school-based qualitative and ethnographic educational research, particularly when participants are youth from BIPOC and nondominant communities. This is all the more important given the problematic legacy of dehumanizing practices often used in research with regard to nondominant communities. The editors of this book articulate a definition for care-based research that draws from a range of disciplines, methodologies, and theoretical conceptualizations of care as well as their own empirical studies. They locate the need for care by engaging in historical literacy and naming, with details, some of the historical challenges in educational research, particularly with young people from BIPOC and nondominant communities. This book emphasizes that care is a radical and necessary component of school-based research, as is the use of decolonizing research paradigms that can disrupt the status quo deficit approaches often found in educational research with nondominant youth. Emphasizing a praxis of critical dialogue, action, and reflection to create knowledge and consciousness about oppression and ultimately dismantle it, this book stresses the importance and responsibility of being good humans and exposes the hurt that comes when we conduct research under the myth of objectivity with our youth participants. In short, this book serves as an important reminder that research involving youth participants must be conducted *with* them, not *on* or *about* them. This book shows us how to enter ethical, emotional partnerships with the youth participants in our research and, in the process, how we can potentially foster the ideas and values of social justice in schools.

Care-Based Methodologies: Reimagining Qualitative Research with Youth in US Schools provides an intimate view of caring practices among researchers who work with youth in America's schools. It allows us to witness when and how youth flourish in their roles as researchers and activists when care is the center of the research agenda. There is no one way to prescribe or describe care in all educational research, but this edited volume—which I imagine will be celebrated among graduate students, emerging and seasoned researchers alike—reminds us how essential and contextual care is, and should be, in our research endeavors. The work of the scholars in this book helps us to visualize care without oversimplifying and valorizing it—reminding us that to care for our youth participants is arduous work. It takes courage, strength, and stamina to bring one's heart *and* mind consistently in alignment while engaging in research with youth. *Care-Based Methodologies: Reimagining Qualitative Research with Youth in US Schools* invites us all to do just that—bring our minds and our hearts to school-based research. This book also contributes to research on culturally relevant care, noting the power of care when everyone involved shares a commitment to improving the community (Pang, 2001). Explained another way, care in our research with youth is a form of kinship created between youth and researchers. As we see in the studies in this volume, this kinship is characterized by listening, support, and collaboration (Siddle Walker & Tompkins, 2004), where genuine care reflects an understanding of, respect for, and response to the cultures, ways of knowing, and realities of young people. Howard (2001) explained that culturally connected care entails creating a community with rituals and practices that are reflective of students' home lives. This type of care builds trust, enacts *warm demanding* (Ware, 2006), and integrates the cultures and experiences of community members. What my colleagues and I found in our own research (Jackson et al., 2014; Watson et al., 2016) was the possibility for teachers (and us as researchers) to help create a school community where young Black and Latinx males exhibited greater levels of care for each other—care that helped them challenge the status quo of limited expectations and pernicious stereotypes for them.

Given the challenges faced by youth of color in schools and society, researchers desperately need to operationalize care as activism for the young people involved in their research. This book, aptly named *Care-Based Methodologies: Reimagining Qualitative Research with Youth in US Schools*, provides examples of care that are provocative and inspiring—displaying the beauty and strength of research that is concerned with the lives of its youth participants. Collectively, the research in this volume shows that when researchers are present for the small and large events that happen in the lives of youth, everyday moments of humanity occur and can potentially change the school and societal environment for everyone.

Introduction: Caring in Research with Youth in Schools

Veena Vasudevan, Nora Gross,
Pavithra Nagarajan, and Katherine Clonan-Roy

DENISE: *"You're like an equal—you're like one of us."* (Conversation with Veena, May 2016)

CHARLES: *"You understand—you talk to me, ask questions. You're always there ... No other teachers do that."* (Interview with Pavithra, June 2017)

SOFIA: *"[The research] brought people together. An adult and girls. Usually, girls don't really trust adults enough. But since that person actually cares and they always meet up, yeah ... You're like a girl, too."* (Interview with Katie, March 2015)

HAZEEM: *"You really got to know us [me and my friends] personally and built deep relationships with each of us, it's even some stuff we trusted you with so we told you instead of each other."* (Instagram direct message to Nora, October 2020)

Youth like Denise, Charles, Sofia, and Hazeem[1] have taught us, the four editors of this book, lessons about the possibilities of practicing and enacting caring through the research process. Qualitative researchers occupy unique positions in school buildings as we can become implicated in the quotidian patterns of youth's day-to-day lives and privy to their internal struggles, their likes and dislikes, their intellectual eccentricities, their family dynamics, and other facets of their personal lives. Getting to know students, learning about the many roles they play in and out of school, and hanging out in the spaces where they feel comfortable are essential to the work of school-based researchers, particularly those who engage in long-term, immersive qualitative research projects. There is, however, little training in graduate schools or within professional organizations on how to navigate complex interpersonal dynamics and relationships with youth.

An inherent challenge in conducting school-based research is that it can be extractive when it comes to the lives of children and youth:[2] researchers arrive to collect data on youth's learning, social relationships, and lived experiences but may think little about the implications of their presence in young people's lives. Youth from nondominant communities[3] are the subjects of countless social scientific and educational studies, but the processes through which researchers come to make meaning of youth's lives and their well-being during and after a study often go unquestioned and unexamined. Thus, in this book, we advance a care-based research methodology as essential to qualitative and ethnographic research in school settings, particularly when participants are youth from nondominant communities.

Care-based research methodologies recognize the youth who participate in research not as *subjects*, but as *people* first—whose full selves must be considered, taken seriously, and prioritized at each stage of the research process. Care-based research involves offering close attention to youth, treating youth with consideration, regard, and affection, responding to their needs in the moment and honoring their humanity. In doing so, school-based researchers can conduct rigorous and responsible research that simultaneously improves our understanding of youth's lives, cares for their well-being, and works toward dismantling the systems that oppress them.

***

The seeds for this book were planted in January 2018 when a social media post by one coeditor asked how other researchers "think/write about your own potential impact as caring/interested adults on young people's lives." The virtual exchange that followed, about negotiating care and concern for youth's well-being within and beyond the boundaries of our research, catalyzed a series of conversations across our editorial team and led us to organize several conference sessions in 2019 (Vasudevan, Gross, & Nagarajan, 2019a; 2019b; Vasudevan, Gross, Nagarajan, & Clonan-Roy, 2019) to critically examine the role of care in research. In these formal presentations and during many informal conversations, we explored how and why our respective school-based research projects had challenged and complicated our understanding of researcher-participant relationships and the research process. Collectively, we began a serious examination of what we had each experienced as ethnographers conducting multiyear studies of preteens and adolescents (ages 10–19) within a range of school contexts (e.g., public, private, charter, single-sex, and coeducational).

While our research questions and project aims differed, we were each motivated by a commitment to better understand facets of youth's lives through deep engagement with the goal of contributing to larger academic conversations about teaching and learning, teacher education, social and emotional well being, programming for students, education policy, and more. Prior to our lives as researchers, we had worked with youth in classrooms as K-12 teachers (Pavithra, Katie), in formal in-school academic programs (Nora), and in informal and after-school settings (Veena). These experiences had revealed the systemic inequities built into American schooling and partially motivated our pursuit of doctoral studies and our dissertation projects.

Through our conversations as an editorial team, we learned that each of us had similarly experienced moments of uncertainty, anxiety, and panic—alongside the joy and exhilaration—of engaging in long-term school-based research engagements. We found that our graduate training and other professional work had not prepared us for how messy, complicated, and unpredictable school-based research could be. We worried about the young people we were coming to know: their social and emotional well-being, their academic achievement, and their personal trajectories. We felt the urge to shield them from unfair disciplinary practices or delegitimizing academic experiences. Often by just *being there*, we became to some students a source of support and care in ways we did not anticipate, and that sometimes stretched our own personal capacities.

As the four of us shared our stories with one another, we generated questions about our research practice: what happens when students confide in us? When they come to rely on us? How do we make sense of challenging conversations about our identities, our motivations, or a lack of shared positionality with our participants? When and how is it appropriate to intervene on behalf of a young person in need? In any given moment, how do we balance the goals of our data collection with a request for attention from a student? What happens to our relationships with these youth when our studies end? How can we enact care responsibly both during and after our projects?

In an effort to answer these and other questions, the idea for this book began to take shape. We were deeply moved by the responses we got to our call for chapter proposals. In each of our chapter authors' stories of research with youth—the complications, successes, and pitfalls—we discovered new ways of seeing and understanding care within research relationships. We learned together with the authors in this book how to make ideas of caring that may have been implicit in our work and practices more explicit—and, we hope, accessible and informative for readers. This book is the result of true collaboration, not just between the four of us and the mentors and scholars whose work we build on, but among our twenty-nine named chapter authors—and, perhaps most importantly, the many young people across all of our studies who continue to teach us how to care for and with them in our research.

Uncaring and Caring in Schools

As an editorial team we have witnessed youth experiencing the joy, promise, and possibilities of schools as well as the sadness, humiliation, and sense of impossibility that sometimes fill American school buildings. It is well documented that nondominant youth are often the recipients of uncaring practices and attitudes that make schools isolating and fraught: over-disciplining and bodily control, frequent police presence, standardized curriculum focused on testing and "drill and kill" learning, policies that push them out, and school reform strategies that prioritize measuring grit and "quick fixes" (Anyon, 1997; Ferguson, 2020; Fine, 1991; Love, 2019, p. 86; Valenzuela, 2010). These youth are often silenced in schools and classrooms in both explicit and implicit ways, from literally not being able to speak up or express the fullness of their emotional selves (Clonan-Roy, Gross, & Jacobs, 2020; Kirkland, 2013) to being expected to talk, think, act, and dress in certain ways, and in experiencing curriculum that seeks to obscure their cultural practices, literacies, and ways of meaning making (Gonzalez, Moll, & Amanti, 2006; Nagarajan, 2018; Sealey-Ruiz, 2016; Yosso, 2005). Black and Brown children, as Bettina Love (2019) poignantly writes, experience "spirit murdering" in the American education system, which she describes as "the death of the spirit, a death that is built on racism" (p. 2). Schools and schooling can dehumanize youth, reproduce social injustice, reify racism, sexism, ableism, and so on and ultimately traffic in systemic oppression becoming, at their most extreme, sites of "suffering" and "emotional abuse" (Dumas, 2014; McKenzie, 2009).

And yet we also know that schools *can* be places where children thrive and feel supported, affirmed, and cared for. There are school models that, in their mission, prioritize the autonomy and agency of young people and put resources toward vulnerable students' mental, physical, and emotional health (see Garcia et al., 2021; Gray & Chanoff, 1986; Meraji & Demby, 2017). There are schools and classrooms that value the identities, cultural practices, and funds of knowledge of their students and families (see González, Moll, & Amanti, 2006; Ladson-Billings, 2009; Pacheco, 2009; Warren, 2021), teachers who understand that students need to learn in relationships (see Gross & Lo, 2018; Nelson, 2016), and informal institutional structures like mentoring groups and youth participatory action research (YPAR) projects that affirm and value young people's contributions (see Carl et al., 2018; Watson, Sealey-Ruiz, & Jackson, 2016). And there are approaches to education, as Freire (2005) offers a continual reminder, where teachers become "student among students" seeking "mutual humanization" (p. 75) and students become agents of their own liberation. These serve as reminders that schools can—and should—be places of care.

Conducting Qualitative Research in Schools

Just as schools can be both caring and uncaring places, the enterprise of research itself also presents opportunities for care and attention to the well-being of young people, but also—and too often—has a tendency to marginalize, neglect, and even harm vulnerable youth and communities. People from nondominant communities have been subject to cruel and inhumane treatment under the auspices of advancing knowledge production (e.g., The Tuskegee Study [1932–1972], the Stanford Prison Experiment [1971]) (National Commission for the Protection of Human Subjects of Biomedical and Behavioral Research, 1979). Even more innocuous studies of children and communities can often be extractive and exploitative and rarely result in any change for the communities (Tuck, 2009). The aforementioned problematic and persistent research legacies engender understandable mistrust, skepticism, and fear of researchers on the part of potential participants. This requires that researchers see our responsibility as more than to "do no harm"; indeed, we should seek to do good through our research (see Friesen et al., 2017; Mackenzie, McDowell, & Pittaway, 2007; Tilley & Thomas, 2018).

The intent of qualitative and ethnographic research is to reveal features of the human condition from the perspective of participants through documenting the fullness of individuals' lives by highlighting the personal, the evocative, and the everyday. Qualitative research is an inherently relational process—and, in school contexts, as this book focuses on, these relationships are multifaceted, complex, and often perpetually burdened with the layered dynamics of power and the historicity of schools (Galletta, 2013; Hays & Singh, 2011). Understanding schools requires *being there*, getting to know community members, students, and staff. Researchers have to identify and cultivate relationships with gatekeepers to gain access and negotiate ever-changing relationships with youth. Researchers embedded in school life learn the rules, rhythms, and expectations of these complex institutions. While it is beyond the scope of this introduction to explicate all the facets of qualitative research in schools, we highlight a few specific dimensions of school-based qualitative research that come up throughout the book: the way researchers navigate school spaces, negotiate multiple roles and relationships, and experience their own and others' vulnerability.

When researchers enter schools, one of the early decisions they have to make is where to be; they must find ways to exist in institutional and informal spaces in respectful, reflexive, and responsible ways that will allow them to see what is happening. School ethnographers describe their approach as "nomadic" as they go about trying to understand the context, inhabiting the public spaces of school buildings, like hallways and stairwells, as well as the physical spaces where usually only youth hang out (see Eckert, 1989; Lewis, 2003; Morris, 2012). Through these processes, some researchers become part of the scenery (see Ferguson, 2020); others may be mistaken for social workers, therapists, teachers, parole officers, or even students (see Eckert, 1989; Flores-Gonzalez, 2002; Pascoe, 2011). In addition to the standard decisions about specific research methods and instruments, a researcher's choice about where, when, and how to *be* has significant implications for the relational outcomes of a study, as well as its findings (Horvat, 2013).

School-based researchers also negotiate multiple roles and relationships, often simultaneously, and balance responsibilities to multiple stakeholders in a school. Scholars like Eckert (1989)—who examined youth cultures in a high school—grappled with the challenges of multifaceted research relationships, arguing that her "main job in impression management ... was maintaining a separation from the norms and the authority structure of the school" (p. 29). She sought to cultivate a researcher identity that differed sharply from other school adults, like teachers or administrators, so that she could gain students' trust and learn about their lives in a fuller way. Relatedly, some scholars have written about cultivating a "least-adult" identity (see Bettie, 2014; Pascoe, 2011; Van Ausdale & Feagin, 1996) to implicitly express to youth that they are on the same level. However, others like Lewis (2003), who studied elementary age children, found that "for children ... to see me as someone who was 'on their side' or sympathetic to their point of view did not [require] subverting my adult position. Rather it meant having genuine conversations about their lives, listening to them carefully when they spoke, helping them when they were confused, and expressing care" (p. 202).

In addition to the decisions researchers make about how to occupy space and how to show up for people, they must also negotiate their own and others' vulnerability in the research process. Many researchers working with nondominant communities lack shared positionality along at least some key dimensions of identity, including race, ethnicity, socioeconomic status, gender identity, sexuality, or class. Learning about others' lives, especially across lines of difference, often requires researchers to make themselves vulnerable, since immersive qualitative research involves "try[ing] to understand people by allowing their lives to mold your own as fully and genuinely as possible" (Desmond, 2014, p. 561). In her study of Hmong high schoolers, Lee (2005) found that being open about her own background, even when it differed from her students', and "sharing bits of [her] own identity and history" as she also "[kept] students' secrets" helped her to "gain the confidence of a range of students" (p. 18–9). Moreover, scholars have found that being honest, authentic, and transparent about their values has supported the work of building meaningful relationships with youth (see Dance, 2002; Khan, 2012).

Becoming students' secret-keepers, confidants, and sources of support also comes with myriad ethical considerations, as many of the chapters in this book will detail. Researchers have to make quick decisions about how to respond to a problematic or worrisome situation and whether or not to intervene (see Lareau, 2011; Pascoe, 2011; Rios, 2011). Informed consent from young people is not, as Khan (2012) argues, a "one-time event" (p. 202) but an ongoing process, and researchers interacting with youth often need to stay attentive to how young people might reflect later on what they have exposed about themselves through the research relationship. As Eckert (1989) reflects from her own work with teenagers, "it is not that difficult ... for a reasonably attentive person to get people to tell all kinds of things about themselves. But we frequently do not know, once we have gone away, the kinds of regrets they may have for having told us these things" (p. 30). One of the challenges in rendering youth's perspectives, experiences, and practices is to engage responsibly and ethically so that youth never feel they have to perform or share what they think researchers *want* to hear (Tilley & Thomas, 2018).

Conducting qualitative research with youth in schools is a complex and messy process, requiring thoughtful decision-making, relational and ethical attention, and much "improvisation" (Green, 2014). These approaches sit in contrast to positivist notions of research that assume that researchers can arrive at an objective, universal truth. Positivists have traditionally been concerned with empirically testing existing theory, replicating methods across disciplinary areas, and generalizing knowledge to a population. In the pursuit of these goals, positivist researchers aim to maintain objectivity in research design, set clear and distanced boundaries with participants, avoid discussions of values among those involved in the research, and control contextual variables that impact studies (Hays & Singh, 2011). An emphasis on positivism continues to linger in graduate education, within the demands of Institutional Review Boards, and the allocation of funding opportunities through professional organizations, and in the use of post-positivism as an interpretive paradigm by some qualitative researchers.

Beyond the ethical and methodological issues we see with positivist approaches to research in schools, we also worry that when training emphasizes this orientation; it leaves novice researchers without the tools to navigate the complex ways relationships with youth play out in the field. In that sense, we echo Paris and Winn's (2014) concern that "continued and longstanding efforts to make the process and product of qualitative inquiry fit into positivist notions of what research is and how it should look often silence and minimize what it is we actually do in coming to know and know about the youth we spend months and years with" (p. xix). This book aims to pull back the curtain on these processes of coming to know and know about youth and the ways we do so with care.

Toward a Framework for Care-Based Research Methodologies

In developing their approach to research and designing a particular study, qualitative researchers must distinguish between methodologies and methods. Methodology refers to the theoretical considerations and philosophical assumptions that shape how researchers engage in the process of conducting research. Methods, on the other hand, refer to the tools that researchers use to collect data (such as interviews, observations, focus groups, etc.) (Creswell & Poth, 2018). Methodologies are driven by assumptions or beliefs about the nature of reality (ontology) and knowledge (epistemology), and the role of values (axiology) in research. In this and the following section, we clarify how interpretive paradigms, philosophical assumptions, and theoretical considerations that foreground caring relations shape our methodological orientation, and in turn, how they shape the methods a care-based researcher carries out.

Broadly, inviting care into methodological practices is to suggest that our axiological commitments to caring for participants, their communities, and the material conditions of their lives are inextricably linked to our research. This methodology is rooted in a transformative (Creswell & Poth, 2018) or critical theory (Hays & Singh, 2012) paradigm, which orients research toward addressing inequities and promoting justice. Specifically, in our care-based methodology we acknowledge the role of power and oppression in shaping what we know; emphasize that reality can be changed and power dynamics can be challenged through research and the actions it inspires; practice rigorous reflexivity in order to consider our impact on individuals and communities; and appreciate and honor the standpoints and values of participants.

Ethic of Care in Pedagogical Relationships

Nel Noddings, a critical care ethicist, articulated an ethic of care as essential to relationships between students and teachers in educational settings. She proposed that relationships in schools signaled something key about humanity—that "to care and be cared for are fundamental human needs" (1984, p. xi). When we "care," we worry about what happens to people in our everyday lives and we attend to them—to their individual needs, perspectives, and interests—by asking the basic questions: who, what, where, when, and why. For Noddings, the answers to these questions may bring a level of consciousness to the ways in which we receive, recognize, and respond to others and ourselves. Noddings urges educators and scholars to organize our work around caring—caring for human affections, weaknesses, and anxieties—to know people in all of their particularity.

When teachers care and try to cultivate a caring relationship, they can see the product of those efforts in how students respond or reciprocate. Noddings (2012) argues that an "ethic of care binds carers and cared-fors in relationships of mutual responsibility ... [which] requires each of us to recognize our own frailty and to bring out the best in one another" (p. 235). A relational view of caring—within teaching relationships—requires a dynamic closer to equality between teacher and student, one that does not assume that one knows best or holds all the knowledge. For Noddings, relational care can lead to trust and deeper understanding about who students are and what matters to them (Noddings, 1992).

Beyond Noddings, and often building on her work, care has been further theorized in education in relation to pedagogical relationships between students and their teachers or other adults (i.e., social workers, therapists, coaches) in the school building. Authentic caring (Valenzuela, 2010) in educational contexts requires attention to the fullness of youth's lives, including the way their lives are shaped by their social identities and societal structures of oppression and who they are (and want to be) beyond their institutional role as "student" (Antrop-González & De Jesús, 2006; Rolon-Dow, 2005). We draw on these scholars' work on care within adult-youth school-based relationships in developing our conceptualization of care-based research.

Care and Love in Research Relationships

In the last decade or so, orientations of care have become increasingly visible and explicitly articulated in the work of qualitative researchers and methodologists. These scholars have theorized the ways *participants* and *researchers* become "something new for and with each other" during the course of a qualitative study and beyond it (Kinloch & San Pedro, 2014, p. 36). Indeed, the process of research itself can be "humanizing" (Paris, 2011; Paris & Winn 2014); it can make participants—and especially those who are dehumanized in so many other ways and spaces—feel seen, heard, understood, and "worthy" (Winn & Ubiles, 2011). Some scholars have written about this form of attention to another's life as *love*. Carspecken (2018) asserts that

> by doing social research we are making an implicit claim that other human beings concern us emotionally as well as intellectually, and that their well-being *should* concern both authors and readers. We are tacitly positing an ethical ideal, a value on which the other values build, although it is not one we ever fully live up to. I translate this ideal as love.
>
> (p. 2)

The relational nature of research is central to Carspecken's conceptualization of love for participants. Similarly, Laura (2016) describes her research participants as "my people" (p. 218). Expressing love toward participants is "an action of caring" (Winkle-Wagner, 2018, p. 153). Engaging this "care-in-action" in our fieldwork can involve activities ranging from "problem solving with participants [and] helping find resources" to "self-disclosing or being vulnerable" (Winkle-Wagner, 2018, p. 156). Laura (2016) similarly argues that "when we understand loving practice as the foundation of our research, then we may begin to establish the conditions for the production of valuable knowledge that shapes and informs the way we think, speak, and act" (p. 218). Care allows us to cultivate openness to "intimate inquiry" (Laura, 2016) even outside of actual familial relationships, and love offers some of the tools to do so.

In the specific case we take up in this book of research with youth in their schools, we must be care-ful to ensure we are engaging with human beings responsibly. We must take responsibility for our actions, knowing that our presence and our role in a school context have implications. Critical scholars offer important lessons to never "use human beings as a means to an end. We do not gain rapport and trust to simply get the data and then run in order to accomplish our own goals while leaving subjects vulnerable or feeling exploited" (Madison, 2011, p. 85). Carspecken (2018) writes that "good" ethnographers (or, we would argue, caring researchers using any method) "listen, they attend to sensory and symbolic details, they acknowledge and respect insiders' perspectives, they work to enhance communication, they are reciprocal, and they are willing to be changed and to recognize change in others" (p. 3). In other words, *how* we treat youth participants has implications for their lives.

As researchers, we also bring our own subjectivities and past experiences into the work; our work is "unavoidably subjective" (Laura, 2016, p. 219) and unavoidably emotional. In cultivating relationships and connecting with our research participants, we make space for our own vulnerability—and as a result, we have something on the line too. Researchers working with vulnerable populations and in contexts of uncare, as several of the chapters throughout this book suggest, are subject to their own "wounding," grief, heartbreak, and burnout (see Behar, 1996; Benoot & Bilson, 2014; Gillespie & Lopez, 2019; Winkle-Wagner, 2018). On any given day, researchers feel sadness, hope, exhaustion, exhilaration, joy, love, frustration, anger, sometimes all at once. To care for and love others within these research endeavors, therefore, requires a level of caring for and loving oneself, and practices of self-reflection and reflexivity.

Care-Based Research Methodology

A care-based research methodology requires that care must be present in both our methods and our practice. Questions about care should emerge both at the outset of a project, in our research design and approach to our methods, and in our day-to-day practices in the field. As a **method**, care shows up in how we make choices about *what* data we will collect, *when* and *how* we will do so and by engaging with *whom*; *why* we will focus on particular phenomena over others; and *how* we prepare to handle the big questions of prioritizing youth's well-being throughout a study. Care is central to decisions about framing research that can contribute to or improve participants' lives so that we are not only extracting information that is useful for our research (Duncan-Andrade, 2007). It also orients us to the approaches we take to cultivating relationships with participants (Paris & Winn, 2014), our understanding of *active* processes of youth informed consent (Khan, 2012), and ongoing, transparent dialogues with participants about what "data" will be shared and in what contexts (see Ravitch & Carl, 2019), and how data is interpreted and articulated, such that researchers "extend knowledge," not "perpetuate ignorance" (Tuhiwai Smith, 1999, p. 176).

Care also shows up in our day-to-day **practice** as researchers, including the stance we take in conversations with youth, the way we engage with them, the in-the-moment decisions we make, as well as the small offerings of care that might be visible through bringing a snack or offering a ride. Practicing care, with youth in particular, requires researchers adopting an orientation that implicitly and explicitly proclaims that youth matter, that researchers care about them as people (Noddings, 2005a), and that researchers are willing to be vulnerable and open to learning (Brayboy et al., 2012; Kinloch & San Pedro, 2014; Winn & Ubiles, 2011).

Researchers in schools often traverse complex ethical minefields as they engage with youth in the field. Taking up care in our method and practice means that when we face situations that pit project against participants, we must opt to uplift youth and center their needs, not ours. At other times, we may choose not to disclose details about a participant, even if we have their permission and even if the details might strengthen our arguments, if disclosing would be harmful to the participant. In other moments, we might decide to close our notebook or put our camera away to fully participate in moments that require attention, connection, and care.

Finally, we propose that care-based research is also inherently **critical** in that projects are designed, as Fine (2018) describes, "to trouble the common sense about unjust arrangements that seem so natural or deserved; to destabilize what we think of as 'normal'; and to reveal where resistance gathers and were radical possibilities might flourish" (p. 6). Of course, a research project cannot dismantle oppressive systems or undo centuries of injustice—and we owe it to our participants to be transparent about the limits of our research—but, by taking on a critical stance, our approaches can put pressure on systems in the places that need change and work toward dismantling and disrupting inequities.

Below we articulate components of a care-based research methodology with youth in school settings:

Care is being there, showing up and bearing witness for youth's meaningful moments, including their challenging ones. Caring means that we do not stand on the sidelines but are actively engaged with students, acknowledging and participating in moments of significance—and the everyday, simple moments— both related to *and* beyond the scope of research.

Care is expressing genuine interest for youth's individuality and seeking to understand who they are. Caring means expressing to young people that they matter, that we want to understand them, and that their thoughts, lived experiences, and ways of being are valued and important. Through our words and actions we must also demonstrate that our care for young people is not just about what they can offer to our research.

Care is treating youth with dignity, respect, and kindness, and acknowledging our shared humanity. Working with youth requires researchers to actively acknowledge youth's full range of emotions and their expertise about their own experiences, not dismiss or discredit them, and treat them with the same respect and dignity we would offer anyone else.

Care is being transparent with youth about our goals and intentions. As researchers, we must be forthright and clear with our participants about what research means to us, the intent of our project and what we expect to come from it, and when, how, and for how long we are engaging in the research process.

Care is questioning the conditions of schools that detract from youth's well-being. When working in schools, we must consider the histories, the material conditions, and the cultural factors that mediate youth's experiences and not only work to understand how our role in the complex cultural landscapes of schools impacts youth, but actively work to oppose oppressive conditions.

Care is honestly communicating and acting with an understanding of the limits of reciprocity between researchers and youth. We need to be honest with participants about the ways we can and cannot personally support them, what research can do and for whom, and acknowledge that research disproportionately benefits researchers.

Care is putting our youth participants before the research. We must put the well-being and needs of participants above the research, and avoid pitting projects against participants.

Care is attending to our own needs while doing work with youth. When we care, we leave ourselves open and vulnerable to being affected, so we must make time and space to be reflexive, reflective, and caring to ourselves and, when we work in research teams, to our colleagues and collaborators.

Our conceptualization of care-based research here is only the beginning; each of the chapters in this book builds out this multifaceted concept and approach in unique ways. Collectively, they offer a range of examples of how care can be practiced and what care-based methodologies can help us achieve, both in research outcomes and in relationships with youth participants.

The Book Ahead

We have divided the book into four thematic sections, described below. We intend for this book to be pedagogical and useful to novice researchers embarking on their first foray into the field, seasoned scholars looking to integrate care into their research toolkits, and anyone in between. To that end, each chapter's author(s) conclude with some form of methodological guidance drawing from the lessons learned in their work.

We are trained to be researchers through graduate school coursework, reading methodological texts and empirical examples, mentorship of advisors and principal investigators (PIs) on research teams, and—as we alluded to at the start, especially for those of us doing qualitative work—trial and error, coming upon unexpected problems in the field and then seeking solutions, consulting with peers and mentors as we go. Each of the chapters in **Part One, "Re/Unlearning Our Orientation to Research: Critical Frameworks for Research in Schools,"** acknowledges the varied ways that formal methodological training can fall short, especially in preparing us to study youth in their schools with care. The chapter authors acknowledge how their initial training left them without a full toolkit to handle relationships with youth as well as the multidimensionality of their lives. Instead, these authors discovered that more individualized, critical, and caring research also led to a deeper, more nuanced understanding of what was going on in young people's lives. In response to the lack of preparation—or, in some cases, preparation for uncaring research—these authors show us how we can unlearn and/or relearn our orientation to qualitative research with youth in school settings and develop critical research frameworks that respond more fully to youth's needs.

In Chapter 1, Natalie R. Davis and Alaina Neal-Jackson express dissatisfaction with their graduate school methodological training which often invited them to do "just enough" and left them on their own to consider the ways their commitments as practitioners, researchers, and political agents might work in concert in support of the Black youth who were the focus of their work. Their chapter, *"All or Nothing:* Demystifying the 'What,' 'When,' and 'How' of Participant Observation in School-Based Research with Black Youth," details the critical ethnographic approach they each developed as participant observers engaging in everyday acts of caring with Black youth and then as critical friends and "co-thinkers" with each other.

In Chapter 2, *"Platicando entre Compañeras:* The Use of *Pláticas* to Navigate Ethical Dilemmas in Ethnographic Research with and for Latina High School Students," Bianca N. Haro details some of her early graduate school encounters with traditional and critical ethnography whose protocols, she found, often failed to leave room to explore the fullness of young people's lives. As she embarked on her own project, Haro responded to these limitations by developing a Chicana/Latina Feminist Ethic of Care and drawing on *platicás*, as both a methodological framework and an alternative approach to interviews with Latina youth.

In the third chapter, "Care as Resistance and Epistemological Necessity in YPAR," Meagan Call-Cummings and Melissa Hauber-Özer, a professor and doctoral student team, offer a peek into the relational challenges and opportunities of complex research teams—in their case comprised of both university-based researchers, young people, and their teacher conducting Youth Participatory Action Research (YPAR). In reflecting on what it means to care *with* youth, rather than just to care *for* them, Call-Cummings and Hauber-Özer think through the pressures on early career scholars trying to succeed in the academy through the lens of care. They challenge what they describe as the neoliberal concept of reciprocity as they reach toward a more genuine, mutual practice of care through YPAR design and enactment.

Researchers entering a school and a set of relationships with youth inevitably become part of a complex hierarchy of power, embedded with all the problematic histories of unethical research as well as all the fraught adult-student dynamics that haunt so many school settings. The authors in **Part Two, "Collaborating and Co-Creating with Youth: Caring Through Sharing Ownership of the Research,"** detail the conscious and unconscious choices they make in developing caring relationships with youth across lines of difference and power including age, race, gender, class, and religion. In these relationships, young people's experiences are witnessed, their stories affirmed, and their creative ideas honored and supported. These processes forged collaborations, new creations, and research processes and products that are shared.

In Chapter 4, "From Hallway Conversations to Making Together: How Care Can Shift Relationships with Young People in Schools," Veena Vasudevan establishes the critical role of "being there"—being present, being helpful, being supportive, being curious, and being vulnerable—in research relationships with youth. Situated in a brand-new school with an innovative mission and a lot of chaos, Vasudevan cultivated relationships with students and teachers by helping where she was needed and spending time in youth spaces. The chapter details the collaboration and co-creation that emerged from a hallway conversation with a student, which led to shared action and long-term reciprocal caring.

By engaging children through play, Ariana Brazier treated her young participants with dignity and respect, taking children's voices seriously when they told her they could make decisions about their participation in the research. In Chapter 5, "'The Life of Julio Good': The Black Ratchet Imagination and Messy Methods as Caring Ethics," Brazier describes how she used her research notebook to invite not only collaboration with children but their ownership of her research. Drawing from her perspective as a scholar of the humanities, Brazier details the good "messiness" of collaborating with children and the way they challenged her and held her accountable to her model of care.

In "The Reception and Reward of Relationship-Building and Enacting Care with Black Boys," the sixth chapter, Pavithra Nagarajan recounts her research relationships with two middle school boys she came to know over the course of her year-long ethnographic study at their school. She joins the students in their worlds—meeting them in the spaces where other adults do not spend time. Through an innovative photo elicitation methodology, Nagarajan creates opportunities for youth to teach her about the things that matter to them. Nagarajan explicates a three-part framework that is rooted in anti-racist research practice for enacting care in youth spaces.

In Chapter 7, "Developing Sustainable Partnerships between Researchers and Youth Participants: Fostering Shared Learning across Time and Difference," a researcher and a youth participant together reflect on how their relationship has been shaped over time and across lines of difference. From researcher-researched to cowriters, Matthew R. Deroo and Ilhan Mohamud explore how a researcher's caring orientation toward a student in his dissertation study laid the foundations for new ways of working together, critically examining the nature of reciprocity, and experiencing the evolving nature of research relationships that move beyond the scope of traditional research.

Even in the most uncomplicated contexts, research relationships with youth are never static. In **Part Three, "Negotiating Emergent Tensions: Developing and Sustaining Caring Relationships with Youth,"** chapter authors explicate how they felt youth received, reciprocated, and made sense of the care expressed through research relationships. These chapters highlight the ways that conducting care-based research is not just about the times when young people feel affirmed, supported, and loved but just as importantly about how we handle tensions, missteps, and missed opportunities. How we respond flexibly and nimbly to momentary or long-term relational shifts. How we make decisions about when to intervene or break confidentiality and how we show up for the young people in our studies even when it is less convenient or more confusing to do so. These chapters also underscore the need for researchers to communicate effectively with students and with appropriate transparency while still fulfilling the expectations and goals they have as scholars. The models these chapter authors offer are, of course, not one-size-fits-all, but they do provide useful insight into what it takes to sustain relationships of dignity, respect, and empathy with youth.

In Chapter 8, "Intervening through Intimate Inquiry with Youth," Katherine Clonan-Roy theorizes the role of love and care in her research with adolescent Latina girls in an after-school girls' group space. She describes how those frameworks guided her through a set of complex decisions in navigating her role as a mandated reporter when an adolescent participant confessed to engaging in self-harm.

In "A 'Friend' or an 'Experiment'?: The Paradox of Ethnographic Relationships with Youth," Nora Gross tells the story of two student research participants with whom she established caring relationships, who became hurt and frustrated when they felt they had become less important to her as her research focus shifted over time. In Chapter 9, Gross recounts the work necessary to repair these relationships and affirm her care for the teenagers, highlighting a paradox inherent in the unique forms of friendship that might develop between researchers and participants.

The tenth chapter, "Unraveling a Researcher's Practices of Care with One Disabled Youth," puts the ethics of care in conversation with disability studies in education scholarship. Katie Scott Newhouse walks through her process of forging a relationship with one youth participant, noticing along the way moments when she does not feel she gets it quite right as well as the choices that seem to make a difference for the research and the relationship, allowing researcher and participant to move from superficial interactions to deeper engagement.

In Chapter 11, "Culturally Responsive Caring and Emergent Tensions in a Bilingual Mentoring Program in a Diverse School," James S. Chisholm, Melanie Jones Gast, and Ashley L. Shelton describe their experiences as part of a research team working in partnership with a high school student who had designed a program to support her school's English language learners. In hindsight, the researchers came to realize that the temporally drawn-out process of academic research, undefined roles in the field, and communication challenges of various kinds constrained their ability to intervene in support of the student and enact the culturally responsive caring they deemed necessary.

When care is practiced in institutional partnerships and relationships, there is potential for longer-term engagements, more responsible research, and more just outcomes. The chapters in **Part Four, "Collaborating with Universities, Communities, and Schools: Navigating the Challenges of Caring Research Partnerships,"** collectively demonstrate what it means to develop and implement care in collaboration. In particular, these chapters examine the role institutions play in reinforcing (or refusing) care-based approaches to research. This section also deals with pedagogy, returning us to some of the questions from which this project began about the way that school-based research methods are—and should be taught—to prepare novice researchers for the unique challenges of engaging with youth in school settings.

In Chapter 12, "Conceptions of Care and Graduate Student Researcher Positionality: Struggling to Reconcile 'Researcher' Care with Personal Moral Commitments," Van Anh Tran, Errol C. Saunders II, Shamari Reid, and Lum Fube describe methodological and interpersonal conflicts that emerged for them as graduate student researchers on a large school-based research team, whose leaders seemed to prioritize research outcomes over the well-being of the youth with whom they worked and required the researchers to silence their instincts to practice care. As peers and collaborators, the authors came to rely on each other for support and affirmation of their individual notions of care and the moral commitments that emerged from their own positionalities—even when it meant uncomfortably pushing back against the power dynamics and hierarchies inherent to academic research teams.

In "Pedagogical Reflections: Teaching Care in Qualitative Research Classrooms," Chapter 13, Stephanie Masta and Ophélie Allyssa Desmet demonstrate the pedagogical possibilities of bringing care into the graduate methods classroom. Written jointly from the perspective of a qualitative methods professor and graduate student, their chapter explores the value in expressing and teaching with care to reinforce the role and necessity of care in research contexts.

Chapter 14, "Establishing, Executing, and Extending Caring Community-Based Research Partnerships," written by Charity Lisko, Katie Woolford, and Rand Quinn, offers another model for what teaching and practicing with care can look like. Their chapter articulates the ways in which caring was taken up among key stakeholders in a community-based participatory research practicum at various stages of the teaching, learning, and service process giving readers a pragmatic understanding of how to develop care-ful relationships with community partners.

In the final chapter, Chapter 15, Samuel Finesurrey, Camille Lester, Sherry King, Michelle Fine, and the Intergenerational S2 Research Collective detail a multilayered care-ful research partnership that spans university, middle school, and community partners. In their chapter, "*Just* Inquiry Rooted in Critical Care: Participatory, Intergenerational Research Tracing the Legacy of School in the Square," the authors show us how caring can proliferate across multiple levels of partnerships and how centering youth in the work, practicing transparency, and prioritizing justice lead to rigorous research experiences and meaningful change.

In sum, in the chapters that follow, our authors transgress traditional research paradigms, they challenge conventional understandings of reciprocity, and they help us to see what it means to walk *with* youth (Vasudevan, 2020). They illustrate what care can look like at different stages and levels of the research process, and they highlight a range of models of collaboration—from complex, intergenerational research teams to peers who can become co-thinkers, as well as all the ways our research participants are also our collaborators. And, most importantly, these chapters reveal the ways that caring methodologies lead to new, richer ways of knowing young people and their lives that are reflected both in the relationships that are cultivated and the research that is completed.

Part One

Re/Unlearning Our Orientation to Research: Critical Frameworks for Research in Schools

1

All or Nothing: Demystifying the "What," "When," and "How" of Participant Observation in School-Based Research with Black Youth

Natalie R. Davis and Alaina Neal-Jackson

Introduction

We are two Black women who, as graduate students, grew dissatisfied by the ways that scholarly research was often framed as invitations to do "just enough." Whether it was *just enough* to finish the dissertation in a timely manner or *just enough* to gain and demonstrate expertise, the political and ethical implications of *just enough* for the Black youth we were studying were seldom taken up in formal discussions of our doctoral student research responsibilities. Aware of our privileged positions as university researchers and our practical responsibilities as graduate students, we embarked on our journeys as critical ethnographers wanting to bring our full and best selves to the work. Our attempts to exceed what we perceived to be the baseline expectations as (then) novice ethnographic researchers surfaced many, unanticipated questions and tensions. As friends, we thought together about what it meant to participate and observe in schools as more than guests on the periphery. We considered the smaller, everyday "moves" that characterized our engagement as judicious and resolute in our efforts to care for the Black children in our research contexts. As our work with Black children progressed and frequently defied traditional researcher roles, we grew increasingly attuned to how our commitments to justice called for us to engage as critical ethnographers in nuanced ways.

In this chapter we define care as the recognition of, and response to, the needs of individuals that acknowledge both their present *and* the more liberated futures we hope to make possible. In line with a cadre of critical and humanizing scholars (Paris & Winn, 2013), we draw a distinction between research that demonstrates caring about people (researcher-centered) and forms of participation as researchers that prioritize the building of dignified, loving relationships between researchers and participants (Noddings, 2002; San Pedro & Kinloch, 2017). When the researcher's "compelling sense of duty and commitment based on moral principles" (Madison, 2005) includes responding to a call to meet the needs (immediate and future) of the young people with whom they are in relationship with, how do we make sense of the designation "participant observer"? What does this look like over the course of a project with Black youth? How does the practice of participant and observation morph and subtly shift in moment-to-moment interactions? When and how are such shifts generative and indicative of care? Drawing from our own experiences in the field, a range of ethnographic information sources and extant scholarship that has helped to elucidate the complexities of engaging as qualitative researchers when the stakes of engagement are high (Ladson-Billings, 2013; Swartz, 2011), we offer insights toward demystifying the "what," "when," and "how" of participant observation in critical ethnography with Black youth. We argue that a critical, caring approach to ethnographic research requires scholars to complicate the idea of practitioner, researcher, and political agent as necessarily distinct and move toward conceptualizations that recognize and embrace the simultaneity of the three.

Theoretical Grounding

Critical Ethnography and Participant Observation

Critical ethnography is a methodology for conducting research focused around participatory critique/analyses, empowerment, and social justice (Trueba, 1999). While traditional ethnography aims to describe the complexity of *what is*, critical ethnographers also consider what *could and should be* as a means of challenging conventional ideologies and unearthing issues of injustice for historically marginalized peoples (Anderson, 1989; Carspecken, 1996; Thomas, 2003). Borrowing from Madison (2005) and her applied work in Africa, critical ethnographers utilize tools (e.g., participant observation, reflexive journaling) that enable them to ethically go "beneath surface appearances, disrupt the status quo, and unsettle both neutrality and taken-for-granted assumptions by bringing to light underlying and obscure operations of power and control" (p. 5). This approach is particularly important for Black youth and communities, who have histories of being "othered" and superficially represented in research (Baldridge, 2014; Edwards et al., 2016; Tuck, 2009).

Within ethnographic education research, participant observation is a highly popular mode of data collection. We define participant observation as a methodological technique where the researcher investigates a group or culture by witnessing and engaging in everyday activity. This form of immersion in the spaces and social situations (Emerson, Fretz, & Shaw, 2001; Lichterman, 1998; Spradley, 2016) of participants is particularly useful in educational research where researchers are focused on the development and meaning making of youth. Although Kusenbach (2003) writes that participant observation is "often characterized as the most authentic and reliable ethnographic method" (p. 461), we emphasize that this does not absolve researchers of their responsibility to reflect upon the political and ethical dimensions of their engagement (e.g., Behar, 1996; Green, 2014). When done with care, sustained direct engagement with young participants should enable deeper insight into their perspectives and educational experiences.

Participant observation in schools may pose unique challenges for those guided by the tenets of critical ethnographic research. This is because a critical ethnographic framework disallows merely fitting into a space if such assimilation perpetuates existing or new injustices in the lives of those we study and care for. However, the language of "participant observer" does not readily avail itself to such a stance. *Observation* suggests passivity and watchfulness without intervention, while *participant* suggests that the researcher is actively engaged in a manner consistent with the customs and prescribed roles of the space. Yet critical researchers must be able to shift and act outside of the prevailing norms and take a more active or disruptive stance when warranted. Across various contexts where access to a research site comes with the expectation that adults "behave" or participate in particular ways according to fixed roles (e.g., custodian, classroom teacher, student, principal, and, in some cases, volunteer), critical researchers face the added task of negotiating present expectations with their charge to advance justice. Such conditions may make it difficult for critical ethnographers to continually shift and (re)define roles in a manner consistent with their goals of empowerment. Nonetheless, this shifting in pursuit of better conditions is necessary, especially when working in solidarity with Black youth to combat oppressive forces inside and outside of schools.

Accounting for Improvisational, Discretionary, and Everyday Acts of Caring in Critical Ethnographic Research

While participant observation is a key methodological tool, there are few empirical accounts of research practice that offer insight into the complexities of engaging as participant observer within a critical ethnographic design framework. With some notable exceptions (e.g., Paris & Winn, 2013; Green, 2014; Winn & Ubiles, 2011), underspecified are the ways that critical ethnographers navigate the fulfillment of research goals while prioritizing forms of active membership (Adler & Adler, 1987) that demonstrate care in everyday interaction. We aim to contribute insights that would help bring analytical and conceptual clarity to what constitutes caring, critical participant observation in school-based ethnography with Black youth.

As participant observers in critical ethnography, we are fundamentally concerned with the ways that researchers move from awareness of inequities to in-the-moment actions that care for and advance justice in the lives of those studied. Noddings (2002), as articulated in Shevalier and McKenzie (2012), argues that in order for researchers to act upon the moral responsibility that comes from caring about societal inequities, they must engage in practices that demonstrate authentic "care for" participants. This is accomplished through relationships that prioritize recognizing participants' immediate needs *and* responding to them. Such work demands perceptiveness, intentionality, and dexterity on the part of researchers. As the needs that surface will necessarily be as varied as the participants themselves and the contexts in which they are embedded, there are no prescribed methodological rules to follow. In these spaces researchers must make constant judgment calls about how to respond in both word and deed based on what they have learned from participants and their own ethical and political subjectivities (Vossoughi & Zavala, 2020). These become the moments when ethnographers actualize and build toward, or not, their commitments to participants and the larger goals of critical ethnographic work.

Our stance toward participant observation as everyday acts of caring and attunement also draws from Green's (2014) framework of double dutch methodology (DDM). DDM is a metaphorical methodological approach to critical ethnographic research that accounts for the grounded, improvisational, and "contextually stylized" nature of participant observation (Green, 2014). Green's (2014) framework is important in that it situates the balancing of priorities and shifting roles within critical ethnography not as problems to overcome but rather as dynamics to expect, embrace, and leverage for the well-being of youth. Green's (2014) recounting of her research study as akin to the multidimensional, collaborative, and embodied practice of double dutch jump rope also helps us to understand how engaging as researcher requires more than just attunement to the major event under study (i.e., jumping). An ability to recognize, honor, and respond to subtle cues in real time is crucial to the overall success of the jumper (and as we argue, the researcher). Informed by the DDM framework and the understanding that justice and caring occur in the everyday, discretionary spaces (Ball, 2018) researchers become embedded in, we turn to describe two concurrent critical ethnographic projects wherein our participation defied normative conceptions of participant observation. Our analyses of research practice demonstrate how fluid roles and seemingly minor interactions with young participants can advance an ethos of care and open up new relational and pedagogical opportunities (Davis, Vossoughi & Smith, 2020).

Data Sources and Analysis Procedures

Data was derived from two projects employing a critical ethnographic design. The first project was Natalie's two-year study of Black student agency across two elementary school contexts (Davis, 2017). Children attended either an African-centered school (John Hope School of Excellence[1]/JHE) or one enacting a place-based model (Mission City School/MCS). The corpus of data included ethnographic fieldnotes, sixty-one child drawings, and seventy semi-structured interviews with 4th/5th grade students and school staff. I (Natalie) began as a volunteer teacher and facilitator for an afterschool "sister circle" girls' empowerment group. Drawing from my past experiences teaching in an African-centered elementary school, later work included leading weekly math groups, tutoring individual children, substitute teaching, attending school meetings/assemblies, and chaperoning field trips. The total time spent volunteering, observing, and collecting data is estimated at over 540 hours. The nature and structure of participation varied, an ebb and flow of taking on formal responsibilities and "just being" in the space. An important dynamic of the study design is that I returned "home" to "Riverview" to conduct this ethnographic work and considered myself to be a part of the city community. Riverview, a city once regarded as a bustling Midwestern metropolis and epicenter of Black culture and life, was/is in the process of rebuilding from enduring social, educational, and economic challenges. In addition to exploring the relationship between the pedagogical design and cultural practices within each school and students' sociopolitical meaning making, I also saw this work as an important opportunity to foreground Black children's ideas and vision(s) for Riverview.

The second project was Alaina's two-year ethnography of Black girls' educational experiences in one school, James High School (JHS). JHS struggled to meet the academic and social needs of its Black student population generally and Black girls in particular (Neal-Jackson, 2018). Given that my (Alaina's) own complex experiences navigating a predominantly Black secondary school as a young Black woman are not adequately reflected in academic scholarship, I was drawn to engage with the Black girls in JHS. Initially invited to engage as a volunteer, over the course of 600+ hours spent in JHS, my engagement evolved to include the roles of assistant director of the Restorative (Justice) Center (RC) and facilitator of *RISE*, a Black girls' empowerment group. As assistant director of the RC, I assisted JHS in their transition from a traditional school disciplinary model to a restorative justice model (Winn, 2018) focused on fostering a deeper sense of community among students, teachers, and staff. As facilitator of *RISE*, I co-created a space for the Black girls in JHS to get academic support, nurture their developing critical consciousness, and most importantly, just be themselves—a freedom they were not allowed throughout JHS more broadly. Ultimately the data corpus for this project included (a) over 100 fieldnotes, (b) interviews with teachers and staff, (c) videos, memos, and artifacts from *RISE* meetings, and (d) documents constituting the print culture of JHS.

The research described herein occurred concurrently from 2014 to 2016. Importantly, we are both Black women teacher-scholars who seek to center the voices of Black children and youth in their scholarship (Akom et al., 2008). As colleagues and friends, we often had informal conversations around the nature of the critical ethnographic work in which we were engaged. While we conversed about the day-to-day happenings of the school in line with our formal research foci, we more often privileged conversations about the affordances, constraints, and complexities of our membership in these contexts. Through these conversations, it became clear that our individual and collective work defied traditional notions of participant observation in that we occupied ever-shifting roles and actively intervened with a sense of political clarity (Beauboeuf-Lafontant, 1999). As we continued informal discussions about our work, we also began to engage in reflective journaling to take note of themes and questions about our process(es) and role(s). This preliminary analytic work set the foundation for more systematic analyses. During data collection, each of us developed thematic memos as a means of further interrogating our tentative assertions in relation to our research questions and methodological process. When data collection concluded, we each read through their corpus of data to "review, re-experience, and re-examine" (Emerson, Fretz, & Shaw, 2011, p. 144) our time in our respective schools. Of particular interest were the instances in our data when we noted fluidity or tension in our roles or when participants described the nature of our participation. During this reexamination, we looked for patterns of typicality and atypicality (Erickson, 1986; 2004) in relation to our conceptions of our roles and engagement within each school environment.

Qualitative analysis software was used for data reduction and thematic coding for each of the larger projects. We used a shared folder to compile documents (e.g., reflective memos, representative data, and fieldnote excerpts). After identifying core themes such as "dynamic and shifting role(s)–participants' assessments" spanning across our respective projects, we then began to discuss the nuances and context of relevant examples. We discussed and wrote about our process, feelings, and priorities throughout the process. Analyses of our ethnographic fieldnotes, interviews, and reflective memos revealed that complicating the binary between researcher and political agent required shifting from a research-first orientation to one that foregrounded the needs of Black children. Furthermore, it required fostering meaningful connections by intentionally leveraging the seemingly minor interactions (i.e., passing in the hallway or quick exchanges between the authors and young people during one-on-one interactions) as opportunities for ethical and pedagogical encounters (Vossoughi & Zavala, 2020). Below, we report on these themes, commenting on how our approach to participation surfaces possibilities for reenvisioning what it means to engage with integrity and agency as critical ethnographers.

Detailing the "What," "When," and "How": Participant Observation as Everyday Acts of Caring and Agency in Critical Ethnographic Work

When we initially engaged in our respective research sites, we did so as volunteers. Beginning as a volunteer communicated to staff our genuine desire to work collaboratively and support initiatives already in place at the school. Volunteering also created an opportunity to become preliminarily acquainted with Black children and the complexities of their day-to-day schooling experiences. We tried to enter into our respective research contexts with grace and humility, understanding that allowing educational researchers access comes with risks that schools/participants have no obligation to take. By the conclusion of our formal research processes, we found that our participation had evolved far beyond what was typical for volunteers or researchers for that matter. We were perceived as productive members of the school community who played key support roles. This was evidenced during the following exchange with Ms. Mann, a teacher in JHS, who situated Alaina as the primary source of support for Black girls.

> ALAINA: Okay. Right. And so when [Black girls in the school] get in this rut, who typically helps them out?
> Ms. MANN: You. [Laughter] ... You are helping them out.

Anastasia, a 10th grade Black girl, supported Ms. Mann's assertion when she expressed her frustration that while Alaina was gone for a week she had no one to help her "deal" with her "irritating" teacher (FN: November 2015).

During interviews and in passing, Natalie also noted how frequently children and staff would comment positively on her role in the school, as evident in the following conversation with a 4th/5th grader:

NATALIE: Okay. So now I want you to talk to me about your teachers ....how you describe them, well who's your favorite teacher, let's start there.

BLAIR: Well, you're one of my favorite ones ... because, how do I put [it]. Okay, let's say we were outside at recess, like, you can play with us sometimes. Like if we ask you, like, do you want to come watch us dance or you want to play jump rope, like, you'll come with us.

In addition to affirming her role as a teacher, Blair indicated that Natalie was among her favorites. Also important here is how Blair described their interactions and what stood out in everyday practice. Blair saw Natalie's role as dynamic and encompassing more than passive or formalized participation. Relatedly, student Juliana referenced feeling seen throughout the research process in her interview when she said to Natalie, "You make me feel welcome wherever I am. Every time I think of you, it's just one spot in my heart that makes—that just fits you inside." Juliana's reaction demonstrates the type of deep relationships Natalie had developed during her time in the field.

This high level of regard expressed by key school partners (i.e., teachers, school staff, and students) was not a happenstance product of our simply *being* in the space. We argue that it was also not solely attributable to our long-term commitments as justice-oriented scholars. Importantly, the perceived value we brought to our respective research sites was directly connected to *how* we engaged in the *everyday* as critical observers and active participants.

Care in Passing: Notes from the Hallways

We engaged as critical observant participants first by shifting from a research-first orientation to one that unabashedly put Black children first. While we were always aware of the focus and goals of our projects, we tried to prioritize, and meet, the immediate needs of the Black youth as they emerged in real time. This included stepping in as a substitute teacher on a number of occasions, providing homework help during interviews, leaving classroom observations to attend to students in crisis, and much more. Natalie recalls a recurrent feeling of being immersed in the flow of the school day, so much so that participating teachers would encourage her to "not worry about [the present activity or student request]" and "go do your interviews."[2]

Passing in the hallways often became significant opportunities to engage with young participants with care and critical intentionality. This was especially true at Mission City School, where the organization and culture of the school often allowed for frequent hall passing and dynamic hallway activity. In January 2016, Natalie wrote the following description in a fieldnote, "The carpeted hallway makes it impossible to disconnect, or to separate. You hear and see everything." Upon entering the school, Natalie typically spent several minutes greeting children and school personnel. Hugs, compliments, and questions were exchanged. One day, Natalie entered the building to find Gabby in tears in the hallway, seated next to a peer Jimmie. She documented in a fieldnote, "My heart aches as I glance at [Gabby]. I say 'oh no' in a concerned tone and ask her if everything is ok. She looks at me but doesn't respond. I am not surprised because [Gabby] usually isn't very vocal when she's upset" (FN: January 2016). Despite being late to facilitate her weekly math groups, Natalie prioritized Gabby's needs and silently joined in the efforts to console her. Student Jimmie also witnessed Natalie's efforts to be with both of them in a challenging moment. Hastily overlooking this instance in the hallway and proceeding as scheduled would have subtly communicated to both Jimmie and Gabby that the primary concern was academics or teaching in an institutionalized sense. Here is an example of a "passing" moment with potentially far-reaching implications for relationships with young participants.

The organization of JHS also presented Alaina with opportunities to critically care for Black girls in the hallways. Though much of Alaina's days were occupied with facilitating restorative circles and gatherings of *RISE*, she was often able to make time to be in the hallway during passing periods. This was a time filled with warm hellos and updates on grades, weekend shenanigans, and relationship dramas. In a fieldnote from November 2015, she documented the following:

> During the passing period I am standing in the hallway right outside of the RC with Dominique and Opal. Mr. E, the community liaison, refers to them as "city slickers" who skip school and will ultimately get kicked out. With visible confusion about the term on her face, Dominique turns and says "I ain't that." I respond, "That's right girl, you ain't gotta be something that you don't agree with."

In this moment Alaina did what so few adults in JHS did—she denounced pejorative narratives about Black girlhood and affirmed Dominique's right to push back against deficit labels. By emphasizing Dominique's ability to define herself on her own terms, Alaina's critical care took the form of nourishing a developing sense of agency and advocacy that could live long beyond the immediate moment. In another instance, much like Natalie, Alaina answered the call to care for a student in crisis. She documented finding:

> Jana [sitting] on the edge of the bench outside of the office, backpack on, and head in hands. She is crying so violently that her body is shaking. I rush over and begin to hug her and rub her back. Later I ask what is wrong. As she cries, and does not answer, I repeat how sorry I am about whatever is going on.

Alaina recounts sitting with Jana until she was ready to move forward with her day. Prior to this encounter, Alaina had been preparing for a restorative circle. Yet she recognized a need to delay the restorative work and make herself available to acknowledge and respond to Jana's distress. In shifting her priorities and deviating from the preestablished plan without hesitation, Alaina demonstrated the usefulness of dexterity in providing critical care.

Given work in our respective field sites, we argue that researchers who wish to practice care must first shift their orientations to put (Black) children first, over and above any perceived research need or inclination to be passive. Doing so opens up opportunities to develop genuine connections that might otherwise not be possible. Though these "passing" moments could have easily been overlooked, we see a clear connection between these interactions and the subsequent candid and rich conversations we had with children during interviews and other one-on-one moments.

Teaching while Researching: Leveraging Pedagogical Moments to Build Critical Capacity

As we worked to meet children's immediate needs, we did so with our political sensitivities at the fore. Though we hoped the products of our work would move our field forward in theorizing and understanding the nuanced (and too often, disenfranchising) experiences of Black children in schools, we did not take for granted our own agentic potential in these spaces. As such we leveraged the insights we gained from our various forms of involvement to support the students in navigating their school and communal contexts in *real time*. By utilizing in-the-moment interactions to help the students build a critical awareness of the inequities they encountered in and out of school, we were intentionally advancing justice consistent with our goals as critical ethnographers. It was sometimes challenging to make these judgment calls to know when to lean in and what to prioritize. Nonetheless, we relied on our intuition and experiential knowledge to delve into discussions with youth around the issues they were *already* grappling with.

Alaina often used restorative meetings as an opportunity to help Black girls understand the broader inequities that drove their challenging interactions with teachers. Though de-escalation and relationship building were the primary purposes of restorative meetings, Alaina felt it was important to use these private moments away from their teachers' gaze to build the young women's critical capacity. On one occasion Alaina facilitated a restorative meeting with Candace and Jana after they had been suspended following a dispute with their math teacher, Mr. Clark. In the meeting Alaina first recognized a need to acknowledge and validate the girls as they shared their frustration with being kicked out of school due to a misinterpretation of their words. Although in her role as assistant director of the RC Alaina worked with teachers (Mr. Clark included) to grow their skills in working with Black girls, she knew that many still struggled. Once this meeting ended, the girls would be returning to classrooms where they would likely have similar experiences. As such, she felt it was necessary to teach them about the underlying power dynamics at play, telling them:

> I'm not saying you did anything to get caught up; what I'm saying is that he laid out all of these traps ... You got caught because of what he was laying out. And I know you aren't going to like what I'm about to say because you shouldn't have to do this. But you have to say (exhales deeply) I'm walking into Mr. Clark's class and I know that if I do A, B, C, or D he's going to interpret that as me having an attitude, me being upset, me talking about him, me being this or that. So although I shouldn't have to alter what I do and I shouldn't have to think about these things because other kids don't have to, because I don't want to get suspended, because I don't want to get kicked out and I want to be here, I am going to try not to do A, B, C, and D because I know that he is going to have a problem with it. Totally not fair; totally not what other kids have to do and it's BS, but that's the way to avoid

coming up against this ... And because he is the teacher, he has the power to write a referral. There aren't student referrals are there? You don't get to write those.

By explaining how their (white) teacher's likely reliance on negative perceptions of Black girls unfairly served as "traps" that made it likely to "catch them up" in the disciplinary system, Alaina hoped to contribute to their developing critical consciousness. By dissecting Mr. Clark's "traps" she hoped to provide a basis for why the girls should not internalize his characterizations of their behavior as unequivocally true. She also hoped the girls would develop the code-switching dexterity to avoid negative disciplinary interactions in the future in the absence of the removal of these traps. Despite being frank, Alaina thought about the necessity of not demonizing the teachers with whom she had developed a strong working relationship with. To avoid this, she encouraged Candace and Jana to think beyond individual teachers to the larger structures that elevate teachers' voices while simultaneously silencing student voices within the referral process (Neal-Jackson, 2020). In thinking about their futures, Alaina knew it was essential that they have knowledge of the structures that made these negative disciplinary interactions possible. By the end of the conversation, Candace and Jana had plans in place to advocate for "student referrals" that would hold teachers accountable and make visible the kinds of inequitable treatment they were experiencing.

Natalie's child interviews were designed to support Black children in making latent considerations about race, sociopolitical inequities, and their own agency more explicit. Many of the children had never been asked to articulate their understandings of racism or describe (in a proleptic sense) what they might do to solve the social problems they identified. Natalie deemed it important to position Black children as agents and experts in their own rights. At the same time, Natalie anticipated that her role as critical researcher would involve leveraging pedagogical moments to encourage and co-construct ideas, clarify misconceptions, and/or intervene. Often this looked like responding to children's *I don't know*s with compassion while inviting participants to dwell and think aloud. "Yeah, that's a big question that maybe you've never been asked before," Natalie would say. "Let's try to think about it together. Have you ever heard the word ____ before? ... " These subtle cues respected Black children's reluctance in the moment without presuming a lack of knowledge or capacity. As both political and pedagogical work, these cues helped to reframe any feelings of uncertainty as reasonable given the nature of the question, all while continuing to encourage and validate Black children's ideas.

In other instances, caring participation took the form of intervention. Consider this excerpt where 4th grader Chase was articulating a possible individual response to a local robbery:

CHASE: Say, I was at a place and—and I came in and order some pizza and it took five minutes. These two guys came in with guns and I was talking to them saying, "What if this person get hurt? And you're going to go to jail and that's not a good thing" and maybe, maybe they will walk away.
NATALIE: Ah. Now, in real life, I want you to be careful with that, okay?

CHASE: Uh-huh.
NATALIE: Because if somebody has a gun, I want you to just make sure you keep yourself safe first, okay?
CHASE: Uh-huh.
NATALIE: Alright. But that's a good idea because sometimes that does work to be able to talk to people. I just don't want you to try it if guns are involved, okay?

Above, Natalie affirmed Chase's thinking but also treated it as a critical pedagogical and political encounter (Vossoughi & Zavala, 2020). Natalie intervened as necessary for Chase's protection and to support a deeper, co-constructed understanding of the risks involved with the solution he envisioned. The sense of responsibility to assert agency as someone who cared most about Chase's learning in that moment (as both a developing activist and human being/Black boy whose life matters) took precedence over any concerns about moving the interview along. In the moment, Natalie was trying to respond in a way that sat at the intersection of criticality and care. The examples in this section are evidence of researchers' efforts to engage with the implicit, "hidden" dynamics at stake for Black youth. In large and small ways, we were taking a proactive stance in facilitating the acquisition of critical knowledge pertinent to Black youth's ability to combat individual and systemic barriers in their lives.

Here Goes Nothing: Stepping up and into Paradigm Shifting Forms of Participant Observation

The analyses presented in this chapter move toward a framework that reconceptualizes the transformative possibilities of participant observation within critical ethnography. Critical research necessitates action, intentionality, and a nuanced understanding of how different ways of being at particular moments work toward or against equity and care. Our attention to the what, when, and how of our work helped us to notice everyday opportunities to (re)define what it meant to practice ethnographic research with care and integrity. Through this lens, carrying out caring ethnographic research becomes less about whether one is acting as practitioner, researcher, or political agent. Rather, it shifts our focus to a deeper consideration of when and how stepping up and into roles (that are always overlapping) creates openings for pedagogy and relationality.

We entered into our respective school sites as Black women committed to educational justice for Black children. It is important to acknowledge this as our starting place. However, regardless of one's racial identity or positionality, it is important for researchers to cultivate an ethos around their work that considers how everyday interactions present an opportunity to engage with youth in ways that are affirming at present *and* that help them visualize liberating paths forward. While we are reluctant to propose a set of concrete guidelines, we offer the following as ideas and questions to think with. Critical ethnographers who aim to practice care might begin by first taking inventory of instances where youth in their research context demonstrated a need for adult affirmation, advocacy, and/or intervention. For these moments recalled and documented in fieldnotes, was there a response? What did the responses (or lack thereof) communicate about the researcher's role and priorities? Taking inventory of normed practices over the course of a day or week might illuminate opportunities to shift in ways that better align with practicing care. Additionally, rather than simply documenting present problems and emergent understandings, we invite researchers to pay closer attention to the near-futures of youth. Some key questions to consider for educational ethnographers are these: What critical sensitivities and perceptiveness do I/we possess as researchers that would be beneficial to share with participants? Am I withholding knowledge in my daily interactions that could support students' agency, savvy, and critical awareness *right now*?

We would be remiss to not recognize the inherent messiness of this work. In our school-based research, interactions with Black youth sometimes felt unresolved and left us perplexed about immediate next steps. And yet these tensions and questions were generative and further indicated our care and growth as novice critical ethnographers. Through these moments of uncertainty, we gained a deeper sense of what it meant to study and nurture youth in real time.

Finally, we return to where we began this chapter by establishing ourselves as coauthors, co-thinkers, and friends. It is important for critical ethnographers to cultivate friendships and coalitions with others who have similar commitments but otherwise vary in expertise, identities, and approaches to teaching/research. Particularly if you are a non-BIPOC scholar doing ethnographic work in a BIPOC community, it may be important to seek out opportunities to have explicit conversations with scholars of color about ethics, positionality, and other important dimensions of the research. Relationships with colleague-friends and participants sharpen our sensitivities to the nuances of the spaces and people we study. By embracing shifting modes of participation and attuning to everyday experiences, we gain insights that enable us to tell stories about (Black) youth that are representative of their meaning making and brilliance.

2

Platicando entre Compañeras: The Use of *Pláticas* to Navigate Ethical Dilemmas in Ethnographic Research with and for Latina High School Students

Bianca N. Haro

Valentina: So yeah, I didn't come Friday cause I was jumped and TBH, I was like paranoid, and I was all bruised up. I didn't want people to ask. I know you were in my class. Sorry I didn't show up.

(*plática*, July 17, 2018)

Over a *plática*, the Spanish word that refers to both a conversation and the methodology (Fierros & Delgado Bernal, 2016) I employ in my work, Valentina,[1] a sixteen-year-old Latina high school student, shared she was "jumped" on her walk home from summer school. In addition to the trauma inflicted on her and her family, this event impeded her from attending school the next day. The perpetrator had left Valentina with physical scratches and bruises that she attempted to cover with a red long-sleeved turtleneck upon her return to finish the last week of summer school. As a first-generation Latina of Mexican descent and born to working-class parents, Valentina faced numerous systemic barriers that could possibly push her out of school. Yet her bravery and desire to finish high school and attend college was far greater.

My approach to research—the use of *pláticas* as a method and methodology and what I call a Chicana/Latina feminist ethics of care—allowed me to respond to Valentina's physical attack in a humanizing way and care for her holistic life, despite the incident occurring outside of the "research site." Caring for her holistic life meant I prioritized her emotional and personal needs throughout the research inquiry. I prioritized our human relationship and the well-being of Valentina. In caring for her holistic life, I also worked with Valentina to find solutions that provided her the safety she needed to attend school.

In this chapter, I detail how I came to the decision to employ *pláticas* as a graduate student based, in part, on the limitations of traditional ethnography and critical ethnography. I then introduce *pláticas* (Fierros & Delgado Bernal, 2016) as a method and methodology in more detail and conceptualize a Chicana/Latina feminist ethics of care. Thereafter, employing three out of the five principles of *pláticas*, I walk through my decision-making process as a researcher and *compañera* (friend/colleague) that ultimately led to me embracing a Chicana/Latina ethics of care. I draw from a two-year critical ethnographic dissertation study that focused on the factors that push Latina high school students out of school (Haro, 2020). I end the chapter with a discussion on the significance of disrupting Eurocentric research practices that assume objectivity, neutrality, and are rooted in the history of colonialism that Western scholars have used for years. In disrupting these research practices, I end with ways researchers can start to decolonize qualitative research and navigate the research process with care, attending to young people's holistic lives.

Challenging Qualitative Research Methods as a Chicana Graduate Student

As a Chicana critical ethnographer examining the factors that push young Latinas out of school, my approach to research is driven by Chicana/Latina feminist methodologies. These methodologies challenge many of the Eurocentric research practices I learned in a mandatory, qualitative methods three-part series course for my doctoral program. The methods employed to conduct ethnographic work, specifically the process of interviewing, seemed fairly straightforward. Researchers develop a protocol that aligns with their research questions. Researchers then recruit participants and follow the protocol for each participant. The instructor suggested that when a participant deviated from the original protocol question, our responsibility as the researcher was to redirect the interview in order to gather "data" that would answer the larger research questions.

As a graduate student researcher, I started to employ what I was learning in the course. Prior to my dissertation work, I began conducting interviews for a larger study.[2] In particular, this experience taught me that qualitative work was much more complex than the instructor had conveyed. As I had learned it in class, the act of interviewing was merely a process to extract information from young people. During an interview I was conducting with an African American young man, Anthony, he spoke about the absence of his grandmother. Almost in tears, he expressed how, although she had recently passed, she was his motivation to do well in school. As I listened, Anthony's body displayed profound pain and grief. I wanted to engage in a deeper conversation about his grandmother—the ancestral wisdom she passed onto him—and share that I too had recently lost my grandmother.[3] Yet the conversation I wanted (and felt he wanted) to have was not part of the protocol nor did it answer the research questions of the larger study. Thus, the conversation about our grandmothers would be considered "unnecessary" audio recording. I was conflicted. Should I redirect the interview? Stop the recorder?

I decided to stop the recorder. Our "interview" thereafter was a rich *plática* that truly offered a holistic insight into Anthony's life—beyond his educational experiences. I noticed his body ease and, in remembering his grandmother, his face brightened with joy. In turn, I shared the wisdom my grandmother had gifted me. After spending some time uplifting our grandmothers, culturally connecting the feminine ancestral wisdom passed onto us, I asked him if he was willing to continue the "interview." Anthony smiled and agreed.

In that moment, I realized qualitative research methods as they were being taught to me—especially the process of interviewing—were rigid and limiting. More importantly, they were exploitative, extractive, and emotionally harming. I left the conversation with Anthony eager to find the tools that allowed for collectivity and a deeper connection between collaborators and researchers; tools that offered the possibility of conducting research that went beyond extracting "data" from young people like Anthony included him as part of the research process, and validated the mutual exchange of lived experiences amongst researchers and collaborators.

Consequently, I decided to take "Chicana/Latina Feminist Methodologies in Education," a seminar taught by Chicana feminist scholar Dr. Dolores Delgado Bernal. This class both challenged Eurocentric research practices and affirmed the uncertainties I had with my qualitative methods course. The course offered methods and methodologies that connected to my community and to my ways of knowing as a daughter of immigrant parents, and as a first-generation Chicana college student and scholar. I learned how Chicana/Latina feminists conceptualize and use methodologies that "situate the researcher-participant in a reciprocal relationship where genuine connections are made between 'academic' and community members" (Flores Carmona, 2014, p. 118). Through this course, I developed the methodological approach I would use in my dissertation.

The Use of Critical Ethnography to Counter Limitations of Traditional Ethnography

The use of ethnography can be traced to late-nineteenth-century anthropologists "who engaged in participant observations in the 'field'" to understand the culture of a group through thick description (Merriam, 2009, p. 27). Ethnography has been a widely used approach amongst education and sociology scholars to examine the effects of school pushout, or most commonly known as the "school-to-prison pipeline" phenomenon (Annamma, 2018b; J. Flores, 2016; Morris, 2016; Nolan, 2011; Rios, 2011). For me, traditional ethnography falls short—in that—historically excluded youth are positioned as subjects of research with the researcher merely observing them to theorize their experiences (see Nolan, 2011; Simmons, 2017). The use of "research subject" (see J. Flores, 2016; Nolan, 2011; Simmons, 2017) and similar language is ever-present in ethnographic studies, and qualitative research at large, that focus on Students of Color (SoC). Such language reflects the way ethnography and the methods employed for "data collection" (such as interviewing) extract from young people, without reciprocity. Paris and Winn (2014) further note:

> The history of qualitative and ethnographic work seeking, at worst, to pathologize, exoticize, objectify, and name as deficient communities of color and other marginalized populations in the U.S. and beyond, and at best, to take and gain through research but not to give back, stretches back across the 19th century and forward to the current day.
>
> (xvi)

For this reason, my work employs *critical ethnography*, a framework that is committed "to producing and performing texts that are grounded in and co-constructed in the politically and personally problematic worlds of everyday life" (Denzin, 2003, p. 270). Moreover, a critical ethnographer "does not use words like data, or abduction, or objectivity. These words carry the traces of science, objectivism, and knowledge produced for disciplines, not everyday people" (p. 270). Perhaps most important to critical ethnography is the "critical," which is the "praxis, taking action for change by challenging marginalization as a result of what the participants have shared" (Flores Carmona, 2014, p. 117).

Critical ethnography, however, does not take into account nor is it framed under a Chicana feminist epistemology (CFE) (Delgado Bernal, 1998). Delgado Bernal (1998) argues that Chicana researchers have different worldviews that equip us with unique cultural tools in research, what she describes as "cultural intuition." This cultural intuition relies on four major sources: personal experience, existing literature, professional experience, and the analytical research process itself. My CFE has ethical, political, and feminist orientations that guided my research process and my relationship with Valentina. I highlight the absence of a CFE in critical ethnography to acknowledge my Chicana feminist ways of knowing and engage in methodological interventions that align with my and Valentina's epistemologies (Delgado Bernal, 2020).

Pláticas is one of the many methodologies Chicana/Latina feminist scholars use in their approach to disrupt mainstream qualitative research practices (Delgado Bernal, 2020; Fierros & Delgado Bernal, 2016; A. I. Flores, 2016; Garcia & Mireles-Rios, 2019; Vega, 2019). As Delgado Bernal and Elenes (2011) explain, "the term *plática* comes from Spanish and means conversation of dialogue" (p. 111). *Pláticas* are different from interviews—they are *shared* exchanges in which participants are collaborators and creators in the production of knowledge and the research process. In other words, *pláticas* are not used to extract information; rather, they allow researchers and collaborators to simultaneously reflect and theorize their own lived experiences.

Fierros and Delgado Bernal (2016) identify five principles of *pláticas* as a methodology:

1. *Pláticas* draw upon Chicana/Latina feminist theory and other critical theories;
2. *Pláticas* honor participants as co-constructors of knowledge;
3. *Pláticas* interlock the everyday lived experiences and research inquiry;
4. *Pláticas* provide a potential space for healing; and
5. *Pláticas* rely on reciprocal relationships, vulnerability, and researcher reflexivity.

In short, critical ethnography supports the limitations of ethnography and *pláticas* acknowledges my CFE, all of which contribute to the disruption of Eurocentric research practices, notions of objectivity, and support my unique ways of knowing. I braid together the commitments of critical ethnography and *pláticas* methodology to bring forth what I call Chicana/Latina feminist ethics of care.

A Chicana/Latina Feminist Ethics of Care

A large body of literature explores the ways teachers embody care through their pedagogical practices and relationships with students (Cariaga, 2018; Calderón et al., 2012; Valenzuela, 1999). Valenzuela (1999) demonstrates how teachers can engage in "authentic care," care that is tailored to meet the needs of individual students. This authentic care considers the holistic life of students, outside of school. For example, a teacher may provide flexibility on assignments for a student who works to support their family. From the standpoint of a CFE, care also embraces the academic, emotional, and personal needs of students that then transform and disrupt the power relations between teacher and student (Cariaga, 2018; Calderón et al., 2012; Prieto & Villenas, 2012). How, then, do Chicana/Latina feminist researchers engage with care and attention to their research collaborators?

For Chicana/Latina feminist scholars, researcher reflexivity is critical to the disruption of Eurocentric research practices (Calderón, 2016; Cervantes-Soon, 2014; Flores Carmona, 2014; Flores Carmona et al., 2018; Villenas, 1996). It is precisely in the practice of researcher reflexivity where Chicana/Latina feminist researchers "search the possibility and explore the contradictions of being 'Malintizin researchers' and how we are replicating oppressive acts" (Flores Carmona, 2014, p. 114). It is this reflexivity that allows researchers to find ways to care for their collaborators beyond the research inquiry.

A Chicana/Latina feminist ethics of care (CLFEC), then, means being in a constant state of reflexivity—at every phase of the research. Similar to employing pedagogies of care, this reflexivity for one invites researchers to contemplate power dynamics between them and their collaborators and then consider ways to disrupt them. This inspires researchers, even those from historically excluded communities, to recognize their position as colonized/colonizers (Villenas, 1996), as well as pay close attention to how we can subjugate and further disenfranchise our own communities. This reflexivity is a constant process, a continuous praxis that generates *action* to disrupt damage-centered research (Tuck, 2009).

For instance, engaging in a CLFEC has the possibility to disrupt language that reinforces the researcher-participant binary. Chicana/Latina feminist researchers have reframed words like "research subjects." For example, inspired by Sara Lawrence-Lightfoot (2005), A. I. Flores (2016) refers to her "research participants" as collaborators. Garcia and Mireles-Rios (2019) recategorize their "participants" as co-constructors and Vega (2019) as *co-madres*. The use of such words challenges hegemonic qualitative research language and the categories used. It recognizes the cultural connectedness of the researcher and collaborators and the significant role of collaborators in the research process. This simple action transforms our approach to research, how we engage with collaborators in a way where they feel empowered, cared for, and, consequently, prioritize the needs of collaborators and not the research study itself.

For me, referring to Valentina as a *compañera* (friend/colleague) was engaging in a CLFEC as I conceptualized the larger study and reflected on the approach to research in previous studies. Referring to Valentina as a *compañera* acknowledged her role in the research process and in turn, informed the care for her holistic life beyond a "research participant." For me, Valentina's needs, rather than the research study itself, were front and center—a reflection of CLFEC. When Valentina was explaining her physical attack, I reflected and asked myself, "What does she need in this very moment to feel safe and secure?" Thus, engaging in a CLFEC not only disrupted the researcher-participant dichotomy and challenged hierarchies of difference, it also made possible the culturally rooted companionship and care between Valentina and me and influenced the actions I took.

Dolores Huerta High School

The narrative of Valentina derives from my critical ethnographic dissertation (Haro, 2020). For two academic years (2017–2018 and 2018–2019) and one summer session (2018), I conducted critical ethnographic research at Dolores Huerta High School in Southern California working with a total of twelve Latina students. The student body was primarily Latinx[4] (55.5 percent) and Black/African American (40.5 percent) (California Department of Education, 2018). The school is located in a predominantly working-class area and 76 percent of students receive free or reduced lunch, indicating economic disadvantage. Within the larger study, I aimed to understand the factors that push young Latinas out of school.

Valentina and I engaged in numerous *pláticas*. These *pláticas* centered on understanding her educational experiences. At times, our *pláticas* were also about college applications, tension Valentina had with friends, and her frustrations with particular teachers and school staff. I audio-recorded and transcribed all *pláticas*. The bulk of the data for this chapter draws on *pláticas* with Valentina and self-reflexive journal entries I incorporated as part of *pláticas*. I also blend fieldnote observations with narrative to fully capture events. In the next section, I introduce Valentina and detail an ethical dilemma I encountered while working with her.

"I Got Jumped"

After her sophomore year, Valentina decided to attend summer school to get a higher grade in her English class. Her goal was to strengthen her transcript for college applications. During the third week of summer school, I walked into her English classroom rather nervous. Students were required to write ten poems and create a poetry portfolio for their final project; I had volunteered to share a poem I had written during my undergraduate studies to inspire Valentina and her peers. Reading the poem was one of the ways I employed the fifth principle of *pláticas*—reciprocal relationships, vulnerability, and researcher reflexivity—I sought to reciprocate Valentina's vulnerability and all the other students who would present their poems.

As usual, I sat in the back of the classroom and waited for class to start. As I took out the poem, a pen, and my small notebook for fieldnotes, I noticed Valentina was not in her seat. I waited for the bell to ring; "Perhaps she went to the restroom," I thought. The bell rang and class started. Ms. Johnson took attendance and after calling Valentina's name she looked at me and said, "She might be absent today." I decided to text Valentina fifteen minutes into class. She quickly responded and shared, "Oh yea, I didn't go to school 'cause there was an incident that happened yesterday. I got jumped and my chain stolen when I was walking home." I was in utter shock—I immediately stepped out of the classroom to call Valentina. Since she was unable to answer, we continued our conversation via text.

> BIANCA: Valentina! Are you okay?
> VALENTINA: My mom wants me to move schools, at least I didn't get stabbed or shot but I have scratches and bruises. I touch them and they hurt. I have some on my arms that turned purple.
>
> (texting, July 14, 2018)

After Valentina described her injuries, I was speechless. In particular, her words "at least I didn't get stabbed or shot" reveal the systems of oppression she confronts in the everyday, and give context to her neighborhood, a community where majority African American and Latinx people have been historically disenfranchised and are faced with low-resourced schools, worn-down parks, and police brutality. I was quickly reminded of the ways I have experienced and continue to experience the same systems of oppression. In previous *pláticas* with Valentina, she described her neighborhood as "hot," especially during summer. Depicting a neighborhood as "hot" was a word young people at Dolores Huerta used to describe their neighborhood as dangerous with heightened criminal activity. As a Chicana researcher, connecting Valentina's everyday lived experiences outside of Dolores Huerta High and the research inquiry was vital to understanding her holistic life—a reflection of the third principle of *pláticas*.

In that text exchange, I had no words to comfort Valentina. I was aware I did not have the power to dismantle and resolve the root cause: systemic racism that has continuously marginalized Communities of Color, crime, and violence. This moment required me to challenge dominant research practices and be attentive to my CLFEC that would inform how I would care for and support Valentina. This event urged me to be reflexive in the moment and ask, "What is my responsibility to Valentina, who welcomed me into her life? Is how I engage with her a reflection of my approach and commitment to social justice research?"

Employing *Pláticas* to Navigate Ethical Dilemmas

Integral to honoring Valentina as a co-constructor of knowledge, the second principle of *pláticas*, my relationship with Valentina as a *compañera* challenged power dynamics and the researcher-participant dichotomy. I also recognized the physical attack Valentina experienced outside of the "research site" as connected to the larger study, the third principle of *pláticas* which braids the everyday lived experiences and research inquiry. To honor my approach to research and my commitment to work with care to Valentina's life beyond a "participant," I decided to prioritize being her *compañera* rather than the researcher that had been attempting to understand her educational experiences.

> BIANCA: Would your parents be okay with me taking you home after school? I am already here and I definitely would not mind taking you. I don't think it is safe for you to walk home. Ask your mom and then let me know.
> VALENTINA: Yeah, I can ask. I am sure she fine with it. But she wants me to move schools but [I am going to] finish summer school here.
> BIANCA: Did you file a police report?
> VALENTINA: Yeah, we did, but they haven't done anything. My mom will be going to the office Monday morning to show them the police report 'cause I didn't go to school today and she wants me to move schools.
>
> (texting, July 14, 2018)

After Valentina's last text, I shared I would be in touch with her over the weekend. I went back into Ms. Johnson's classroom and shared my poem. Employing the fifth principle of *pláticas* and a Chicana/Latina feminist ethics of care, I used my journal entry to reflect on my role as a researcher and *compañera* and the physical attack Valentina experienced.

> Today I left Dolores troubled and shocked of the realities my *compañeras* live, day in and day out. Valentina being physically attacked on her way home and unable to go to school today was a reality check for me, of what I do not experience as a "researcher" despite "fully immersing myself" as an ethnographer. More importantly, it was an insight to her life beyond school.
>
> (journal entry, July 14, 2018)

As much as I attempted to engage with Valentina as a *compañera* and co-constructor of knowledge, the second principle of *pláticas*, the physical attack Valentina experienced made a clear distinction between her and me. As the researcher I had the choice of immersing or completely removing myself from Dolores Huerta High and her community at any given moment. Valentina did not have that choice. As a Chicana critical ethnographer, this was important to recognize. Although my approach to research attempted to disrupt power dynamics within research, power still manifested—even as I engaged with my own community (Villenas, 1996). This journal entry amplified my commitment to a CLFEC and humanizing research (Paris & Winn, 2014), and most certainly, my relationship with Valentina. How, then, did *pláticas* and my CLFEC ensure I did not engage in oppressive acts while working with Valentina?

As a first step, acknowledge the physical attack. Fierros and Delgado Bernal (2016) share that "instead of ignoring or minimizing lived experiences as if they do not relate to the research inquiry, a *plática* methodology draws them in as part and parcel of research inquiry" (p. 112), principle two. In my journal entry I made sense of this interconnectedness. Doing otherwise would mean I was engaging in research that ignored and replicated the subjugation Valentina was already experiencing in school and more generally. In that same journal entry, engaging in a CLFEC I reflected, "What did this experience mean for Valentina's education moving forward? Would she finish summer school? Continue at Dolores Huerta High?" Despite the attack occurring outside of Dolores Huerta High, I recognized it and reflected on how it would affect Valentina.

I texted Valentina the Sunday of the same week of her physical assault to confirm she would be at school the next day. In that same text exchange, I briefly explained that while I was more than willing to drive her home after school, I would feel more comfortable doing so if I spoke to her mother in person. She agreed and shared her mother was willing and able to speak to me. Ten minutes before school on Monday morning, I met Valentina's mother right outside of Dolores Huerta High. Her mother was a light brown-skinned woman of short stature with bags under her eyes, conveying stress and exhaustion. We shook hands and greeted each other in Spanish; I have translated our dialogue.

I explained to Valentina's mother that I was a graduate student at the University of California, Los Angeles, working at Dolores Huerta with Valentina and other Latina students to understand their educational experiences. Her mother nodded and said, "Yes, she told me all about you." Without prompting, Valentina's mother shared, "We filed a police report, but I doubt they will do anything or find the person who attacked her. She is all bruised and scratched." Her voice broke as she spoke. Her eyes filled with tears. I acknowledged her pain, nodded, and thereafter expressed I would be happy to drive Valentina home after school. I emphasized that although my role limited me to the premises of the school, I was invested in Valentina and the other girls beyond what occurred inside the school. I also shared I would only be able to drive Valentina for the 2018–2019 academic year. Valentina's mother nodded her head in affirmation. "It is not a solution to the root cause, but a band-aid," I acknowledged to both. My CLFEC reminded me to be reflective of my researcher positionality in real time, as well as honest, not over-promise, and remain transparent.

I explained another concern I had was school staff finding out I was driving Valentina home as I would be overstepping the formal agreement I had with the district and could face legal repercussions from my university's Institutional Review Board or the school district. Yet, the safety of Valentina outweighed these fears, or the risk of being forbidden into the school and unable to proceed with the study. Valentina's mother quickly assured me, "This is between us," with Valentina following, "Yeah me neither, I ain't telling no one." We agreed I would drive Valentina home the remainder of summer school and next school year. Then, the bell for first period rang—Valentina and her mother headed into the main office, and I met another *compañera* with whom I was working.

That same day, Valentina and I ate lunch together and had a *plática*. I highlight the *plática* that opened this chapter to share in more detail how the principles of *pláticas* manifested. In sharing this *plática* a second time, I attempt to highlight moments that expose principle two, honoring Valentina as a co-constructor of knowledge, and three, connecting the everyday lived experiences of Valentina to the research inquiry. However, it is important to note that the principles of *pláticas* are continuous and do not occur in chronological order, nor are they a clear and defined application. At times, principles occur concurrently in one sentence. For the purposes of this chapter, I **bold** the moments that represent principle two and <u>underline</u> the moments that represent principle three. I **<u>bold and underline</u>** moments where principles are occurring simultaneously. That day, Valentina initiated the *plática*.

> VALENTINA: **So yeah, I didn't come Friday cause I was jumped and TBH, I was like paranoid, and I was all bruised up.** I didn't want people to ask. I know you were in my class. Sorry I didn't show up.
>
> BIANCA: No need to apologize! Really. I am truly sorry that happened to you. <u>I'm more concerned about you, not the work we agreed to do. I want to reiterate I am truly invested in you, even beyond Dolores Huerta High, like I told your mom earlier, and your well-being is most important.</u>
>
> VALENTINA: Thank you. **Yeah, we [are] *compañeras*, right?** That's the word? [chuckles].
>
> BIANCA: Yes, exactly! I am glad you remember that.
>
> VALENTINA: My moms was happy to meet you. She sent me a text after you and her spoke. <u>She was really scared and doesn't want me walking home from school but I gotta finish summer school.</u>
>
> BIANCA: Yeah, I can imagine. You are really courageous. We don't have to talk about it. <u>I am sure it is still fresh. I wanted us to check in about how you were doing, being your first day back since the incident, and then arranging where we will meet today after school.</u>
>
> VALENTINA: I mean, **I don't mind talking about it with you**, cause I trust you and you care. **<u>This is my neighborhood. I can give you a tour of it if you want, but driving, not walking [chuckles]. Then you will know about my school and neighborhood</u>**.
>
> (*plática*, July 17, 2018)

By this time, Valentina had a good sense of the larger study, her role, and what we would ultimately accomplish. Collaborators like Valentina understanding the larger project and her position as a *compañera* is critical to *pláticas* methodology, especially when working with young people. Her words shed light to the possibilities of young people feeling empowered, cared for, and validated in research. Valentina initiating the *plática* is reflective of principle two, how *pláticas* challenges power dynamics between researcher and participant. I valued Valentina and saw her as the holder and creator of knowledge which translated to her leading the *plática*. Along the same lines, Valentina challenges the researcher-participant categories and reminds me we are *compañeras*, a word I used to explain our collaboration, co-constructing knowledge about her and other Latina students' educational experiences. Moreover, she recommends a tour of her neighborhood and defines the approach to it.

I employ the third principle at the beginning of the *plática*—the connection between her everyday lived experiences and the research inquiry—acknowledging my concern for her well-being after the physical attack. Thus, when *pláticas* is used from within a Chicana/Latina feminist perspective, "the holistic life forces of contributors matter for the research inquiry and are not only welcomed, but understood as necessary" (Fierros & Delgado Bernal, 2016, p. 112). Therefore, I reiterate to Valentina that our relationship transcends the larger study and, in that moment, that I was much more concerned about her well-being than "interviewing" her to "collect data." That day, my CLFEC, the self-reflection I had done in my journals, manifested in action—I engaged in a *plática* with Valentina to check in on her rather than extract "data" related to the larger study. Towards the end, Valentina braids principle two and three by encouraging me to spend some time getting to know her school *and* neighborhood. Her words "this is my neighborhood" speak to the pride for her community despite the attack, and suggest it is a key component of her lived experiences, of who she is. Our *plática* disrupted Eurocentric research practices and moved us to employ a CLFEC, together, as *compañeras*.

After our *plática*, Valentina and I walked to her English class. That same day I drove Valentina home. Initially, the drive was rather quiet. She directed me when to turn left or right. Once we were on the main street, Valentina broke her silence by retelling the incident as we drove through the exact location of where the assault happened. I listened. After I dropped her off, I drove a couple of blocks and parked. I needed a moment to breath, to sit with my feelings. Valentina retelling her narrative was gut-wrenching. I then decided to audio-record myself and describe what Valentina had shared with the intent to listen and reflect on it once I arrived home.

> "This is where the guy jumped me!" she pointed to the right side of the street [...] the man initially stopped her to "spit some game." After she ignored him, he started to follow her and suddenly ripped her gold chain and pushed her to the ground. "Luckily he didn't take my phone." [...] I apologized repeatedly and listened. "I am sorry that happened to you. It should never happen to you or anyone." She reiterated her words "TBH,[5] just so glad I didn't get stabbed or shot."
>
> (Bianca's audio-recording, July 17, 2018)

I was heavy-hearted my entire drive home. I replayed the incident in my head. Once I got home, I wrote a journal entry to make sense of our first drive to her home. This was my way of employing the fifth principle of *pláticas*—researcher reflexivity—simultaneously practicing a CLFEC.

> The words "just glad I didn't get shot" echo inside my head. I admire Valentina's courage and fearlessness to walk home every day, especially during summer despite her knowing her neighborhood is "hot." I was uncomfortable as she shared her physical attack in the car, mostly because I did not want her to (re)live it. It had only been three days since the incident. I did not expect her to share so much detail. I am reminded that *pláticas* as a methodology provide a potential space for healing and gave me the tools to engage with Valentina with care and compassion. To merely listen.
>
> (journal entry, July 17, 2018)

In that same journal entry, I reflected on the "critical" in critical ethnography—the action(s) we take as researchers to disrupt the marginalization of our collaborators

(Flores Carmona, 2014). The journal entry helped me reflect on the complexity of my role as a researcher and *compañera,* and affirmed the decision to drive Valentina home every day, through summer school and the next academic school year. More importantly, it reminded me of my commitment to humanizing research, research that goes beyond the extraction of "data," and to remain true to Valentina as a *compañera.* I was well aware that driving Valentina home after school each day wouldn't necessarily change the systemic challenges she faced, but it gave her the immediate care and safety she needed to finish summer school and continue onto her third year at Dolores Huerta High.

Our drives home thereafter gave us the space to enhance our CLFEC and consider potential solutions to her final year at Dolores Huerta. During the last week of the academic school year, Valentina confided that she was potentially going to move schools. I offered my support and encouraged her to stay in touch. The last day I drove her home I had the opportunity to briefly thank her mother for the opportunity to meet her and Valentina. I shared how I admired Valentina's fearlessness and affirmed she had a bright future ahead. I drove off saddened, realizing it was potentially the last day I would see or hear from Valentina.

Conclusion and Methodological Guidance

In this chapter, I highlight the limitations of mainstream qualitative research practices, and more specifically ethnography. I demonstrate what critical ethnography and *pláticas* methodology afford. With the use of a CLFEC as part of my research praxis, I was able to further challenge "the rigid constructions of how to do research" (Flores Carmona et al., 2018, p. 46). I was able to reimagine my relationship with Valentina, listen, interpret, and learn from her with intention and care for her beyond the research inquiry, and drive her home every day after school. I attest to the possibilities of a CLFEC to inform and guide the research practices we choose by and with historically excluded young people, and more importantly, challenge destructive damage-centered ethnographic research practices (Tuck, 2009). Similarly, I encourage ethnographers of different ethnic and racial backgrounds who are attempting to disrupt Eurocentric qualitative research practices, to practice the following:

1. Engage in researcher reflexivity. This can begin with reflections on the self,[6] the self in relation to others,[7] and the self in relation to the system[8] as you conceptualize your collaboration. Thereafter, this researcher reflexivity becomes a constant practice, what I call a CLFEC. At times, this reflexivity occurs in the moment, as I demonstrated in this chapter, and other times it can be practiced in isolation with journal entries.
2. Search for methodologies that disrupt power dynamics between you and your collaborators. I relied on critical ethnography and *pláticas,* a methodology that aligned with who I am as a Chicana, my commitment to social justice research, and included Valentina in theorizing her own experiences.

3. Challenge hegemonic research categories and use language that connects to our commitment to humanizing research that empowers young people. For example, I used *compañera* to acknowledge Valentina as a co-constructor of knowledge, that challenges the researcher-participant dichotomy.

In my attempt to provide tangible practices, I want to be clear that by no means are these the only practices I encourage others to take on. They are merely some of many steps researchers can engage in to reimagine an approach to research that is empowering, holistic, and caring for young people like Valentina.

3

Care as Resistance and Epistemological Necessity in YPAR

Meagan Call-Cummings and Melissa Hauber-Özer

As a form of critical pedagogy, youth participatory action research (YPAR) engages adults and children—often educators and students—in a praxis of dialogue, action, and reflection (Fals-Borda & Rahman, 1991; Freire, 1970). The goal is to raise consciousness about and ultimately dismantle systemic injustices and structural oppression. This mutual education and collaboration process upends hierarchical power dynamics dominant in traditional schooling to conduct research with youth rather than on or about them (Fox, 2019) and requires overcoming the adult/child binary dominant in traditional schooling and educational research (Dennis et al., 2019). In order for this to occur, YPAR researchers must build trust and mutual respect (Dennis et al., 2019; Garnett et al., 2019) and intentionally create space for youth agency and autonomy (Cahill et al., 2019). Caraballo and Soleimany (2019) call for the creation of "transformative third spaces" (p. 84) in which to address power dynamics, renegotiate roles, "examine and interrogate the social injustices and disparities" (p. 85) that youth experience, and advocate for change (Caraballo & Soleimany, 2019). DeNicolo et al. (2017) call this "cariño conscientizado," a culturally grounded praxis of care that disrupts "hegemonic and racist policies" (p. 502) and practices. In other words, an ethic of care informs a pedagogical praxis defined by equitable relationships and roles, mutual respect, and justice-oriented action.

Within and beyond the classroom, care praxis requires understanding, valuing, and creating space for youth's multiple identities and needs while exhibiting both high standards and support for holistic development (DeNicolo et al., 2017). Like YPAR, this praxis is rooted in critical pedagogy (Freire, 1970) and demands collaboration with youth, families, and communities toward consciousness, liberation, and transformation (DeNicolo et al., 2017). In their arts-based YPAR work with undocumented Latinx youth, Cahill et al. (2019) describe how building relationships based on mutual responsibility rather than similarity empowers the collective to commit "acts of resistance and refusal" against the "neoliberal racial capitalism" (p. 578) that often shapes relationships and practices in schools.

Here we take up this commitment to a culturally grounded praxis of care, building on our prior work that examines the nature of participation (Call-Cummings, 2017; Call-Cummings & Dennis, 2019) and the role of care in YPAR (Call-Cummings et al. 2019). Engaging a praxis of care as a form of resistance against neoliberalism, or the "privatisation and marketisation of the education system and the devaluation of professional knowledge" (Fuller, 2019), this chapter highlights moments over three years of a YPAR project as we have worked to build, maintain, and honor the shifting and evolving identity and associated goals of our research collective. We present three vignettes that help to illustrate our own collective's experiences as we have moved from engaging an either/or, dualistic approach to caring toward a collective one. First, we offer a vignette when the authors exhibited care *for* youth co-researchers; that is, when we made methodological decisions that prioritized the needs of the youth members of the collective over our needs as adult academics. Second, we reflect on a moment when our youth co-researchers displayed care *for* us; that is, when they prioritized Meagan's needs over their own individual needs. Third, we offer a vignette when we, the authors and youth, cared *with* each other; that is, we made methodological decisions that prioritized our collective identity and goals in an effort to create change. We reflect on how this move from caring *for* to caring *with* exemplifies the necessary shift from a transactional, albeit well-intentioned, approach to caring to one that can help YPAR collectives resist typical forms of interaction in schooling and research contexts.

YPAR: Enacting a Praxis of Care

One of the more challenging aspects of YPAR is the need to create a true research collective, that is, a group of individuals who may differ in terms of age, gender identity, race, occupational, immigration, or socioeconomic status but come together around a common concern or goal. Working together across difference can be difficult in any context, even more so in an intergenerational YPAR collective. The diversity of backgrounds and identities and the complex power relations between members can lead to a "messiness" (Lather, 2006) that might threaten the unity of the group.

Often, as scholars, we focus on "navigating" differences as if we are trying to work in spite of them. Yet those who engage in YPAR commit to an epistemology—a way of knowing—and an ontology—a way of being—that is rooted in equitable and democratic action as well as a critical praxis of care that resists transactional research relationships and moves toward transformational, caring inquiry relationships. These epistemological and praxis-oriented commitments require that we as university-based researchers move beyond navigation of relationships and power dynamics to the intentional engagement of difference toward mutual recognition and understanding (Cahill et al., 2019; Habermas, 1998, 2003). This chapter seeks to illustrate how university-based researchers who engage in YPAR can take steps to enact this epistemologically informed praxis of care.

Context

Since 2017, students and teachers at a large, public magnet high school in Northern Virginia, USA, Forest Park High School[1] (FPHS), have partnered with faculty and doctoral students at a nearby public university to conduct a YPAR project on student voice. Compared to many suburban high schools, FPHS is atypically diverse along racial/ethnic lines, with 14 percent of students who are listed as "Asian," 34 percent "Hispanic," 17 percent "Black," 30 percent "white," and 5 percent "Two or more races" (Public School Review, 2020). FPHS is also diverse along socioeconomic lines, with about a third of students eligible for free or reduced lunch (Public School Review, 2020). Our YPAR research collective has always included about ten students, one veteran high school teacher, one university faculty member (Meagan), and up to five doctoral students (including Melissa).

One of the complexities of engaging in YPAR is that youth have many other demands, responsibilities, and talents and so get pulled in lots of different directions. This means that the membership of our research collective has constantly shifted since 2017, but it has from the beginning been representative of the gamut of identities and experiences in large, diverse public high schools in the United States. The high school students involved have identified as Latinx, Bangladeshi, Trinidadian, Liberian, Ethiopian, Sudanese, white, Black, second-generation immigrant, American, cisgender, queer, gay, straight, able-bodied, having a disability, religious, not religious, straight-A student, fifth-year senior, working class, middle class, combinations of these identities, and more. Our host teacher, Mrs. Lea Beakman, is a white, cisgender woman and thirty-year veteran of the school. Meagan has been the lead university-based researcher associated with the project and identifies as a white, cisgender, middle-class woman. Doctoral students have come and gone as a part of the collective. They have identified as Black, Asian, white, Pacific Islander, Latinx, LGBTQ+, straight, first-generation immigrant, second-generation immigrant, American, working class, middle class, able-bodied, having a disability, religious, not religious, and more. At the time this chapter was written, Melissa was a doctoral candidate and worked for Meagan as her graduate research assistant. She identifies as a white, cisgender, middle-class woman and has been involved in the YPAR project from its inception in various ways.

In the summer of 2017, Meagan set up a meeting with the principal of FPHS. It was the end of her first year on the tenure track, and as a participatory action researcher, she knew she needed to find a research "home"—a site where she could work with students and teachers to develop a long-term project. She decided to approach FPHS because it was her children's own high school and because her university had an existing partnership with the school. At the meeting, Meagan introduced the principal to YPAR, described its emphasis on equity and shared power, and talked through a few examples of school-based YPAR projects with which she had been involved. Meagan then asked the principal if anything came to mind as she was talking about YPAR that he was interested in pursuing but simply hadn't had the time to dedicate to it. The principal expressed concern about the school's lack of cohesion. As a magnet school drawing students from a relatively large area, it was difficult for students to participate regularly in after-school sports or other extracurricular activities, which, along with other complicating factors, he felt had led to the students feeling a lack of community. After receiving permission to move forward, Meagan worked with a teacher hand-picked by the principal to reach out to students and other teachers interested in pursuing a YPAR project on this theme.

Over the next month, Meagan and two of her doctoral students held an informal meeting with fifteen teachers from the school to hear their thoughts on possible directions for a YPAR project. The teachers, including Mrs. Beakman, immediately identified issues of concern that aligned with those the principal had discussed. At a similar meeting for students, over forty students shared similar concerns about the school's lack of cohesion. The students, however, felt that a root cause of the problem was administrators' and teachers' lack of respect for and understanding of the voices and experiences of students of color. After this meeting, we formed a research collective and narrowed our focus to a single research question: "What can schools do to help students feel like their voices are heard and honored?" We named our project Courageous Conversations in the hopes of hosting and inspiring critical conversations around issues that are important to youth but often silenced within school walls.

During the first year of our YPAR project (2017–2018), our research collective created a school-wide student survey that garnered over 500 responses and conducted over thirty interviews and five focus groups with students. During the second (2018–2019) and third (2019–2020) years of the project, we based much of our YPAR work in arts-based inquiry, engaging in Theatre of the Oppressed (Boal, 1985), spoken word poetry (Fisher, 2007; Jocson, 2008), Photovoice (Greene et al., 2013; Wang & Burris, 1997), and other narrative techniques to honor and amplify students' perspectives on how school needs to change. We met on a biweekly basis during the academic year and held annual day-long arts-integrated research workshops that included time for data collection and analysis and performances and exhibits of data and findings.[2] Throughout the project, we have remained committed to the flexible, iterative nature of YPAR work. While, during the first year, we spent two months reviewing and training youth co-researchers on research methods, we have chosen to forego that approach, finding that it instantiated unequal power dynamics (knowers/learners; adults/children) that we sought to reject. Instead, we moved toward methods the youth were interested in using and/or methods that they already used in their everyday lives. This shift equalized power dynamics considerably.

In considering how we could best represent our learning about caring through and with this collective, we chose to focus on three vignettes we had noted in our own research journals, which challenged us to think about and enact caring as an intrinsically methodological praxis and as inherently tied to YPAR epistemology. We want to clarify that to this point in our scholarship we have almost exclusively focused on YPAR epistemology as anchored in goals of uprooting systems of power and inequity. We chose to share these three vignettes because they helped us clarify how a critical praxis of care is in fact one aspect of YPAR's epistemology.

Caring *for* and Caring *with*

Although the membership of our research collective is in a state of constant flux, we have attempted to enact a praxis of critical, culturally responsive care (DeNicolo et al., 2017) through learning about and continually centering our youth co-researchers' identities and concerns. We offer these vignettes to illustrate how we have seen this caring praxis evolve (in a nonlinear way) from a more transactional caring *for* to a transformational caring *with* that characterizes the trust, mutual respect, and solidarity

(Cahill et al., 2019; Dennis et al., 2019; Garnett et al., 2019) needed to create a safe and productive "third space" (Caraballo & Soleimany, 2019) within an intergenerational research collective.

Vignette 1: Caring *For* Co-Researchers, Resisting Academia

In our short time as a university faculty member and doctoral candidate, we have often experienced that we must negotiate whom we care for and when. Meagan came to her current (and first) faculty position with the commitment to engage in participatory inquiry no matter the context. From the beginning, even during the interview process, she received wise, knowing smiles and told something to the effect of "Ah, yes, that is wonderful to hear. Remember, though, that you will need to get tenure." The not-so-subtle implication seemed to be either that participatory inquiry wouldn't be seen as rigorous or that it would take too long, so she wouldn't have the requisite number of publications to be successful in her bid for tenure. In fact, she had heard this refrain before: when describing her plans to co-create a digital dissertation with her YPAR collective, one committee member responded, "Meagan, that's all well and good, but remember, you need to get a *job*." Again, the message was that there were limits to participatory research/approaches if she wanted to be "successful" in the academy.

While working on Courageous Conversations with high school co-researchers, we have often wondered about—and ultimately ignored—those supposed limits in favor of caring for our youth co-researchers. One telling example of this came when a paper we had worked on for six months was rejected for publication. We had struggled to honor the epistemological underpinnings of YPAR to foreground and honor the knowledges, experiences, and priorities of the youth members of the research collective, meeting multiple times over six months to engage in different approaches to participatory data analysis. Meagan also met with the youth co-researchers at their school every other week to hold informal focus groups, during which we read through the data we had collected together, talked about what students were communicating about their lives through their art, and began to theorize what we saw and felt. We spent months working to accurately reflect those processes and the findings that came out of them in forms that would be deemed useful and worthwhile by a scholarly journal, meticulously documenting how often we had met, who had been present, how we accounted for and challenged power structures, how we maintained the transparency of the process, and on and on.

This rejection was particularly rough. Along with useful feedback, one issue stuck out as inescapable for participatory inquiry. The reviewers critiqued the analysis process as not rigorous enough. It was difficult to grasp why the reviewers seemed to not understand what we were after, and their questions made it clear that they were not interested in critical or participatory processes of meaning making, even though the journal clearly stated in the "aims and scope" section of its website that it valued critical work. Rather, they were interested in representing whatever process we went through in a linear way that made sense to them—not to those involved or readers who do similar work.

We were baffled. We wondered how we could get some of our work published in order to facilitate Meagan's hopeful tenure and Melissa's prospects on the job market while accurately representing and honoring the work we—most especially the youth members of the collective—had done. Most importantly, how could we do this with the youth in a way that continued to honor their wishes and goals? They had told us it was cool to have their name somewhere, but really, they didn't care much about publishing. It was something they were doing because it was important to us and for us.

The tension between caring for youth and their knowledges and priorities and caring for ourselves, the writing process, and our career aspirations became central to our decision about how—or even if—to move forward. In the moment, it seemed almost impossible to strike a balance between our competing demands—caring for youth or caring for ourselves. We recognize that caring for our own career trajectories is not inherently a bad thing. Indeed, it is good and important to care for oneself and to work toward our goals. Yet, in weighing options and balancing priorities, it felt impossible to care for both equally and simultaneously. We felt that we had to choose between prioritizing ourselves and, therefore, the neoliberal, capitalist practices of production that structure academia and prioritizing the youth, which would be an act of resistance against those practices. If we cared for ourselves first—that is, if we prioritized our publications and asked the youth to continue working with us through the revisions process—we worried we would lose our participatory footing and revert to the power dynamics we worked so hard to diminish. If we chose to care for the youth co-researchers first and prioritize what they had clearly articulated to us (*not* the publication process but the project itself), then we would lose out on a publication, or at the very least, our timeline would be set back significantly.

Eventually, we made a choice. We erred on the side of our original commitments to our student co-researchers and what *they* cared about. We chose resistance. We chose to focus less on the publication process and engage in the arts-based inquiry activities that were important to them. Other researchers may have made different decisions, and perhaps there may have been a way to strike a balance, but in that moment, we believed that resisting academia's insistence on production over everything else was crucial. Caring for the youth meant not prioritizing the academic writing process but continuing to focus on the project that would (hopefully) have a real, tangible impact on their lives and their school.

Vignette 2: Caring *For* Each Other, Resisting Reciprocity

About a year after we began our YPAR work at Forest Park, our collective began to discuss what we had accomplished as a group—what changes we had realized, what goals we had accomplished. While we knew we enjoyed the project and had engaged many students from high schools across the region in knowledge production that helped them see the value of their own voices, opinions, and experiences, it was hard to pinpoint one or two concrete *changes* that had occurred because of our work. No new policy had been introduced. No teacher had suddenly been transformed. No administrator had miraculously allowed us to have open conversations on controversial topics during the school day. What had we accomplished? What had all these surveys and interviews and group dialogues been for? One of our collective members, Jeffrey, who had been with Courageous Conversations since the first student meeting in 2017, summed it up poignantly: "We've been together now for a year? Eighteen months? And … what?" He shrugged his shoulders, his hands outstretched, as if trying to grasp any real change our work had spurred.

The conversation turned to the possibility of bringing the project to an end. It had been a good run, we seemed to be saying—or at least that is what we as university-based researchers were hearing. We were somewhat relieved, as it had been difficult to get youth together recently due to competing schedules, parent demands, and the like, but we were also concerned, because we knew there was still so much more that could be done with this collective. As we started to feel rather sorry for ourselves, there was a lull in the conversation. Then Kate, a senior who had been a leader in the collective over the preceding several months, spoke up: "Well, what do *you* guys need?" She nodded toward us, the university researchers. We had made no secrets about the demands of academia we were under, so Meagan understood that Kate wanted to make sure we had gotten what we came for in order to be compensated and rewarded professionally.

"Oh, no, no, no, we're fine," Meagan began, trying to shift the focus back to the needs of the students, but at the same time wondering if it wouldn't be better if we just did move on. "We're good. We've got lots of papers to write. What about *you* guys? What do *you* think is best?" "Well," Kate started, with a few of the youth co-researchers looking at her and nodding as if in agreement, "you guys have done the stuff that we wanted to do, for us, and for the school, we just want to make sure that you guys get what you need to for tenure and stuff." It was said so matter-of-factly, almost transactionally: *We got what we wanted. Did you get what you wanted?*

We ended the meeting by agreeing to think more and to communicate via email and group text message. Meagan felt uncomfortable about the gesture of care offered by Kate and the other youth researchers but couldn't really figure out what she wanted to do or why. This caring act of reciprocity, while often hailed as something good, like evidence of mutual benefit, in academic literature, felt more transactional to Meagan. It didn't feel like an equitable give-and-take moment. It felt like Kate was caring for Meagan but in a way that was rife with complication and power.

A few days later, Meagan recorded in an email to Mrs. Beakman how torn she was feeling about Kate's offer and about wanting the project to continue but also not wanting the "push" to come from her and her agenda as a university-based researcher:

> I've been thinking a lot about [FPHS], you, the students, our conversation the other day …. I am just not sure where I am/we are in this. I don't want to put you in a position (and I fear I already may have) where you feel like you have to or need to (or even want to) continue with this process because you like me or we somehow want to egg these students on toward …. something. Or maybe the students are generally interested but just can't practically put in the time or effort or …. time to make "it" (whatever "it" is) what "it" could be … whatever that is.
>
> (September 20, 2018)

Mrs. Beakman wrote back the next day:

> Ahhhh, where to start and what to say? I love what we are doing. I love working with you. I love the kids and the space we have created. And I'm not sure what to do next. I think we are needed more than ever. I guess I am not ready yet to pass this on to someone else. I don't believe that anyone else will be able to do what you and I and the kids have done (see, that's the ego). But I also know that I will get tired, that you can't keep up your pace indefinitely.

In this email, and often in informal conversations during and after research collective meetings and activities, Mrs. Beakman expressed this care for Meagan and the doctoral students that were involved—not wanting to impose, knowing we had lives outside of this project. But, as an educator committed to the same power sharing and equity that YPAR is anchored in, Mrs. Beakman continued:

> I don't know where we should go next. I don't know if we will get any more kids involved and if this thing we are trying can grow to be self-sustaining. I do know that every kid who is touched, even tangentially by some of our conversations, is interested and engaged.
>
> (Email September 21, 2018)

Upon receiving this email, Meagan realized that in being open and honest about feeling unsure and uncomfortable with Mrs. Beakman, Mrs. Beakman was free to expose her own feelings and thoughts. At the next meeting, Meagan more clearly shared with the group how she felt and that she wanted to continue but didn't want the students to feel forced or obligated. Kate and the other students agreed that they wanted to continue working together but sometimes simply wouldn't be able to attend because they had other things to do or were simply tired. The collective agreed to be okay with whatever each person could give. This open dialogue once again equalized the power dynamics and moved the act of *caring for* from a transactional idea of give-and-take to openness and understanding of each person's expectations, interests, possibilities, and limitations. In other words, working through that moment of discomfort helped us to recalibrate our expectations and interactions, resisting a neoliberal concept of reciprocity and reaching toward more a genuine, mutual practice of care.

Vignette 3: Caring *with* a Collective, Resisting Either/Or Duality

We heard about the mass shooting at Marjory Stoneman Douglas High School in Parkland, Florida, as soon as it happened. News outlets seemed to be reporting nothing else. Mrs. Beakman texted us about how students were reacting and what administrators were doing in response. A few days later, we received word that students in the school district were planning a walkout in solidarity. The school district at first responded that walkout participants would receive detention but then retreated, deciding they would "let" students walk out for the last ten minutes of the school day. Some participated, some did not. It was, by all accounts, all very orderly. Sanitary.

During our research meeting the next week, we asked students in the collective what they chose to do during those ten minutes and how they were feeling. They talked about being terrified just walking into the building in the mornings, laughing with each other in a way that only those who share the same visceral fear can. When we talked about the walkout, they joked that "it was ridiculous" and "it meant nothing" to walk out at the end of the day. Then Iviana, a junior who had been active in the group for the whole year, spoke up:

> I heard a teacher say, "Congrats on doing literally nothing." That's why I feel like teachers don't care, because they treated us like that, with the walkout and stuff, teachers were like, "you did literally nothing, you didn't do much, you didn't do this or this, you don't have a voice or blah blah blah."

When Mrs. Beakman responded that she "never heard a teacher say that," Iviana identified the teacher by name and said she heard him say it with her own ears "when he was holding the door open" for kids to walk out of the school.

When the others heard this, they were not surprised. They commented on how their own teachers responded, how they did nothing to support the students or the walkout, and then Chloe, Iviana's best friend, added:

> Yeah, my math teacher was asking, "Like, do they realize that Mr. Blotter [the principal] …" Like, she thought the impression was people were walking out around the nation to convince their principal to do something or something. And she was like, "Everyone just remember, everyone walking out today, Mr. Blotter can't do anything about gun law legislation," and I was like ahh [screaming out of frustration].

Mrs. Beakman responded with frustration as well, adding that "as teachers, we're not allowed to have a voice." Our conversation, which happened to be recorded and transcribed (not all were), moved between frustration with these particular teachers and frustration with a system that threatens punishment of teachers who support students, who openly discuss political issues in class, or who act as role models for students to take sociopolitical action.

This conversation became a turning point for our collective. Up until this point, we had cared individually. That is, we had cared *for*. We had repeatedly vacillated between caring for ourselves or caring for members of the group. In this moment, though, our course shifted from one of caring *for*—asking what the students wanted to do, or what they cared about, and then working to support them in that direction—to caring *with*—joining together with a common purpose, working toward dismantling a common, oppressive and unjust system that harms us all, not just students.

Our collective decided to focus less on students and what students can or need to do to change systems of oppression, inequity, and injustice, and more on the roles teachers and school adults can and should be playing to initiate and support social change within and beyond the walls of their classrooms and schools. As we began to care *with* and better understood how youth and adults were mutually implicated in the processes of inquiry and change, our focus shifted. Together, our research collective realized that our YPAR work had placed huge burdens on students to identify inequity and initiate change. We had placed one layer of blame on teachers and administrators for not doing better but another layer of blame on students for failing to make change in the first place.

In subsequent collective meetings, we discussed the implications of this shift, realizing that our methods would need to change again. We needed to invite teachers into the collective rather than excluding them, which would be difficult because of inherent power dynamics between teachers and students. Yet, upon reflection, we realized that the year spent engaging in arts-based methods was useful because it helped students see and hear the value of their own voices, knowledge, and experiences. Our youth co-researchers were now better equipped to resist silencing structures of schooling and to express their identities and concerns. They were now in a position to invite teachers to actively participate with us in our courageous conversations, rather than remain on the outside as subjects of critique. Ultimately, our collective was inviting teachers to care—and resist—with us.

In this way, we learned that caring *with* may at first appear as a seemingly simple, practical, or logistical switch. Yet it is actually methodological in nature. Indeed, caring *with* is central to YPAR because it cannot be fully enacted without committing to a mentality of collectively oriented caring *with*. Of course, caring *for* is not inherently bad, but it buys into a neoliberal agenda of reciprocity that is not in keeping with YPAR's underlying epistemology. We learned that we needed to resist this tendency of reciprocal, give-and-take caring and move toward a more relational praxis of care among the collective and beyond.

Discussion

When we have had difficult or uncomfortable experiences in the context of YPAR or other research, we have often thought of caring as *either/or*. Should I care or should I not? Should I exhibit care for this person/interest or for the other person/interest? Should I prioritize my own interests or their interests? Our quandaries are often dualistic—and individualistic—in nature: we are thinking purely in terms of an individual. In our minds, socialized by neoliberal agendas and capitalist ideologies, the answer to ethical and moral quandaries must create, in very simplistic terms, one winner and one loser.

In this chapter we have aimed to move our thinking around a praxis of care beyond this dualistic approach to caring *for*. We have reflected on *how* and *with whom* we care, anchoring our thinking in the ontological (ways of being) and epistemological (ways of knowing) tenets of youth participatory action research. Caring is rife with culturally bound difficulties and seemingly natural hierarchies, particularly between adults and youth. In YPAR, this needs to be foregrounded and complicated because of the central epistemological conviction that youth have valuable expertise, which is too often diminished and disregarded. As we have stated, researching *with* and not *for* youth in order to hold educational decision makers accountable for their failures requires a dynamic of mutual trust and respect (Caraballo & Soleimany, 2019; Dennis et al., 2019; Fox, 2019; Garnett et al., 2019)—and of care. By enacting a critical care praxis in our YPAR work, we seek to more fully understand the identities, needs, and priorities of the collective as a "transformative third space" (Caraballo & Soleimany, 2019, p. 84) from which to take social and political action.

This move to caring *with* permeates all aspects of YPAR—not just the methods we choose for data collection or the ways we engage in data analysis. It is a methodological imperative that even in the everyday interactions we have with our youth or school-based co-researchers we frame our actions by resisting a caring *for* approach. This is not easy. Caring *for* can appear natural, even desirable. Of course, we want to be kind to others—especially those who are in positions of relatively less power than us, structurally and culturally. But being kind can create or reproduce patterns and systems of inequity, even unconsciously and even with good intentions. A praxis of care rooted in resistance to inequity is paramount—in YPAR and beyond. Indeed, moving toward a caring *with* creates a space for mutual resistance, which is a critical aspect of the democratized alliances we seek to build in, through, and beyond YPAR.

Implications for New Researchers

Learning to care with our co-researchers is crucial to resisting adult/child binaries and to challenging deficit models of schooling and broader structural inequalities (Dennis et al., 2019; Fox, 2019)—that is, caring *with* is crucial to enacting YPAR epistemology. However, pushing against a normative, dualistic framing of care can be difficult, especially in the academy and amidst today's schooling policies and practices. As Cahill et al. (2019, citing West, 2008) express, "To struggle against, and within, neoliberal racial capitalism is an exhausting, ongoing and uphill battle—and yet we engage in it together with a sense of 'critical hope'" (p. 585). It is when we work in solidarity with those who have been pushed to the margins that the YPAR collective becomes a "site of radical possibility, a space of resistance" (bell hooks, 1989, p. 206). As we have tried to illustrate in this chapter, this evolution of solidarity is not a linear progression from caring *for* to caring *with*, but a constant struggle to engage in ways that foreground transparency, reflexivity, dialogue, resistance to dualistic and individualistic patterns of thinking, and an interest in the collective. We see this ongoing negotiation and repositioning as part of embodied research that manifests our commitment to resisting the marginalization of youth perspectives and experiences (Fox, 2019).

To be clear, we take the stance that it is not enough to simply care for the same things youth care for, joining them in whatever cause they choose. Barad (2007) helps us understand the possibilities and potential of an entangled existence:

> To be entangled is not simply to be intertwined with another, as in the joining of separate entities, but to lack an independent, self-contained existence. Existence

is not an individual affair. Individuals do not preexist their interactions; rather, individuals emerge through and as part of their entangled intra-relating.

(p. ix)

To engage in YPAR is to relinquish one's independent, self-contained existence as a researcher. So, as new researchers, we must make the decision carefully. Can we do this? Are we deeply committed to this messy, difficult process of entanglement and collective self-discovery? Are we prepared and willing to resist external measures of productivity, profitability, and pace? Are we ready to redefine success, validity, and rigor? Our hope is that as we commit to resisting the status quo we will be in a stronger position to enact the solidarity, anchored in a critical praxis of care, so many of us feel.

Part Two

Collaborating and Co-Creating with Youth: Caring through Sharing Ownership of the Research

4

From Hallway Conversations to Making Together: How Care Can Shift Relationships with Young People in Schools

Veena Vasudevan

As I think of my work as collaborative and embedded so deeply in a school community that is continuing to emerge and develop, it feels wrong to "pop in" but I imagine others feel like they are popping in a lot more. **I feel like I have to maintain both physically and emotionally a connection to the community and want to be there as much as I can in all the ways I can be. Part of it is the urgency I feel to help them be successful. I care deeply about the kids and even after a few days felt so invested in their lives, in their dreams, and aspirations.** *I care about the teachers who I think are putting a great deal of effort into this work and seem unmoored and slightly dejected after a tough several weeks. I feel for the city, not for the bureaucrats or other noisemakers but for the human beings of a city that has historically treated them like garbage. The discrimination and utter disdain for human beings by virtue of their race, class and geographic location sickens me.*
—Excerpt from field memo October 14, 2014

I wrote this memo six weeks into my fieldwork at a new high school that opened in September 2014. I was a member of a design-based ethnographic research team and, within minutes of the first day of school became, along with my other team members, enmeshed in the everyday rhythms of the school. As I recount above in an excerpt from a field memo, as a novice educational ethnographer I was overwhelmed by the sense of responsibility to students and staff. While I always understood research with youth to be relational, it was not until I was immersed in a school community and increasingly part of the social fabric of a school that I realized how personally implicated I could become in the lives of young people.

Instead, I began my dissertation fieldwork filled with excitement and anticipation at what I might come to know about students' identities in relation to a new educational approach that centered making as a way to facilitate learning. I was determined to *be there* (in the field) and understand the ethnographic context, just as I had been trained to do. I was ready to listen, look, and document what *was* happening versus what was not (Heath & Street, 2008). I was also determined to be in conversation *with* students and document their learning, sensemaking, participation; I *cared* about what students had to say and I wanted to understand their lived experiences.

Despite what felt like substantive training, I was unprepared for the realities of relational ethnographic practice with youth. Even with a deep embrace of participant observation (see Atkinson & Hammersley, 1998; Creswell & Poth, 2016), my conceptions of ethnographic work were challenged and changed through caring about the lives and well-being of students at my field site. I was also unprepared for how a strong urge to support and hold up a fledgling school, and ensure that the young people who were just beginning their high school journeys were *okay*, would complicate my understanding of ethnographic research and the roles that youth participants and researchers were meant to play. In the end, caring about what mattered to students and trying to understand their school(ed) lives led to new ways of relating and working together and *with* each other. In this chapter, I share one such story about how Denise[1]—a young Latinx student at my field site—and I began a journey that started as student and researcher and, through caring by *being there*, the nature of our relationship shifted to become more dialogic, and over time, the care between us became reciprocal.

Care as Being There For and With Youth

In this chapter I conceptualize caring as *being there*, both *for* and *with* youth. Being there *for* youth is to be present, to be available to support and help, and to express care and love for youth. Being there *with* youth is to be working with one another, to be in step with each other, to share in their triumphs and tribulations. Being there for and with youth work in tandem as an expression of care. I elaborate on my conceptualization of *being there* below.

Caring as *being there* **for** youth is to engage in what San Pedro and Kinloch (2017) describe as projects in humanization where "educational researchers willingly center the realities, desires, and stories of the people with whom we work. We must situate their stories in relation to our stories, lives, and research projects in humanizing ways" (p. 374S). Being able to receive and make space for youth's stories, for the sharing and exchange that occurs naturally between researcher and participant can then cultivate a shared human connection. A commitment that Paris and Winn (2014) suggest is "critically important it is to respect the humanity of the people who invite us into their worlds and help us answer questions about educational, social, and a cultural justice" (p. xv). Sharing stories, creating connections, and cultivating trusting relationships through actively engaging with one another create new opportunities for relating; it is also the basis for cultivating love and care. In sharing our stories, as researchers we make ourselves vulnerable and make space for youth's vulnerabilities, thus unseating traditional researcher-participant paradigms (see Brayboy & Deyhle, 2000; Paris, 2011), and acknowledge that work with youth is "unavoidably subjective" (Laura, 2016).

Caring as *being there* **with** youth is a kind of witnessing. Laura (2016) describes witnessing as "act of love, involves the deliberate attendance to people, seeing and taking notice of that which they believe is meaningful" (p. 219). So, by being there, one can begin to observe, attend to, and build awareness on what matters. Being engaged with other people by actively participating in their lives, we make meaning with them, while also bearing witness to what she calls "phenomenon of collective interest" (Laura, 2016, p. 219). Attending to what others think is meaningful is more possible when we are in fact immersed in a place and open and aware of how we are implicated within the lives of our interlocutors. Laura (2016) also suggests that witnessing is particularly important in relation to people who have experienced marginalization, because bearing witness to people's pain validates their experiences and affirms their right to "peace, justice, and humanity"(p. 219). For young people whose experiences have been historically fraught, the act of witnessing can actively illustrate that they matter, they are loved, and cared for, within school walls.

Finally, just as teachers and students can cultivate dialogic relationships rooted in love for people and the world, researcher-participant relationships can emulate this openness and vulnerability that suggest each person in the relation has something to offer and something to learn (Freire, 1970; Noddings, 2002). There is then a possibility to move from witnessing to with-nessing (Vasudevan, 2016), which allows for care and love to open new possibilities for relating and working *with* one another and unseats traditional adult-youth and research-participant relationships.

Methodology

Finding My Way to the School Site

As I looked for a dissertation site in the spring of 2014, I found out about an innovation network launching in the local public school district consisting of three new high schools. Each of the three schools was embracing maker-oriented learning, part of the educational zeitgeist at the time that sought to nurture youth's identities as makers and for their formative educational experiences to be about making to learn such that they were able to play, tinker, fail, iterate, and reflect (see Vossoughi & Bevan, 2014). In doing so making to learn sought to supplant the traditional didactic approaches to education with a dynamic that positioned students and teachers as collaborators who worked *with* each other.

Each school was open enrollment so any interested students in the city could apply; there were no tests or other admission criteria.[2] One of the schools, the Design School, happened to be partnering with a professor at my graduate school on a design-based research project examining the literacies youth engaged in three high school makerspaces. Given my interest in understanding and exploring how maker education could shape students' identities, I asked this professor if I could conduct my dissertation at the school site. Being part of this team legitimized my presence in the school and made it possible for me to participate in student recruitment and orientation activities, summer teacher professional development, and eventually in the daily life of the school.

The Design School

The Design School was situated in a large metropolis in the northeast. It opened in the fall of 2014 amidst a slew of school closures and massive budget cuts in the school district. The inaugural class had ninety-nine students.[3] The study body was 82.8 percent African American, 14.1 percent Latino, 1 percent white, 1 percent Asian and 1 percent other. Students with disabilities made up to 13.1 percent of the student population, and 100 percent of the students were economically disadvantaged. In its second year, the demographics mirrored the year prior, while the number of students increased, as the school added a new group of freshmen, bringing the total to 172 students. In the first year there were six teachers (ELA/digital humanities lab, history/civics lab, science, design lab, mathematics, special education), one school secretary,[4] a dedicated guidance counselor,[5] two school security guards, one maintenance staff person for the entire building, and two noontime aides. In the second year, they added four additional teachers (humanities, digital humanities, science, and Spanish), and a dean of students who dealt with school culture and issues related to discipline.

The founding school principal, Mr. Greene, wanted to reimagine urban education for high school students. He lamented the overuse of worksheets, arbitrary deadlines, and the lack of independence in high schools, things he had been frustrated by in the previous nine years as a high school history teacher. Thus, he sought to implement a program of education that was driven by students' interests and knowledge (student-centered), allowed students to learn at their own pace (asynchronous), and wanted grading and evaluation to be grounded in evidence-based (competency-based) learning. The teachers who founded the school (save for one) were very invested in nurturing and supporting students in their own ways. The educators and staff also aspired to create a school environment that nurtured and encouraged youth leadership, used restorative justice over antiquated and over-used disciplinary measures, and supported students' social-emotional development and growth.

Data Collection and Analysis

For my larger ethnographic research project, I conducted a multimodal ethnography (see Dicks, Flewitt, Lancaster, & Pahl, 2011). To do so, I wrote multimodal ethnographic fieldnotes, collected photographs, recorded short films and audio recordings as well as interviews with students and staff. I also collected student-produced artifacts and school materials (e.g., announcements, student memos, assignments, digital compositions, and more). The students in my study were 13–15 when the study began and 16–18 years old when the study concluded. In my study, I had six focal students and another ten students with whom I worked closely with over the course of two years both in the youth-led spaces and in other educational and out-of-school contexts. For the data that I share in this chapter, I focused my analysis on ethnographic fieldnotes, memos, student artifacts, and student interviews, specifically tracing my researcher-participant relationship with one student participant, Denise, in relation to caring as being there for and with her.

Negotiating Researcher Positionality by Practicing Care

My ethnographic project was concerned with trying to understand how young people made sense of their learning lives. To do so, I wanted to make sure that what I was learning was true to youth's perspectives. How else to do that but to try and be *with* students in spaces that mattered to them? Thus, I began my ethnographic exploration in earnest, wanting to be at the school and immerse myself in the everyday rhythms of the space. In the short vignette below and subsequent paragraphs that follow, I unravel how I came to practice care and cultivate a positionality as a member of the school community.

> *On the first day of school, I hurry into the building, dressed in maroon capri pants and a charcoal grey blouse, and tan flats. My chunky necklace bounced as I ran up the stairs to the second floor and popped my head into the main office, it was 7:00am. I see Mr. Greene, the principal, and ask how I could help, he tells me he needs someone in the cafeteria to greet new students. So down I run, with a sharpie, a poster paper, and a sheaf of name tags. As the school day officially started, the security guards started letting students and the occasional parent, through the metal detectors, down the stairs, and into the basement cafeteria. As students arrive, I greeted them warmly and likely with too much energy for timid freshmen: "Good morning! Hi! How are you? I'm Ms. V" shaking their hands and asking how they are doing. I was ebullient. I was one of the first adults the new students encountered at the Design School, especially if they had not attended previous orientation events.*
>
> (Vignette, based on fieldnote September 2014)

As I recount in the above vignette, the first few days of the school opening, I supported teachers, staff, and students, in any way I could. I helped teachers circulate the room as students tried new activities, helped them prep for classes, shepherded students, and obliged when the guidance counselor, Ms. Colson, asked me to make the student IDs to free her up to do other things. I went to lunch with the students, hung out in the hallways, and helped anyone and everyone out whenever I could. Most importantly, I engaged students in dialogue, I asked them questions, and I told them about my work. It was through these interactions that were initially facilitated by the institutional and practical needs of a school that allowed me to *be there* in youth spaces.

As the days turned into weeks, I continued to help students think through new assignments, walk students to and from places at the request of teachers, and offered an extra set of hands in any classroom I was popping into. When in classes, I would crouch by students' desks or sit in a vacant seat to help them work on assignments—be it an essay, math problems, art projects, or whatever came my way. Amidst helping with assignments, I would check in with students, ask them how they were doing, how they were making sense of their new school, ask them about their interests, and life in general, and sharing anecdotes about my life and interest with them. I would also walk students to classes and act as a go-between between students and teachers during conflicts related to disciplinary issues or other emergent challenges. Our design-based research team was constantly in communication in those early months. When one of us would arrive, we would pick up where the previous team members left off—often emailing updates about which students had done what work, where files were saved, or what challenges we might help solve together.

Our team worked most closely with the three lab teachers, which included Mr. Richards. He was warm, easy to talk to, and was open to our research team being in his classroom space. We quickly built a rapport and I got increasingly comfortable going in and out of his classroom. He would often find me when he needed more support with a student or asked for my (or another research member's) support in designing and delivering lessons. Being often situated in the humanities classroom meant that I was often helping students with writing, revising, or composing and thus we were often *making together* within academic spaces.

As the weeks wore on, I established a routine. I would walk from the train station to the school and hit the buzzer and wait for Ms. Rodriguez or whomever else was available to buzz me in. Then, I climbed two flights of stairs to the main office, where I would chat with the Ms. Rodriguez and whomever else was in the main office and signed myself in via the visitor log. Sometimes Ms. Rodriguez would mention that a student was looking for me, and I would wander down the hall to find them. Other days, I would simply pop in to classrooms or other spaces like the lunchroom. Each day, as I walked through the halls, I said hello to every student by name. I would ask, "How you doin', kiddo?" (Over the years, students would often tease me calling out "Hey kiddo!" when they saw me around).

I spent significant time speaking with students and asking them about their interests and their impressions of school. One of the things that students were immediately frustrated by was the absence of activities available. They had anticipated that there would be sports teams, clubs, a gym for activities, and other opportunities. There was even major concern that this high school did not have lockers, high technology, or the other trappings of the futuristic school many had anticipated based on admissions conversations.

So when students with whom I cultivated relationships started to ask for support to start clubs to fill gaps in activities that were not available at the school, I agreed to help with whatever I could. Over time I supported several students in bringing to fruition three youth-led spaces (a dance team, a youth activism group, and a film club). I showed up to practices, meetings, acted as a sounding board, and vouched for students, making it easier to do things that would otherwise be challenging without adult support (e.g., use school spaces, gather before and after school, use school resources, leave class for special events).

As a South Asian woman whose life experiences, affect, and language were markedly different than the students', my time within the Design School community forced me to constantly contend with these differences. I came to realize that students read me as white because of how I spoke and dressed and my overall affect. So even though I had always walked in the world as a person of color, the students' rendering of me was understandably different. In the early months of field work, as I exchanged stories, I asked students about their own lives and witnessed conversations among students. I grew increasingly aware of how my middle-class upbringing (Me: "Oh, I love London." Charles: "Ohh, you got money"), advanced education (I was seeking a PhD; many students would be the first to graduate college in their families), and overall privilege created space between myself and students.

I often peppered my fieldnotes with words and phrases I didn't know and wrote memos about what I was meant to do, how I should be engaged with students, on what to do when I felt confused, concerned, emotionally exhausted (and there were lots of days like that). I was constantly trying to make sense of my role, my interactions with students and staff, and how I could most effectively and respectfully engage in the work. However, it was practicing care, through *being there* through witnessing, sharing, and receiving students' stories, and remaining vulnerable, that I believe sustained and strengthened my relationships with students.

Case Study in Being There: Caring, Connecting, and Creating with Denise

Meeting Denise

Denise was fourteen years old when she started her freshmen year at the Design School. She self-identified as Latinx and white. She had a wide smile, her hair was always done in different styles (and colors), and her voice got really wispy and soft when she got excited about something. She talked faster when she was emphatic and would punctuate sentences with "MY POINT!" when she expressed agreement. She could lose herself in a book or some movie, or a music video, or playing around with a new app. She was earnest, kind, and always willing to help out. She also, especially in her younger days, would get angry or impatient at perceived impertinence or disrespect from her friends, which at times would lead to arguments. But Denise was loyal and would always find ways to make amends with people she cared about. Most of all, Denise was kind and compassionate, determined, and full of energy and ideas to make the world a better place. But I didn't know any of this when I first met her. Below, I highlight two moments early on in my fieldwork that connected me to Denise and how *being there* with students, as a helping adult and as a researcher who could traverse youth spaces, created opportunities to work with one another.

On the fifth day of school (during freshmen orientation) after a rocky start, with many students being frustrated that the high school they were attending was *not* what they had imagined, our design-based research team and teachers hastily put together an interactive learning experience to introduce students to competency-based learning through a series of embodied activities like writing poems, designing artifacts, and more.

That morning, I saw Denise and several other students frantically working on completing a long list of activities, which had students working on mini-projects that highlighted key competencies. Each mini-project earned them a stamp on a passport. As I stood in the hallway chatting with some of my research team members while students worked, I wondered out loud if students would complete the activities while Denise was within earshot. She overheard me and decided to take on the challenge, incredulous that someone would believe otherwise. I remember the look of determination she had as she raced down the hall. After lunch, when most students had lost interest or stamina, Denise kept going. Somehow we bet that if she finished I would bake the entire student body cookies, and with that as extra motivation she filled out her passport minutes before the school day ended. She was triumphant and reveled at the thought of me baking cookies for the entire student body.

A couple of weeks later, Denise was elected as one of two student representatives from her advisory class, joining ten others. The elections were hasty and informal with students nominating themselves and each advisory teacher overseeing a quick vote. The elected students trekked down the hall and, led by the science teacher, Ms. Oliver, were first tasked with writing the school's first constitution. As students tried to take on their newly assumed leadership roles—many for the first time—the mood in the room fluctuated between frustration and conflict, to excitement and ultimately triumph. Creating the constitution and sharing their frustrations about what they wanted in their high school inspired the group to do more—they deemed themselves a sort of student council that would effect change on behalf of their peers. The students asked me if I could support them, and I happily accepted. Over the next couple of weeks, we gathered for lunchtime meetings, practiced for a back-to-school night performance, and simply hung out and got to know each other. The group, whom I referred to as "the constitution kids," eventually disbanded. However, it was the first opportunity for me to collaborate with students and help them bring their ideas to fruition. It was in those meetings that Denise and I got to know each other and I demonstrated through *being there* that I was an adult that youth could count on and call on when they needed support.

I share these seemingly mundane moments from my fieldwork because it was being there to bear witness to these small moments that ultimately led to larger moments. I turn to one such moment in the next section.

Creating New Researcher-Participant Dynamics Through Collaboration

In the early months of that first school year in 2014, I was at the Design School regularly. I continued to show up in classes, meet with students, hang out before and after school, always checking in and supporting. As Denise and I got to know each other, and as the aforementioned Constitution Kids group ended abruptly, Denise mentioned she wanted to continue student-led work. She came up with an idea for a youth group and enlisted my help in bringing the group together. One afternoon during advisory, Denise decided to take a leap of faith and recruit members to her group by making an announcement. As she stood in the middle of the room, she said to her peers, *"we're trying to create something like beyond the boundaries of our school—we're trying to make school better for ourselves—like not just goin' by the teachers' rules. We wanna have something better"* (fieldnote, November 7, 2014). She was ecstatic after she made this announcement.

A week later, I was at the Design School walking with students back from lunch when Denise asked me if I could help her with a poster for the student group that has been percolating in her mind. I share excerpts from a much-longer fieldnote below, during which I was **being there** *for* Denise and *with* her.

> *I'm walking back with students from lunch, we are chatting and laughing along. I see Denise, whose hair is again crimped, bordering on curled. Her blonde and red highlights are still visible in the back and she dons a thin stretchy headband around her forehead that is reminiscent of the 60s. Her grey sweater and black pants run counter to this nostalgic hair style. Somehow we end upon the topic of working on the poster for Breaking Boundaries in advisory. She also, mumbles under her breath about something that happened in lunch. She assures me that she can do work during part of advisory and when Ms. Oswald shows up we ask her about that. Ms. Oswald says that Denise has more than enough reading hours so she can work on the poster with me.*
>
> *As we stand out in the hallway while students move to class, Denise recounts her exchange with Gordon, who I had just noticed was seated on the perimeter of Ms. Oswald's classroom, black hoodie and black pants, hoodie covering his face, face down and music blaring from his chrome book. It's some kind of heavy metal or screaming music. Denise goes on to explain that Greg was listening to his music and she at first politely asked him to turn it off but he ignored her. She says, he listens to that music where they scream, you know? I respond with an equally pained expression, yeah, I'm not a huge fan, hurts my ears (or something like that). Then she said, in a soft but rapid tone, so then I cursed him out and he still wouldn't turn it down. She said then she felt bad and tried to apologize but in the meantime Ally, who wasn't involved in the situation somehow recounted it to Ms. Colson and the noontime aide. "Why she gettin' other people involved? This is an A and B conversation C yourself out of it!" she said. I was surprised, remarking that they were all friends. "Yeah, but I don't know why she got involved miss." At one point, Mr. Greene comes up to ask what's happening and she says to him, "Nothing." "Well obviously something is wrong," he says looking at her quizzically. I respond, "well she had an issue at lunch." Denise tries to brush it off.*
>
> *We [Denise and I] decide then to sit down by the bathrooms, at the tiny desk in the hallway where Ms. Jewel usually was seated.*
>
> *"Miss, because I'm nice you can have the rolly chair," says Denise. "You sure?" I confirm. "Yeah," she says. So, we start talking about the "what" of Breaking Boundaries. "What is this going to be about?" I say out loud. I ask her if she wants to type but she says she's happy to just spout out the ideas. I open up a PowerPoint file and start to type things as she brainstorms.*
>
> *She says she's conflicted; she wants to help the school but also do outreach at other schools. At one point I go to interject and then I say, "I'm going to refrain so I don't color your thoughts." She smiles and says, "miss you can color my thoughts or whatever." We talk as students walk up and down the hall coming in and out of possis,[6] mostly because the mask making projects are going on throughout the building. At one point Sloane and Bella come down the hall to wash their hands and rinse out their paint for their mask making projects. She shares what she's up to and*

> they offer ideas. Bella suggests that we could do fundraisers to raise money for the group and that we could do posters that encourage people not to bully or hurt people. Sloane suggests they might be able to raise money via a walkathon.
> (Excerpt from fieldnote, November 14, 2014)

I have often reflected back on the afternoon I recount above as a valuable illustration of how caring relationships can experience a shift, from centering things that matter to young people to working collaboratively to engage *with* them. That afternoon in November, I was there, not as an observer or a passive participant, I was living life with students and participating in the everyday rhythms of youth's lifeworlds; going to lunch, walking back as we gossiped and joked around; and stopping in the hallway to debrief on stressful encounters. Denise made herself vulnerable to me by telling me about what happened with her friends. I was there to receive her anger and frustration by listening and talking things through with her versus advising and recommending a specific course of action. Then we sat side by side to work together—me as the scribe and sounding board and she as the leader and visionary for the work she wanted to do at her school.

In the days that followed, we again sat side by side, collaborating on a poster design, Denise as art director and visionary and me again as sounding board and co-designer. A few weeks later, we gathered for the first meeting of the group, and I joined Denise and several of her peers, in a circle as Denise nervously led the first meeting of her youth-led group. She would name the group, Breaking Boundaries. The group's mission was to support younger students in feeling comfortable in their own skin and as she wrote in her opening speech *"show you are an amazing and beautiful person inside and out."* What I took away from this experience and the work that followed with the youth-led group was that caring about what Denise cared about and caring for her when she needed someone to listen, support, or give love meant that we built a relationship that created opportunities for us to do different kinds of work.

Winn and Ubiles (2011) argue that "when students and researchers work side by side, the bonds of mutual respect and understanding allow a new practice to evolve in which the researcher is fellow traveler, journalist, critic, and contributor" (p. 9). For Denise and I, the bonds of mutual respect were built through working together to bring the group to fruition, and in the small moments along the way, that positioned us as collaborators and interlocutors.

You Are One of Us: Rethinking Researcher-Participant Relationships

During my fieldwork, Denise would often find me when I arrived and just say, "Miss V, I need to talk to you!" and we would find somewhere to sit, or I would follow her to class or wherever she was headed. On one such occasion, during her second year of high school (in the spring of 2016), Denise and I sat together after school in the principal's office, a sprawling room that was often used for meetings and had a general open-door policy.

That afternoon, Denise started to open up about things that were creating stress and anxiety for her. She told me that she might have depression and shared some intimate details of her family life, particularly digging into her relationship dynamics with her parents, some of the stressors she had dealt with throughout her childhood like housing insecurity and some experiences that have made it difficult for her to have faith in adults in her life. One particular story she tells me is about police raiding her house, revealing some things about her family she had previously shied away from sharing. I asked her if it would be worthwhile to speak with the school guidance counselor. Denise tells me that she doesn't want to be judged or treated differently if she were to share all of the personal things she just related to me. I ask her, "*So why did you tell me?*" She responds, "Well you *might* treat me differently but ...." She stopped and then gestured with her hand. Denise said, "So it's like a pyramid: kids are at the bottom, the principal is at the top, then the staff and teachers." She drew imaginary lines in the air to signal the sides of the triangle. "Where am I?" I ask. She responded, "You're like an equal—you're like one of us." Denise's meaning, as I understood it, was that she felt like she could be herself with me, that I was at the same level.

Over the course of our relationship, Denise would come to confide in me and rely on me for support. Sometimes it was to share (i.e., "Miss V! Veena! OMG guess what?!"); sometimes it was help on academic things (i.e., a link to a Google Doc with a note "Ms. V, can you help me edit this?"); sometimes it was advice on life (i.e., "Miss V, I got this e-mail from the college board, what do I do?"). Even after I left the field in a regular capacity, we would speak often—via text or occasionally even a phone call. I remember one night she called me in tears the night before the PSATs in the fall of 2015 because no one had prepared her for what to expect. A year later, two of her classmates left her in a random neighborhood because they wanted to keep hanging out and she wanted to get home. She had called her aunt to come pick her up and then called me just to talk while she waited for her ride because she was terrified of sitting on a random stoop alone in the middle of the night. In her sophomore year, Denise started missing a lot of school and was having trouble with some of her teachers and started avoiding them. I followed up with her teachers, reached out to the principal, and connected with Denise to figure out what was happening. Eventually, she started showing up again and started to refocus on the dreams she came into school with, which were obscured when life happened.

The care went both ways. I could count on Denise. Over the course of my research and beyond, she listened as I shared my frustrations about the dissertation process, or spoke excitedly about the media festival I was helping lead, or was always there when I needed someone to organize and oversee big events like the school talent show. She expressed her care by showing up for me.

These boundary-crossing moments, what many educational researchers would likely consider out of the ordinary, emerged out of a relationship that was centered on care and love. I felt a responsibility, a kinship (hooks, 2001), that I did not take lightly and I think she felt that same connection to me. Even now, years after my fieldwork concluded and Denise has graduated from high school, we are still in conversation, expressing care, sharing updates.

Reciprocal Caring

After I finished collecting data in June of 2016, I continued to return to the Design School, spending the 2016–2017 school year doing member checks and hanging out with students. Almost every time I would walk through the doors in that third year, after giving hugs, and checking in with students, someone would inevitably ask, "You done with that book yet?" I would laugh and say that I wasn't, but I was slowly getting there. At times when my energy and confidence would flag, but I was reminded that I had committed to finishing, not just to myself or my committee, but to the students, whose lives I was trying to responsibly story San Pedro & Kinloch (2017). Finally, in the spring of 2017, I defended my dissertation. Shortly after I left the room, I texted a selfie to Denise and the other students with whom I was close to tell them I had passed. They were enthusiastic and supportive. I promised her I would come visit that week.

When I arrived at the school two days later, I walked to the literacy lab, where I often hung out or helped students with work. When I opened the door, I saw that the room was full: almost every student with whom I had worked closely over three years was crowded into the room. On the long conference table where I had spent many afternoons doing homework help, there was a big sheet cake with bright yellow scalloping on the edges and celebratory plastic balloons with "Congratulations Dr. Veena" written in blue icing. Students in the room were singing and cheering. Then, without any warning, several students, many of whom I had worked with in a student-led dance team (see Vasudevan, in press), performed a short piece of choreography, and there were so many hugs and notes of congratulation. I was astounded and incredibly moved.

After most of the students had dispersed, Denise revealed she had purchased the cake on her own and went around to invite everyone she knew I had worked with closely, even those people with whom she was not friends. Denise had stepped outside of her comfort zone to go talk to students from all over the school to make the day special for me. Denise's actions and those of the students at the Design School to come together to celebrate what was on its face, my accomplishment, illustrated just how shared it was.

Making Relationships Together

In reflecting back on my relationship with Denise, I came to realize all the ways that care was implicated in our shared work together. I bore witness (Laura, 2016; Winn & Ubiles, 2011) to the everyday moments in her life that over time became our shared school lives. It was through the ordinary and mundane that I would come to know the lengths Denise would go to attend a concert for 21 Pilots (her favorite band), or her practice of reading the last pages of a novel before reading the middle, or the reasons why her own personal struggles with who she was, inspired her to help younger students through starting Breaking Boundaries. Caring and connecting led to moments of possibility and catalyzed journeys where I got to support students and practice with-ness (see Vasudevan, 2016) as we navigated what it meant to cultivate youth-led spaces.

Wissman (2007) in her work with young women writers alluded to Audre Lorde's notion that we should be "here" or in the present, so that students could be "visible, acknowledged, and heard" (p. 348). And what I found is that *being there* had the potential to lead to many new possibilities of working with young people to co-create things that matter to them. It also expanded my understanding of how researchers could conduct responsible and caring studies that centered who youth were, what mattered to them, and how they made sense of their lives.

As a scholar who came to this work trying to reimagine new ways of designing and implementing curriculum in schools, caring for and with youth by being there, helped me to reimagine what research-participant relationships with youth could be in school.

5

"The Life of Julio Good": The Black Ratchet Imagination and Messy Methods as Caring Ethics

Ariana Brazier

Seeking to elevate the profundity of Black child play at the center of my dissertation research, my three-year-long (2017–2020) ethnographic study highlights how Black children within a school-cluster negotiate meaning in housing insecure conditions in Atlanta, Georgia. Black children are making critical contributions to their community's survival through systematic interactions known only to children within this and similar communities. The systems of play and exchange provide children with a self-confident value in their abilities to create and contribute to their community's culture via reciprocal relationships as they teach their community [sub]cultural knowledge and conscientious forms of care through self-assertion and social critique. The forms of play I witnessed cultivated collective imaginations, challenged social perceptions, and demonstrated self-efficacy at Blaze Rods Elementary School, Flower Elementary School, and Fun Middle School;[1] essentially, their play revealed how they cared about and were cared for by their larger communities.

My dissertation, primarily situated within the fields of English, critical and cultural studies, analyzes the intersection of Black child play and protest in order to illuminate the way their play and joy are methods of developing and channeling collective responses to their everyday experiences of institutional anti-Blackness and intergenerational oppression. I consider how Black child play and Black joy are reflective of a relationship between ratchet, a term commonly used to define the precarious and fluid realities of poor and working-class Blacks, and womanism, a community-oriented form of Black feminism situated within the everyday.

The first year of my ethnographic study, spanning May–August 2017, consisted of relationship building (while awaiting IRB approval for my research) within the school community. I worked closely with school parents, mostly mothers, as a member of the team of parent-liaisons employed by the school-cluster. With IRB approval and a familial love for members of the school community, I returned to the cluster the following year in May 2018 to continue learning from and loving on the students as they unconsciously responded to one of my core research questions: how do Black children come to know and be known by their communities? The vignettes presented throughout this chapter were collected during this second year, spanning May through August.

Blaze Rods and Flower Elementary Schools as well as Fun Middle School[2] are in a predominantly Black neighborhood within Atlanta, Georgia. Focusing on 2nd–6th grade students, I used students' descriptions of their own behavior and opinions to conduct this analysis. I chose to work across the three schools because, while children may attend separate schools, many families compose the same kinship networks, as attending one or more of the cluster schools is a generational legacy for families throughout the neighborhood. Additionally, the summer camp program (June–July 2018) in which a few of the experiences recollected in this chapter occurred consisted of students from all three schools. I decided to observe 2nd–6th graders because students in this age had demonstrated a developing understanding of their environment and the contextual circumstances that impact their living conditions. They can articulate their experience in terms that are meaningful to them.

As a Black-Filipina woman in my early twenties with familial ties to Atlanta and experience as an after-school counselor at Blaze Rods, I was aware of my insider-outsider positionality (Merriam et al., 2001) within the school community. The students knew that I was always willing to break for play, and the parents knew that I was always willing to help—these truths had become evident to them throughout summer 2017. However, as a graduate student raised within a predominantly white, middle-class suburb, I was distinguished by my dialect and the fact that I was always reading and carrying a book. So, while some families trusted me with the details of their personal lives and diverse interactions with their children, others did not.

For example, Ocho Jinks, a 6th grade student at Fun Middle School, was initially distrustful of my research, particularly my note-taking, as he would regularly ask, "Why you write that?" "Who's gonna see this?" "You gonna tell my momma?" When his peers explained the nature of my research—that I was "writing a book on what kids do" (as one student informed), Ocho Jinks began taking ownership over my research as well. On multiple occasions, Ocho Jinks would get off the bus and ask me, "Where's our notebook?" "You got our journal?" or "You takin notes, Ari?" Sometimes, he would dictate his own notes in the notebook. I later noticed how his demonstrable concern for "our" research and the personal insights he shared about himself and his community reinforced how children's writings must be situated within "the social and ideological complexity of children's lives and contemporary times" (Dyson, 1997, p. 13). Ocho Jinks's writing, in conversation with his sometimes-incomprehensible actions (he was known for fighting and was low-key silly) and the recollected systemic violence in his earlier childhood in the adjacent neighborhood, revealed the complexity of his life at this current moment in time.

Beginning that summer (2018), students expanded their own intellectual proclivities through playful, or ratchet, performances as they carried, exchanged, protected, and contributed to my field notebook. In this chapter, I exhibit how students used my notebook to perform as ethnographer, note their observations of me, reveal private information that may have contradicted their public selves, and investigate their own interiority (Quashie, 2012). Through the collaborative use of my notebook, students affirmed their intellect by documenting experiences in casual language that invoked laughter and invited me into the dialogical practice of relationship building. Essentially, they inserted Black joy, redirected my initial inquiries, and expanded research possibilities as they subverted institutionalization and created space for analysis, laughter, and joy through their responses to and self-insertion within my research.

I structure this chapter by first describing the Black Ratchet Imagination (BRI), defined by Bettina Love in her article, "A Ratchet Lens: Black Queer Youth, Agency, Hip Hop, and the Black Ratchet Imagination." I situate care within the BRI as a framework to consider how the children in my study resist the institutional limits placed on their observable interactions and the meanings of those interactions; care invites, without judgment or agenda, the messiness of vulnerability. With the conceptual framework outlined, I recollect my initial research interactions with students as I sought to acquire consent/assent within the fraught constraints of institutional bureaucracy. Then, I share a series of vignettes that explore my process of aligning with the "messy" ethics of the students as my research collaborators. I exhibit how students used my notebook to perform as ethnographer, complicate their public identities, and investigate their own interiority as demonstrations of someone who cares and is cared for. I conclude with a reflection on my consent/assent, my analytical process, the notebook, and caring relationships.

Conceptual Framework

The word "ratchet" was popularized through hip-hop culture between 1999 and 2004 as a representation of the complex and fluid realities of working-class Blacks in the southern region of the United States (Brown & Young, 2015, p. 2). L. H. Stallings introduced the BRI to name and elevate the queerness of Black youth occupying contemporary hip-hop cultures and the ways its "unreality and performance of failure" is contributing to a movement that "interrupts the order of knowledge" (2013, p. 136) and is divorced from notions of Black respectability. Elaborating on the fluidity of hip-hop's above- and below-ground Black liberatory movements, Stallings advocates for the consideration of hip-hop through the lens of queer theory as a means of illuminating "transitional bodies in transitional spaces, rather than a fixed body in transitional spaces" (2013, p. 135). Ratchet connotes "messy, meaning it has no straightforward definition; it is contradictory, fluid, precarious, agentive, and oftentimes intentionally inappropriate" (Love, 2017, p. 540). Ratchet is disruptive, nonnormative, ageless, gendered, and always raced. The BRI examines the experiences of Black youth who exist at the intersections, within the contradictory—positioned simultaneously as invisible and hypervisible, criminal and innocent, adultified and infantilized, hypersexualized and desexualized, threatening and passive—and lean into the liberatory terrain of hip-hop culture in the United States.

Applying this messiness at the heart of the BRI to her field research, Love (2017) constructs the BRI as a methodological perspective that parallels narrative inquiry; however, unlike traditional narrative inquiry, which centers itself around the researcher's questions, concerns, and interpretations, within the BRI, researchers must decenter both adults and themselves to give platform to youth experiences in the formation of narratives and the production of knowledge (p. 542). Decentering the researcher-self and adults from the outset of the study enables the co-construction of safety, thereby moving against the sociological whiteness/rightness model (Willse, 2015) that produces deficit narratives. In doing so, the BRI reveals Black youth's social consciousness, the concerns that plague them, and the practices they employ in collectively acknowledging and addressing these concerns. Creativity, pleasure, and movement have been integral to Black survival. The BRI "[recognizes] the importance of creativity, laughter, joy, love, and innovation to all participants and communities, regardless of race, ethnicity, and gender" (Love, 2017, p. 545). The BRI is designed to create space for an ever-evolving understanding of a particular Black youth subculture and its relationships to the culture of hip-hop and the history of the participants' city.

The BRI encompasses both the "messy, incomplete findings, which are not generalizable" (Love, 2017, p. 541) as well as the Black joy in play and communication. Because his engagement with my research began at the tail end of summer 2018, Ocho Jinks's aforementioned engagement with my research felt "messy and incomplete," but I now recognize how he used my inquiries about "what kids do" to share his interests—what brings him joy, what he cares about—and used my notebook to gesture toward an interior life and create multiple identities in and through my research. He demonstrated a level of trust in me, and my consistent listening practice and personal inquiries demonstrated my care for him.

Ocho Jinks's engagement with me and investment in my research was evidenced by countless students included in the study. Through my interactions with students, I nurtured genuine and mutual relationships with their families that then catalyzed my research on and through an ethic of care founded in love for the entire community. An ethic of care mandates that the research paradigm decolonize and radicalize, while also supporting the construction and expansion of alternative models of resistance. The embrace of messiness and joy within the BRI aligns with my conceptualization of care as a practice of "holding space," which, according to Jacqueline Roebuck Sakho, "means, my vulnerability meets your vulnerability with an open heart for the purpose of creating a safe moment in time where we can express authentically, courageously and vulnerably in any way we choose; free of judgement, agendas and expectations" (2017, p. 14). Care, performed and extended, establishes reciprocal relationships that invite nuance and fluidity and, thus, augments self-expansion and communal exploration. In this way, care contributes to the interruption of social scientific research that has historically been self-invested in the objectification of Black lives (Willse, 2015) by opening new pathways to a multifaceted preservation and celebration of Black childhood.

Play is how I extend love and, thereby, practice and embody an ethic of care. Play is the means through which experiences, behaviors, social and cultural expressions are merged and transformed into a practice that catalyzes self-interrogation and communal exploration (Hale & Bocknek, 2016, p. 88). The knowledge generated and exchanged through play is often culturally responsive, in that play forms are reflective of the habits, customs, and institutions that dictate the daily routines in a specific community. For the Black children with whom I studied, the BRI was embodied through and grounded in play—the vehicle through which joy and laughter is generated, social critique is provoked and realized, games are created and accolades are acquired, burdens are alleviated, and self-care is practiced, and humans can be fully acknowledged for the personal experiences, historical narratives, and cultural practices that they bring into the space. Play founds and organizes peer culture. So play is our earliest form of "holding space" as care for another person.

Local Ethics and Child Agency: Complicating Research Consent/Assent

In May of 2018, I sent introductory letters home with each child in the 2nd–5th grade at both elementary schools. The letter contained information about me, a brief overview of my research, and a photo of me. After obtaining parental consent, I reintroduced myself to potentially assenting students. I proceeded to inform them that I wanted to learn about their interests and the games they play at school, home, or in the neighborhood. I explicitly stated that for at least the next four months I was their student and they could teach me anything they wanted.

Productive ethnographic work with children, particularly children who are not white and middle class, demands that the ethnographer be open to accepting the role of the student and position the child as the expert. Positioning children as experts provides the space for a rebalancing of expert knowledges that are often in tension with each other as adults are conditioned to prioritize the expertise of the researcher over the expertise of the child who exists within and acts upon their own subculture(s). My reconfiguring of the researcher/subject binary at the onset of my research produced immediate results. Within the first week I learned from many parents that my letter never made it home. Yet students across grade levels at both schools approached me in the cafeteria, on the playground, and during after-school with comments like, "I heard you wanna learn about games," "I signed the paper [assent form]. When does your thing begin?" "I read your paper with your picture on it. What's that thing again?" "I told my mama about your thing and she said I could sign myself up." Students had read my letter and/or been in conversation with their peers, and they all understood that the research was about them and the games that belonged to them and wanted to sign themselves up for my study.

I grappled with the problem of denying students the opportunity to share knowledge produced by and belonging to them on the premise that I did not have their signed parental consent. A denial would undermine the expressed competencies and agency of the student and signify my alignment with adult authority (Heath et al., 2007, 415). While I do not refute the need for fundamental participant protections, these students' inquiries into my research contested the ethical grounds on which consent forms are established, as the prioritization of parental consent in a play-based study reinforces the stereotype of children as vulnerable, unaware, and helpless. As one Blaze Rods parent noted, "[You] got kids doing grown up stuff like changing diapers, making dinner—so when they come to school and they get talked to like a child, it's a step back or disrespectful." Her comment forwarded the fact that "ethical practice is tied to the active construction of research relationships and cannot be based in presupposed ideas or stereotypes about children or childhood" (Heath et al., 2007, p. 484). Obstructing students' participation could potentially be interpreted as disrespectful as these children were inviting me to participate in their own cultural expressions.

Students' proclaimed desire to participate can be read as moments of self-assertion and institutional disruption. Whether I was an adult or not did not concern the students—whether adults consented or not was not a concern—as one Blaze Rods 5th grade student questioned, "Why my mama got to agree if you're writing about me?" A few weeks into my study, the same parent remarked, "The kids notice loyalty—they will respect that … They respect people [who respect them] not status." Student responses to my consent process and this parent's comments emphasize the significance of local standards and identify that these standards value respect and loyalty over age and status. To learn what the students wanted to teach me about their play practices and cultural expressions, I had to move within *their* locally constituted ethical framework.

Considering that consent/assent is an ongoing process that occurs differently in various contexts, researchers must rethink the priority we give to parental consent if we are to practice a care for the agency of our child participants. Read together, the student and parent commentary reinforce the necessity that researchers who enter research relationships with Black youth understand local history, structural inequalities, neighborhood dynamics, and Black youth precarity *prior* to the commencement of research (Love, 2017, p. 545). Consciously engaging my research question about play practices and their neighborhood structure, students had taken a route to this engagement that seemed to be preparing me for *their* concerns about my accountability, the stakes of their participation, protection of their interests, and an awareness of my own positionality in relation to other existing social actors, especially their parents and teachers (Christensen & Prout, 2002, p. 482).

Ultimately, I resolved first to contact directly the parents of students who identified themselves for participation in the study. Parents with whom I had established relationships assisted me with recruitment by walking me through the neighborhood and introducing me to other parents. Second, I decided to document only communal interactions of students who had expressed a desire to be included, but whose parents could not be immediately contacted. Given that students from both groups were constantly engaged in conversation or some activity with each other, my protocol became far more communal with documented interactions rarely occurring in groups of less than three. I would announce each time I was about to document a comment or observation in my notebook so that students could interject. This shared practice of documentation ensured that sensitive information was not revealed and that consent/assent remained ongoing, which allowed me to operate within the constraints of my IRB protocol while maintaining an alignment with the students. Students were affirmed by this shared practice because it displayed my care and regard for their concerns and my desire for their participation.

JaQuan and JaCobee: Reconsidering and Sharing the Notebook

During the first week of the study, which was also last week of the 2017–2018 school year, I joined a cluster of students during their lunch and recess breaks at Flower

Elementary. I jotted down their corny jokes, fabricated stories, personal interests, dating advice, imaginative games, and social critiques. Within a few days of people learning of the purpose for my notebook, someone, usually a child, would instruct me to "make sure you write down," "write this down in your book," "don't write that down." But, after a few days of watching me take notes on their conversation in my notebook, one 3rd grade boy, JaQuan or JaCobee (not sure which twin), told me, "I can just write it down for you." After I agreed and forfeited my notebook, it seemed, every 3rd grade boy was asking to write in my notebook. During that lunch, JaQuan and JaCobee wrote in fractured sentences across the page:

> We watch trollhunter
> We watch nigos
> My mius is migos.
> We play basketball
> and football and baseball and
> kickball. We love to
> watch all the shose
> show on tv. We love
> are faimly.
> - I'm a fan of Stephen Curry.
> - He is a fan of Kyeri irving.[3]

> fornite

With these notes, JaQuan and JaCobee initiated the unexpected direction my research would take as more students desired the opportunity to write and speak for themselves in a project that extended beyond their immediate community. Their knowledge of this extension was made clear to me when one twin introduced me to their teacher; he excitedly announced: "This is my best friend! She's writing a book on us." I believe his comment signaled that he felt cared for in our interactions and that his contributions to the community were being recognized and explored because those contributions were singularly invaluable.

Allowing students access to my notebook to record their responses to my questions about their favorite games decentered my voice as the adult/researcher. Hence, in the act of documenting their own play practices, the students repositioned themselves as active co-constructors of our research project. Before I left the cafeteria, I scribbled a header of sorts in my notebook documenting the location and grade. I did not add any comments to their notes. Instead, I continued my observation notes for the remainder of the day on the next page.

Beginning the next day, I added a header that identified the location and grade whenever I entered a space. Then, I would announce to the students with whom I was sitting or playing that I was taking notes or I would immediately proceed to take notes once instructed to do so—whichever came first. In this single notebook, their notes, which often consumed pages of their own, became commingled with my own notes, distinguishable by their large handwriting and use of first-person pronouns.

DeSiree, Meme, Bri-Bri, and Kendra: Ethnographic "Participant-Observers"

DeSiree agreed to participate in my research study in May 2018 before her 4th grade school year ended. We subsequently bonded at the summer camp program. I learned of DeSiree's gigantic personality during our first field trip. Thereafter, I frequently sat next to her at lunch throughout summer camp and spent the most time with the girls in her class during the after-school program at the beginning of her 5th grade school year. She was the first student to ask me what I had written about her—even though much of what I had written from our interactions she had dictated herself. She would tell me, "Write this down," "Take this note." DeSiree was also the first student to initiate a sort of role reversal in my field research when, holding my notebook while I conversed with Angel Gist, a rambunctious 3rd grade student, DeSiree wrote:

> What do you want Angel Gist?
> – Ari
> *Ari is pretty.*

The dialogue she started with and through my notebook enacted a core component of the BRI: "youth must play a vital role in data analysis and member checking to ensure the research captures all the textures and layers of their lived experiences" (Love, 2017, p. 545). I believe my attention to DeSiree's behavior and DeSiree's attention to my notebook invited the curiosity and enthusiasm of her Black girl classmates. Throughout my last week at Blaze Rods, DeSiree and three of her classmates requested my notebook, which I provided without question or instruction.

They observed and recorded the following notes about each other in my notebook. Meme was the first to record her observations:

> DeSiree is being werid with
> carrots. She stuck a carrot in Bri-Bri ear, and nose.
> Bri-Bri pushed me =| and
> it was werid to.
> Now were dancing =)
> DeSiree a is dancing crazy.
> Meme is going crazy.

Bri-Bri mimicked Meme's actions and responded to Meme's notes that same day:

> DeSiree was acting ~~wear~~ crazy today
> (august 21, 2018) Meme was
> So So crazy so, I push
> her. Not on purpos it's
> because her stinky butt
> was on Me! That crazy!

Two days later, Kendra added her own observations of the group, but she included me in her notes too:

> DJ is being so weird and she
> keep making weird nosies.
> Ari is the best and hope she has a good year(s) at school.
> DJ (DeSiree Jones) she keep being so, so, so, so, so weird.
> Meme is mad because Ari won't walk with her.

Rather than remaining adhered to traditional notions of "participant-observer" in which I was the primary investigator, this series of role reversals smudged the lines between researcher/subject and even adult/child as I was included in Kendra's observation as more of a peer, associated equally with DeSiree and Meme.

Their written engagement with me as researcher and subject, each other as researcher(s) and subject(s), positioned my notebook as the conduit for new forms of interactions. Together, the students initiated a multilayered form of communicative labor. In structuring my research, I intentionally avoided traditional social scientific or classroom models of student knowledge production/acquisition, which often take the forms of surveys or interviews. Instead, I sought to make space for various forms of students' creative knowledge production and data analysis. As a result, students actively participated in both production and analysis as they documented and responded to their own observations and each other's. The critical analysis of the notes, one another, and my research was in their playful intellectual engagement with each other.

The girls' literal act of writing themselves into my research study was also an act of writing themselves into the institutions through which my research will traverse. Relatedly, Aimee Meredith Cox calls for an increased awareness of the ways that "Black girls develop their own rhetorical performances and creative strategies" (2015, p. 27). If researchers, and adults everywhere, examine how Black girls perceive themselves and their relationship to institutional and social spaces, we can understand how their actions may be constrained, but nonetheless self-disciplined. DeSiree, Meme, Bri-Bri, and Kendra's collaboration in our shared ethnographic explorations reveal how institutional and social spaces are continually transformed by their presence and activity (Cox, 2015, p. 234). Their requests for my notebook, observations, and documentations were self-initiated, self-directed, and collectively analyzed. We cared about each other as friends and research collaborators. They forced an insertion of the BRI as they subverted the limits placed on the types of interactions able to be studied by researchers, as well as the corresponding meanings of those interactions. They made the notebook a shared space rooted in care for our collective and individual creativity, laughter, and joy.

Julio and C.J.: Co-constructing Research Agendas and Relationships of Accountability

Brothers Julio and C.J., 7th and 6th graders at Fun Middle School, similarly exhibited a shared ownership over my research. After about a month of sporadic questioning about graduate school and my research (like, why did I choose them and what will I do with my notes), Julio and C.J. (but mostly Julio) began taking a singular interest in the content of my research.

Julio and C.J. spent their after-school hours in the Blaze Rods library while their younger siblings attended the after-school program. Julio, C.J., and Ocho Jinks would come into the library and share the most interesting part of their day. During these two hours together, Julio would direct his attention to me and assert authoritatively, "I'ma give you some notes. What you need to know?" Julio would then proceed to answer my research questions directly, indirectly involving C.J. and Ocho Jinks in the conversation as well. One day, Julio shared aloud that he and his siblings enjoy, "Fortnite; Call of Duty; GTA; NBA2K; Connect 4; Sorry; playing with their scooters and bicycles; and trampoline games like 'Flip Master' and 'Flip Contest.'" The next day, Julio provided the rules for Flip Master and Flip Contest, which were games he and his brothers created in their backyard. Throughout our time, Julio would share his favorite foods, his perception of the adults in his daily life, as well as common terms and concepts he and his peers used daily. Often, these perceptions and definitions were more speculative than definitive. Yet, in these encounters, Julio used literal play and explanations of play practices to share about his life, confront unfair notions of childhood, and highlight the significance of his sibling relationships.

Two specific dialogues between myself and Julio are emblematic of Julio's unique engagement with my research. After a summer of him observing me "observe" him, Julio randomly informed me of a plan he had hatched. The conversation went as follows:

JULIO: I'ma start taking notes.
ME: What you gonna take notes on?
JULIO: How grown ups live.
ME: How do grown ups live?
JULIO: For instance, they tell us to clean up the house but its they house. ... Since grown ups made you, they tell you what to do.

The next day, Julio told me, "Since you're writing a book on me, I want it to say [on the cover] 'The Life of Julio Good.'" Through his comments and assertions, Julio expressed a consistent awareness of the socially constructed childhood scripts that assume obedience to adult-sanctioned norms. In declaring that my book shall be named in his honor, Julio rebuked "the black experience of anonymity, the estrangement of being without a name," which "has been one of living in the oblivion of society's inverse, beyond the dimension of any consideration at all" (Roberts, 1999, p. 303). Julio forced a full consideration of himself as an individual, not merely one child in a multisite research study. I postulate that Julio resisted the associated constraints and debilitation of those childhood scripts as he engaged a form of cultural and social criticism and knowledge exchange. This criticism and exchange of knowledge was masked as culturally informed play and interactions in which he directly involved me as an unquestionable equal.

Julio effectively denies the possibility of me overlooking his engagement by utilizing my research as an opportunity not only to share his knowledge of Black child play but also to share a larger critique of the conventional cultural hierarchy in which children are at the bottom. Julio compelled me to consider how certain ethical standards and research design foreclose the possibility of accessing particular knowledges before the study begins. For example, had the research study not allowed the inversion of the researcher/subject binary, Julio's critique and subsequent decision to surveil adults in the same way adults surveil children might not have occurred. His critique provided alternative routes to understanding how Black children protest oppressive institutions and unfair conditions. He strategically revealed this knowledge as he casually denounced the assumed childhood dependency on grown-ups to indict the form of imperialism most immediately visible in his daily life. In so doing, Julio verbally asserted his own agency as a declaration of personal power.

Julio was conscious of the fact that he possessed the knowledge I was seeking. Treating me as his mentee, to whom he bequeathed his knowledge of the world, Julio decentered me as the adult and centered himself and his siblings as the experts. He disallowed me the choice of simply recording what I thought was important, and thereby, rendering him an object to be exploited in my research. Moreover, recalling my definition of care as the co-construction of safety for vulnerability that is messy—free of agendas and expectations—Julio manifested his care for me and our research through accountability. You must care for a person to be in accountable relationships with them. Julio challenged me to uphold my commitment to honor his knowledge and play by decentering *my* research agenda and co-constructing one that was representative of his experiences, not merely my interests.

Lauryn: Honoring Messy Engagement and Multiple Identities

Lauryn, a 4th grade student at Blaze Rods, provided an intimate engagement with my research through her self-initiated and self-directed entry in my notebook. Although her mother had prodded me all summer to include Lauryn in my research, Lauryn's skepticism of my research was unmistakable in our early encounters at the start of the 2018–2019 school year. During the after-school program one day, I told her and the 3rd–5th grade girls that I was writing about the "cool things they do." Lauryn side-eyed me and told me that she didn't believe me, but she shared about her experience living in the neighborhood anyway.

Over the next few days during and after school, Lauryn and I discussed books we like to read, her career aspirations, our experiences as middle children in our families, and how we both have a lot of emotions that we usually write about in our journals. One day shortly after these conversations, I approached the lunch table where I had left my notebook in the possession of a 3rd grader. As I walked up, I noticed that Lauryn had my notebook and was shielding other students from reading the notebook as she wrote. When she returned the notebook to me, she said, "I wrote in it like I write in my journal." Her entry is below:

> This girl in my class don't like me
> Because i don't know. I think it's about
> my group i got KKL that mean all my
> friends. Do you no What's wrong
> with her. They Stare at me, I will
> turn around an look ~~bh~~ behind me
> and ~~there~~ they will look carzy.
> Is that Petty to Look back
> I don't think so. I belive that
> That's ok Katelyn is always in
> mess i don't know Why but she
> Is. ~~Her teacher wasn't her because~~ Her teacher wasn't here
> and she had to come to my
> class I thought it was going
> to be ok but she was Just
> then she got in mess and
> start calling ~~al~~ out my group
> KKL, KKL an I was so mad
> So i started to get mad.[4]

Lauryn exhibited a heavy and somewhat esoteric reflexivity in her writing that indicated the presence of an expansive interiority. Kevin Quashie defines interiority as the "quality of being inward, a 'metaphor' for 'life and creativity beyond the public face of stereotype and limited imagination' … The interior is the inner reservoir of thoughts, feelings, desires, fears, ambitions that shape a human self; it is … 'the locus at which self interrogation takes place'" (2012, p. 21). In this regard, to possess an interior is to be conscious of the essence of one's own existence and one's place in the larger social stratum. Lauryn appears to make a conscious attempt at opening an analytical discourse on her social positioning in relationship to her peers. Rather than verbalizing these musings aloud about her friendships–the "mess" Katelyn (who is identified later) creates, and her socioemotional responses to this "mess"–Lauryn repurposes my notebook from an object used for my external investigation of the lives of Black children, to the "'the locus at which self-interrogation [can take] place'" for herself, a Black child.

Lauryn's appropriation of my notebook and her reflective writing reaffirms the "need for a concept of interiority, that … can support representations of blackness that are irreverent, messy, complicated" (Quashie, 2012, p. 23). Her entry attests to the need for the BRI, as the framework invites the messiness and honors the hyper-locality evident in Lauryn's modest, yet unrestrained, anonymous, yet dogmatic, expression of interiority. Lauryn's gesture toward her interior and her articulation of her ideological, social and emotional positioning in her peer-governed world contributes to a larger ethnographic imaginary (Kidd, 2002) that might otherwise seek "to smooth over contradictions, conflicts of interest, and doubts and arguments, not to mention changing motivations and circumstance" (Abu-Lughod, 2008, p. 153) or romanticize

Black youth resistance. In her one entry, Lauryn contests external valuations of her person by a peer and valuations of her by white patriarchal hierarchical institutions that marginalize Black children, especially Black girls. As researchers, we must care enough to notice and value the messiness of their insights and experiences, which ultimately requires us to educate ourselves about the social and ideological complexity of students' lives (Dyson, 1997, p. 13) and their local communities.

Katelyn: A [Research] Ethic of Love

Katelyn, the 4th grader at Blaze Rods previously cited as always "in mess" by Lauryn, also used my notebook to invite me into meaningful dialogue with her. Katelyn usually "doodled" drawings of hearts, flowers, and girls in the pages of my notebook (Figure 5.1).

Like the other students, Katelyn flattened the researcher/subject binary by interacting with me, through my notebook, in a raw manner characteristic of intimate peers. In one specific instance, she refers to me in her "fieldnotes" by name; Katelyn wrote:

> You is pretty and You is
> so smart. I love you so much Air
> U is nice al the time when I ask
> You for you book

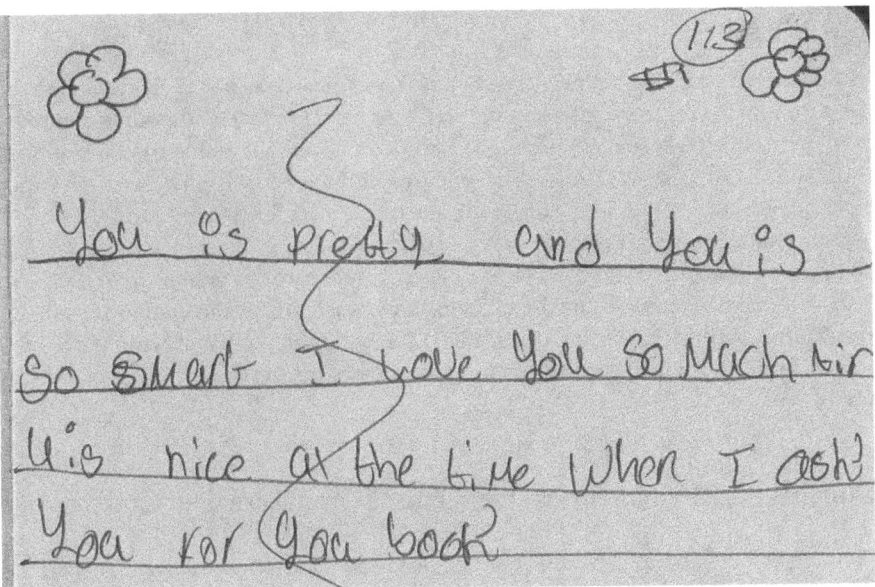

Figure 5.1 Katelyn's writing and drawings in my notebook

> I
> Show respect

She continues on the top of the next page:

> When I first meat you, you
> had a smile on your face
> I thought you was shy sometimes
> but you always look so cute and

She trailed off and did not finish, but evidently, she had been studying me. Katelyn took up an extreme amount of space in my research as her notes and doodles consume almost eight pages in my notebook, more than any other student.

We must consider how Black girls are both hyper visible and invisible and continually in the process of mediating the space between the two. As a result, living within their Black child bodies often means "generally being seen and not heard" (Cox, 2015, p. 215). Katelyn, however, transformed my notebook into a site of agency in which she was self-determining and free to utilize the space of each page as she chose. Considering how institutions have historically denied Black children, especially Black girls, freedom of signification, Katelyn's entries can be read as obvious forms of resistance. Ruth Nicole Brown notes that too often, academic research defines Black girlhood as absence (2013, p. 8), and instead of addressing this violent falsehood, Black girls are "routinely disciplined into taking up less and less space" (2013, p. 2). Katelyn seizes an immense amount of space in my notebook. There were no stigmatizing tropes or debilitating expectations prescribed for her on the pages or anywhere else in the notebook. When you feel seen and understood, you feel free to take risks and take up space.

So Katelyn scribbled out new directions for my research as her open declaration of her emotional investment in me would not have been possible without my summer-long effort to transform "ethnographic practice into ethnographic praxis (action)" (McClaurin, 2001, p. 61). This praxis allowed me to see fully this Black girl and, consequently, she employed my notebook as a mechanism for establishing a sisterhood with me. Katelyn reminds me that "the ethic of [love] that ultimately engenders 'political communities rooted in a radical ethic of care' occurs through action" (Cox, 2015, p. 232) or praxis. Extending this discourse of love-based ethics and care to include all the children in this chapter, we can see how centering intentional expressions of care can expand the bounds, considerations, and reach of our research beyond our initial vision.

Conclusion: The Notebook, the Analysis, and Care-Full Community

Through the collaborative use of my notebook, students affirmed their intellect by documenting experiences in casual language that invoked laughter and invited me into the dialogical practice of relationship building. Students' control, exchange of, and notations within the notebook became the foundation for my analysis of Black child play as their reflections, insights, and critiques were emblematic of marginalized conversations happening across Black studies, childhood studies, and literary studies regarding the urgency of centering Black children's experiences and knowledge. Acting on their self-initiated momentum, I began preparing myself to ask scaffolded questions that provoked investigative and communal responses about both play and research as a means of laying the foundation to ask more specific questions about cooperative play and their role in the local community. I began preparing questions for the next interaction based on previous interactions—I would hand them the list of questions to read aloud to each other. The interactions and dynamics between myself and students were fluid and intentional.

I did not write up full fieldnotes after my interactions with children. I did not physically comment on children's fieldnotes in my notebook until I returned to my university in August. At this point, I had opened pathways to direct communication with entire families in the community and remained in communication with teachers, parents, and students. I shared theories I was working through, and they kept me updated about changes in the neighborhood and inside their school. In this way, the analysis was created in community while the research continued to build upon itself as families continued to notice, think about, and respond to my questions throughout the year via phone calls, texts, and social media exchanges.

Ultimately, as I have evidenced in this chapter, by utilizing the BRI, researchers can mobilize a repositioning of Black children as community gatekeepers and invaluable collaborators. Through this repositioning, we redefine and redistribute representational power. We can experience Black children's cultural praxes and work collaboratively to promote and refine a relational culture that equips both researchers and students with the knowledge and skills necessary to thrive. We can be in an authentic community—contributors to and recipients of a network of care—with students and families.

The BRI, however, compels researchers to reckon with our relationships to institutions founded on whiteness and violence. Researchers must practice an intentionality that is rooted in a consciousness of our collective struggle against imperialist, capitalist, white supremacist patriarchy (hooks 2004, p. 21). To assess fully all risks that our studies may pose to students and their communities, we must speak to the ways in which risk is racialized, gendered, and institutionalized before we initiate the study. This requires that we be willing to complicate our own methodological approaches while leaving space for children and youth to develop their own understanding of the study and determine their role within it. We are not unlike our [potential] participants, in that we cannot account for the full implications of our research at the outset of the study. However, locating ourselves as the risk and in the mess is how we decolonize our research and manifest care that critiques, nurtures, and mobilizes individual and shared experiences of safety and vulnerability.

My perception of research with children, and my relationship to these children specifically, was radicalized through each of these interactions. Essentially, they made space for me and modeled a practice of care and reciprocal investment that subverted institutional and hierarchical oppression. When you care about people, you care about what they care about and vice versa. I cared about these students, the games they played, and their community. And in return, the ways in which the students invested in my research, built friendships, and protected my notebook exhibited a relationship with me and the research they were now co-constructing that centered reciprocal care.

6

The Reception and Reward of Relationship-Building and Enacting Care with Black Boys

Pavithra Nagarajan

Introduction

I'm sitting on the floor of the gymnasium during Morning Town Hall helping Danté go through his backpack to find his consent form which he says has to be in there somewhere. The teachers are standing against the wall lining the periphery. Maurice approaches us and starts telling Danté about two other boys who were fighting before school. Danté says, "yo, you're going to tell me this with Ms. N right here?" Maurice responds "It's Ms. N!" and starts laughing, and Danté joins in. I ask why they're laughing, and Danté says, "I was just kidding. We know you're good and you got our backs, plus you were probably there."

(excerpt from fieldnotes, November 2016)

My years spent as a classroom teacher were formative, and as I have now learned, inextricable from my research orientation and praxis with youths in schools. In teaching, and later in my research, I positioned myself as a learner so I could learn about my students' in and out-of-school lives. I was basically a youth myself when I started teaching—an eager, yet very much naive, 21-year old who wanted to ameliorate the educational opportunity gap. It was this context through which I first developed my orientation to and methods of teaching, learning, and relating to youth from nondominant, historically marginalized communities.

As a new 6th grade teacher, I was still getting my bearings with solid pedagogy and instructional practice. I was new to the community, and did not share racial/ethnic or gender similarities with my all-male, Black and Latinx students. I knew I had a lot to learn. I felt deep care for my students, and believed my curiosity and genuine interest in their lives would translate to students' reception of that care in the classroom, and with it, trust in me as a teacher. This orientation did serve me well for my teaching career and it stayed with me as a researcher. I placed a great deal of importance in building relationships and demonstrating care with the boys who participated in my research, so that they would trust me as a researcher in their lives.

In this chapter, I first provide a framework for how to enact care in schools as a researcher. This framework is based on reflecting on some of the choices that I made that helped foster a sense of care with the boys who participated in my study. I then use this framework to examine the research relationships that I developed with two of my participants—David Sanchez and Isaiah Edwards—by highlighting moments that I now, upon reflection, recognize as contributing to boys' articulated notions of care. Next, I describe how my research benefited from the care that I enacted with the boys—creating space, uncovering truths, and deeper knowing that otherwise would have been foreclosed to me without practicing a care-based research methodology. Lastly, I consider the broader themes and implications of enacting care-based research.

Background

I draw from a research study I began four years after leaving the classroom: a yearlong, qualitative study in a 6–12 public single-sex school, Sankofa Collegiate,[1] in a large Northeastern city. This study was motivated by my time as a teacher at a school much like Sankofa Collegiate both in terms of its single-sex setting and school population, predominantly Black and Latinx boys, the majority of whom were navigating poverty.

Sankofa Collegiate, like many other public single-sex schools formed over the last two decades, is positioned as a respite from traditional, public schools for historically marginalized (e.g., Black, Latinx) students navigating poverty. In addition to providing a tailored space to support students' academic and social well-being, these schools seek to dismantle the normalized "rightness" of white, middle-class perspectives, knowledge, language, and behavior by centering and uplifting those students who may not otherwise be centered in public institutions (Carter, 2005; Noguera, 2009). Sankofa Collegiate primarily serves Black boys from low-income communities. In order to improve boys' academic outcomes, Sankofa and many schools like it seek to organizationally (re)define Black masculinity for its students such that it is positively academically oriented (Fergus and Noguera, 2009).

Through my study, I sought to learn how Sankofa organizationally (re)defined masculinity through practices, policies, and rituals. I also aimed to learn how boys negotiated, participated in, and made sense of these organizational definitions, and how school practices affected boys' sense of self-perceptions, identity, and agency. My ethnographic observations included observing whole-school practices, shadowing 6th grade classrooms and students, and attending extended day and after school activities, and field trips. I interviewed eighteen school-based staff including school leaders and educators. I selected thirty-four students for in-depth interviews and photo elicitation narrative projects.[2] It is from the experiences with students (i.e., observations, interviews, and photo narrative projects) from which I draw my reflections on how I enacted care for this chapter.

Enacting Care: A Three-Part Framework

Care-based research requires a radical revisioning of what is possible in research. This revisioning, first, necessitates an expansion of the traditional bounds of a researcher's "responsibility" to the youths that share their lives with us in this distinct and personal way. Enacting care requires a commitment to disrupting systemic racism, which can be thought of as a "machine that runs whether we pull the levers or not, and by just letting it be, we are responsible for what it produces" (Oluo, 2019, p. 30). To avoid being complicit in racism, we as researchers must actively reject the comfort of neutrality and find opportunities—both in the planning and in the execution of research—to shift traditional power relations in schools and institutions that uphold the primacy of whiteness.

Caring requires reimagining the role of power in research relationships, and how that power could be repurposed toward individualized attention and affirmation, acknowledgment, and affectionate connection with youths. Researchers must be, therefore, anchored by intent and action toward dismantling racism and ending racial equities or committed to an anti-racist research praxis (Gillborn, 2006; Perry & Shotwell, 2009). Engaging in such a praxis requires directing action and reflection toward structures that need to be transformed in order to disrupt and dismantle racism (Freire, 2014).

Engaging in research with youths with an anti-racist research praxis requires first, and consistently, prioritizing the dignity and care of youth participants through relationship-building, or what Django Paris and Maisha T. Winn (2014) term "humanizing research." Paris and Winn (2014) note that humanizing research requires a researcher to be vigilant in order to actively monitor and ensure that research activities respect and honor the humanity of those who "invite us into their worlds" (p. xv). This vigilance is especially necessary when conducting research with youth from historically marginalized communities and in instances in which there is not shared positionality (e.g., racial/ethnic, geographic, gender, sexual orientation, socioeconomic) between researchers and the youth with whom research is conducted. Difference, in and of itself, is not problematic; rather, it is how those differences are rendered through the process and the outcomes of our research that can characterize the enactment of and possibilities for care in our research relationships. Researching from a foundation of respect and humility is not only anti-racist; it is a fundamental ethical and justice-oriented responsibility.

Below, I articulate each of the three key components of the framework, grounded in anti-racist research praxis, that I took toward enacting care in the aforementioned research study. These components are parallax; affirmative witnessing; and reception, not reciprocation, of care.

Parallax and Space

"Parallax"—a term from the Greek words parallagé, "alteration," and parallassein, "to change"—refers to an apparent change of an object's position against a background due to a change in an observer's perspective upon viewing that object along two different lines of sight (Greenwood, 2008; Sameshima, 2007). School-based ethnographers have the ability to inhabit spaces that may otherwise be unusual, or impractical, for typical school adults (e.g., teachers, counselors, school aides) to be present. These spaces include places of transience, such as passing interactions in hallways or stairwells, or more sustained interactions in nonacademic settings (e.g., student lunch or recess) in which adults typically do not participate.

Parallax provides a useful concept through which to consider how a researcher's choices of physical and spatial positioning have ethnographic implications for not only who or what is observed, but *how*, or through what perspective observation is cast. Observing in spaces that students themselves choose to occupy allows researchers additional sight lines into youths' lives and decenters adults, including the researcher, in the process. This decentering provides "a platform to youth experiences in the formation of narratives and the production of knowledge" (Love, 2017, p. 542). Love (2017) further argues that creating this metaphorical and physical space fosters the "co-construction of safety," and as a result, can push against the primacy of whiteness in institutional spaces that positions youth from nondominant communities squarely within a deficit frame.

Affirmative Witnessing

Qualitative research with children requires an ongoing act of witnessing or "deliberate attendance" to and taking notice of what is particularly meaningful to the youths with whom we work (Laura, 2016). Witnessing can take many forms (see Winn and Ubiles, 2011), but here I focus particularly on a curiosity and a willingness to be led by youths in a quest for knowing. This might include demonstrating a genuine interest in youths' interests and lives, within and outside the scope of the research aims, including asking questions and seeking to understand. Bearing witness requires the consistency of "being there" emotionally and physically over time such that youths can assess whether our curiosities are genuine and well-intentioned. As such, affirmative witnessing signals a researcher's care and respect, and further empowers students by "legitimizing their 'voice' and visibility" as important, special, and worthy of attention (Gay, 2000, p. 49). Researchers therefore have the ability to render the personhood of youths more visible, and in doing so, can affirm their importance and rightful presence in the world. Youths do not want or need researchers to tell their stories for them, but they do deserve to interact with adults who care enough to listen to their stories, or even, to be in the stories that they tell. Youths are more than the data they provide.

Reception, Not Reciprocation, of Care

A researcher's care need not be reciprocated in equal measure, but simply received by youth. Care should be given without expectation of its return given the inherent power imbalances between researchers and youth participants and the privileges that researchers hold. These power imbalances hold regardless of demographic background, but are especially salient across a lack of shared positionality between a researcher and youth participants, especially when those youth participants are from historically marginalized racial and ethnic groups and/or low-income communities. In line with Noddings (2013) and Rolon-Dow (2005), I argue that caring intentions are necessary, but not sufficient to constitute care; rather it is the felt impact of intentions being received that constitutes care. Reception of care can be indicated by what

Winn and Ubiles (2011) term "revelation": a felt mutual respect as an outcome of the collaborative working together of researchers and youth participants to co-construct and advance knowledge. There are critical implications for reconfiguring traditional power relationships through witnessing and care: youths can be affirmed that their perspectives are valid, important, and have value well beyond the "information" they provide to our research.

Enacting Care

Below, I reflect upon how I built research relationships with two of my participants: David Sanchez and Isaiah Edwards. I chose David and Isaiah, in particular, because they were two boys for whom my care appeared to be especially well-received due to the trust that they came to have in me. Reflecting upon my actions helped me most decisively, and retroactively, identify how I demonstrated my care and what in particular of those actions led to that care being received. David and Isaiah were both students who described feeling as though they did not fit in to Sankofa, and described the school as an unwelcoming place.

David

David Sanchez was an exceptionally quiet student who mostly kept to himself when the school year first started. He had one to two close friends with whom I'd see him sit at lunch and occasionally play during recess. David would rarely participate in class. Often, I'd see him talking to himself during class, typically at a higher volume than a whisper, which would regularly attract disciplining from teachers for creating noise during class or being off-task. The reason I first started talking to David was because he was regularly in the hallway and in the stairwell when he "shouldn't" have been. I'd pass him during times when class was in session whether it was while I was running an errand for a teacher, switching between classrooms, or walking to the bathroom. He'd often catch me by surprise; pacing the hallway, sitting in a stairwell—always by himself and typically talking to himself in frustrated tones.

    I chose to practice parallax here: leaning into these moments I would find David "out of place" and engaging him in those places, simply to connect. As a former teacher, this was very difficult for me, because I had to resist my urge to ask him, "Where are you supposed to be?" with an agenda of getting him back to that "where." Instead, I intentionally shifted toward affirmative witnessing by asking him "what's going on?" or "what's wrong?" The latter questions would actually tell me more about David—not just "where" he was supposed to be but "why" he chose not to be there. An example of the typical interactions I'd have with David is below, an excerpt from my fieldnotes:

> *I run into David as I'm walking through the hallway. I see him storm out of a classroom, the door slams and he walks in my direction ... I ask him "What's wrong?" and he's breathing really heavily, fists clenched, backpack on, and pacing through the hallway. It's hard to get him to pause, I look him directly in the eyes, a hand on the shoulder, and I tell him to breathe in and breathe out. He does, and after his*

breathing slows, maybe 30-45 seconds later, he says "thanks, Ms. N—okay, so this is what happened ..."

In this instance, as with most other interactions with David, he walked out of his class because he felt he was being disrespected by his teacher. Often, he'd name one particular teacher who disciplined him "unfairly." David would argue that the teacher "didn't see what happened and blamed me," and that the teacher "doesn't know me like that." Over the year, he continued to have struggles with this teacher, such that instead of even going to class he'd stand in the stairwell. Once I spotted him in the stairwell as I was in the hallway watching the other students line up to enter their classroom. I opened the stairwell door and popped my head around, and asked him, "What's going on?" David told me, "He doesn't listen to anyone, he just doesn't care." David regularly would leave people and places he found "uncaring" such that he could calm himself down, recalibrating his emotions by taking literal and metaphorical space to protect himself from a lack of care. Choosing to observe David in spaces that adults typically do not inhabit offered me an additional insight into David's intentions and actions that would have otherwise been obscured to me had I not, quite literally, met him where he was. Specifically, if I did not choose to engage David in the hallway and learn that he took space to calm himself, rather than say something disrespectful in class, I would not have understood how deeply sensitive David is and may have viewed his actions to leave, or not even enter, classrooms as simply willfully disobedient.

In the classroom, as well, David took note of my witnessing as a way to affirm what he was experiencing. During classroom instruction, I would typically take a seat at the back of the classroom taking notes and periodically walking around the class and talking with students when it wouldn't be disruptive. On one occasion, with the teacher he described above, David repeatedly called "Ms. N" to get my attention in the back of the classroom. I looked at him immediately, and we had the following exchange:

> David asks me, "Do you see this?" David gestures to his raised hand with the other. I do note that he has been raising his hand for three minutes, and has been holding his paper up in the air to signal he needs help. David says, "I've been raising my hand and [the teacher] doesn't even notice me. I nod at him, and look toward the teacher who is helping another student. When I look back to David he says "forget this" and crumples his paper. I pick up the crumpled paper and walk over to his desk.

In calling my attention to his situation David initiates, or confirms, that I am indeed witnessing the events, or seeing what he is seeing. The affirmation that he has, indeed, been raising his hand without acknowledgment demonstrates that I do see what he is seeing, and I hear his frustrations. When I chose to pick up the paper and walk over to his desk, David met my gaze and I asked him how he was feeling and encouraged him to continue to try hard, not for anyone else, but for himself. He picked up his pencil and continued to work.

I believe my efforts to care were received by David. He sought me out during the school day to say hello and to talk to me about things that were troubling him. Any time I approached him when he was upset to ask him how he was doing, he did not refuse my questions and participated fully in the conversation. David described how my care was indeed received by him: during his interview I asked him the question, "Is there an adult at school you would talk to if you had a problem and needed to talk to someone?" David responded "no" fairly quickly with a laugh and then sat up a bit and said, "But I mean, I would talk to you if I had a problem. It's 'cause you ask questions, or you notice we're upset. You come over to us and you care if we're having a good day or not." In his description, David acknowledges my efforts to demonstrate care, including noticing when he is upset and my genuine interest in his life and well-being. In this description, David also uses the word "us" to signal that my caring efforts are not just tied to him, but are visible in my approach with other students.

Isaiah

Isaiah Edwards came to Sankofa with a number of friends from his elementary school who remained his close friends throughout the year. Several teachers noted that Isaiah was very smart and that his work was excellent, but also found that he wasn't always consistent with finishing his work and sometimes his behavior or temper got in the way of his academic success. Isaiah certainly experienced difficulty with the disciplinary code at Sankofa: he regularly broke the rules because he didn't understand their rationale, and would describe the rules as being "unnecessary." For example, Isaiah would regularly wear a zip-up sweatshirt on top of his uniform because he said "I'm still who I am, why can't I just be who I am?" Like David, Isaiah would also become frustrated with his teachers, but also his peers, during classroom interactions. Rather than walking out however, he would move his desk to a corner, and disengage from class by putting his head down or actively reading a book or doing something other than his schoolwork.

Isaiah would regularly call out to me during classroom instruction when he seemingly wanted a witness of what he was experiencing in an interaction with his peers or with his teachers. If, for example, a classmate was teasing him in class, taking his belongings without his permission, or distracting him or if the teacher wasn't acknowledging his participation, Isaiah would catch my eye, wave in the general direction of the person that he was feeling affronted by and say, "you see this, right?" As with David, it is not only witnessing, but the confirmation of that witnessing in the moment, that was important for the boys. Actually seeing what was frustrating to the boys, when it was occurring, may have helped the boys feel like they had less to explain to me, or that I would be able to understand because I had seen it with my own eyes. Additionally, the consistency of my presence allowed me to be a constant spectator to their lives. I could bear witness to things that upset them throughout the course of the day, such that boys could reference those things with me in later moments using a short-hand, acknowledging not only that I had seen what they had seen, but I understood what they had seen in the *way* that they had seen it.

On a separate occasion, after I entered a classroom for an observation, I saw that Isaiah was sitting at his desk with the hood of his sweatshirt pulled over his head which he had rested on the desk. Here is an excerpt from my fieldnotes about this interaction:

> Isaiah is folded over his desk with his hoodie pulled over his head. He's hiding his face (his face is facing the floor). I go over to Isaiah's desk, put a hand on his shoulder and crouch down to ask him, "what's the matter?" Isaiah doesn't move his head from it's spot, nor looks at me. Instead, he talks to me through the space in his arms he's created as his face is parallel to the ground. Isaiah tells me he hasn't been feeling well and that the teacher thinks that he threw a pencil at him, when it was actually (according to Isaiah) another classmate, but the teacher didn't listen to him.

In order to enact care, I needed to meet Isaiah, quite literally, where he was. In doing so, I had to accept that my actions may not be reciprocated as Isaiah may not turn his face to speak with me, or even acknowledge my presence. To learn more about what was upsetting Isaiah, and signal that I cared, I needed to simply demonstrate that I was there to witness and to listen. I needed to physically position myself such that I could look up to Isaiah's face in order to provide him with eye contact and have a conversation. Parallax, here, is not only choosing to inhabit different spaces for a different perspective, but creating new opportunities for space and conversation that may not otherwise exist. Without engaging Isaiah in this way, I would not have known what caused him to rest his head on his desk, and might have made false assumptions about his actions based on other (mis)information (e.g., from his peers, his teachers).

Aside from being a consistent presence who could witness these moments, I also asked a lot of questions beyond these moments of stress. On another occasion, I stood in the hallway while the boys were waiting in line for class. When I came to Isaiah, I asked him, "What are you up to this weekend?" To which Isaiah replied, with a laugh and a shake of his head, "You are *always* asking questions, Ms. N!" I smiled, and told him, "Of course! I'm interested in what you have to say." Isaiah laughed again and smiled, and said, "Yeah, I know, that's why I tell you everything!" In this instance, Isaiah recognizes my curiosity, and seems to indicate he believes it is authentic as he smiles and mentions that this is why he is willing to share so much with me.

Isaiah's description of choosing to share with me indicates that he had, indeed, received my efforts of care. Like David, Isaiah did not name an adult in the school he would go to if he had a problem. Below, I present our conversation around this interview question:

PN: Is there a teacher you would talk with at school if you had a problem?
IE: No one, except for you.
PN: Really? Why me?
IE: You're always where I am. When I was sick in class, when I was in [detention]. You're always there, so I know you care.

Isaiah's willingness to come to me reflects the choices I made regarding how I occupied space, and how through using it differently from other adults, I was able to build trust. As Isaiah mentions, this regularly happened in the detention room, in which adults, except the disciplinary dean, rarely entered. Given my unique role, I visited detention for explicit research purposes (i.e., to observe, to schedule interviews) but also just to check-in with students. I typically would enter this room and ask boys,

"What happened?" not only because I wanted to know what got him in trouble for my research but out of concern. Notably, asking "what happened?" was an unusual question to ask at Sankofa. Teachers send students to detention and memorialize their reasons for the Deans; students rarely are asked for their side of the story. Asking Isaiah for his account signaled my care and curiosity, especially given how he characterized Sankofa as an uncaring place.

Received Care Creates Trust and Deeper Knowing

Enacting care is more than a responsible methodological choice; caring also produces better research. When enacted care is received, care creates the possibility of and foundation for trusting relationships between researchers and youth. An indicator that care is received is a collaborative relationship: built on mutual respect between researchers and youth participants as they work to co-construct and advance knowledge, or what Winn and Ubiles (2011) term "revelation." Revelation indicates that youths believe that we as researchers care about them as people, but also, that we will treat their stories and what they share with us with that same care. Choosing to trust is a decision by youths to take a great risk on us as researchers. Revelation, then, requires not only youths' respect, but their trust.

Without enacting care, the insights that I gained about David and Isaiah, as with other participants in my study who received care, may have otherwise been obscured. Below, I present excerpts from my interview data, including photos from David and Isaiah's photo narratives, to illustrate the increased trust and deeper knowing facilitated by their reception of care. I pursued using photo narratives in my methodology to serve as an element of anti-racist research praxis and counter-storytelling (Perry & Shotwell, 2009; Solórzano & Yosso, 2002). Through taking pictures, boys had the opportunity to frame and define their own realities, with minimal researcher influence (Clark-Ibanez, 2004; Harper, 2002). Interviews were grounded by photographs, which positioned the boys as the one with the undeniable expertise in the conversation, as they were the ones more undoubtedly "in charge" of the intent, meaning, and interpretation of the photos that they had taken.

While caring ought to begin as an ethical commitment, caring can also increase the validity of research as it encourages youths to safely grace us with greater and fuller access to their lives (Paris, 2011). The authentic care that I enacted supported boys' vulnerability and increased access to their lives as demonstrated by boys' photo narrative and interview data. As a researcher, these expressions of boys' openness encouraged me to take latitude to ask more follow-up questions and pursue opportunities to learn more about the boys, their stories, and their experiences. Research that is conducted with care therefore engenders deeper knowing and greater surety in the data collected, and therefore, more responsible and truthful renderings of participants.

David

My interview with David took place after the school day in an empty classroom. We sat next to each other in two student desks with an array of the photos he took for his

Figure 6.1 David Sanchez's photograph in response to the prompt: "Take a photo of a place where you feel comfortable or that you belong"

photo narrative scattered between us. David took a number of creative and personal photos, but his response to one question in particular took me by surprise for its vulnerability and self-reflection. The photo (Figure 6.1) David took in response to the prompt, "Take a photo of a place where you feel comfortable or that you belong," and the respective conversation we had over the image allowed me to gain greater insight not only into David's out-of-school life, but also into David's way of making sense and coping with the world.

After I asked David to show me his photo response to the question of where he felt most comfortable or belonged, he began looking through the array of photos scattered between us. Initially, he pulled out a photo he took of his bedroom, and then quickly discarded it. He then selected the above photo and handed it to me. Our exchange is below:

DS: The place I do feel most comfortable is Home. No sorry, it's this one—[pulls above photo out]

PN: In the park? Is it ...

DS: No, not in the park—on top of this building right here [points to below the image]. It's like a short building, it's not even that tall, anybody—well I guess not *anybody* could jump off of it, some people could jump off of it.

PN: Okay, and how do you get up there?

DS: You know most of the time, the police ladders are lowered down, we took them [David begins smiling] and we climbed on top of them. Or sometimes

I climb a tree, or a tall tree with the ladder and I'll tell my friends to move the ladder—people will look at me and think like "how am I going to get down?" but it'll be a really long tree. All I do is tell them to move, and I jump and I grab a branch and I just jump off. But I sit there and I just lay down [pause, begins staring off, dreamlike] and I just feel comfortable there [eyes focus back on me]. I've never told anyone that.

David sharing this photo, and the motivation behind taking this photo, demonstrates David received the care that I had for him—as he articulated to me, something private, and trusted me with this information. As the only person to whom he had revealed this information as well, David himself recognizes that the received care permitted him to share information about himself that he may not have otherwise shared without the protection of a caring relationship. Beyond the image and the related conversation, the rest of the interview that followed allowed me deeper knowing about David. In the conversation that followed, David continued to describe how when he feels overwhelmed, upset, or angry, he likes to be by himself and as far away from what bothers him as possible, so he can calm himself down. David talked about these moments of "feeling peaceful," and it also allowed me further insight to David's common occurrences of leaving the classroom unannounced, spending time in the hallway rather than other places he was designated to be, and seeking out the stairwell—these moments were not, to David, acts of defiance but rather attempts to find calm.

When we passed the hour mark, I mentioned to David that we could pause our interview and chat again over the next few days, but David shook his head and simply said "no, I like talking to you and I want to tell you more about things." We continued the interview, and in my time at Sankofa that followed David would seek me out, wave me over in the hallways, and ask when we could continue to talk more. In future conversations, David provided me more updates on his out-of-school-life, including his activities in the park, his friends, and even conflicts he had in the neighborhood or with members of his family. In this way, the care that contributed to David's vulnerability and openness during the interview created even more opportunities, many initiated by David, to learn more about him and feel confident about the accuracy of observations and impressions.

Isaiah

Like David, I met with Isaiah at the end of the academic day to conduct our interview. I told the boys that interviews depend on how long the conversation lasts, and could be anywhere from 45 to 60 minutes. Isaiah's interview was easily my longest interview, as we chatted for nearly 90 minutes, so long that he had texted one of his friends an hour in to ask them to bring him a snack from a local deli. Like David, Isaiah was very thoughtful about the photos he chose to take for his project and was eager to explain each photo to me. In particular, I was really struck by Isaiah's response to the photo prompt, "Take a photo of something that represents 'Manhood'"[3] (Figure 6.2) and the conversation that followed.

Figure 6.2 Isaiah Edwards' photograph in response to the prompt: "Take a photo of something that represents 'Manhood'"

Isaiah presented me with a photo that was a screenshot of the poster for the 1991 movie *Boyz N the Hood*. When I asked Isaiah about why he chose to take a screenshot of this image to serve as his photo for manhood, he explained:

> Just the story—it's about what a regular Black man goes through. Not all the stereotypes, just like real [nods while closing his eyes]. It's growing up in the hood, being Black, it's what we go through … there's racism, it's like … ok, let me explain it to you because you'll listen and you'll get it.

Isaiah's willingness to share with me his identification with the movie *Boyz N the Hood* demonstrates that even across my lack of shared positionality with him, he believes that I am capable of understanding something so personal to him: as Isaiah puts it, "you'll listen, and you'll get it." Isaiah volunteers an explanation of the movie as he is confident that I will listen. In this way, Isaiah's photo, and the subsequent conversation, demonstrates care in a few ways. First, Isaiah feels cared for such that he is willing to share information with me, and secondly, that he is willing to push past and engage with me, despite my lack of shared positionality. Isaiah anticipates that I will want to learn more about him and about a movie for which he cares deeply, and believes that I have the capacity to understand, in his words, "being Black, what we go through."

I told Isaiah I was ready to listen as long as he liked, but I did confess that I hadn't seen the film in years and didn't remember it well. He looked aghast, as he slammed his palms on the table and exclaimed, "What!" and then without hesitation, began to describe the entire plot of *Boyz N the Hood* to me scene by scene with incredible detail, such that when I later reviewed my interview notes, I realized that he had spent nearly fifteen minutes alone telling me the story of this movie believing that I would be interested in understanding something with which he deeply connected. While I of course could have figured out the plot of this movie on my own time, in the moment I could see that it was important to Isaiah that I not waste another moment not knowing more about this movie. In this instance, I let him lead me, and while at the start of this conversation, it wasn't clear how tied to my research purposes this conversation would be, I let curiosity and respect be the drivers in this interaction.

Serendipitously, when I came home from fieldwork that day and sat down to dinner, I saw that *Boyz N the Hood* was just about to start playing on television. I watched it that night. The next morning at school, I approached Isaiah excitedly in the hallway to tell him that I watched the movie we had talked about in such great detail. His eyes lit up when I told him as he asked, "You did? Yes!" I told him I thought it was a good movie, but it was so incredibly sad. In response Isaiah said, "It's not sad, it's life. When can we talk about it more?" This interaction, demonstrating my interest in watching the movie Isaiah so diligently narrated to me, allowed Isaiah further affirmation that I was authentically interested in his life, and wanted to understand him better. Isaiah responded to my efforts here with excitement about future opportunities to talk together, an opportunity that may have otherwise been foreclosed to me had Isaiah not initially received care to open up to me in this way, and if I had not demonstrated interest in what he had shared with me.

Broader Themes and Reflections

In order to enact care in my study, the boys and their choices were the compass that guided my parallax and positioning: I engaged boys in less "academic" spaces such as hallways and stairwells to have conversations and created opportunities to lean in to conversation, rather than shy away from it. I prioritized building relationships such that the vast majority of my research participants singled me out as an adult in the school to whom they could turn if they had a problem. These testimonies signaled that through my affirmative witnessing, I prioritized their well-being and cared for them well beyond my research agenda. Enacting care was more than an ethical and responsible research practice: when boys received care, it created moments of revelation in which I gained greater insights into boys' inner thoughts and social lives.

David and Isaiah were among several boys in my study who described Sankofa as an uncaring place, and for those boys I was the only adult whom they identified that they could trust. It is possible that for youths who do not find school to be a welcoming or safe place, our work as caring researchers is not only more necessary, but even more felt.

Reflecting on my relationships with David and Isaiah also provides space to reconsider what I could have done differently for others who may not have received my care as deeply, if at all. As relationships grew and bonds formed with certain students, I didn't always make the difficult, or uncomfortable, choice of engaging or spending more time with other students who were slower to warm to me. Care is not easy; it takes a considerable amount of patience, time, and awareness to enact. The choices I made with my time and energy had consequences with how effectively I was able to honor all of the boys and their stories in my research.

Implications

The most responsible, caring researchers use their research as protest – disrupting long-standing norms of our disciplines and training that harm students from nondominant communities who have been historically marginalized by institutions, including by the educational system writ large, and exploited by both the process and outcomes of research. As researchers, regardless of our socio-demographic backgrounds, we undoubtedly carry a level of privilege as we enter into school communities to conduct research. It is important to consider how this privilege intersects with youths' historical and current realities of oppression. If researchers conduct their work in schools without care, we run the risk of reproducing and further entrenching the marginalization of nondominant, historically marginalized youths and their interests, knowledge, stories, and experiences. It is through authentic and affirmative relationship-building that we as researchers can enact an academic and ethical responsibility to treat youths, and their stories, with deserved care. This relationship-building allows researchers to access deeper, fuller, and more accurate knowing about our social world. It is in these opportunities that we as researchers can advance transformative change: not just in our research studies, but at our fieldsites and in our broader disciplines. As researchers, we must research for the communities, and world, we wish for; to do so, we must commit to engaging in practices that actively model and create care.

7

Developing Sustainable Partnerships between Researchers and Youth Participants: Fostering Shared Learning across Time and Difference

Matthew R. Deroo and Ilhan Mohamud

I have often thought about the power of listening. Often what we want as human beings is to have someone hear our stories, connect with us, pay attention to us.
—Kinloch & San Pedro (2014, p. 4)

Sometimes I find I can't talk about politics, or religion, with my family members or my friends because they will think I need to shut up or I disagree with them.
—Ilhan to Matt in an interview

Educational researchers learning with and from youth may create spaces for personal sharing centered in care. But these researchers must also grapple with and attend to varying factors across intersecting points of difference. In short, the inherently colonizing and damaging nature of research as historically understood is one where care for research participants and communities has been disregarded. In the case of our collaborative work shared within this chapter, we argue that care, while supporting a dynamic and sustained relationship across time, must also attend to contrasting identity markers, including gender, race, religion, and age, between researchers and research participants. From these varying identities, we seek to build with and further examine what it means to create space to listen and respond across differences. We draw upon relevant methodological literatures underscoring our collaborative process. Specifically, in this chapter, we investigate how principles of dialogic listening (Kinloch & San Pedro, 2014) and humanizing approaches to research (Paris, 2011) may provide avenues for researchers to enact care in their qualitative studies with youth. We find this especially productive as youth share about matters of personal importance to them, such as their religious being.

In the sections that follow, we begin by tracing the origin of our shared collaboration which began in spring 2017 when Ilhan, a Black, Muslim transnational youth, was a high-school junior and Matt, a white, Christian male doctoral student, was engaged in his dissertation research. Next, we discuss more deeply how a Project in Humanization (Kinloch & San Pedro, 2014) approach has grounded our ability to engage this work together. Specifically, we highlight how multivocal textual analysis (Tobin, Hsueh, & Karasawa, 2009) served as a means to engage in rich listening and learning as Ilhan shared about her social media use at a time of increased concerns about privacy and surveillance. Finally, we close our chapter by discussing how we have sustained our relationship since "leaving the field"—when our initial collaboration in the research process came to a close, but a lasting friendship and coauthorship relationship began.

Her and His(story): How We Came to Develop a Relationship of Care

While this chapter ultimately traces our shared learning over time, we harken back to our initial interactions that took place within and beyond a social studies elective course at a multilingual, ethnically and racially diverse Title One public high school in the Midwest. That is, in order to tell the story of our ongoing collaboration, we want our readers to clearly understand where this relationship began. Ilhan remembers:

During Mr. Denker's (pseudonym) class, we often took part in whole group conversations following presentations from guest visitors or as follow up to the films, like Munich we had viewed in class. I was aware that Matt sat in a student desk next to Mr. D's desk, occasionally raising questions or sharing ideas as a participant observer during classroom conversations. Sometimes Mr. Denker would have groups of students do a Socratic Seminar, and we would sit in circles and have a dialogue about current events or topics related to religion and politics (i.e. The Israeli-Palestinian conflict; President Trump's executive order constituting a "Muslim Ban"). During these conversations, I was interested in what was being discussed or felt as I identified with these topics as a Somali-American Muslim, regardless of whether the topics we discussed were global or domestic issues Muslims faced. After one class period, Matt asked Mr. Denker about certain students he might reach out to interview for his dissertation work.

Recounting the earliest days of our collaboration, I (Ilhan) did not know how much I could contribute to Matt's study about immigrant youths' social media use. I remember the $50 Amazon gift card for my participation in Matt's study initially led me to want to join his work, but I was not quite sure what to expect. At that time, I was formulating ideas both personally and on my social media regarding what it meant to be the daughter of refugee parents and a Muslim. My interests in global politics were developing because I believed that my character as a Muslim female was a matter of interest to those who knew little about me and my way of life. Classroom discussions, interactions outside of class, and on the TV screen—all of these left me to feel as though I needed to be heard and understood. In short, I sought an outlet to share my views with others in a way that would be received without judgment. I originally thought I was preparing for an interview with some sort of questionnaire where I would have to give the "right" answers, because that was my understanding of how research worked at the time.

I also remember, *in the space of the multicultural studies class, it felt like all eyes were on me. I was working through my identity, following my decision to wear the hijab, [because] before that, I could pass. Like, unless you knew my name, you might not know*

I was Muslim and Black. When talking about pressing social issues in the class, like #BlackLivesMatter, refugees, or religion I felt like the class was opening space for me to respond, but I was not always comfortable with how others might receive what I felt I had to say.

When I think back to those initial moments and consider care, I believe that care can be rooted in settings where youth feel like the adult (in this case the teacher or researcher) is not analyzing their every word, in an attempt to combat their ideas. I think of care as a space where the student feels as though they are being listened to, or the classroom is a courageous or safe-space for their voice, ideas, and sharing to be heard in ways that others know what is said matters and will not be dismissed. For me, caring meant an adult who would mediate my ideas, and not silence me (see Kinlock & San Pedro, 2017). In some classes, when interacting with other adults in positions of authority, I found myself trying to be "politically correct" and was conscious of trying not to say the wrong thing to my teachers and peers when class conversations focused on racism. I wanted to use words like "white privilege" but was worried how they would be perceived because of my identity. I didn't expect to be completely understood in the way I felt about certain topics concerning race. Therefore, when I decided to start talking to Matt, an outsider and an adult, about my life and experiences, I was uncertain and cautious. I remember, initially when discussing race or religion, I wanted to center the conversation on experiences I had, or when discussing opinions and current events, to actually talk about how certain events or policies affected *me* or those I love—and you (Matt) listened and affirmed those experiences. Following the first few interviews, I no longer assumed that what I would say would be "misunderstood" or that I needed to say the *right* things but could share how I genuinely felt.

***

In seeking to learn with and from transnational youth, I (Matt) was very aware of the power differentials that would underscore my research. Having been a student in Dr. Paris's graduate seminar that centered humanizing approaches to research (see Paris & Winn, 2013), I used the space of his class to work through considerations for how my privileged positionality (white, male, Christian) might affect my interactions at Ilhan's high school (Deroo, 2018). While I had been an active participant at Hallandale High (pseudonym) for four years by the time I started my dissertation work, my approach was continually informed by care understood as both a noun and a verb:

- serious attention or consideration applied to doing something correctly or to avoid damage or risk. (n)
- feel concern or interest; attach importance to something. (v)

That is, as a researcher, I understood how prior research endeavors had harmed communities or put research participants at risk. Therefore, due care was needed to protect those I was learning alongside. Simultaneously, I wanted the transnational immigrant youth who shared with me to know I was interested and concerned about the important work they were doing in online spaces to resist marginalization—that I cared about their advocacy and agency. While I had originally planned on conducting four interviews with Ilhan, we ended up talking across ten weeks. Initial interviews following a semi-structured protocol gave way to conversations. Each chat led to more things to be shared, especially as they related to widespread anti-immigrant and anti-Muslim sentiment across news media—topics both Ilhan and I were interested in.

***

Having developed a sense of trust in sharing with one another, we engaged in ongoing conversations based on Ilhan's perception of Matt's listening and care for Ilhan's experiences. Ultimately, these conversations were a form of giving back rather than taking, as we have sought to amplify the stories being shared with broader publics. We believe care is made manifest by re-lensing expertise in light of the hegemonic, uncaring history of research. Through our partnership, we seek to promote social change toward social justice by highlighting the promises of coauthorship between research participants and researchers.

Theoretical Framework

What makes the work of caring and being there possible, especially sharing that sustains and extends across time? For Matt, the scholarship of Paris (2011) and Kinloch and San Pedro (2014; 2017) have been especially helpful in supporting his learning with Ilhan over time. That is, Matt's approach to research would likely not have been as intentional or grounded in care without these scholars.

In his work with multilingual and multicultural youth, Paris (2011) framed humanizing research as a methodological stance that seeks to develop relationships of care and dignity between both participants and the researcher as they dialogue with one another and engage in consciousness-raising over time. Humanizing approaches to research are broadly being taken up by emerging scholars. For example, Harris Garad (2017) used Paris's humanizing approach to investigate how narratives from immigrant and refugee educators shape academic and proverbial discourses. In interviewing Luula, Bunu, and Annie, three female instructors diverse in age, race, religion, and ethnicity, Harris Garad centered collaborative knowledge-building based on reciprocal listening and storytelling. Player in her dissertation work (2018) explored the process of building solidarity with eight female youth participants of color—the "Unnormal Sisterhood," a name the girls gave to define themselves. Specifically, the Unnormal Sisterhood established a shared sense of reciprocal support and self-confidence that collectively allowed the young women to confront and critique environments of oppression. In his work, San Pedro (2018) called upon humanizing approaches to research during a three-year longitudinal, ethnographic study with indigenous students. San Pedro supported youth as they shared personal stories and sought to heal wounds of the past and cultivate new, stronger identities through listening and sharing. Collectively, these studies center the power of humanizing approaches for researchers who engage in studies with traditionally marginalized youth.

The work of this chapter also builds upon Kinloch and San Pedro's scholarship (2014, 2017) including calls for dialogic-listening and Projects in Humanization (PiH). According to Kinloch and San Pedro (2014), dialogic-listening frames the interactions between researcher and youth participants as a relational construction of knowledge that takes place together as opposed to separate from one another. Specifically, PiH seeks to build relationships that "on the one hand, emphasize our shared desires for racial, linguistic, educational, political, and social justice in schools and communities and, on the other hand, emphasize those same desires in our professional and personal lives (Kinloch & San Pedro, 2017, p. 347). Central to the aims of this approach are sustained relationships grounded by "the human capacity to listen to, story with, and care about each other" (Kinloch & San Pedro, 2017, p. 373). By centering shared learning through listening between researcher and research participant, Kinloch and San Pedro (2014) highlight how trust may be established in the "in-between space" (p. 30). Specifically, this space represents a sort of a comfort zone that emerges through listening and dialoguing, a grey area in which the participant in the study is able to open up his or her feelings, vulnerabilities, and emotions (Kinloch & San Pedro, 2017).

The concept of dialogic listening has been taken up by scholars like Wargo (2017) who applied the approach as he analyzed how Jack, Zeke, and Camille, LGBTQ youth, represented their literate identities across social media posts. Kinloch and San Pedro's (2014, 2017) work has also supported researchers working with youth who hold multiple marginalized identities, such as Annamma's (2018a) learning with girls of color, who were differently abled and incarcerated. Through shared listening and speaking with Annamma, youth drew on their complex intersectional identities to share counter-narratives that spoke back to patterns of oppression, marginalization, violence, and inequity. Since our inquiry is similar to that of Wargo (2017) in regard to social media use and Annamma's (2018) examination of marginalized identities, we appreciate how dialogic listening opens space for sharing that extends beyond traditional interview practices. We see the work of this chapter extending existing conversations about care to address and hopefully move beyond the hegemonic past of research work and its dehumanizing practices. We affirm and build with dialogic listening and PiH to create space where individuals from varying identity backgrounds may listen to and learn from one another to experience care (understood as both a noun and verb) across the process.

Methodology

The collected data in this chapter come from Matt and Ilhan's shared learning. Initial data collection began in spring 2017, during Matt's qualitative dissertation study at Hallandale. After Matt and Ilhan graduated from their respective schools in spring 2018, they engaged in conversations that have continued to the present through texts and FaceTime. Therefore, this chapter is somewhat autoethnographic (Boylorn & Orbe, 2014) even as we reflect upon what was originally empirical data Matt collected from Ilhan and her peers.

In this chapter, we draw on longitudinal data sources: transcriptions of ten audio-recorded interviews, researcher memos, and thirty-seven participant-observation field notes of classroom observation from Matt's dissertation study in spring 2017. Additional data sources include notes and conversations in a shared writing folder on Google Drive and ongoing conversations between Matt and Ilhan from spring 2018 onward, including one retrospective conversation we recorded in February 2020 as we recounted our ongoing research partnership. We focus most closely on the first two interviews and conversations we had about Ilhan's social media posts as a high school junior, because these initial interviews established and affirmed Matt's sense of care for Ilhan's sharing and served as a catalyst for our longer-term relationship.

Positionality

Although aspects of our positionality appear elsewhere in the chapter, in reflecting back on our initial conversations in spring 2017 with a critical lens, we recognize an oversight in that we did not specifically engage in direct discussion about our varying identities with one another. This is something we encourage other researchers to consider. While Matt and Ilhan both identify as having transnational relationships to friends, family, and communities outside of the United States, and as bilingual (Matt, Chinese; Ilhan, Somali), the contrasts in our identities reveal inherent power dynamics and difference in access to power and status that remain to this day despite our coauthorship. Even though Matt lived in China for ten years prior to beginning his doctoral studies, his life and time outside of the United States varied greatly from that of Ilhan, whose parents immigrated to the United States before her birth due to factors outside of their control. We challenge other researchers to continue to attend to how their positionality and access to power impact their work and learning with youth (see Paris & Winn, 2013).

Ethical Considerations in Support of Caring for What Youth Share

Despite the affordances of a calling upon Projects in Humanization and employing dialogic listening to the research design, Matt had to carefully consider how he could protect youths' identities in his dissertation work. That is, since the context of Matt's study was around transnational immigrants' social media use, and participants were minors from immigrant and refugee backgrounds, he intentionally took care and precautions so that the topics he discussed were not traceable back to youth. Specifically, Matt used a modified version of multivocal textual analysis, first employed by Tobin, Hsueh, and Karasawa, (2009) in their work with preschoolers in China, Japan, and the United States. For their study, researchers used hours of video-taped data from their work in preschools across the three countries, not as a source of data, but as a springboard for discussion.

In the context of Matt's dissertation, rather than making claims about Ilhan's actual Tweets and Instagram posts, we discussed the ideas and motivations informing those social media posts. This aligns with a multivocal approach, in that the posts engendered discussion that became data rather than serving as published, and therefore possibly traceable, data themselves. For example, we discussed Muslim identity in response to a Twitter thread on Ilhan's feed in which various users were debating responses to a viral YouTube video showing a young woman twerking on the street in the UK while wearing a hijab. Therefore, as we engaged in back-and-forth communication about the broader conversations that Ilhan was taking part of through her Twitter feed, we enacted what San Pedro (2013) termed "a dialogic spiral" or movement back and forth and up and down to extend prior understandings between listener and speaker. A key affordance of this approach was protecting Ilhan's identity and building trust while also allowing her to center and share topics of interest.

Findings

In the section that follows, we draw on exchanges across two conversations that took place between Matt and Ilhan at the start of Matt's dissertation study. These examples demonstrate mutual sharing and reflective listening in ways that made Ilhan feel care and safety in discussing topics close to her multiple identities as a Black, female, Muslim youth. In short, the exchanges reflect the importance, concern, and interest Matt ascribed as he listened to Ilhan's share. Both examples highlight the multivocal textual approach (Tobin, Hsueh, and Karasawa, & 2009) and demonstrate enactments of dialogic listening (Kinloch & San Pedro, 2014). That is, by using Ilhan's social media account as a catalyst for discussion, we engage in back-and-forth reflections in response to Ilhan's lived experiences.

Conversation #1
MATT: I am wondering if you could share a little more about what's been on your Twitter feed lately.
ILHAN: The other day, I don't know if I still have it favorited or not, but, somebody replied back to someone what they tweeted, "do you agree with this, this, and that about Muslims?" This girl tweeted back and she was like, "I am tired about people who aren't a part of some religion telling other people what they believe in." For me, it's not on [my feed] anymore. But for me, it's kind of like out of ignorance. Where did you get that from? I think in the original tweet, some guy was like, "the Muslim girls are married at a really young age and they're property of their husbands now and the men can do anything now, like they can beat them if they want." And I am like, where are you getting this from? It's basically like propaganda, you don't know anything about Muslims, it shows how ignorant you are.
MATT: Earlier you made a comment about trolls. I want to go back to that, given these tweets and what you've shared. How does one deal with trolls on Twitter?
ILHAN: When they come at us on Twitter, [they] think they know what they're talking about, but really they don't. For me it's kind of sad, like who taught

you that? Where did you get that from? It's not what we believe in. But, but you have to question people's intentions when they are asking you something when it comes down to religion. Are you curious? Are you ignorant about something and you want to know more? Or are you just trolling and one thing will lead to another problem with what I believe in?

The above example highlights how our initial conversation created space to discuss topics that extended beyond the curriculum of the multicultural studies class where Ilhan was a student. In seeking to center Ilhan's experiences as a Black female Muslim youth, Matt engaged in active listening as Ilhan testified to her experiences. Given our different religious identities (Muslim; Christian), centering conversation on how Muslim identity is positioned and framed by those outside the faith supported shared meaning-making for how marginalized identities may be understood. This approach, rooted in care and central to humanizing approaches, attends to youths' religious practices as fundamental to their identities. Moreover, since Matt is a member of a dominant religious group in the US context, care was needed to not reify positions of power when listening to the experiences Ilhan recounted about the ways that others falsely portrayed her religion.

Specifically, in this exchange Ilhan responded to inaccurate positioning of her faith. In conversation with Matt, she processed how, if at all, she should respond to those who were misinformed about gendered roles within her faith tradition. While these tensions were unresolved for Ilhan at the time, our conversation provided space to question whether some people engage in bad-faith efforts to "troll" people for their religion or if they are "curious" or "ignorant" and seek better understanding about the Islamic faith. By processing the event with Matt in conversation, Ilhan vocalized and made sense of how she may choose, or not, to push back on harmful online discourse.

Next, we turn to an additional exchange occurring one week later to further center the dialogic listening as informed by Tobin et al.'s (2009) approach.

Conversation #2

MATT: I saw on Twitter that yesterday was like, "The National Day of Prayer."
ILHAN: [laughs] Oh, godly men are in the White House. I remember when [Trump] was claiming he had been reading the Bible, Two Corinthians, and people were saying, like, "Ah I don't think he's read certain passages." And on Twitter people like quoting it back. Obviously there are people in the White House, they are spiritual and stuff like that, but I don't know ….
MATT: So, in light of this, has anything stood out on your social media feeds in regard to religion?
ILHAN: Myanmar's leader, she was saying, I saw it on the *Al Jazeera* feed, I don't know how to say her name, but [she] has rejected the UN's decision to investigate crimes towards Rohingya Muslims, and I was like, if you don't have nothing to hide, why won't you let them investigate. In an interview, she was like, "There are Muslims who are killing other Muslims." It's like what I was saying [earlier] about Bernie Sanders and a video questioning why he signed a letter against criticizing Israel's human rights violations.

MATT: Yeah, that's so interesting, and then we have to consider the United States' own human rights violations ...

ILHAN: I think that is a quick shot for people to not focus on those problems, to not speak on it because they feel a different way, so they will just be like, "Look at this [violation]." Why are you so focused on that [one]? There are problems in both—we need to discuss that and fix that.

Ilhan remembers the above conversation as centered on her dislike for US-based cable news, because world events (i.e., conflict in Syria, genocide in Myanmar) at the time were not being mentioned. In short, it seemed to Ilhan like no one cared (verb form—to be concerned, interested in, or attach importance to the event) to cover the topics and issues that mattered to her. Ilhan recounted learning a lot from Twitter about what was going on in the world, through an international, networked online community that cared about these issues, compared to the silence from the US news media—which felt, to her, like an erasure of those issues.

Throughout Matt's study, we were able to use Ilhan's social media feeds as a catalyst for discussion, as we did in the example above. The back-and-forth interactions as we listened to and learned from one another raised awareness for Matt, specifically in regard to the topics of importance to Ilhan and directly related to her identities. In short, it provided space for Matt to enter into a place of care about the plight of Muslims in Myanmar. Moreover, since traditional US news media sources were not covering these events, Matt started to search the terms and issues Ilhan raised in order to be in better conversation with her. At that time, Matt had never heard of Rohingya Muslims and was unaware of the persecution taking place. Thus, dialogic listening led to raised awareness and a shift in perspective. This, in turn, provided an opportunity to engage in an extended capacity for care. Specifically, open and vulnerable sharing from Ilhan about a sensitive topic provided space for us to teach each other new perspectives—especially as our conversations centered topics not covered or given attention to in the curriculum of Ilhan's social studies class.

Sustaining Relationships over Time

While researchers consider what it may mean to "exit" the field, we see the work we have engaged in as traveling far beyond the walls of Hallandale High where this partnership began. Specifically, as Matt sought to publish his learning from Ilhan beyond his dissertation in academic journals, he did not feel comfortable writing Ilhan's stories on his own. This led to an important shift, or evolution, in our partnership as we moved from researcher and participant to coauthors. Because care may also be understood at the maintenance and protection of something or someone, our shared commitments align with this definition of care. When we reconvened in summer 2018 to begin moving our shared experiences to press, we quickly found ourselves back in a rhythm of sharing about our social media feeds and topics of mutual interest. These ongoing conversations were rooted in the care that comes from the dialogic relationship that served as a foundation for our prior exchanges. We now have weekly or biweekly check-ins that have cultivated and sustained a friendship across distance and time. This relationship has been further sustained, in part, by the lengthy publication process. Below, we offer our reflections about our ongoing partnership from a recorded conversation in February 2020:

> MATT: Ok so we're trying to think about the way we have been able to sustain our relationship since we both moved out from when you were in high school and I was in graduate school. I'm wondering if you can just tell me some of your thoughts about what it has meant to continue to be in conversation and to write together and, you know, we've changed a lot since that time.
>
> ILHAN: Yeah, I think talking about, like, school-wise and how that really changed me going from obviously high school to a big university, taking different classes and in shifts within obviously different parts of my life, my religious life, uhm, how I use social media, my interests, how that's hinged in my identity. We talked about like, at first when I was expressing my identity in new ways, wearing a headscarf and being Muslim. Now, I no longer felt like I had to cater or to apologize for things that have nothing to do with me, personally. That I am not a spokesperson for my faith. I think that, that is maturity, that all of that was growth, so yeah …
>
> MATT: So, it's kind of interesting because I think that a lot of my commitments in my normal life are just sustaining relations over time, like to be in contact with people I've known. This past weekend I was in Nashville and saw some friends that I first met twenty years ago, when I had gone to teach in China after university. We were able to pick up from where we left off. So that's why, a year later, when we were both about to graduate, I reached out to you formally, so we could talk about if we might want to coauthor.
>
> ILHAN: Yeah, initially I thought it was just gonna be it, like we talked about, it was the gift card and I was super excited, I told you I spent the whole thing on books. In talking about research, headed to college and thinking about my future goals, like I can participate being a part of something I am interested in. I want to be a doctor and that involves research. I actually don't mind having a conversation one hour or two hours a week, just catching up and then writing through something because it's natural, it's like my experience, but like, I am really appreciative about we can take what I say and it becomes like so much more.
>
> MATT: Yeah I really enjoyed the process of writing in a Google document together at the same time, and thinking back of our thoughts before, and processing, uhm … you know, what we've done. Did you think like you would be in contact years later?
>
> ILHAN: When you switched your teaching in Florida I was actually, "oh well, you know, I don't know how this is necessarily gonna work, like I don't know if he, if he's still doing more research around this particular topic." So at first yes, it was different being on FaceTime than meeting in person, but I just got used to it.
>
> MATT: Yeah, there's, we can see each other's faces and hand gestures and expressions. It feels kinda like we're in a similar space even if there is a virtual

distance. And I know at some point this collaboration, it will, you know come to a close, but I think about the fact you are probably about to head out, after you graduate university, to become a doctor, and like you said, the idea of the skills you have for research now will help you later on.

ILHAN: I know, that's why I always say that I am appreciative of, like, seeing the process, and thanking us for our work, because I have never known how difficult it is even to get something published and to write through things, and how all that writing can become a reality. I'm not saying that I'm gonna get a Ph.D., but you know, even if I do want to participate in a lab, it's long-term learning so ...

As noted above, we recognize in our shared learning across time that we have not moved away from the fundamental care that comes in listening to one another as we share about topics important to us. Before each writing session, we continue to check in on our personal lives before turning to the task of writing. In short, we are fully aware of how one process (mutual sharing of daily life) informs the other (scholarly writing). For example, in revising the work of this chapter ahead of publication, we stopped to process a microaggression that a patron at the pharmacy where Ilhan works directed toward Ilhan and her hijab. In taking the time to process what is happening across our lived experiences, we continue to grapple with how our collaborative writing and scholarship can push back against the ongoing marginalization of Muslim identity.

While we both understand research projects are fixed and finite, our partnership has transcended traditional research approaches of data generation, analysis, and reporting of findings. Therefore as we continue to grapple with the issues we face in our daily lives, our process has come full circle. Despite the fixed identity characteristics that remain for both of us, including the marginalization Ilhan continues to face within the broader US context, we trust caring research partnerships where shared learning across difference is widely disseminated might lead toward social change. As we have moved from researcher and research participant to coinvestigators and friends, we engage in scholarship that speaks back to negative framing of Muslim identity. Ultimately, we hope that others might look upon our shared experiences and interrogate their own beliefs and assumptions, such that our collective sharing could lead people toward more equitable and just interactions across social settings.

Recommendations for Future Research

Building on our experiences, we offer the following recommendations for those who desire to cultivate a sense of caring in their qualitative work with youth participants.

First, we understand the importance of clear communication about the process, aims, and outcomes of research. While youth may be less interested in the promotion and tenure-related aspects of academic publishing, (the importance of) their role in the knowledge production of academic writing should be made clear and explicit. We further believe that a genuine, shared interest in the research topic (in our case: religious identity, immigration, and policies as informed by politics such as the so-called

Muslim ban) is important for both the researcher and youth participants. Moreover, we find it productive for educational researchers to take a posture of humility as they interact with youth participants and learn from them about the issues most relevant to their lives. Collectively, researchers and research participants might take inventory of the ways that youth use their own perspectives and experiences to guide and instruct researchers to topics salient and real, but overlooked by others. Specifically, for the research process to feel worthwhile and productive, both researchers and research participants who coauthor should have a sustained interest in continuing to explore lines of inquiry that matter to both individuals.

A second and connected implication is that the "reward" for research matters differently to the researcher and the participant. In the case of our research partnership, the gift card for participation in the study was an initial draw for Ilhan. However, as the conversation/research continued in alignment with broader anti-Muslim rhetoric and domestic issues concerning Ihan's racial and religious identity, she felt inclined to continue the discussion. Knowing that there was more to say about certain subjects, and to share with broader audiences, emboldened Ilhan to write with Matt. Therefore, we can collectively draw upon our varying identities to address topics less examined in the research literature. Moreover, when we center care in research relationships, that relationship has the power and potential to transform other domains in our lives such as Matt's work as a teacher educator where he has shared with pre- and in-service teachers and at academic conferences how Ilhan engages in counter-storytelling. In highlighting how Ilhan has used her social media feeds to resist and write back to dominant narratives that seek to marginalize her identities, teachers might investigate how youth in their contexts engage in similar practices.

Third, we appreciate the ways that technology has been able to support, mediate, and sustain dialogic listening across distance. For example, as users of Apple devices, we have mainly stayed in touch via iMessage and FaceTime which have provided us with a secure connection as we correspond across time and space. Furthermore, in coauthoring manuscripts, we use a shared Google Drive. This approach allows us to leave notes and comments for one another, gives us the ability to track changes we have made in our writing and offer suggestions to one another. We can also revisit former archived versions of our work, to see how our ideas and shared meaning-making have shifted over time. Use of technology is an important and sustaining source of connection, especially when researchers and research participants leave the initial, shared field of study.

Finally, given our varied backgrounds and different identities, we believe it is crucial that when having conversations with those who come from marginalized or minoritized backgrounds, the person whose identities offer less societal power feels they can have a sense of control over the conversations when discussing matters surrounding their identities. Shifting power-dynamics in adult-youth relationships are key, which is why we build with Kinloch and San Pedro's (2014) dialogic-listening approach as critical for supporting these types of interactions. Often the researcher takes the lead, and the research participant is the one who answers in response. However, we challenge researchers to not only listen, but to ensure, in the spirit of dialogical listening, that they are actually *hearing* what is being shared.

While it may be difficult to cultivate a relationship that allows for candor in discussing topics surrounding race, religion, and politics, Ilhan found her assumptions about research were challenged when Matt did not feel the need to insert what may be perceived as corrective viewpoints into the discussion. Moreover, we believe that when participants believe their sharing and words are listened to and valued—when dialogic listening is meaningfully enacted—youths' concerns that their sharing may be met with disapproval or judgment are likely to subside. While we understand that our interactions are unique and not generalizable to those of other researchers and research participants, we firmly believe that similar relationships which support a sense of caring based on shared interests and commitment are possible and may become more common.

Part Three

Negotiating Emergent Tensions: Developing and Sustaining Caring Relationships with Youth

8

Intervening through Intimate Inquiry with Youth

Katherine Clonan-Roy

In the spring of 2012, a few months into my ethnographic research, one of my Latina adolescent participants, Sofia[1], messaged me on Facebook asking, "Hey … Can I ask you something? … Is it wrong to cut yourself?" I met Sofia when I helped to launch an after-school girls' group program for Latina girls at her school, Marshall Middle School (MMS). In the fall of 2011, MMS staff reached out to me for support in creating an after-school girls group program for Latina girls, because they were concerned that their Latina students were dating older boys, having sex, becoming pregnant, surviving sexual abuse, and experiencing mental health challenges, at higher rates and earlier ages than other racial/ethnic groups of girls in Marshall. The deficit-based concerns originally made me feel very apprehensive, as a researcher, about creating a program that educators hoped would "reform" Latina students. In the fields of education and youth development, practitioners are often tasked with creating programs or interventions that are designed to support "vulnerable" or "at-risk" youth. Often, a goal of such interventions is to change or "fix" subgroups of youth or compensate for the barriers they face. I wanted to co-create a space for research and practice with girls, where they could explore and analyze their experiences and find support and affirmation from peers. Inspired by feminist literatures, I strived to work with Latina girls to create a homeplace, grounded in love and care (hooks, 1990).

Between 2012 and 2015, I served as the adult facilitator in this girls' group and also conducted research within and beyond the group. Over these three years, I developed close relationships with my participants, as we spent time together in school, the after-school girls' group, and the community of Marshall (at restaurants, parks, their homes, nail salons, etc.), collaboratively exploring intimate topics that were incredibly formative to their lives. In this chapter, I focus on my close relationship with Sofia and how research intervened upon both of our lives when Sofia disclosed to me that she was engaging in self-harm. Through our shared story, I define my conceptualization of love and care in qualitative research, demonstrate the complexities of caring as a researcher and mandated reporter, and illuminate the academic and personal products of care-based research.

Love and Care in Education

Care and love in educational spaces and relationships are important for youth, especially because schools are often sites of othering, abuse, and suffering for students from nondominant communities, due to structural inequities ingrained in school systems, histories of segregation and racism, and biases held by educators (Dumas, 2014; Lewis & Diamond, 2015; Love, 2019; McKenzie, 2009; Zirkel et al., 2011). Noddings (1992) argues that "to care and be cared for are fundamental human needs" (p. xi) and that when we care about others we attend to them and their needs, perspectives, and interests. hooks (2001) encourages us to consider love as an act and a choice, not simply a feeling, and inextricable from justice. In choosing love, or acting in accordance with love, we "learn to mix various ingredients—care, affection, recognition, respect, commitment, and trust, as well as honest and open communication" in ways that shape our own and others' lives (p. 5). Brooks (2017) also advocates for a conceptualization of love rooted in justice and healing and argues that love must be "embodied for social justice" and "tend to the whole person" (p. 102). Based on hooks' and Brooks' conceptualizations, I argue that care is one ingredient that comprises our love for others.

Researchers conducting work with youth in schools are in unique positions to exercise care and love for youth due to their lack of academic and disciplinary responsibility and authority. Drawing upon hooks (2001; 2002), Laura (2013) defines love in research as "an exercise of will for the satisfaction of human needs" and emphasizes that love in research is "good" if "it enhances, protects, and alters another's life" (p. 290). Laura (2016) also emphasizes that when we "understand loving practice as the foundation of our research, then we may begin to establish the conditions for the production of valuable knowledge that shapes and informs the way we think, speak, and act" (p. 218). In this way, to care and love in research is an axiological stance and a consistent choice or act that we must dedicate ourselves to. Laura (2013; 2016) calls researchers who engage in this stance intimate inquirers. Intimate inquiry is "messy and moving, publicly affirming and personally empowering, humanizing and unabashedly interventionist, precisely because it is governed by a different set of values" (p. 218).

San Pedro and Kinloch (2017) affirm many of Laura's (2013; 2016) arguments and advocate for researchers to move beyond normalized constructs of social science and to center the stories of participants while situating them in "relation to our stories, lives, and research projects in humanizing ways" (p. 374S). These authors explain that when only one person (the participant) is asked to reveal themselves, we reinforce an unjust power dynamic in the research relationship. Instead, researchers should acknowledge the potential for whom we can become in relation to other people and how research can transform both researcher and participant in a variety of ways. In intimate inquiry, interventions involve reciprocal impacts on adult researchers and youth participants. Such interventions can be emotional, psychological, personal, and academic. While caring is not a prerequisite for relational interventions, it can deepen or broaden the type of intervention that might transpire and make the product of the intervention more meaningful to those who experience it.

Love and Care in Intimate Inquiry

My conceptual framework for care-based research integrates hooks' (2001) and Brooks' (2017) conceptualizations of love and Laura's (2013; 2016) notion of intimate inquiry. As depicted in Figure 8.1, hooks (2001) identifies seven *ingredients* for love and Brooks (2017) outlines what I am labeling as six *commitments* in a critical theory of love. According to Brooks (2017), if love engages these six commitments, it resists erasure and dehumanization, within and beyond educational spaces. In this chapter, I argue that *our intimate inquiry* (Laura, 2013; 2016) *should be guided by the love that* hooks (2001) *and* Brooks (2017) *describe, and we should show that love through the acts of witnessing, engaging, and laboring.*

Laura (2013) explains that love acts "are driven by the notion that every human being deserves to live fully and freely in the world, and that each of us is an expert on the qualities of our own experiences" (p. 291). According to Laura (2013), qualitative researchers who choose love in their work choose to witness, engage, and labor with and for "the individuals whose lives our research aims to shape" (p. 291). *Witnessing* involves "deliberate attendance to people," and "seeing and taking notice of that which they believe is meaningful" (Laura, 2016, p. 219). To witness in our participants' lives is to affirm and validate the existence of stories and to protect "their places in the world" (p. 219). When we act as witnesses in research, we participate in learning and knowing about others, we engage with constructions of truth, and we communicate what we have experienced and learned to others. Similarly, Hansen (2017) explains that witnessing invokes justice, remembrance, and documenting the facts of violence and emphasizes that witnessing is not complete until it has been shared and acknowledged by others.

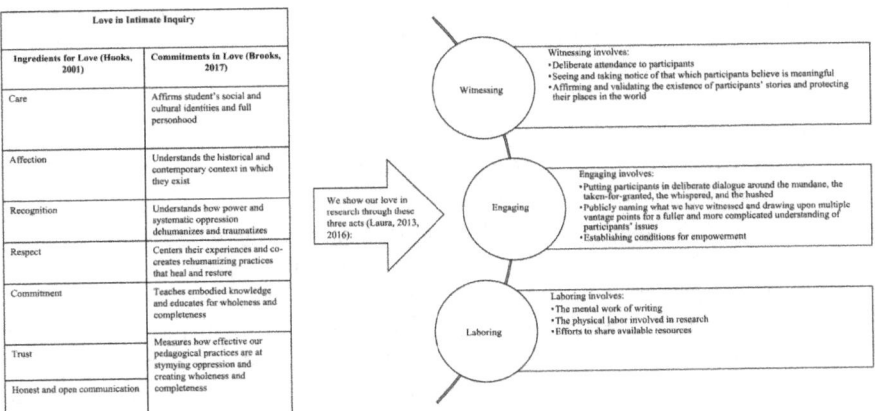

Figure 8.1 Conceptual framework for care-based research

Engaging "points us to the posing of problems and the highlighting of contradictions that are inherent to all experiences of the peopled world" (Laura, 2016, p. 219). To engage in intimate inquiry "is to put people in deliberate dialogue around the mundane, the taken-for-granted, the whispered, and the hushed" (p. 219). When we engage, we publicly name what we have witnessed, and draw upon multiple standpoints (including that of the researcher), for a more complicated and nuanced understanding of people's experiences. Through this love act of engaging, we establish conditions for empowerment for both participants and researchers. Finally, *laboring* "encompasses the mental work of writing, but also the physical labor—the work of the hands and the bodies—of sharing available resources" (p. 219). This can take on a variety of forms in research, depending on the research context and methodology.

Methods

Marshall is a town of 35,000 residents in the mid-Atlantic United States that experienced a rapid increase in its Latinx population from 1990 (3 percent) to 2010 (28 percent). Similarly, between 1990 and 2016, the Latinx population in the Marshall School District grew from 3 percent to 37 percent. I conducted ethnographic research in the Latina girls' group program, MMS, and Marshall from 2011 to 2015. The Latina girls' group was launched in January 2012. Until June 2015, I facilitated semester-long sessions of girls' groups and worked with a total of seventy-two Latina girls who were in 5th through 8th grades. The groups were segregated by grade and each group was composed of eight to ten girls.

Most of the girls with whom I worked in Marshall either migrated to the United States when they were young children and experienced most of their schooling in the United States (1.75 generation), or they were born in the United States to parents who had recently migrated there (second generation) (Rumbaut, 2004). My participants lived in economically marginalized households, and their parents often worked multiple jobs in landscaping, hospitality, or custodial services. While most were Mexican immigrants or children of Mexican immigrants, many girls had one or both parent(s) from other countries in Central America.

I began my research in Marshall after leaving my position as a high school science teacher in D.C. Public Schools. I am a white, middle-class, highly educated, heterosexual, cis-gendered woman, and as I began my work with the Latina girls' group at MMS, I consistently reflected on how my past teacher identity shaped my researcher identity and on the imbalances of power that characterized the research process and the girls' group. To decenter these dynamics, I encouraged the group members to create a girl-centered space: girls directed our meetings, determined group rules, and were positioned as the experts of their experiences. We regularly examined the similarities and differences in our experiences of life, privilege, and marginalization. I strived to be as helpful to MMS staff as possible, while making it clear that I was an ally to the girls with whom I worked and that I would not breach their trust outside of mandated reporting responsibilities. Although I was very transparent about the research I was conducting, girls often positioned me as a mentor or therapist. I regularly reminded them that I was a mandated reporter, and that while I wanted to support them, I was required to report specific concerns. In the ethnographic story that unfolds, I flesh out some of these role complexities, as they relate to loving and caring research.

Intervening through Intimate Inquiry

In the following analysis, I will trace how love and care, through the acts of witnessing, engaging, and laboring, shaped my research, the girls' group and my evolving relationship with Sofia. I will specifically focus on the experience of going through the mandated reporting process with Sofia, and at the end of this section, I will raise questions regarding mandated reporting, intervening in our participants' lives, and the dangers in the intimacy of ethnography.

Love and Care in the MMS Latina Girls' Group

In the fall and winter of 2011, I conducted dozens of hours of participant observation in Marshall and its schools, researched the history of migration to Marshall, and met with girlhood studies leaders who helped me to design a loose and student-centered structure for the girls' group. My excitement for meeting and working with the girls was growing, and as I prepared for the girls' group to launch, I practiced some of Brooks' (2017) commitments in love: (1) I aimed to develop an understanding of the historical and contemporary contexts in which my participants existed, and (2) I outlined a structure for the girls' group that would center the girls' experiences and allow for the co-creation of healing and restorative practices.

The first meeting of the MMS Latina girls' group took place in early February 2012, and the first group of girls I began working with was in 8th grade. We held our meetings at the MMS library, and on that first meeting day, I remember arranging tables, materials, and snacks, so that we could sit in a circle throughout our meeting, then nervously awaiting the girls' arrival. Girls began trickling into the library in small groups. Sofia was in the first small group that entered and she had long, straight, black hair down her back, and wore a beanie, an oversized sweatshirt, and skinny jeans.

As girls continued to trickle in, we began engaging in casual and friendly introductions. Sofia introduced herself by saying, "I am Sofia and I am weird." I laughed and jokingly asked her if she was weird in a "good or bad way," and she replied, "Both ... no ... good," and giggled. She said that outside of school she liked to eat and then asked if she could eat a snack. The other girls laughed with Sofia, as I replied, "Of course!" Sofia struck me as warm, goofy, bold, and a leader among her peers.

Throughout that first meeting, we developed community norms and a list of topics that we wanted to explore together. These collaborative activities were foundational to the ways that the girls' group was run with this cohort of girls and cohorts to come. In developing community norms, we practiced the ingredients for love that hooks (2001) discusses: *recognition* of individual and collective values, *respect* for what the girls thought and valued, *commitment* to each other and certain ethical and moral standards, and *trust* that we would uphold these standards.

The topics that the girls generated included: "drama" with girls, sexuality, engaging in healthy relationships with boys, self-esteem, body image, racism, dealing with sexual harassment, loss, family, and setting positive personal and academic goals. By positioning the girls as leaders in determining what we would focus on, I hoped to help create a space that affirmed girls' social and cultural identities and centered their experiences (Brooks, 2017). This list of topics and group structure set the foundation for *witnessing* and *engaging* (Laura, 2016): it allowed me to pay deliberate attention to the girls and take notice of what they believed was meaningful; it put us in dialogue around topics that were meaningful to them but often framed as mundane or superfluous by others (such as "drama" with peers), and; it allowed for collective affirmation of the girls' stories and experiences.

Our girl-centered and collective governance of the girls' group allowed for love and care to flourish in the girls' group, between the girls, and the girls and myself. Most girls' group members had 100 percent attendance at girls' group meetings and they looked forward to staying after school and meeting with me and their friends. In an interview, Sofia expressed that the girls' group was important because "it brought people together. An adult and girls. Usually, the girls don't really trust adults enough. But since that person actually cares and they always meet up, yeah ... You're like a girl, too."

While feeling like I was "a girl, too" allowed for the flourishing of care, respect, and trust in the group, it did complicate the multiple roles that I played: researcher, mandated reporter, and girls' group facilitator. When I had met with MMS staff in the fall of 2011, they positioned me as a mandated reporter and instructed me to work with the two MMS counselors if I needed to report any information. During my first meeting with Sofia's cohort of girls, and during the first meeting of every girls' group session to follow, I tried to explain my role as a mandated reporter as clearly as possible to the girls. I promised the girls that I would not share personal information about them with others, unless they told me that they were hurting themselves, being hurt, or hurting others. I told them in that case, I would have to tell an adult at school. I reminded girls of this role when we discussed sensitive topics like sexuality or loss. Unfortunately, this complicated our ability to have totally honest and open communication and my ability to bear witness to and engage with (Laura, 2016) the challenges they experienced.

Learning about Cutting from Sofia

In the first few months of my research, girls found me on Facebook and began initiating friend requests, including Sofia. In this period of time, I became more and more aware of how important social media was as a developmental and social arena. I obtained Institutional Review Board (IRB) approval to engage in virtual participant observation with the girls' group members on social media and began to accept girls' friend requests on Facebook and Instagram (I never initiated "friend" or "follow" requests).

Through this social media research, I had my first introduction to the serious emotional and mental health realities that my participants were grappling with. In the spring of 2012, Sofia messaged me on Facebook and asked if she could ask me something:

KATIE: ya, girl. what's up?
SOFIA: is it wrong to cut ur self
KATIE: i don't think that is a right or wrong question, ya know.
KATIE: i think if someone cuts themself, then that probably means that they are feeling sad or bad ... but i don't necessarily think it is wrong, i just think it is kind of dangerous ya know?
SOFIA: Yeah ...

Up until this point, I had heard the girls mention cutting as something that some of their peers did, but I had not had individual conversations with girls about cutting and/or observed signs of self-harm. I immediately became nervous and suspicious that perhaps Sofia was engaging in cutting and that she was about to disclose this information to me. My care for Sofia sparked anxiety and many questions in my mind: Is Sofia okay? Should I ask Sofia if she engages in cutting? If I do, and then I need to report this, should I tell Sofia on Facebook that I have to engage in mandated reporting, or might that upset her and encourage her to engage in cutting? What is the most caring and loving response? I decided I had to ask her if she ever engaged in cutting and braced myself for the complexities of the intervention that might have to take place.

KATIE: do you know people who cut?
SOFIA: Yeah ...
KATIE: I had a girl in my class this past fall who used to cut and she was writing a paper on cutting ... have you ever cut? or thought about cutting?
SOFIA: Yeah I kinda cut [my] self
KATIE: aw girl, really? I never saw it on you. do you cut your arms? ... I don't think you should feel wrong for doing it, but it makes me worry about you girl
SOFIA: Yeah but most of them are gone but 3 tbh yeah
SOFIA: I cut am [my] arms and legs so tht [my] mom doesnt see them
KATIE: it kinda makes me worried about you though, ya know? I would never want anything to happen to you bc you are SO awesome;(Do you ever talk to Cici about this stuff?
SOFIA: Ik I Been ok now & no she ... knows tht I cut myself
KATIE: wait, what did you mean in that first part? that you're feeling better lately?
SOFIA: Yeah
KATIE: oh good! what do you think is making you feel better?
SOFIA: Idk
KATIE: well that is good that you are feeling better. you know you can talk to me whenever you want to, right? are you feeling ok right now?
SOFIA: A lil
KATIE: Do you want to have lunch on Friday and chat?
SOFIA: sure I would like to but can Cici come
KATIE: ya of course
KATIE: would you want to chat about this type of stuff in front of Cici or no?
SOFIA: Yeah

> KATIE: ok. sounds good. are you going to be alright tonight girl?
> SOFIA: Yeahh I'm [eatin'] a grill cheese sandwich lol I like cheese
> KATIE: lol mmm i LOVE cheese
> SOFIA: Same lol
> KATIE: maybe ill bring some cheese to our lunch on friday and we can have a cheese party
> SOFIA: Ard [OK] but only for me cuz I love cheese lol
>
> *Facebook conversation, April 2012*

Our conversation concluded after an hour. I chose not to remind Sofia, at that moment, of my mandated reporting duties. Looking back, I should have, but at the time, I worried that that reminder, across the virtual divide of Facebook, could have dangerous consequences (such as prompting her to cut) if Sofia was experiencing distress. I tried to wrap up the conversation on a positive note, with a plan for a special lunch meeting.

Sofia seemed to turn to me with this information because she trusted me and recognized my commitment to her and the other members of the MMS girls' group. By engaging in the love act of persistent witnessing (Laura, 2016), I had shown deliberate attendance to Sofia and her peers, taken notice of what she found to be meaningful, and affirmed the importance of her stories and experiences. The love act of witnessing, unfortunately, had laid the foundation for this moment. Although I was anxious and uncertain in the moments after this conversation, Sofia's disclosure made me feel her care and love for and trust in me, which made the idea of mandated reporting all the more heartbreaking. In that moment, I wished there was a way for me to intervene and co-create practices that would heal and restore (Brooks, 2017), while not making her feel like she was getting in trouble or like I was betraying her trust. However, my role as a mandated reporter had been defined, and so I immediately reached out to my graduate school advisor and an MMS counselor, named Mr. Drake, to identify next steps.

Intervening in Sofia's Life

On my way to MMS to visit Sofia, I stopped at a grocery store to buy cheese and crackers, and I hoped that this small love act of laboring (Laura, 2016) would demonstrate my care for Sofia, despite the challenging afternoon we might have. When I got to MMS, I found Sofia and CiCi in the cafeteria, and we took their lunches up to the library to talk. After eating lunch, cheese, and chatting, I told Sofia, with my voice shaking and hands sweating, that I really appreciated what she had shared with me and that she trusted me with that information. I then asked her to remember back to the beginning of the girls group, when I had discussed confidentiality and my role as a mandated reporter. I told her that, although I did not want to disappoint her or break her trust, I had to tell Mr. Drake about what she had told me. CiCi was quiet, and with wide eyes, watching Sofia for a reaction. I apologized for not reminding Sofia of my mandated reporting status during our conversation, and I emphasized that at that time I was not sure what to do. Sofia looked at me fairly blankly and replied, "Okay." She did not become upset as I had feared; she was calm and agreeable but seemed nervous about what was to come. We cleaned up the lunch and cheese, parted ways with CiCi (who went on to her next class), and walked down to Mr. Drake's office. I asked her if she would like me to stay with her when we spoke to Mr. Drake, and she said yes.

I had contacted Mr. Drake previously, and he was aware of the fact that Sofia and I would be coming to visit him. Mr. Drake was a warm man who related well to students, and he opened up the conversation by welcoming Sofia, making small talk, and then asking what we wanted to discuss. With Sofia's permission, I described the Facebook conversation we had. Mr. Drake was gentle and caring in his follow-up questions. First, we talked about Sofia's feelings and experiences and Mr. Drake tried to decipher why she engaged in cutting. Sofia explained that two of her brothers were deported earlier in middle school, and she had been very sad since that happened. Mr. Drake emphasized that we could help her to find safer ways to process her emotions. This conversation, although difficult, brought us to new realizations of the ways in which oppressive policies had translated to trauma in Sofia's life. As Sofia told her story, Mr. Drake and I engaged in the love act of witnessing (Laura, 2016); we listened without judgment and aimed to affirm and appreciate her experiences, rather than dismissing her experiences and engagement in cutting as a dramatic, adolescent response (which I had heard other educators do).

After listening to Sofia, Mr. Drake called the school nurse, who came to look at Sofia's cuts, which the nurse noted were superficial and healed. Then, Mr. Drake went to find Ms. Chavez, MMS's Latinx Community Liaison,[2] to call Sofia's mother. While Mr. Davis looked for Ms. Chavez, Sofia and I went into a resource room to talk more. I continued to apologize for having to take these steps, and she quietly reassured me that it was okay. She seemed tired from talking about cutting at this point, so instead we talked about her family members from Mexico who had just visited and how much fun she had had. We eventually returned to Mr. Drake's office, and Ms. Chavez greeted Sofia and asked her some questions so that she could relay correct information to Sofia's mother. In Spanish, Ms. Chavez calmly explained to Sofia's mom that this was not Sofia's fault and that Sofia's mom should be supportive. Ms. Chavez set up a meeting with Sofia's parents and the school for next Monday morning. Before Ms. Chavez left, she hugged and kissed Sofia and tried to be very comforting. Mr. Drake explained to Sofia the next steps in terms of finding a counselor and he said that he would make a referral and discuss next steps with her and her parents soon.

At this point, there were only fifteen minutes left in the school day, and Sofia and I just walked around the building and then went outside. Sofia said that she was feeling better that she told people about it, because she had been thinking about telling her mom anyways. I asked her if she was going to tell CiCi about the afternoon. She said yes and joked that she was going to tell CiCi "not to tell me stuff anymore." Although she laughed and smiled at this, I wondered if this was in fact what she was going to say to CiCi. The bell then rang and students were rushing outside. Sofia started talking to some of her friends and I gave her a hug and told her to message me if she needed to.

A few weeks later, Sofia was paired with a clinical social worker at MMS and she was able to meet with him during the school day weekly. She had an incredibly positive relationship with him, looked forward to her appointments, and continued to see him weekly until the end of the school year. Sofia learned more about trauma and mental health, and coping strategies that she could exercise to support her resilience. Later that year, I observed her post text on Facebook that encouraged other girls to seek support with their mental health if they needed it. Thankfully, my and Sofia's relationship continued to flourish: she continued coming to the girls' group and engaged enthusiastically, we rebuilt our trust, and we stayed in touch through 2016, when I graduated and moved to Maine for a job. The love acts that produced this moment were persistent witnessing, engaging, and laboring (Laura, 2016). Witnessing allowed me to discover the trauma that Sofia was struggling with, and engaging and laboring with Sofia, MMS educators, and Sofia's family, fostered the sharing of mental health resources and created conditions for empowerment for Sofia.

Sofia Intervening upon Me

San Pedro and Kinloch (2017) argue that in order to decolonize and humanize educational research, we must "willingly center the realities, desires, and stories of the people with whom we work" and "situate their stories in relation to our stories, lives, and research projects in humanizing ways" (p. 374S). Thus, it is critical to situate Sofia's story, in relation to my own. Throughout this section, I will explore how the loving, intimate inquiry and relationships that Sofia and I co-constructed intervened upon my life.

Love in the research allowed for me to develop deeper understandings of what Sofia and many of her peers believed to be meaningful. Bearing witness to Sofia's experiences exposed me to realities that I had not yet uncovered and complicated and sophisticated the ways that I thought and wrote about immigration, trauma, and adolescence. In the coming months and years of research, more girls turned to me to disclose that they were struggling and engaging in self-harm. From 2012 to 2015, seventeen of the seventy-two Latina girls that I worked with (24 percent) reported engaging in cutting. This is probably a low estimate because I lost touch with many girls at some point due to district mobility, changes in girls' group membership, etc., and because some girls may not have disclosed their cutting behaviors to me due to my mandated reporter status. Bearing witness, engaging, and laboring in this intimate inquiry (Laura, 2016) allowed me to show love to the girls I worked with and arrive at a level of deeper knowing that would permit me to make important recommendations to scholarly and practitioner audiences regarding how to best support Latina girls in schools.

Witnessing, engaging, and laboring with Sofia also brought me to new methodological realizations and helped to transform my relationships with MMS gatekeepers (educators). I was skeptical after hearing the deficit perspectives some staff at MMS voiced about Latina girls, and I realized that I was not positioning Mr. Drake and other staff as experts and allies. Witnessing the love and care that Mr. Drake and Ms. Chavez showed Sofia and her family made me check my assumptions. After Sofia got on her bus the day we reported her cutting, I went to see Mr. Drake, and I expressed how nervous I had been in handling the situation. He asked, "Don't they teach you about mandated reporting in graduate school?" I had not been taught about how to navigate the complexities of being a researcher and mandated reporter in graduate school, and ignorantly, I had not expected such issues to arise. That afternoon, Mr. Drake sat me down in his office and we discussed steps we could take and collaborate on if future situations were to arise. That conversation was incredibly informative for my work as a researcher; it better prepared me to show love and care through intervening with girls who were cutting in the future and filled an important gap in my graduate training.

This episode also impacted me personally, emotionally, and psychologically. In 2010 (less than two years before I began my research at MMS), a student of mine in the public school where I taught was brutally murdered by a family member, whom I had met and conferenced with many times. I was still grieving and traumatized by that loss and angry with myself for not having been able to protect my student. When Sofia disclosed that she was harming herself, I experienced severe anxiety and ruminated endlessly about her accidentally cutting too deeply, and what could happen if I failed to protect and support Sofia and other girls. I realized, through my relationship with Sofia, that my identity and experiences as a researcher would be inextricable from my past identity and experiences as a teacher. This encouraged me to memo more regularly on these overlaps in identities and experiences, and how this overlap produced both assets and challenges for my work as a researcher. This experience also inspired me to go to therapy. Therapy aided me in developing understandings of how to support youth in research without experiencing intense anxiety when something under the purview of mandated reporting came up. Finally, while loving research produced interventions that often felt challenging, it also produced joy. Doctoral study can be grueling, isolating, and defeating. The love, care, and closeness that I experienced in my research relationships with Sofia and other girls got me through graduate school and supported my own resilience.

Dangers in the Intimacy of Ethnography

As Laura (2013) explains, love in intimate inquiry is "good" if it is a choice, if it "enhances, protects, and alters another's life," and if it is "personally empowering, humanizing, and unabashedly interventionist" (p. 289). Love did these "good" things for Sofia and me. However, as Judith Stacey (1988) emphasizes for feminist ethnographers, intimate inquirers need to grapple with the dangers in the intimacy of loving qualitative research for a variety of reasons. First, she emphasizes that ethnographic methods subject participants to greater risk of exploitation, betrayal, and abandonment by the researcher than does much positivist research. Although Sofia and I built a caring, trusting, reciprocal relationship, I still betrayed her trust due to my role as a mandated reporter and made her rethink telling me things in the future. There are limitations to the trust and confidentiality that adult researchers can offer, and researchers have to be honest and transparent about those limitations. While I tried to be cautious and clear in explaining my roles, complexities nevertheless arose and I never knew if my explanations were clear enough for middle schoolers. Finally, although I tried to stay in contact with Sofia after I graduated, the job market took me to Maine and then Ohio, and in a sense, I abandoned my relationship with Sofia and the other girls that I worked with.

Second, and relatedly, Stacey (1988) emphasizes that fieldwork and its textual products represent an intervention into a system of relationships that the researcher is far freer than the researched to leave. While the interventions that occurred in the MMS girls' group were relational, reciprocal, and long-lasting for many of us, I still existed beyond the system of relationships that Latina girls remain immersed in, in Marshall. My reporting of Sofia's cutting impacted her relationships with her family and educators in a long-term way, while the interventions that I experienced were largely private and internal. Additionally, Stacey explains with concern that "the lives, loves, and tragedies that fieldwork informants share with a researcher are ultimately data, grist for the ethnographic mill, a mill that has a truly grinding power" (p. 23). As intimate inquirers, we must at the very least question the reduction of human lives, loves, and tragedies to code-able data. Stacey also warns that the "ethnographic method appears to (and often does) place the researcher and her informants in a collaborative, reciprocal quest for understanding, but the research product is ultimately that of the researcher, however modified or influenced by informants" (p. 23). So, although the research interventions in my and the girls' lives were caring and fairly reciprocal, I still produced a product that would advance my career, while the girls were not left with such a product.

Conclusions and Methodological Recommendations

At the beginning of my dissertation research, I was apprehensive about thinking of the girls' group and the research as an intervention. However, through research experiences and consultation with the literature, I learned that loving, caring research is unabashedly interventionist (Laura, 2013). It is important, however, that we recognize the commitments that we have in the love that we exercise. hooks (2001) and Brooks (2017) provide us with ideas that support a critical theory of love: the love that we exercise in research should be grounded in an affirmation of our participants' identities; understanding of historical and contemporary contexts and power dynamics which shape our participants' lives; and committed to social justice, to humanization, and towards centering our participants' experiences. Such a love can be shown, as Laura (2013; 2016) explains, in intimate inquiry through the love acts of witnessing, engaging, and laboring, which can lead to deeper knowing and establishing conditions for empowerment. Finally, as Stacey (1988) emphasizes, through engaging in such loving relations and inquiry, we must stay "rigorously self-aware" for the dangers in the intimacy of ethnography and simultaneously be transparent with participants about those precarities and try to address them.

For researchers who are engaging in similar projects, I conclude by offering the following pieces of guidance, which I wish I had prior to beginning my ethnographic project:

- When navigating access to a site, researchers should have clear conversations with gatekeepers and advisors (if relevant) about whether the researcher is seen as a

- mandated reporter, and if something comes up that needs to be reported, what the best pathway for action is.
- Relatedly, researchers should have clear and consistent conversations with youth to remind them of their role as a mandated reporter (if relevant).
- In qualitative methods classes, we must include thorough discussions of relationship building, maintenance, and leaving the field, and how notions of care and justice should shape these phases of research. Offering panels of researchers in classes who can discuss their relational and caring practices in different contexts would be immensely helpful.
- Many qualitative researchers in the field of education are former teachers, and it can be tricky to determine roles and boundaries as an adult researcher working with youth. Again, in methods classes, we should equip our students with readings and guest lectures about differences and similarities in those roles and boundaries before graduate student researchers begin fieldwork.
- Finally, an important qualitative practice is memoing. I would encourage researchers to integrate memos responding to the following questions in their qualitative practice:
  - How do I define love and care? In what ways is that love and care connected to humanization and justice? How will I practice these values in my research process? How will I communicate these values to my participants?
  - Do I understand the historical and contemporary contexts in which my youth participants exist? How am I bringing that knowledge into the ways that I build relationships, show care, and engage in methodological practice?
  - How am I practicing care and investment in my youth participants' lives and full personhood? How am I or how am I not affirming their social and cultural identities?
  - In what ways might my research allow for the co-creation of rehumanizing practices that could heal and restore?
  - How have I seen power and systemic oppression dehumanizing and traumatizing my participants? What action can I take? What intervention can I/my research make into these systems of power?
  - How are my research relationships intervening upon me—emotionally, psychologically, and academically?
  - What practices could I engage in, on my own and in collaboration with my participants, to monitor the dangers in the intimacy of ethnography?

9

A "Friend" or an "Experiment"?: The Paradox of Ethnographic Relationships with Youth

Nora Gross

About eighteen months into my ethnographic fieldwork at an all-boys' Philadelphia high school, I found myself having a long, difficult conversation with seniors Yaja and Siah,[1] two of the central participants in my study. The three of us sat together in the windowless office by the school's front door, which I had taken over as an interview room, to have this heart-to-heart, which extended for more than three hours on a Tuesday afternoon. About an hour in, Yaja offered earnestly, "I really don't want to be a part of your research [anymore], I just want you to be a really cool friend."

Yaja went on to say that his experience of our dynamic—of adult researcher and student participant—had shifted over time and he had come to feel that being "part of the research ... took away from the genuineness. Instead of you being my friend, and talking to me as a friend, or somebody that cared, it was like, now everything I'm telling [you] is for [your] research." Similarly, Siah, who had once felt a sense of importance and validation when I wanted to *interview* him, now pointed to my periodic use of that word to describe our conversations as he questioned whether I considered him more of an "experiment" than a "friend." Although the close personal relationships I had enjoyed with both Yaja and Siah for more than a year at that point began because of and within the context of my research at their school—and would never have formed if not for the project—the two young men were suggesting that being a part of the research had, over time, come to feel like an invalidation of my care for them.

I felt I had entered the school and conducted myself as a researcher with deep and genuine attention to the needs of the young people I was studying—expressing respect toward their ideas, identities, and lived experiences; gratefulness for the time and stories they shared with me; and care for their well-being and comfort. I was committed to this both in the daily practice of my ethnographic research *and* in the very research questions I had come to the school to answer: how Black adolescent boys coped with the deaths of friends to gun violence and how they experienced their grief with peers and at school. But Yaja's and Siah's comments, within our extended conversation that afternoon, led me to wonder how much my own care-based methodology mattered if my participants—or even just these two boys—did not feel cared for.

I have reflected since then about how researchers ought to respond to shifts over time in research relationships with youth. How do we ensure that our feelings of care, both within and outside of data collection processes, come through continuously to our participants? And what responsibilities do we have to rectify relationships that go bad over time, especially if doing so might come at the expense of other research plans? In outlining how I answered these questions in my own project, I propose that there is an inherent paradox in the relationships built with youth as a school-based ethnographer: the same relationships that are made possible through the unique positionality of a long-term researcher in a school can also be threatened by the very research premise through which the relationships were built. As researchers, any commitment to sustaining caring relationships throughout a study requires us to acknowledge and reckon with this paradox.

In this chapter, I explore this paradox and the methodological questions it raises through the lens of my shifting relationships with two research participants over two years of research. I identify important moments for intervention in research relationships that sour and argue that truly caring for young people who participate in research sometimes means prioritizing those relationships over data collection.

A Vacuum of Care and the School Ethnographer

The scarcity of resources in so many US public schools serving students of color often leads to a parallel scarcity of care. When administrators, teachers, and counselors are stretched thin—often just getting by without the time, money, or support they really need and with the weight of centuries of educational inequity bearing down—they may be forced to cut corners in their individualized relationships with students. These tradeoffs can lead administrators to prioritize disciplinary personnel over mental health professionals (Whitaker et al., 2019), teachers to forge relationships based more on evaluation than on care, and school cultures of "tough" love to unwittingly contribute to students' "emotional abuse" or "suffering" (Dumas, 2014; McKenzie, 2009; Rickwood et al., 2005; Zirkel et al., 2011).

In these contexts, schools may be overly focused on "aesthetic caring" that positions students as *in need* or reinforces the institutional status quo (McKamey, 2017; Noddings, 2005b; Valenzuela, 1999). Aesthetic caring can be practiced without the "authentic" or critical care that is truly responsive to students' dynamic needs or acknowledging of the oppressive structural forces that shape their lives (Rolon-Dow, 2005). And in school environments that are hyper-focused on testing or prone to blaming families for students' under-achievement, individual caring teachers who understand the structural basis of their students' challenges may not feel safe or supported in "practicing transformative humanizing pedagogies" (Lynn et al., 2010, p. 317). All of this leaves some young people grasping for the individualized attention, affirmation, and affection of caring relationships with adults in school.

Enter the school ethnographer: a new adult with an unfamiliar job title. To students, she may kind of look like a teacher, but she doesn't stand at the front of the classroom or give grades. She may roam the hallways freely without a specific classroom schedule like the school support officers but doesn't discipline students for breaking rules. She may ask questions like a newspaper reporter but doesn't leave after a quick visit or few interviews. She is not a peer, but sits with students in the cafeteria and texts or communicates with them on social media. She is not a therapist, but she promises confidentiality when they share secrets or seek advice. And importantly, by nature of the job, a school ethnographer is inherently curious and interested in students' lives, likely taking the time to listen, ask questions, probe for more, and follow up.

Though most of the literature that has shaped conceptions of critical care in schools centers relationships between *teachers* and students, a researcher embedded in a school long term also contends with similar relational opportunities and challenges. If "a critical care praxis begins by acknowledging that, to care for students of color in the United States, we must seek to understand the role that race ethnicity has played in shaping and defining the sociocultural and political conditions of their communities" (Rolon-Dow, 2005, p. 104; see also Antrop-González & De Jesús, 2006; Valenzuela, 1999), then a critical researcher armed with research questions about the racialized forces that shape students' lives is well positioned to enact care both within individual interpersonal relationships and in more systemic ways. This approach, according to Rolon-Dow (2005), also involves developing relationships with students that recognize their fullness and complexity *beyond* the limited sets of roles they play at school.

School ethnographers, then, have an opportunity to not only care *for* and *with* student study participants, but also, as McKamey (2017) describes it, to *care within* the systems that shape youths' lives. An ethnographer's positionality in, but not of, the school allows her to practice care that "recognizes the ways interactions occur within a larger social structure or historical context," including the fact that her own "beliefs and actions may be oppressive to others" (221). Positioning herself as learner, not teacher—there to observe and become "engrossed" in students' lives (Noddings, 2005b)—the researcher, in her interactions with students, can disrupt the typical power dynamics of adult-young person school relations. In the case of Black boys, who were the central focus of my study, researchers also have the flexibility and potentially the time to practice the kind of culturally relevant care Warren and Bonilla (2018) describe as "persistent concern for [youth's] holistic well-being" and "willingness to extend ... beyond the limits or confines of ... professional duties" (14, 18).

But there is an important caveat here—the basis for the paradox I am introducing. Because the ethnographer is at the school to do research, conversations and interactions with assenting students are potentially data—and really everything we see and hear colors our understanding of the life of the students and their school. While collecting data and enacting care are not mutually exclusive, it would be inaccurate and even deceptive to ignore the fact that relationship-building is a necessary part of the process of conducting qualitative research and researchers may have multiple simultaneous goals. These goals might compete for the researcher's time and attention and/or they may feel incongruous or uncomfortable to the researcher or a participant.

Study Context and Methods

I entered Boys' Prep, an all-boys, all-Black charter high school in Philadelphia, with care as unstated but integral to my research design. Care was, in some sense, the very point of the work since my research questions were about how schools were caring for vulnerable students experiencing loss—specifically the loss of friends to gun violence. These questions were pressing to school leaders, teachers, and the students themselves as Boys' Prep had, just months before my arrival, lost a freshman boy to gun violence in the neighborhood. And, over the following two years that I was immersed in school life, the school community would continue to be directly impacted by violence. During my two years of ethnographic research from 2016 to 2018, I spent over 600 hours in the school building, observing in classrooms, hallways, the cafeteria, academic and administrative offices, and schoolwide events. I interviewed sixty-five students and more than thirty teachers, administrators, and parents. I also observed students' peer interactions on their social media accounts.

It was clear to me within a few days of being at Boys' Prep that my relationships with students would go beyond my research questions. Before I had even figured out the most efficient routes through the building to get to particular classrooms or learned the names of all the school administrators, students started seeking me out to talk. I think for some students, my presence was a novelty, and spending time with me in hallways and the glorified closet I co-opted as an interview room was a change of pace from regular school life. Students seemed to appreciate the extra attention that I gave them and the interest I showed in their lives. Some would text or call me on weekends or evenings to check in or tell me about something going on. Others would comment on my Instagram posts since I allowed any student I observed online to also "follow" me. I was somewhat surprised early on by how little it seemed to take for students to open up and share their stories with me and how grateful so many of them were for the caring attention.

Meeting Siah and Yaja

When I first arrived at Boys' Prep in fall 2016, I was invited to attend a student-run group called Freedom to Speak (FTS).[2] A group of about fifteen juniors and seniors gathered during lunch twice a week to check in with each other, talk about the issues on their minds, and offer support to each other. In effect, FTS functioned as an informal peer counseling space. Several school staff had suggested that this group might be a good starting place for my research, and the students were on board with me joining them. I audio-recorded and took notes during meetings and chimed in periodically with questions or with my own opinions or reflections when asked. Eventually, I came to serve as a kind of unofficial advisor to the group.

Siah and Yaja, both part of FTS, were close friends and both juniors at the time: Siah, charismatic, sometimes cocky, and with dreams of being an actor, and Yaja, a natural leader who was popular and respected by peers though privately expressed self-consciousness about being overweight. Just after the conclusion of the second FTS meeting I attended, Siah came up to me as I was packing my notebook into my bag. Our first one-on-one interaction, he introduced himself again and asked to talk. Specifically, he explained, "There was this cheating thing in Math class and I just need to talk about it with somebody and I can't talk with a teacher. Is it okay if I talk to you?" I agreed and we made plans to meet the next school day I would be back at Boys' Prep. We talked through the situation in detail for almost an hour, and I helped him strategize what to do. In this conversation, I also told him more about my research intentions and he agreed to participate. From that day on, I often chatted with Siah individually before or after the FTS meetings and began observing some of his classes.

Yaja was a little slower to open up. My first day in FTS, he had many questions for me about why I chose *this* school and what interested me about Black boys specifically. Though the staff at Boys' Prep was overwhelmingly white (75 percent) and female (56 percent), he was rightly skeptical about the motives of this white woman researcher in an all-Black and all-boys school. Despite his critical lens, Yaja also expressed an openness to getting to know me. A month or so into my time at the school, we spent an unexpected hour together one afternoon stretched out on the floor of the hallway, leaning up against a row of lockers. Excused from his Math class for the period, he was in the mood to talk and I was there. He shared an experience from a few years earlier when he had been shot at and confessed that he was recently told by the school social worker that he might have PTSD. He was grappling with the ramifications of that possible diagnosis. I listened and asked questions, appreciating the opportunity to get to know him better and feeling pleased that he was coming to trust me enough that I could offer support around such a sensitive experience. Although Yaja and I had not yet formally discussed my research and whether he would participate beyond the FTS meetings, I wrote up fieldnotes later that night about our conversation. I figured that, even if he ultimately did not become an official participant in my research study, I was at an early enough stage of my exploration that it was useful for me to keep track of all the new things I was learning even tangentially connected to my research questions.[3]

Our hallway chat had given me strong feelings of respect for Yaja, who was smart, thoughtful, and measured, but also incredibly funny. The conversation also seemed to have an effect on Yaja. A few days later, he texted me: "You earned your Black card. The community recognizes you. Your new name is Norquiesha." Though we could not have known it at the time, this conversation was the start of what would become a special kind of research friendship. A year later, Yaja reflected on that afternoon: "I remember that one time [you and me] was sitting on the floor talking. I forget what we was talking about. I think that's where it started," referring to our relationship. He continued, "It was something real emotional, because I think you ... you had dropped a couple tears."

Indeed, over the course of my first year of research at Boys' Prep, both Siah and Yaja were among the students I spent the most time with. They regularly confided in me and sought my advice. To them, I think, I was a caring, trustworthy adult who was able to offer them more mutuality and respect than they received in their relationships with many other adults they interacted with at school. Care showed up in my consistent and persistent efforts to get to know them, attention to them as full people beyond their roles as students, and engagement with the structural and institutional forces that shaped their lives. In turn, they also supported me both in the ways they helped me refine my research questions and by publicly vouching for me with other students who would become key to my research.

Changes during My Second Year of Research

The dynamics at Boys' Prep and my role within the school shifted during my second year of research, Siah and Yaja's senior year, for two reasons. First, over time, I became increasingly incorporated into the adult-level school community in formal and informal ways. Formally, I was given more access in the school building mirroring that of teachers and administrators. Though I continued to store my belongings in a student locker—which many students found wildly entertaining—I also now had a master key, which allowed me to open any classroom door, the main office, and the private adult-only bathrooms. Informally, I also began to develop closer relationships with several teachers. Whereas I had not spent any out-of-school time with teachers during the first year, the second year I had coffee or drinks on at least four occasions with teachers in ways that were as much social as they were research based. I was also invited to the faculty holiday and end-of-year parties, asked to be an adult chaperone at prom, and included in the procession of school staff at graduation.

Second, a series of disturbing and destabilizing events during the year dramatically shifted my role at the school. In November, one of the boys who had been part of my study was killed; his death was followed, a few months later, by the murder of a second student, both victims of gun violence. Given the goal of my study to understand the grieving experiences of victims' friends and school communities, these events opened up new layers of my research and led to relationships with new groups of students who were impacted by these losses. While it is inevitable in ethnographic work that research priorities shift and studies evolve, this evolution came with heightened emotions on all fronts. As both the number of students who leaned on me for support and the depth of their needs in the face of so much loss grew, it stretched my time at school thinner. There were often three different places I wanted to be at any given hour of the day, and I became less available for impromptu hallway conversations. In hindsight I can see that when conflicting demands—combined with my own grief—maxed out my emotional capacities or left me feeling on edge, I sometimes defaulted to "teacher mode," trying to help settle the chaos by offering students direction or behavioral suggestions.

Though FTS continued to be a touchstone of my time at Boys' Prep most weeks, my evolving research focus meant that I began prioritizing interviews with new students or spending time in the classrooms the deceased students had been in—which sometimes conflicted with FTS meetings. The FTS students kept me clued into the pulse of the school and I tried to make it clear that I remained available to support them, but all these changes certainly must have made me seem less present to those boys with whom I had initially been so close.

Conflict with Siah and Yaja

By the middle of the second year of my research, it was becoming evident that the changes in my role at the school were affecting Siah and Yaja, and they were feeling differently about my relationship with them. Two excerpts from my fieldnotes, from March and April 2018, illustrate this:

> On the way out of a class I've been observing that Yaja is in, I check in with him and suggest that we're overdue for a catch up. He seems less warm with me than usual and says, "we used to just hang out but seems like everything you do is for your studies now."
>
> I see Siah in the stairwell. He says, "I miss Ms. Nora. This year, you're Ms. Gross." I must have made a face that suggested I was hurt by this and he immediately took it back, saying he was just kidding.

More than a year after telling me I had "earned [my] Black card" following the care and commitment he may have felt was demonstrated by our impromptu "hang out" and deep conversation in the hallway, Yaja now felt like things had changed. For Siah, a similar sentiment was illustrated by the way he referred to me. Upon arrival at Boys' Prep, I had told students they could call me Nora or Ms. Nora, whichever they preferred, but now, Siah implied I was acting more like a teacher whom he would refer to by last name.

The person inhabiting this strange role of school ethnographer no longer seemed to them like a trusted friend. Now, it seemed, they were more aware of both my goals of collecting data and my adultness. This is the paradox I shared at the start of this chapter: it was only in my role as researcher, a role embedded with the goals of getting to know students deeply in order to produce new knowledge about the patterns of their experiences, that I was able to develop relationships that were so special and different from the typical student-adult relationships in school buildings. And while these relationships were and are genuine, there is no avoiding the fact that their foundation was the research project.

The offhand comments from Siah and Yaja, and the changing nature of our interactions over the spring of my second year of research, deeply affected me. On my drives home from school, as I typed up fieldnotes, and even while taking walks or showering, I ruminated on how relationships that had been so strong could have shifted so dramatically. Were my research goals stretching me too thin? Had I taken on too much responsibility for the emotional well-being of the school community during an unimaginably difficult year? And now that these relationships had been interrupted in these increasingly palpable ways, what responsibility did I have, potentially at the expense of some of my research goals, to focus on repairing them? What did I owe these two boys who had welcomed me into their community, helped me connect with and become trusted by other students, and shared so many meaningful conversations with me?

Repairing the Research Relationship

I eventually decided that I needed to make a concerted effort to talk with Siah and Yaja without distractions. It took a few weeks to persuade them and then to find a time when both were free—which required me rescheduling an interview with another student and missing some planned classroom visits—but eventually the three of us sat down together in late April and the boys allowed me to record our conversation. What began as a somewhat forced gathering during lunch turned into a three and a half hour heart-to-heart that took us to the end of the school day.[4]

At the beginning of our conversation, I asked them to tell me more about how they felt our relationship had shifted. Yaja thought for a second and then offered up a vivid memory of when "we really started to fall off":

> YAJA: There was like one time this year, I was on the second floor. I never forgot it and you walked past me, you told me tuck my shirt in. I couldn't tell you if you were playing or not. I was like, "She told me to tuck my shirt in."
> NORA: Oh, wow. I don't remember that. I mean, I'm sure I was joking 'cause I don't have anything in. There's no incentive for me to tell you –
> SIAH: I would say –
> YAJA: I never forgot it. I walked –
> SIAH: You tucked your shirt in?
> YAJA: No, I ain't tucking—I was like, "who the fuck" –
> SIAH: I know.
> YAJA: ... And I was like, "she's starting to get on my nerves."

Here, Yaja holds on to a moment when I said something that represented a different kind of adult role. I had told him to tuck in his shirt, which was a constant refrain from teachers to students about the school uniform.

This little moment mattered to him and, probably along with other similar moments, fundamentally shifted his view of what kind of friend I could be to him. The conversation continues as I try to reflect on why I might have spoken to him in ways I would never have previously:

> NORA: I think that I was sensing a little bit of, like, pushback from you and I think I probably was taking it personally and, like, taking it out on you.
> YAJA: That makes sense. I really felt some type of way.
> SIAH: Y'all are like a corny ass couple. It's like, "This is how I felt." And like, "Okay, well ..."
> YAJA: And I thought about it the entire day, like, "Yo, Nora just told me to tuck my shirt in."
> SIAH: For real?
> NORA: And that was weird because I usually don't.
> YAJA: Yeah.

My reflection on this memory reveals the way research relationships with youth are fundamentally real human relationships, with all their missteps and mistakes. I might have been having a bad day and took it out on him. I might have been trying to make a joke that did not land. And certainly, this was during a stretch of time when I was feeling hurt—emotionally "wounded" in the field (Winkle-Wagner, 2017)—by Yaja's behaviors toward me, and as I expressed here, may have been subconsciously using the power I had as an adult over him. Siah, who is offering commentary on this exchange between Yaja and me, jokes that we sound like "a corny ass couple" as we work through our feelings together.

As the conversation continued, both boys reflected on what was at the root of the hurt they felt and then directed toward me:

SIAH: *I still think you cool as shit, you just got favorites.*
YAJA: *Yeah whatever started the friendship back up, I was like, alright I'm cool. I don't feel no type of way. Oh cause remember, so we was in Ms. X's room and you had said something to me and I was like, you remind me of the staff, or you just like the staff now, and it hurt you a little bit.*
SIAH: *Yeah you was telling me about that, I was like ...*
YAJA: *When you told me that you was hurt by that, I was a little hurt. I was like, damn I did cross the line. I was trying to be an intentional asshole to you.*
SIAH: *Yeah at one point, I was like ... I don't even know if you caught it but I was really like throwing you shade. I wanted to get across like, I don't fuck with you and I need you to know that.*
YAJA: *It was like a heartbreak. It really was. I develop over time. You was a thurl boul,[5] you was a cool friend. I'm like damn like, she really cared about me. She cared about my feelings, all of that.*

In this moment, about an hour into the conversation, something new comes up that had been latent to this point. Siah says that he felt I had "favorites" among the students I was spending time with at school, and implies a bit of jealousy toward other boys who were increasingly receiving more of my attention.[6] Siah is honest about the fact that he wanted me to know his displeasure and change in feelings toward me.

Meanwhile, Yaja also reflects on a time when he had intentionally tried to hurt me by telling me that I was acting "like staff"—a jab he may have known would offend me since I had been so clear with them about my role being *not* as a teacher or disciplinarian. Yaja then felt bad when he realized how much his words had hurt me. He goes on to reflect on the way his perception of my lessening of attention and care toward him over time was "like a heartbreak."

This narrative points to a perspective on care as a necessarily reciprocal act. My intentions of care, recognition, and affection toward students like Yaja and Siah are empty if they are not felt and received (Noddings, 2005b; Rolon-Dow, 2005; Warren & Bonilla, 2018), or if they are perceived as inconsistent. And, although I do not think I could have articulated it as such at the time, my own ability to stay present and caring with students depended, in part, on feeling some respect and care back from them since they had come to play an important role in my own life—and especially at this time of collective grieving.

As our conversation continues, Yaja points to the paradox of research relationships even more directly when he draws out the idea that me being a friend, being "genuine," and "somebody that cared" was in contrast to him being part of my research. For him in this moment, these two relational dynamics are in conflict and cannot coexist:

> YAJA: *I don't want to be part of your research. I really don't want to be a part of your research, I just want you to be a really cool friend.*
> NORA: *… What made you feel strange or not good or indifferent about the research part?*
> YAJA: *Because it took away from the genuineness, instead of you being my friend, and talking to me as a friend, or somebody that cared, it was like, now everything I'm telling her is for her research, and that shit hurt. … People like to be cared for, and the fact that you cared about me was like-*
> SIAH: *… I could have gave you a lot of data. I could have been a good subject.*[7]

For Yaja, the genuineness of our initial conversations when we were first getting to know each other—conversations that I wrote fieldnotes about and considered to be research *as well as* relationship building—reflected my care toward him. As my research progressed and the time I had for him and the way I treated him shifted, he also felt a change in the purpose of our conversations.

Siah similarly felt like the frame of my research now overshadowed the possibilities that our relationship could be an authentic friendship after they both graduated high school. He latched on to a suggestion I made that as part of staying in touch after graduation we could meet up for a follow-up interview at some point:

> SIAH: *A interview? Don't ever. Don't. When you said that just now, I swear to God, me and [Yaja] looked at each other like, "Did she just say we're going to fucking do a interview after we graduate?" … If you going to say we going to have a friendship, say we going to have a friendship. Or just call me a experiment.*

Here Siah expresses a profound critical consciousness in his worry that I viewed him only as an "experiment." His pushback was likely (and rightly) rooted in the sordid history of exploitative research on communities of color, often done by white researchers. In Siah's mind, there was no possibility of overlap between future conversations that were "interviews" and future conversations that were rooted in a long-term friendship.

The Paradox This Illuminates

My relationships with my participants were, in my view, always about *both* collecting data and authentically caring for the boys in their full personhood. The two were inextricably linked for me because the research itself was responding to bigger structural questions of care.

Yet, even before things came to a head with Yaja and Siah, there were momentary conflicts between caring one-on-one relationships and research goals—which usually played out in in-the-moment decisions about how to spend the limited hours I had at Boys' Prep every week. For example: whether to extend an impromptu conversation with a student who seemed to need extra attention from a caring adult or follow through on previously planned data collection activities in a classroom. In my "good enough" research decisions in the moment (Luttrell, 2000), I often prioritized the former or might try to find a way to do both by keeping my scheduled appointments but suggesting another time to follow up with the student in need.

Authentic caring relationships require that both parties know each other beyond the institutional roles through which we met (e.g., researcher and participant) as full, complex human beings, including all the ways that social categories and structures of oppression and privilege have shaped our lives (Antrop-González & De Jesús, 2006; McKamey, 2017; Rolon-Dow, 2005). To feel cared for, then, students must have a sense that they are seen in ways beyond their participation in a research study; they must feel it, not just trust me when I say it.

This presents an ethical, relational, and methodological paradox: It is only in my role as a researcher that I am able to be *in* the school consistently, but not *of* the school—that is, without formal academic or disciplinary obligations, free from expectations for reporting sensitive information, and able to give time and attention to young people. In this role, I could (in fact, it was my purpose in being there) "get to know [boys] personally [and] build deep relationships with each of [them]," as one student recently reflected to me in an Instagram direct message. And yet, it is this very research focus that seems to threaten the integrity of those relationships in the eyes of some of the boys. Being the subject of research can make students feel seen, feel like their life is worthy of study, like their full humanity is being recognized in spaces where that does not always happen. But, as I have learned, there is a very fine line between feeling *seen* and objectified, used, or treated like an "experiment"—and the contours of that line might shift throughout a study.

Reflections for Future Research

Acknowledging this paradox and anticipating the complications it can create in research relationships with youth requires researchers to develop some guidelines for themselves as they plan, embark on, and carry out a study. Below are three areas to consider:

Ongoing informed consent. Negotiating this paradox with care requires having a thoughtful, responsive, and *ongoing* process of informed consent (or assent for minors), rather than viewing it as a "one-time event" (Khan, 2011, p. 202). Most youth do not have any idea what research involves and what its products are, putting the onus on the researcher to meet participants where they are in describing the research process, being transparent about its focus and goals, and trying to predict, as best they can, what the outcomes will be and what will ultimately happen with the stories students share. These conversations involving, as ethnographer Shamus Khan (2011) puts it, "friends [being] reminded that you are part of their life to study it and … not simply to be their friend" (p. 202) are rarely easy, comfortable, or convenient, but researchers need to think about consent as something always subject to renegotiation, including after the research is technically concluded.

Reception of care and research tradeoffs. Commitments to caring and feelings of care do not matter much if the people one is caring for and with do not receive it.

To ensure that care was received by the boys in my study at all times, I would have had to slow down and make some crucial research tradeoffs. A longer study, more days/hours in the field, or fewer participants might have allowed me to be more responsive to individual students' needs as they shifted over time—though this might have required additional funding or other privileges. Relatedly, given the adult-student power dynamics often embedded in schools, researchers aiming to learn about youth's lived experiences must carefully consider the way they publicly relate with adults at school. Every school culture is different, but in buildings where students and adults have antagonistic relationships, a researcher might need to limit interactions with adults to maintain the trust of students. There are, of course, implications for the data collection with these changes, but the bigger picture of caring for youths' well-being demands that researchers are as attentive to the way care is being received as they are to how it is being given.

Responsiveness or relationships over research. As the story of this chapter highlighted, research relationships are not static; they can shift and even sour. Researchers must stay attuned to dynamic relationships as well as changes in how they interact with youth over time. Though research itself can be a caring act, and scientific study of the lived experiences of youth can lead to real material change for them, those outcomes are potentially years away from the actual moment-to-moment time a researcher spends with young people in a school. A caring stance toward those youth means that sometimes a researcher must prioritize the needs of those individuals over the needs of the research. This might mean remaining a caring adult in a young person's life even if he decides not to participate in the study or opts out midway; it could also mean pausing data collection—turning off a tape recorder or skipping a planned research activity—to attend to the immediate emotional needs of a young person.

To some researchers, these choices may seem obvious in the abstract, but when time is tight and research goals are pressing (weighted by all the expectations of life in the academy), they are sometimes harder to remember and even harder to enact. Recognizing the inherent paradox of research relationships with youth—and the unexpected relational shifts it might produce—is the first step to being able to enact care within these relationships. Researchers aiming to practice care-based methodology can plan ahead by articulating their priorities both for data collection and within relationships, working through possible challenging scenarios in advance, and reflecting regularly with critical friends and thought partners.

Epilogue (a Relational Resolution)

About a year after the conversation with Siah and Yaja about their feelings about being part of the research, and after all of us had left Boys' Prep, I ran into Siah on a long Bolt Bus ride. We sat together and immediately started updating each other about our lives. Though he had previously expressed resentment that I might perceive any future conversations between us as an "interview," a few minutes into our casual catch-up, he said: "Did you bring your recorder? I do have things that would help you."

Several months after that, I began thinking through an earlier version of this chapter to present at a conference. A few days before the conference, I shared my slides with Siah and Yaja to get their blessing for what I would present. Yaja responded via group text about reading the slides:

> *It brought back the emotions and feelings of those 3 years, How we met, how I felt about you, From feeling like you was family 😊 to having a crush 😊 to disliking you, to liking you again, back to family, and then seeing you at graduation and feeling like I actually accomplished something 😊 Thank you Nora* ❤

Yaja's narration of our relationship more than fourteen months after the conclusion of my data collection period is a telling reminder of the constant and continued evolution of participants' feelings about being part of a research study—and the researcher's obligation to take these shifts seriously, particularly if they purport to care about participants' well-being.

10

Unraveling a Researcher's Practices of Care with One Disabled Youth

Katie Scott Newhouse

Often educational researchers from the traditional special education orientation collect research *on* participants (e.g., youth identified as disabled) with dehumanizing outcomes (Connor, 2009). Based on my own anecdotal classroom teaching experience and working in community with disabled scholars and community activists, I realized this was not the approach I wanted to take. As I worked to develop the methods for my dissertation study, I read widely in the fields of disability studies, disability studies in education (DSE), and care ethics. I often struggled while developing my study because of the complications I grappled with related to how disabled youth are treated during the process of research. This led to the creation of a research design, which drew from specific theories to develop methods for data collection and analysis, which emphasized researching *with* instead of researching *on*. In this chapter, I describe how my conceptual framework informed my methodological decisions as part of a larger dissertation project.

My dissertation was a multisite ethnographic narrative inquiry that explored the lived experiences of youth who are required to attend restricted educational programs (REPs), either due to receiving a disability classification or court-involvement.[1] The larger project included two separate sites at two different REPs, one was an alternative-to-detention afterschool program for court-involved youth, and the other was an independent school for youth identified with disabilities. Across both sites I wanted to collect and explore the stories youth and adults shared with me from within these spaces. This was primarily because a wealth of prior research (Algozzine, Morsink, & Algozzine, 1988; Causton-Theoharis, Theoharis, Orsati, & Cosier, 2011; Dunn, 1968) has illustrated the impoverished experiences of teaching and learning in REPs and highlighted the negative outcomes for young people who receive their education in exclusionary spaces (Allan, 2006; Bogdan & Kugelmass, 1984; Connor, 2009). Young people who are mandated to attend REPs are often the most vulnerable (cf. Annamma, 2018b; Erevelles, 2011). This is in part due to the process of labeling and classification by which a young person is identified as disabled or court-involved. The process of labeling, though different for each group, is similarly damaging as it forces youth through a system of deficit-oriented assumptions that are often tied to other identity categories such as race, class, and gender. Due to my understanding of this process, I intentionally explored care-based research methods and built moments into my method for reflexive practice, such as audio and written memoing. This was to unearth my own assumptions as a nondisabled white researcher and better inform my decisions throughout the study as I developed researcher-participant relationships.

I use my developing researcher-participant relationship with Sapphire, one of the participants for my dissertation study, as an example of the posture I took up as a researcher. This involved leaving myself open to learn from participants who identified as disabled to help me unravel what practices of care look like/feel like/sound like in a large qualitative research project. This chapter serves as a critical reflection of the moves I made as a researcher toward developing a researcher-participant relationship with Sapphire. I hope to offer some critical insight/learning about how care (as a practice that makes up a larger ethics) is used in research that involves youth participants, specifically those labeled with disabilities.[2] Additionally, I share how using a DSE framework and the ethics of care (EoC) helped me develop a research design, which integrated a relational research practice with youth participants and a strong ethical and moral commitment to researching alongside or "with" instead of "on" said participants.

Introducing Sapphire

Sapphire was seventeen and about to turn eighteen when I first met her in January of 2019. She self-identifies as a young Black woman who is a wheelchair user with low vision and difficulty hearing. Sapphire always dressed in coordinated outfits with small splashes of color: if she had on a pink shirt, then her socks were also a matching shade of pink. She used an electric wheelchair with a motorized switch she controlled to move around the school building. She wore a small cross-body purse positioned over her front right hip. Her school backpack hung over the back of her chair with the large loops firmly pulled behind the chair's handles.

Sapphire rarely wore makeup; however, she shared with me that when she turned nineteen, she planned to wear more eye shadow. She preferred her natural hair[3] and typically wore it braided in two thick braids or pulled back in small puffs on the top of her head. She often came to school with brightly painted fingernails, styled to offer contrast to her outfits. If her shirt was orange, her nails were blue or a light seafoam green. Sapphire's voice was soft and slightly high-pitched; she spoke slowly and clearly, which I later realized was partially due to her hearing impairment.

Sapphire's overall demeanor was calm, friendly, and open. I often saw her smiling and laughing with her friends during the school day. Sapphire was classified on her individualized education plan (IEP) as a young person with multiple low-incidence disabilities.[4] Sapphire shared with me that she began attending the Saturn school when she started 8th grade. To provide a bit more context I share a brief description of the Saturn school.

The Saturn school is organized as a PreK-12th school for youth with low-incidence disabilities (per their organization website). The school offers a range of programs for youth aged 4–21 years old, including specialized classroom instruction, speech and language therapy, occupational therapy, physical therapy, access to counseling, and other medical services, all within the main school building. Saturn remains an independent school but receives funding from the state where it is located because the school only enrolls youth identified with low-incidence disability classifications. Another key feature of the Saturn school is its small student population and class size. The current total student enrollment for the school is 185 youth. Students enrolled at the Saturn school spend 100 percent of their school day segregated from same-age, nondisabled peers. In the following section I discuss the conceptual framework I used for the larger study and this chapter. My purpose here is to highlight *how* I constructed a theoretical framing for this research that led to a conceptual development of care practices I used to develop a researcher-participant relationship with Sapphire.

Ethics of Care

Care, as a practice, is a relational interaction that typically involves one person offering support to another. For example, calling to check on a friend, helping a student reach a learning goal, and bringing food to someone who is hungry are all practices of care. Piepzna-Samarashinha (2018) shares that for people who identify as disabled practices of care may be more complex. This also touches on dominant understandings of intimacies, since the care some people require may involve carrying and lifting bodies from wheelchairs, attending doctor's appointments and assisting with taking notes (p. 40). These practices of care make up a larger EoC, which informs the ways human beings relate to one another, highlighting how people make sense of their world in regard to their moral development (Gilligan, 1982). Following Held (2006), I use the phrase "ethics of care" as opposed to an "ethic of care." Held suggests that there are multiple different practices of care, which make up this ethics. She notes that although "care practices have much in common, their plurality requires the use of 'the ethics of care' as a collective and singular noun" (p. 30). This plurality allows for a range of care practices, which makes up a larger ethics of moral theory, which encompasses care practices of adults and youth who identify as disabled and pushes further commonly held understandings of caring practices in the field of education (Noddings, 2003).

Noddings (2003), building on the work of Gilligan, laid important groundwork in the field of education toward a normative theory of relational care ethics. DSE-informed scholars Danforth and Smith (2005) write, "Noddings asks us to view our mission [as educators] as one of developing moral citizens who care deeply about others and themselves" (p. 95). Noddings (2003) defined 'caring' as a relational practice between two individuals, one providing care (carer) and one receiving care (cared for). Two key features of this caring relationship, according to Noddings, are (1) engrossment, which means the carer offers themselves completely to the cared for without regard for anything except the needs of the cared for, and (2) motivational displacement, wherein the required support for the cared for is "the complete goal for the carer" (Danforth & Smith, 2005, p. 97). Noddings notes that the caring relationship may be imbalanced, especially in an educational context where the carer is more frequently an adult teacher and the cared for is a young person and student. Still, Noddings suggests there is a certain amount of reciprocity, which must come from the cared for in order for the caring relationship to thrive and remain sustainable.

Disability Studies in Education Framework

DSE is a framework that incorporates theories from the field of disability studies (DS) and applies them to educational research and practice (Gabel, 2005). DS has shaped educational research in key ways that widen how scholars of education understand and theorize about disability in both research and teaching (Gabel, 2005). A major contribution from the field of DS is how disability is socially constructed. DS scholars show that disability is more than a biological category or fixed trait within a person, also referred to as the medical model of disability (Oliver, Sapey, & Thomas, 2012). An understanding of different models of disability is especially important to the field of education because many (if not most) public schools, which offer special education programs and services, often take up a medical model. This is apparent in how a young person is classified with a disability, which is part of the process for qualifying for special education programs and services. Often a young person and/or their family must prove that something is "wrong" with the young person in order to receive support in the public schools (Taylor, 2004).

DS/DSE scholars actively engage with research that frames disability as a social process that humans construct through their interactions with their environments (Davis, 2013). This is referred to as the social model of disability.[5] This means many DS/DSE researchers make the distinction between disability (as socially constructed) and an impairment (as a lived reality that a person may require support to address). This is important to the field of education because a DSE framework suggests that disability classifications are not fixed but instead constructed by schooling environments, which include many barriers to access and participation for disabled young people. This understanding of disability as social from a DSE perspective complicates practices of teaching and learning, which may be rooted in medical model thinking. One such practice that runs this risk is care.

Ethics of Care from within a DSE Framework

Historically people labeled with disabilities were institutionalized and/or segregated from general society (Piepzna-Samarashinha, 2018). Often the rationale for these actions was that isolating disabled people was a practice of care, which protected disabled people by keeping them safe from harm. This is why using a DSE framework is essential to research, which also takes up an EoC. There are practices of care, such as seeing a person using a wheelchair and pushing their chair without asking or rewriting a student's paper without their input, which are seemingly well intentioned but may not be received as care.[6]

EoC is further complicated by the work of DS-aligned scholars in both philosophy and political science for two important reasons. One is that practices of care, such as helping a student with an assignment, may establish caring relationships but are not always reciprocal. Tronto (1995) notes that humans care for various living and nonliving beings and objects across their lifetimes. Her point is that several care-based relationships may never offer reciprocity in the normative or linear fashion, which Noddings (2003) suggests. Still, Tronto explains that these relationships bring deep meaning for people though they may lack reciprocal action.

Second is that practices of care are not always received as care (Piepzna-Samarashinha, 2018). Historically, practices of care for disabled people often led to infantilization and the presumption that people labeled with disabilities are not fully human (Kittay, 2005, 2019). Using the DSE framework with an EoC results in a more ethical research method, which allows for the considerations of a range of practices of care. It also acknowledges the dimensions of power that exist in each caring relationship between the carer and the cared for. Furthermore, it suggests that a caring relationship may be established with or without reciprocity. I brought these considerations into my work as a researcher aiming to develop researcher-participant relationships with youth who identify as disabled.

Data Collection

The data collection methods for the larger dissertation project were ethnographic and narrative. They consisted of participant observation, open-ended interviewing, informal conversation, and photography. After receiving Institutional Review Board (IRB) approval and receiving consent and assent from all research participants, I audio-recorded all open-ended interviews and informal conversations. At the first research site, the Saturn school, I collected data over a six-month period, from January 2019 to June 2019. During that time, I visited the Saturn school 3–4 days a week, generally from 9:00 a.m. to 3 p.m., which was about the length of the school day. The research participants from the Saturn school consisted of nine youth from the 12th grade class, three classroom teachers, and three assistant teachers.

Confronting Observational Barriers. I made several intentional methodological decisions as I designed and carried out this project. I generated methods that aligned with my framing from the field of DSE and EoC. Using the DSE framework I relied on the idea that disability is social and often it is the environment that constructs a person as disabled. During participant observation, I never took typed notes on a laptop or other computing device as I felt using a laptop was a barrier to observing how the space was constructed through physical movement and interactions between youth and adults. Instead, I took handwritten notes in my field journal that included sketches and drawings of where participants were physically located in a given space. I also wrote down specific words or phrases that youth used to refer to themselves and/or others in both the classroom space and the schooling spaces outside the classroom.

The EoC helped me to maintain a critical awareness of how practices of care are both given and received as a researcher. At the end of each observation period, I found a private room at the school where I audio-recorded myself dictating the key observations or moments that I had not fully captured in my jottings. Using the DSE and EoC together, I viewed this decision to immediately audio-record my own observations as a more direct way to record observations of interactions within the educational space where I was engaged in participant observation. To maintain a practice of reflexivity, which is integral to a DSE and EoC-aligned study, after I finished with data collection for the day, I listened back to my audio notes while looking over my field journal jottings and then crafted more detailed, typed ethnographic fieldnotes. Later during open-ended interviews, I shared excerpts from these transcribed recordings with research participants to receive their input about how I described and possibly interpreted a given interaction.

When I introduced the study to all the youth participants at Saturn, I made it clear that my plan was to conduct open-ended interviews. However, I intentionally waited two or three months after establishing relationships with consenting participants before actually beginning to schedule those interviews. I made this decision based on one of my first interactions with Sapphire, which I share below.

Sapphire's Cover Story

I start with this moment, from my fieldnotes, to show how my attention to the DSE framework and EoC allowed me to develop a care-based researcher-participant relationship where I moved from superficial interaction (what I refer to as the cover story of Saturn school) to a deeper engagement with Sapphire's day-to-day lived experiences while she attended Saturn.

> *I first observed Sapphire during Ms. Roger's Media Arts class. The students were filming short videos and one featured Sapphire in the role of President of the United States holding a press conference about why schools, such as Saturn high school, an independent school for youth with low-incidence disabilities, required more funding from the U.S. government to continue serving disabled youth in their local communities. As Sapphire listed the positive aspects of the Saturn school, "accessible classrooms, adaptive P.E., making friends, people treat you nice," her voice resembled a cadence that people often adopt when reciting a list of items, in a matter-of-fact tone without much passion.*

After this observation I wrote a reflective analytic memo about how youth at Saturn took up the school's "cover story" (Crites, 1979 as cited in Craig, 2003). A cover story is the narrative that people within a specific location are taught to tell about that place (Craig, 2003). Often the cover story is the curated version of a place that highlights the positives and steers away from any challenges or difficulties that a place may have. At Saturn, the cover story focused on the positive aspects of the Saturn school, the small class sizes, access to an array of related services, and the family-like atmosphere of the interactions between adults and youth. Of course, in reality, the day-to-day lived experiences at Saturn were quite messy, and as a DSE and EoC-informed researcher I wanted to explore the messiness and move beyond the "cover story" of the Saturn school, which I could easily glean from the school's website and other promotional materials.

Sapphire's First Interview. After following the consent and assent procedures, I waited about two months, during which time I spent time observing and participating in Sapphire's English and Media Arts classes multiple times a week. During that time, I introduced myself to Sapphire and sat next to her a few days during her English class to work on writing poetry. After about eight weeks had passed I let Sapphire know that I wanted to interview her and asked again if she still wanted to participate in the research study. Sapphire confirmed that she was interested and as she put it, "happy to talk with me anytime."

The next day, I asked Sapphire if we could do our first interview, she agreed, and we found an empty classroom to conduct the open-ended interview. I showed Sapphire my cellphone and explained that I would use it to record our conversation. Sapphire smiled and said, "Oh that's good because I wondered how you would remember what we talk about." So far, I felt that I was taking up DSE and EoC in my process as a researcher, checking in with Sapphire after the assent process to confirm that she agreed to be interviewed, finding a private place for us to speak, and showing her the recording device and making it clear that I planned to record our conversation and how I planned to record it. I also emphasized that my main interest was Sapphire and her thoughts and opinions about attending the Saturn school. Since all my research participants required pseudonyms, Sapphire and I took a few moments to practice using the cell phone to record her voice and test out a few pseudonyms she chose. We giggled together at the way her voice sounded saying different names until she settled upon Sapphire.

I was now ready to begin our first interview. A key point here is that I was ready, but reflecting back, I *assumed* that Sapphire was also ready. In what I now identify as a fairly novice care-based researcher move, I began by asking Sapphire, "So tell me what you like about Saturn?" Sapphire sat quietly for a moment and slowly began to respond to my initial question. As she responded, I noticed a shift in her speaking voice from moments before when we played with the recording device. Sapphire began speaking in the same cadence she used during the video skit, almost as if she was inhabiting her role as president at the press conference again. This was worrying to me because I did not get the sense that Sapphire was fully invested in the things about the school, which she was describing. In this moment, I felt the DSE and EoC-informed research design I created had completely failed. Still, I was confident that I was developing a caring relationship with Sapphire based on our interactions moments before. Here I was reminded of Tronto (1995) theorizing that care may not always be reciprocal for a caring relationship to be established. I decided that I needed to devote more time to developing a relationship with Sapphire that helped her understand who I was and why I was interested in learning more about her opinions of the Saturn school.

Location, Location, Location: Understanding Why Context Matters for Relationship Building with Youth Participants. I leaned on my reflexive memo practice here and wrote up several memos with thoughts and observations about how to establish a more authentic researcher relationship with Sapphire. Through this process I identified that a potential barrier in our development of a researcher-participant relationship was my own socio-spatial position as a white nondisabled researcher who looked quite similar to many of the adults Sapphire worked with at

Saturn, such as her teachers and teaching assistants. I realized that by occupying space in Sapphire's school, it was difficult to establish a relationship with her that allowed her to perceive me as different from the other adults within this location. I began thinking about how to make the difference between my role as a researcher and not her teacher or support aide clearer to Sapphire. The DSE framework was also helpful here as I strove to presume competence (Biklen & Burke, 2006) and connectedness (Kliewer et al., 2015) with the youth at Saturn. Instead of focusing on predetermined understandings of my youth participants, I sought out organic ways to develop the researcher-participant relationship. One way I did this was by eating lunch every day in the student cafeteria (Figure 10.1).

Early on in my fieldwork, I noticed that the only adults who ate in the student cafeteria were teaching assistants or other support staff (e.g., health aides and feeding attendants). As I familiarized myself with the day-to-day routines of the Saturn school, I came to understand the cafeteria as a space where youth were able to gather with limited adult supervision. The choice to occupy the cafeteria as a site of possible relationship building with youth participants took on qualities of being in-between the strict regulation of the classroom space and a cafeteria space that was less mediated by adults (Tokunaga, 2016). The youth ownership and autonomy of movement from within the cafeteria space were two reasons why I identified this as a space I wanted to inhabit as a researcher for this study specifically to establish relationships with my youth research participants.

Figure 10.1 School cafeteria

Though I had been eating lunch in the cafeteria for about two months, I typically sat at a table on the periphery and ate my lunch alone. A few days after our first interview, which in my mind had completely failed, I noted Sapphire was eating lunch along with her health aide and asked if I could join them and eat my lunch. Sapphire warmly agreed. As I sat with Sapphire, a few other students joined, and we engaged in informal conversation for the remainder of the lunch period.

Deepening the Researcher-Participant Relationship: Eating Lunch with Sapphire. After that, I started eating lunch with Sapphire and a handful of other students every day I was at Saturn. During our lunchtime interactions, I encouraged Sapphire to adopt the role of expert of her own life. DSE-informed research must be participatory (Ferguson & Nusbaum, 2012) and it was necessary I establish a relationship with Sapphire that demonstrated I was working *with* her to collect data for the study as opposed to gathering information *about* her. These conversations began informally across the lunch table, often with long stretches of silence while I hesitated to prompt or guide Sapphire. Instead, I spent time slowly eating while waiting for Sapphire to direct our conversation. This took some time, but, over the course of a few weeks, our conversations developed. These informal conversations, which only tangentially related to my research questions, helped me establish a meaningful connection with Sapphire. This invited the establishment of a relationship that helped her realize I was different from the adults at her school who were teachers and teaching assistants. I share another moment as our relationship developed, which helped me reach this conclusion.

Moving beyond Sapphire's Cover Story

One afternoon when I worked with Sapphire during her English class, she said to me, "Sometimes I need help because it's hard for me to hear and I don't see that well." I was struck by how Sapphire identified, to me, the support she needed. As I reflected back on that moment, I realized that I grossly underestimated Sapphire's capability to identify her own needs. I implicitly assumed that the teacher would identify how to support Sapphire in the classroom. I did not expect that Sapphire would indicate the type of support she needed. This was another important moment of critical reflexivity for me. Later I wrote reflective memos to unearth my own assumptions and address how I understood academic support in the classroom. The way Sapphire shared her support requirements with me was like she was confiding in me, asserting that she was competent but did need some support. This allowed me to adopt a posture as researcher where Sapphire took the lead and I was offering support, based on her own assessment. Sapphire's request was also when I realized I was getting closer to the quality of researcher-participant relationship I wanted.

Sapphire's Second Interview. After about four months of working together in her classrooms and about six weeks of eating lunch together, I asked Sapphire again if she was interested in participating in my study and if I could interview her again. Sapphire agreed and expressed interest at conducting another interview. This time when I asked about her experiences at the Saturn school she provided a starkly different answer from our first interview. She shared,

> I like coming here and sometimes I don't because ... like it's really a nice experience and it's a lot of fun for me and I can make friends and learn new things so that's why I really like it. Sometimes it's too—(pauses and takes a deep sigh) it's too bad. Like the classes are not right, it's math and social studies [but] it's not that interesting. But this year has been good because we went on a lot of trips. Every time they give us a permission slip, I sign it right away because I want to get out of the building.

Sapphire's initial description—"I like coming here and sometimes I don't"—is concise and hints at the larger conflicting stories (or lived experiences) circulating within the Saturn school below the surface of the "cover story." In a later conversation, when I asked Sapphire to elaborate on her statement, "It's too bad," she told me,

> Sometimes I don't really like talking about why [it's bad or why] I don't like it because it's really not gonna help anything, [or] help me in that way. It is hard for me to talk about that. But talking about why I like it [the Saturn school] is easier for me.

By her own admission, Sapphire shared that it was difficult for her to discuss the parts of the Saturn school that she did not like. Though as our conversation continued, she shared some details of her dislike, like the smell and lack of privacy in the school bathrooms. I realized much later this was an important transgression for Sapphire to share with me, a nondisabled person, about an intimate part of her daily routine (using the bathroom) and what made it unpleasant to her. I also more fully understood my initial failings. Though I was informed by DSE and EoC I did not fully consider the ways care as a practice is given and received in the moment with a research participant. As Sapphire shared, "it's not gonna help anything, [or] help me in that way." During our first interview, I realized Sapphire was likely skeptical about who I was and why I was asking her these questions. Her skepticism was fully warranted, but it also showed how important the DSE framework and EoC were to this research. If I took up a different conceptualization of disability and care, I might take Sapphire at her initial words and build an argument that the Saturn school was a happy family-like place for all students.

Later interview data with Sapphire actively disrupted the statements she made during her first interview. Her statement, "Every time they give us a permission slip, I sign it right away because I want to get out of the building," served as a reminder that while the Saturn school might possess supportive and destigmatizing elements, it also limited Sapphire both socially and academically. Designing a research study that drew from a DSE and EoC framework and specifically highlighted the social model of disability and fluid understandings of practices of care allowed me space as a researcher to develop relationships with participants that allowed for a richer qualitative understanding of their lived experiences at the Saturn school.

Developing a Care-Based Researcher-Participant Relationship. Piepzna-Samarashinha (2018) states that practices of care are highly and, at times, frustratingly subjective lived experiences. Through this research with Sapphire I came to understand that a part of how an EoC is conceptualized is almost always through a negotiation of decisions and choices. From this standpoint, using an EoC is always an active process of weaving together practices of care, which are potentially received/given as more or less caring from one moment to the next. Furthermore, these care practices may not be reciprocal, but this does not mean a caring researcher-participant relationship is not being formed. As a researcher I needed to pay attention to these negotiations and consider how my own definitions and understanding of practices of care informed the relationship I developed with youth participants.

Methodological Reflections and Recommendations

I conclude here to share some insights that emerged from developing a researcher-participant relationship with Sapphire over the course of six months. Being guided by the DSE framework and EoC as a researcher with Sapphire allowed the development of a researcher-participant relationship, which moved from a superficial "cover story" to richer qualitative data collection. Given the highly subjective nature of the term "care," I suggest that researchers *carefully* select methods that align with EoC and whichever other theories and concepts are used. I also suggest that researchers maintain a posture of humility and openness, allowing themselves to consider the possible complications involved while establishing a conceptual framework. Finally, I strongly encourage educational researchers to explore using a DSE framework when conducting research with disabled youth. I share a few recommendations for educational scholars conducting care-based research with (or involving) disabled youth:

1. **Time:** While some may view this as a limitation, an important care-based practice I often relied on and illustrate in this chapter is time and patience. This allows for more authentic and organic relationship-building. Over and over again I found myself waiting, sometimes awkwardly, for relationships with my participants to develop. This meant I spent several days eating lunch in the cafeteria where nothing of particular interest happened. It also meant figuring out the right location or context to build researcher-participant relationships. Though it was, at times, frustrating, my consistent presence, in a specific location, over an extended period of time was necessary. Part of taking time also meant waiting for relationships to develop not solely on my terms. As I illustrated above, the time I spent with Sapphire led to much richer collected interview data.

    I also intentionally provided Sapphire with time to determine which aspects of her life she wanted to share with me as a researcher. Using a DSE framework along with EoC meant that my commitment in this study was not to lead with a young person's disability label but to instead wait for the young person to disclose to me how they chose to identify. This decision is an example of a practice of care I enacted as a researcher that was informed by my conceptual framing, which suggests disability is part of a social process. I did not want to assume that I, as the researcher, implicitly knew how Sapphire self-identified. Of course, this also meant I took time for our relationship to develop to a point where Sapphire felt comfortable self-identifying her classification, as she did that afternoon in her English class.

As I shared, when I interviewed Sapphire before spending time eating lunch with her I received very superficial interview data. I underscore the importance of building time into a research design to allow for researcher-participant relationships to develop as it may impact the type of information a participant shares and in turn the type of data that is analyzed. Here I also share another care-related methodological insight; people (and especially young people) rarely tell you their opinion directly, especially when they first meet you. Therefore, time, as a care-based research practice, involves both patience and potentially not working on your own timeframe (as the researcher) but the participants' time as well. I suggest researchers consider building into their research design extra time at the outset of a study for this purpose.

2. **Surfacing Assumptions through Reflexive Practice:** Researchers should sincerely consider how their own assumptions about interpreting disability and practices of care are enacted throughout the research process. As the researcher, I found humility was central: I had to grow comfortable with admitting what I did not know (Kittay, 2019). Here I relied on Tronto's (1995) point that not all caring relationships are reciprocal. Along with Piepzna-Samarashinha's (2018) emphasis on the ways, practices of care are subjective. For researchers planning to conduct care-based research, especially with disabled youth, I suggest critically examining your approach to data-collection practices, as well as considering the possible harm data collection may have on research participants who identify as disabled. For example, the first interview with Sapphire generated superficial data. This challenged me, as a researcher, to think about care-based research practices. By engaging in ongoing reflexive practice (such as memoing) I was always in a process of figuring out exactly how care was given and/or received in the researcher-participant relationship. Instead of basing my developing understanding solely on my own assumptions, I attempted to enter a type of negotiation with Sapphire. This also informed my role as the researcher and what implicit assumptions I carry into the research space, and how I attend to and address these throughout the research process.

There are deep implications in terms of how educational researchers orient toward and defer to youth participants. This requires the maintaining of reflexive practices, such as memoing, audio recording, and journal writing, which aid in the continual addressing of assumptions. Finding outlets for my own (potentially misguided) interpretations was an important piece of this methodological puzzle. Developing a reflexive practice across a research study is one way to maintain an openness to the misinterpretations that may arise. The process of engaging with research from a standpoint of an EoC meant consistently checking in with myself and my participants. This led to an ongoing interrogation of my own assumptions about disability and care throughout the study. The result was a care-based ethical researcher-participant relationship with Sapphire, which provided her space to share her lived experiences at the Saturn school.

11

Culturally Responsive Caring and Emergent Tensions in a Bilingual Mentoring Program in a Diverse School

James S. Chisholm, Melanie Jones Gast, and Ashley L. Shelton

We consider in this chapter tensions surrounding the practice of culturally responsive caring in a bilingual mentoring program, Peers Making Change, in a diverse school in the US South. We highlight the importance of action in Geneva Gay's (2000) definition of culturally responsive caring, which

> focuses on caring *for* not *about* the personal well-being and academic success of ethnically diverse students, with a clear understanding that the two are interrelated ... *caring for* is active engagement in doing something to positively affect it. Thus, it encompasses a combination of concern, compassion, commitment, responsibility, and action.
>
> (Gay, 2010, p. 48)

As we researched and attempted to support Peers Making Change and the emotional and academic well-being of immigrant and bilingual participants of color, we experienced tensions related to undefined roles, unclear expectations, communication challenges, and varying ideas about the needs of those designated as "English Language Learners" (ELLs).[1] These tensions were exacerbated by our limited physical presence at the school site. In short, we were initially underprepared for emergent tensions surrounding our goals to *care for* the program participants. Drawing on the literature on youth-adult partnerships (Camino, 2005) and student-led programs, we provide suggestions for university researchers to navigate tensions and circumvent assumptions that limit the enactment of culturally responsive caring (CRC) in the interest of social-justice research and practice.

Pedagogical approaches to cultivate CRC can help youth of color push back against institutional structures that remove their voices and agency (Cridland-Hughes, 2015). While scholars suggest that CRC is necessary for fostering social justice in schools, educators centering CRC as a practice face difficulties in working against broadscale systems of oppression that marginalize students of color.

Like teachers, qualitative researchers can also practice CRC in schools; yet past work rarely highlights the researcher in this process. Qualitative researchers, unlike teachers, are not typically employed by school districts where they collect data. This outsider status can work against researchers who face difficulties in establishing trusting relationships with participants, but it can also work to a researcher's advantage in centering CRC as a practice. For example, students may find in a caring researcher a listening ear or perceive the researcher as an objective, nonjudgmental, or nonauthoritarian adult as compared to teachers who are in the position to evaluate and discipline students. School officials may find in caring researchers an outlet for candid discussions of the strengths and challenges of working in education contexts in the twenty-first century. Thus, qualitative researchers play a potentially mediating role in centering CRC while seeking to promote social justice, one that can be unique to roles played by teachers and administrators in schools.

Youth-Adult Partnerships and Student-Led Programs in Schools

Youth-adult partnerships (Y-APs) are "relationships in which both youth and adults have the potential to contribute to decision-making processes, to learn from one another, and to promote change" (Mitra, 2009, p. 407–08). Y-APs cultivating the empowerment of youth, especially youth of color, reveal the potential of CRC in practice outside of traditional educator-student relationships. Yet successful Y-APs can be difficult to develop in institutions where intersecting forms of oppression and power and authority hierarchies have strong footholds (e.g., Baldridge et al., 2017). An example of this is the very label of "English Language Learner"—used by our participants, but which imbues stereotypes, additional power limitations, and marginalization in mainstream classrooms.

One approach for countering systemic forms of oppression and encouraging youth agency and empowerment involves cultivating action in Y-APs to recognize and disband traditional power structures. Within Y-APs, adults (often local community members or youth workers) engaging in CRC work alongside youth to mutually reconstruct traditional power hierarchies and prioritize the voices, needs, and concerns of youth marginalized in mainstream institutional settings. This can happen by partnering with and supporting youth so that youth have the power to make decisions and develop programmatic opportunities on behalf of themselves and their peers (Camino, 2000). Adults may help youth in these goals by providing resources, guidance, and knowledge (Camino, 2000) and centering CRC to elevate youth voices and leadership. However, power imbalances may still exist between adults and youth, even in Y-APs seeking to promote change. These imbalances can lead to adults being over- or under-involved, dependent upon the structure, goals, and relationships present. Thus, the literature on Y-APs demonstrates tensions that can emerge for adults engaging in the practice of CRC, as well as possibilities for navigating these tensions to center caring in action.

Gay's (2010) notion of "caring *for* not *about*" is captured in Mitra's (2009) points on building relationships in Y-APs. For caring practices to thrive in educational spaces, adults (teachers/administrators and, we argue, researchers, too) need not only care about youth of color, but adults must also actively create processes and contexts in which these youth can thrive. CRC is "action-provoking" (Gay, 2000, p. 48) and requires "empower[ing] students by legitimizing their 'voice' and visibility" (Gay, 2000, p. 49). This call has clear implications for the roles played by stakeholders in Y-APs. Trusting, caring relationships do not consist solely of checking in with youth and demonstrating compassion; rather, adults' prioritization of students' voices shapes how the culture of a school supports CRC in practice. Without efforts to practice CRC, researchers seeking to develop Y-APs will likely undervalue shared decision-making processes and, ultimately, thwart social-justice goals of empowering youth of color.

Our collective[2] work revealed tensions in practicing CRC with student leaders managing a peer-mentoring program with limited direction and guidance from adults. Student-led programs can be sites for social change as they are often initiated and led by students who can prioritize the concerns, skills, and voices of schoolmates (Jones & Perkins, 2004). Additionally, Espinet et al. (2018) described how, in their study of a peer-mentoring program, bilingual mentors learned to view their own bilingualism as a "source of pride" (p. 131). For these mentors, supporting mentees' learning shaped their own sense of empowerment.

Yet student leaders in youth programs lack the institutional resources, authority, and power of adults and may face obstacles in meeting their goals (Camino, 2005). Research shows that youth programs can benefit from adults who practice the "art of restraint" and know when to effectively give, but also hold off on giving, advice and assistance (Larson et al., 2016). In what follows, we discuss problems surrounding unclear roles for researchers in schools and our "lessons learned" while navigating school-based norms of restraint when working with a student-led program.

Peers Making Change at Riverview High School

Peers Making Change (PMC) is a peer-mentoring program founded by bilingual students, including Leticia, a Latina 12th-grader at the time of study, in a public high school in the U.S. South. PMC involved aspects of a developing Y-AP, although as we later note, our role in the Y-AP was not initially clear. Through PMC, high-achieving bilingual students volunteer their time to mentor and tutor ELLs during unstructured lunch/study hall periods in which mentors lead the sessions; some also tutor mentees during classes for course credit. The mentors come from immigrant families and, including English, they speak Spanish, Swahili, and other languages reflecting the district's growing, diverse ELL population.

Historically, Riverview High was a predominantly white school. Riverview is now a diverse school with about 50 percent of white students, growing immigrant and ELL populations, and a majority of economically disadvantaged students. Due to Riverview's focus on preparing students for postsecondary education or vocations, upon entering, all students choose or are placed into college-going or vocational-preparation tracks. It is likely that this type of tracking affects how educators and students define and understand academic success and boundaries distinguishing student groups. Moreover, the school's history of white dominance affects how school officials discuss race and ethnicity, student needs, and programs like PMC that focus on immigrant students. During 2018–2019, we followed PMC's development by interviewing mentors and educators and documenting mentoring sessions and post-mentoring reflections. We transcribed all interviews and post-mentoring reflections, supported PMC's development, and plan to continue this work throughout 2020–2022.

Leticia and other bilingual students developed PMC after recognizing that the few Riverview bilingual and ELL staff were unable to adequately provide support to the increasingly diverse ELL-student population. As a Latina and former ELL student herself, Leticia had experienced many challenges with learning English as a young newcomer. Entering a mainstream American elementary school was, in her words, "very rough." She felt isolated and disconnected from the rest of the class: "I didn't really understand anyone. No one really wanted to sit with me … like I was definitely in the corner all the time." Leticia felt ostracized and unsupported as a young ELL student, and she drew upon those experiences while becoming involved in social justice-focused activities at Riverview.

Leticia and other bilingual students worked with administrators and counselors to address the critical needs identified at the school through PMC's new peer-mentoring program. Based on teacher and counselor recommendations, student leaders invited other bilingual students who carried a 3.0 GPA and had no significant absences to participate as mentors for ELLs. With the support of educators, student leaders paired bilingual mentors with ELLs, and each dyad met at least twice a week during a lunch/study hall period for mentoring sessions; other bilingual mentors in PMC tutored and translated for ELLs in traditional classrooms. All bilingual mentors received community-service hours for their mentoring.

Although the district has other resources for newcomer ELLs, there are no other local student-led programs quite like PMC. In fact, bilingual peer-mentoring programs appear to be largely concentrated in institutions of higher education, facilitated by professionals, in out-of-school contexts, or part of larger initiatives to support language learning in elementary schools (e.g., Arco-Tirado et al., 2018). The originality and student-led nature of the program excited us as a research team, and we were eager to support the goals of PMC participants to empower Riverview youth of color and address resource and opportunity gaps.

An Emergent Youth-Adult Partnership

The three authors (Ashley and James, white education professors; and Melanie, an Asian American sociology professor) initially met PMC student leaders through Riverview administrators/staff in fall of the 2018–2019 year. Ashley and James knew administrators/staff through teacher-education programs at Riverview. One educator introduced Ashley to ELL teachers, described student leaders' interests in starting a mentoring program, and subsequently introduced Ashley to student leaders over email. Ashley and James met with student leaders to discuss their vision, grant funding, and research-collaboration possibilities. Ashley and James asked Melanie to join the conversations given her expertise and social-justice interests in education. All three authors then asked to partner with PMC students, although, as we later detail, our partnership did not have clearly defined roles from the start.

When we initially spoke with PMC students about our research interests, we explained our interests in observing and interviewing bilingual mentors to better understand how mentors structure academic and social support for ELLs and to inform school-based support and future programs like PMC. We obtained a grant and Institutional Review Board (IRB) approval in the winter of 2019, a couple of months after student leaders started to recruit mentors and mentees. We spent the next several months conducting observations and interviews with bilingual mentors as well as key personnel involved in PMC, including administrators, counselors, and ELL teachers.

As a new program and the only one in the district, PMC did not have officially designated advisors or guidelines to follow. Student leaders received classroom space, administrator approval to run the program, and guidance from administrators and counselors, including support with the recruitment of mentors and mentees. Student leaders created Spanish- and English-language versions of invitation letters and application materials for mentors and mentees, training materials for mentors, and terms of agreement for participants, and they worked with Ashley and James to develop a questionnaire, including open-ended and Likert-type scales to collect data about mentees' views of and experiences in Riverview to guide PMC. The newness of the program and lack of clearly identified adult roles meant that we, as researchers, were often asked by student leaders to support PMC in a range of ways, even while we wanted to ensure student leadership, which we discuss further.

We drew on grant funding to provide food, dictionaries, and other material items like Chromebooks during mentoring sessions. This may have unintentionally created an implicit exchange relationship in which our material support of the program implied the cooperation of PMC students in responding affirmatively to our research requests to interview mentors. We noted examples of how student leaders relied on our funding of material resources in our fieldnotes early on, but we were not necessarily cognizant of how this affected our day-to-day interactions with students and staff. Additionally, we later realized how unclear roles established by administrators/staff affected our relationships in PMC. Although, as qualitative researchers, we were constantly taking notes on conversations, emotions, and emergent issues during the research relationship, we did not systematically analyze and discuss those notes and thematic patterns until the summer after the school year ended. We later realized how our typical once- or twice-per-week interactions with PMC participants and the drawn-out processes of reflective writing and qualitative analysis were insufficient for enacting culturally responsive caring and empowering student leaders and participants in real time. Next, we discuss emergent tensions with trying to promote CRC while also supporting and researching this student-led program.

Explicating Roles and Prioritizing Students' Voices to Strengthen Y-APs

Two main emergent tensions in the developing Y-AP affected our ability to care for PMC participants. One emergent tension materialized because we never explicitly discussed with student leaders the role of the research team in relation to PMC and the mentors. Another tension that interfered with our practice of culturally responsive caring emerged when we realized that various PMC stakeholders held different ideas about the specific needs of ELLs at Riverview. Although we did not realize the significance and consequence of these divergent ideas until much later on, our missed opportunities for prioritizing students' voices weakened the impact of CRC at Riverview. We elaborate on both of these emergent tensions below.

"She Is a Fantastic Leader, So We Let Her Run with It": Unclear Role Expectations and Not Interfering

During initial conversations with Riverview administrators and staff, we heard consistent messaging about the need to be "hands off," which influenced how we understood but did not vocalize our roles, and also how we limited our enactment of culturally responsive caring. Instead of actively and consequentially prioritizing students' voices, we allowed suggestions and perceptions from Riverview educators to shape our responses to students' ideas, needs, and concerns. Riverview educators implicitly stated that researchers with PMC should not take on active roles, which, in essence, complicated our attempts to enact culturally responsive caring.

School personnel regularly positioned Leticia as an unusually talented leader: "She's amazing!" Educators and students alike marveled at her capacity to take on so many responsibilities while keeping up with numerous extracurricular activities. The title of this subsection comes from an interview we conducted with an administrator at Riverview, in response to a question about expectations for PMC. "We let her run with it" captures the way many adults positioned Leticia and other student leaders, especially when considering the lack of an official PMC adult advisor. Perhaps more importantly, this positioning points to the following emergent assumption among adults involved with PMC: adults should not interfere with youth work and goals in a student-led program.

During an initial conversation with teachers and administrators, Mr. T told us that he was quite "protective" of PMC student leaders and worried about researchers or other personnel from the district "co-opting" and exploiting students' ideas and work. Mr. T specifically wanted to ensure that the district would not seek to prematurely replicate bilingual mentoring programs in other high schools before PMC students had the opportunity to realize their vision for PMC. He activated a common narrative among adults trying to enhance youth leadership: Adults should not overstep their roles in youth-led programs (Camino, 2005; Mitra et al., 2013). We were glad that he brought these concerns to our attention, and we explained to Mr. T and student leaders our goals to support the student-led nature of PMC as social-justice-oriented qualitative researchers, as well as our lack of affiliation with the district as university professors. We also appreciated that Mr. T was coming from a place of care in his efforts to "protect" student leaders. However, we continued to be affected by Mr. T's initial hesitancy toward us and felt compelled to not intervene in student leaders' management of PMC. Yet caring for student leaders by protecting them from outside forces that might take advantage of their work and ideas reflects only one layer of culturally responsive caring. In isolation, and in retrospect, this orientation toward care prevented us from enacting CRC by asking student leaders about their concerns and ideas with regard to our role (and that of other adults) in PMC, as we describe next.

The first PMC event that James observed was a training session for bilingual mentors. After qualifying mentors (with a 3.0 GPA or higher and no significant absences) were selected, student leaders designed a mandatory training meeting for mentors, without direct guidance from school personnel. During the training, student leaders described paperwork processes to obtain service-hour credits and delivered a guide for "best mentor and coach" practices culled from another program online. Failing to attend the training session precluded prospective students from becoming PMC mentors. As experienced teachers and education scholars, we could have discussed with student leaders possible consequences that such restrictions for mentors might have on PMC enrollment, as well as on how others perceive mentors and PMC. We could have offered student leaders our support in planning and debriefing the mentor-training session. However, the unclear and ad hoc roles of adults affected why we did not actively practice culturally responsive caring. We "let her run with it" and, in so doing, did not ask for student leaders' voices, concerns, and needs regarding crafting recruitment restrictions and mentor training. Adults can enhance youth agency and learning by restraining the amount and type of advice that is given (Larson et al., 2016). However, the "art of restraint" should involve judiciously sharing advice, providing options, and asking questions to reinforce youth agency while also ensuring that issues are effectively dealt with and that the project is successful in meeting its goals (Larson et al., 2016).

Student leaders were coming from a place of care and wanted the most committed mentors to consistently support English Language Learners at Riverview. As adult partners enacting culturally responsive caring, we could have functioned as a sounding board off which student leaders could bounce ideas. We could have participated as dialogue partners for student leaders to think through appropriate, caring, and equitable decision-making. However, we refrained from asserting ourselves into day-to-day decision-making unless we were asked by student leaders. Like the teachers and administrators we interviewed, we tried not to interfere with student leaders' work other than frequently asking how we could help and if they needed resources for PMC.

Student leaders took on many managerial responsibilities as well as emotional, ethical, and academic issues that came up with this group of about 30 students (12 mentors and 18 mentees). Student leaders were the sole communicators for scheduling mentoring meetings and reminding or updating the mentors and mentees via text messages when the schedule changed. Yet student leaders lacked authority to impose consequences when students did not show up, and student leaders faced difficulties retaining busy or disinterested participants. Some dropped out of the group, and student leaders faced problems finding new mentors or mentees in the middle of the semester. While student leaders appeared to grow in confidence and skills from these experiences, as we heard them discuss strategies for enticing and engaging mentees in PMC, we later realized that mentee attrition greatly frustrated student leaders. At one point, a student leader threw up their hands and said, "What do you do?!," indicating that they felt powerless when mentees did not show up. At the end of the school year, when we formally interviewed Leticia, she shared with us that leading the group was "a lot," but it was not clear whether or not (and how much) she and other student leaders would have wanted earlier help from adults. We recognize that we could have played a more deliberate role in helping student leaders navigate these issues, but we did not fully become aware of their frustrations until the end of the year during interviews. This emergent problem illustrates adults' misguided assumptions that youth have the time, experience, and desire to assume the important responsibilities in Y-APs (Camino, 2005).

Additionally, our interviews with mentors near the end of the school year brought to light their lack of power, resources, and experience in taking on their new roles of teachers/tutors and counselors for ELLs. We observed some mentors, who had not yet applied to college and were not trained as counselors, providing college counseling to their ELL mentees. Others faced difficulties with confronting teachers and intervening in the education of their ELL mentees. Given the amount of time it takes to transcribe and analyze interview data, we were not necessarily aware of the widespread nature of these issues until after the school year. As mentioned, we also had fears of overstepping and interfering with student leadership based on Mr. T's concerns. In summary, the unclear roles of adults, coupled with administrators' directions to be "hands off" in this student-led program, affected how and why we did not initially become more involved in the structure, relationship-building, and day-to-day work and in elevating students' voices, concerns, and needs as part of culturally responsive caring in PMC. For the most part, we did not intervene or provide more active guidance, even while we wanted to support PMC and its social-justice goals.

Unclear adult role expectations and assumptions about the "student-led" nature of PMC also meant that communication lines between student leaders and adults were primarily driven by student leaders. Student leaders used an app to communicate with mentors about schedule changes or PMC events, and they sometimes texted or emailed the researchers and educators. Student leaders could also physically stop by teacher and counselor offices for face-to-face communication. While this demonstrated student leaders' dexterity and initiative, it also meant that student leaders often received information and guidance after making PMC decisions. For example, after hearing about our grant to research and support PMC, student leaders organized an ice-cream social to help mentors and mentees get to know each other. Student leaders assumed they could simply charge the grant for expenses and later asked us about paying for ice cream. We informed them that the funds were not readily available for their direct use. In fact, it took months before we could access funds, and even then, the university's bureaucratic process meant that we (not students) had sole authority to pay for items using university credit cards. An administrator also related a story about how student leaders requested a last-minute bus for transportation for a PMC field trip. The administrator informed student leaders that such a request had to be processed at least a month in advance. Student leaders sought out help from adults, including ourselves, when needed, but lack of early, clear communication about roles and responsibilities meant that student leaders were often scrambling in working out logistics for events or programming where they lacked authority in navigating bureaucratic processes. Thus, student leaders were expected to proactively manage issues and know which adults (and when) to approach for guidance and support.

"[W]e Are Providing Resources That the School Is Not": The Lag between Data Collection, Reflections, and Analysis

The title of this subsection comes from an interview when a student leader was asked to describe how PMC supports ELLs at Riverview. The student diplomatically, yet critically, identified Riverview's gaps when it came to meeting the needs of the growing ELL population. Student leaders, along with educators, recognized the need for additional teaching support for ELLs and issues surrounding district-level bureaucracies and competition with other schools, which affected Riverview's resources for ELLs:

> So many other schools are experiencing this because every time I talk to an administrator ... they tell me about going to meetings where that's literally what they talk about: the need for more instructors, for more ESL teachers ... That's what they keep telling the [district] board. We need more support, and although that's a long-term goal, it's what we need. We need more instructional teachers who are bilingual ... There is a short-term issue of what are we going to do in the meantime because ... kids still need things.

The student leader understood that administrator intentions to pressure the district for more bilingual and ELL support staff did not provide immediate, concrete resources to current ELLs at Riverview. The student leader described a snowballing phenomenon experienced by ELLs: ELLs face difficulties understanding academic subjects, which then negatively affects their test scores and their success in transitioning to college. PMC mentors also mentioned hearing from ELLs their frustrations when teachers did not grade holistically and, instead, favored "English acquisition." Some mentors described how ELLs unfairly received low grades because of struggles with English fluency, despite their efforts to meet assignment requirements. For PMC leaders, supporting ELLs was *the* social justice issue for Riverview.

However, school officials provided more positive views of ELL-school-based support. The sense of urgency with which student leaders wanted ELL support and changes in the school was not shared or perhaps fully appreciated by school officials. For example, Ms. D, a Riverview administrator, described how teachers collaborated to meet the diverse needs of ELL students: "I feel that we have a pretty personalized approach to making sure that if you come to school, you get what you need and you also get a lot of the things that you want. So, I think that kind of makes us special, a special place." Mr. T, described above, noted how teachers were able to serve diverse students regardless of the unique circumstances that characterized their lives:

> The supports that we provide are the supports that a fourteen to eighteen-year-old needs. Independent of all the other factors in their life. And a lot of our kids, they're poor, they're from poor families, again independent of their faith, their culture, whatever, we have those supports that we can provide. I think we do, do that.

Evident in both Ms. D's and Mr. T's responses is the belief that Riverview provides adequate support for diverse students, including ELLs, at Riverview. Social justice researchers who enact culturally responsive caring must recognize divergent perspectives among educators and students in real time in order to prioritize students' voices and advocate with students for structural changes.

We knew, for example, that student leaders recognized that the school was not fully meeting the needs of ELLs. There were more ELLs at the school than the two ELL teachers could support. The school had requested an additional ELL coordinator, but had not yet received that position from the school district. It was not until the end of the year, when we formally interviewed student leaders, that we realized student leaders' struggles with lack of power in changing school structures, such as teacher practices, to support and enhance the school experiences of ELL peers. When asked about the need for classroom mentoring on top of the mentoring sessions PMC created, Leticia said:

> It's just sometimes hard, 'cause I think, even then, [for] a lot of teachers there's an issue between equity and equality in the sense of teachers want to be fair by giving twenty minutes to all students. But sometimes that is not being fair. I think sometimes you have to use equity [to] treat everyone differently in order to treat everyone fair. And in the case of having ESL students in your classroom, twenty minutes for your native speaker might be enough, but for your ESL, it is not enough.

When PMC began, we understood student leaders' views in prioritizing ELL needs and creating change on behalf of ELLs, but we were not initially aware of how teachers and administrators held views that complicated the enactment of care and student leaders' empowerment through PMC. Culturally responsive caring requires researchers to empower students of color by engaging in dialogue and check-ins and centering these students' voices, concerns, and needs. Additionally, researchers enacting CRC can play mediating roles by helping teachers/administrators to bring students' perspectives to light and connect those perspectives to social-justice goals.

Our perspectives as researchers of PMC afforded us insights from teachers, administrators, and bilingual student leaders—but not until months later after we had transcribed interviews, coded and written memos about the transcripts, and discussed the data as a research team. Only then were we holistically aware of stakeholders' different views about ELL needs and how those views could have affected the development of PMC and its goals. It was not until we conducted and analyzed our interviews that we realized how much dominant perspectives among teachers and administrators about ELL needs and school-based practices contrasted with bilingual student leaders' critical perspectives about ELL school-based support. The lateness in which we came to understand these different perspectives and possible tensions affecting PMC and bilingual students' relationships with adults affected our potential for enacting culturally responsive caring with youth participants. Our researcher statuses and emergent roles as adult guides and partners for PMC afforded us the capacity to bring these divergent perspectives between educators and students into conversation. Earlier and more consistent dialogue could have supported CRC and the strengthening of a Y-AP by amplifying students' voices to support the shifting of power dynamics. In our ongoing work with PMC and Riverview, as we attempt to build CRC and the possibilities for a Y-AP, we are prioritizing conversations surrounding the complicated and evolving aspects of caring for PMC participants.

Navigating Tensions and Circumventing Assumptions to Promote Culturally Responsive Caring

We have learned over the course of our now two-year collaboration with PMC and Riverview that there are many well-intentioned adults wanting to support ELL and bilingual youth of color. We recognize, however, in the tensions surrounding communication conundrums, role expectations, and differing perspectives on ELLs' needs, that we have missed opportunities for strengthening CRC and a Y-AP. We reflect below on our developing insights and the pathways we intend to forge moving forward. It is our hope that we may support other researchers, especially those starting out new social-justice projects, in navigating these tensions earlier on in their projects and circumventing assumptions that may prevent CRC from taking hold in schools and youth spaces. We share the following lessons: (1) explicate clear and regular channels of communication, (2) facilitate discussions about power and roles, and (3) determine shared goals while amplifying student perspectives early in the partnership.

Explicate Clear and Regular Channels for Communication

Both the mode and the timeliness of communication channels proved to be consequential in our initial work with PMC. We think difficulties in communication channels were exacerbated by our limited physical presence at Riverview, which is now nonexistent during COVID-19 due to in-person school closures. Therefore, we advocate for (a) ensuring regular, early, and multiple forms of researcher presence (e.g., online/ text messaging) at Y-AP sites, (b) identifying preferred modes of communication with youth, and (c) relating critical information quickly among and between researchers and youth during data collection.

Despite the time constraints of researchers, Y-APs depend on participants' consistent presence and active, regular discussions involving communication between youth and adults (Camino, 2005). Such interactions afford adults the opportunity to fine-tune "the art of restraint" (Larson et al., 2016) and calibrate when and how to weigh in with advice for youth. Researchers must then be regularly available, engage in active and consistent communication with youth, listen to youth and discuss components of CRC and possible researcher and student roles, especially when becoming involved in a Y-AP. Physically being there (online or in the building) more often would have allowed us to more consistently discuss student leaders' work and concerns.

Clear, open communication channels accessible to youth should be identified and used to support CRC. We often used email to communicate with Leticia; however, Leticia often used an app and texts to connect with mentors and physically knocked on doors to communicate with educators. Establishing common communication channels for a Y-AP could facilitate shared understandings of role expectations, program goals, and how to manage issues.

We also suggest that researchers talk with each other and regularly reflect on important perspectives from stakeholders. Had we met soon after each interview or read interview reflections and had we met with student leaders about interview reflections earlier, we could have begun to identify these "emerging tensions" earlier in the process to be able to act on them. Despite constraints on time, building in thirty minutes per week to read reflection notes focused on divergent perspectives on ELLs could have helped us to better promote CRC and actively build a Y-AP involving shared goals and strategies to meet such goals. Enhancing communication among all stakeholders can promote the development of youth and adults alike (Camino, 2005).

Facilitate Discussions about Power and Roles

Camino's (2005) work on Y-APs emphasizes the value of reflection during meetings between youth and adults. Without reflection, partnerships like ours can leave one of the key partners feeling isolated or undervalued. Talking through such tensions can be liberating for Y-APs. Having a mechanism in place wherein reflection could be fostered could have allowed student leaders and researchers to discuss, together, how to align mentoring with program goals and how to bring critical perspectives of the school to teachers and administrators.

Engaging in discussions about power dynamics inherent in Y-APs and schools more broadly could have allowed us to more directly interrogate with PMC students our roles and that of teachers/administrators in PMC. Through such discussions, we could have learned earlier on from student leaders about areas in PMC where they could have used support. Although we discussed emergent patterns and excerpts from interview transcripts with student leaders, we could have created more opportunities to analyze excerpts or notes together in order to interrogate how divergent perspectives might affect the implementation of PMC's goals and student-led work.

Thus, qualitative researchers in schools should seek out opportunities to regularly reflect with youth on the roles they play in Y-APs and facilitate discussions about the ways in which power shapes the experiences of different members of the school community. This is just one way in which qualitative researchers can collaborate with partners who occupy various positions in schools, and how qualitative researchers can navigate moments of conflict between educators and students, while still showing care for students. We recommend foregrounding these reflections for researchers taking up new projects with youth in schools.

Determine Shared Goals Early in the Partnership

Determining early in the Y-AP a set of shared goals between us, as researchers, and PMC student leaders could have helped with more concerted efforts to address the first two lessons learned above. For example, identifying students' and teachers'/administrators' perspectives could have provoked discussions about power and researchers' roles in amplifying student perspectives to school officials. Such discussions could have brought to light concrete ways that we, as researchers, might have helped elevate students' perspectives, concerns, and goals and communicate students' perspectives to educators. Our communication challenges described above might have also been uncovered in a goal-setting exercise. Through such dialogue that honors youth agency and leadership while offering adult guidance, Y-APs can become sites in which CRC is co-produced.

As we seek to center culturally responsive caring in our emerging Y-AP, we call for researchers working with youth to examine the extent to which they enact CRC and interrogate their roles in Y-APs. Mitra et al. (2013) emphasize the importance of adults in Y-APs who understand "how to scaffold the process of increasing youth roles in the partnership. Even more important, perhaps, is that adults sometimes neglect to recognize that they themselves need to change in order to facilitate a partnership relationship with young people" (p. 198). As we continue to examine our lessons learned, we realize that to practice culturally responsive caring, we will also have to change. Specifically, we must actively engage in dialogue about roles and goals, streamline communication channels, offer judicious advice while demonstrating restraint, and support critical conversations about topics related to power dynamics and social justice. By drawing upon the literature on caring, researchers can actively recognize and respond to power inequities and mediate between youth and educators to enact change.

Part Four

Collaborating with Universities, Communities, and Schools: Navigating the Challenges of Caring Research Partnerships

12

Conceptions of Care and Graduate Student Researcher Positionality: Struggling to Reconcile "Researcher" Care with Personal Moral Commitments

Van Anh Tran, Errol C. Saunders II, Shamari Reid, and Lum Fube

Given that graduate students arrive to their programs with well-developed moral and ethical commitments to communities outside of the research team (Weidman & Stein, 2003), the role that graduate students' own positionalities play on research teams is material to the ways knowledge is produced within the academy. Yet the dominant apprenticeship understanding of graduate student education (Sedlacek et al., 2007) often neglects how power dynamics constrain graduate students, since faculty members serve as gatekeepers to the academy, wielding considerable influence over their graduate students' career and research trajectories (Johnson et al., 2018; Lee, 2008). This chapter explores the challenges we encountered, as graduate student researchers (GSRs), in caring for youth on a qualitative research team, which did not discuss understandings of care prior to working with the youth in the school-based study. We argue that it is particularly important for GSRs to understand what moral/ethical/equity commitments they are bringing to a team, grapple with what compromises they are and are not willing to make for the sake of research, and how the power dynamics they encounter doing research might bind their senses of agency. We make these arguments because we believe that how GSRs conceive of care impacts the way that young people are cared for in research, regardless of how our liminality may position us on- and off-site. Furthermore, we believe that research teams will more effectively care for youth in research by proactively developing a collective, inclusive, working definition of care.

As GSRs from marginalized communities, each with significant K-12 teaching experience, we reflect on how identity and power impacted our conceptualizations of care. Our experiences working with marginalized youth in the same school-based qualitative research project revealed discordance between how members of the research team thought of and enacted care. As we explore these discordances, we four authors have been careful to focus our writing on our experiences as GSRs, the power dynamics that those experiences illuminated on our research team, and the necessity of addressing these power dynamics for creating a firm foundation for shared understandings of care when working with youth in qualitative research. Our reflections in this chapter invite conversation on the layered structures, actions, and dynamics that mediate caring for young people in qualitative research, and we hope that researchers take up the charge to center the well-being of young people by partaking in honest discussions around each team member's understanding of care. The power dynamics that complicate each team member's enactment of care could ultimately result in (un)care toward the young people, or failing to disrupt actions that go against our moral and ethical stances. As such, we are also pushing primary investigators (PIs) to treat their GSRs as agents with moral commitments who need to be both respected and cared for, if not for our shared humanity then for our shared commitments to care for youth in qualitative research.

Throughout this chapter, you will notice that issues of positionality and power relations are ever present in the production of knowledge. There may be moments in the chapter when you, as a reader, will have questions or confusion about our nondisclosure of relevant facts. Those moments of nondisclosure are real: they are intentional and necessary for us, as graduate student researchers (GSRs), to navigate the fraught power dynamics inherent in publicly recounting our research experiences.

Conceptual Framework

Positionality

Over the courses of our respective tenures on this research team, power dynamics became visible to us as we observed the consequences of speaking or not speaking, the ways that our agency was stifled when we did speak, and our own resulting complicity in the uncare that we feel was afforded to the youth in the study (Johnson et al., 2018; Lee, 2008). We could not always name the tensions present in the interactions between our actions and identities and those of the communities with whom we were working and for whom we care deeply (Alcoff, 1991–1992). Furthermore, these dynamics did not dissipate on site. Instead, they became amplified as they conflicted with our affective enactments of care toward our student participants, especially enactments stemming from our identities as teachers.

At our core, we four authors are committed to education as a transformative tool for social change that can alter existing social structures (Fine & Weiss, 1996). The Black Feminist Statement by the Combahee River Collective (2015) says, "We realize that the only people who care enough about us to work consistently for our liberation is us" (p. 212). This powerful statement expands the feminist principle that the personal is political and informs our own reflections about how care can be conceived. Yes, our personal notions of care were and continue to be central to the formation of our identities, positionalities, and agency (Biesta & Tedder, 2007). Yet, as graduate students and people of color, both on site and in our team meetings, we did not "suddenly become powerful in our new identities and roles as university researchers; we "carr[ied] our baggage with us" (Villenas, 1996, p. 726). Brayboy and Deyhle (2000) implore us to examine the researcher's dual position of "insider/outsider" and the cultural ramifications of these relationships.

We hope that this chapter complicates that duality: as GSRs we were simultaneously constructed by our PIs as researchers, students, and teachers in ways that reinforced the hierarchical power arrangements that privileged our PIs knowledge above ours while justifying the extraction of our labor for research purposes. As students, our PIs made it clear that we should defer to their understandings with regard to research plans and what aspects of our identities we ought to embody on- and off-site (Lee, 2008). As teachers, we were constructed to have pedagogical knowledge that could be useful on site to enact the curriculum of the research (Biesta et al., 2017). As persons of color, we were positioned for the possibility that our sociocultural identities might help students at the site connect with us (Achinstein & Aguirre, 2008) and the research. Yet our identities as researchers were what sewed together the contradictions of being neither students nor teachers at the school site, only given fragile entry for the purposes of working with youth.

Care

Our positionalities and lived experiences have led us to the following understanding of care. Care for young people in research, motivated by love, must not only embody and enact our moral and ethical stances toward the youth, but it must also interrupt anything that might threaten their humanity. Therefore, ignoring our moral and ethical commitments as critical educators to interrupt all that threatens the humanity of young people with whom we research, to us, might be regarded as (un)care. Our collective conception of care resonates with Sellar (2009) who writes about the embodied, affective enactment of our moral and ethical stances toward the youth with whom we are researching. As such, care for youth is drawn from our internal values and expectations (Laletas & Reupert, 2016) and grounded in our identities (Velasquez et al., 2013). It is also our shared belief that it is possible to have a collective understanding of care but there are different approaches to enacting care due to our unique, individual positionalities.

Methodology

To be clear, the data for this chapter are our experiences as GSRs rather than the data "owned" (Tuck & Yang, 2012) by the research team. We came together as graduate students who had once been GSRs on the same research project and engaged in collective reflexive dialogues (Kahn, 2016; Rothman, 1996) as a practice toward our own healing (Huber, 2009). During our initial conversations, we created a space to tell and explore one another's stories about our different experiences on the research team. These dialogues allowed us to engage in critical conversations about moments of internal dissonance, interrogating our moral commitments to communities made up of people whose lives are shaped by their raced and gendered bodies, native languages, countries of origin, and socioeconomic and immigration statuses (Delgado Bernal et al., 2012). These conversations also afforded us an opportunity to further dive into how our positions as graduate students complicated our practices of agency (Biesta & Tedder, 2007) within the research team and how this manifested in our care for youth participants.

Our explorations took many shapes. We had text and phone conversations, in-person discussions, and produced written reflections. We shared our written reflections using word documents on a shared Google drive and often used the comment function to react personally and intellectually to each other's reflections. Our explorations ranged from our ideas around how identity and power impacted our conceptualizations of care, the ways that care was enacted by the team when working with youth, to how we saw care being practiced in different spaces of the research. After noting the salient themes that arose in our collective explorations, we revisited the data to explore the following questions:

- What are our commitments? What do we see are others' commitments? How did we navigate the boundaries of our commitments?
- How do we understand positionality in relation to the young people on our projects? How did this impact how we engaged with the team and the youth?
- What is the role of power?
- How have young people been impacted by our presence and interactions with them, as well as by the overall research project?

In revisiting our collective conversations, we were able to co-embark on a multi-ethnographic encounter exploring what we learned about enacting care with young people in qualitative research as GSRs. As many other duoethnographers have done (see Sawyer & Norris, 2015), we sought to turn the inquiry lens on *ourselves* and reflect on what we can learn about our own beliefs and ideologies around notions of care, ultimately arriving at new understandings of our experiences with care as GSRs working on a research team comprised of members with different life histories and conceptualizations of care, and what such an exploration means to/for us now (Wilson & Oberg, 2002). What follows is a collage (Sawyer & Norris, 2015) of our positionalities, narratives, and initial reflections followed by a conclusion that flows from our present-day reflections and attempts at making meaning of these conversations.

Positionalities

Lum

During my early adolescent years, I boarded a plane and was transported to a different universe consisting of beautiful, but ideologically complex, worlds with no maps or designated tour guides. In this universe, America, the drawing of settler colonial boundaries was layered with intricately woven ideological boundaries that came crashing into pernicious remnants of ideological and cartographic demarcations from the Scramble for Africa that would come to shape my understanding of self. In America,

I was "African"—a construction that caused dissonance, challenging and reconstructing my notions of self and where I was situated in what I perceived as ideological warfare. Colonial lines were redrawn and all of us who traveled from different places on the continent with varied ethnicities and languages were flattened to being "Africans" and thus began the renegotiating of one's identity. Because of collective experiences in this new universe, my African friends became my brothers and sisters in ways that I could have conceived were we to have remained in our respective countries. Consequently, as a graduate student, when I was presented with an opportunity to work with youth who shared a similar background as mine, I was elated.

Errol

I am a big, gay, Black man. I grew up in Los Angeles on welfare, the eldest of four, and helper to my extraordinary mother who had the misfortune of having the love of her life and father of her children battle with drug addiction over the course of my childhood. I wear bowties and oxfords and loafers with wooden click-clack heels. I code switch and fan-thwap. And I have been a teacher since the dining room table when we kids were all assigned to explain to everyone what we'd learned at school that day ... a teacher since the "mom-work" of library trips, book reports, and reading to one's younger siblings.

Now, as one of a few Black men teaching on a high school campus, I believe that it is both my job and my moral obligation to be my full self in spaces with students. For some, so that they might see part of themselves reflected back to them as the possible foundation of a relationship with a teacher on campus (Watson, Sealey-Ruiz, & Jackson, 2014). For others, so that they might go out into the world with some experiences with a real Black man, a real gay man, a real first-generation college student, a real kid who grew up poor, a real *whatever it is they see in me* (Achinstein & Aguirre, 2008) to combat the inevitable caricatures they will encounter in life.

Shamari

My journey to membership on the research team we explore in this chapter most certainly begins with writing one of the first papers for my doctoral program. Throughout that paper I explored the possibilities of designing, carrying out, and positioning research so that it may serve as a source of therapy for those who have experienced marginalization. That paper is not just a memory, it is my reason. As a cisgender Black gay man from Oklahoma City who learned too much, too early about racism, homophobia, classism, and other insidious forms of discrimination, I came to the academy to heal myself and others. Before coming to the academy, those same beliefs led to my time in classrooms as a teacher working with young people whose lives the white supremacist world wanted me to believe did not matter. The same beliefs that led me to a research team working with young people who had their own relationships with marginalization and oppression. I thought, "how can we all heal together?" Thus, I joined the team with a conception of care that was grounded in a desire to nurture the students' emotional and spiritual growth, and promote their healing.

Van Anh

I see theorizing and practicing care as facilitating access to collective joy (Piepzna-Samarasinha, 2018). Through this lens, teaching means building and creating; learning means sustaining the connections between us. I decided to enter the academy as a high school history teacher because I saw an opportunity to add capacity to the communities in which I lived and breathed, and to continue to practice the agency that being a student organizer and educator taught me. With these experiences and beliefs, I joined this research team as a first-year graduate student, eager to learn from and alongside my peers and the young people with whom we would be engaging. In this moment, I saw the possibility of nurturing the intersection of my identities as a graduate student, as a classroom educator, as a person of color; I saw our time together as learning what exactly it means to lean on each other, to love each other. I soon realized that there were a variety of webs with varying conceptualizations of care that converged within the research space. How do we learn, then, to care for one another in a way that uplifts one another while naming the ways that our notions of care can clash?

Moments of (un)care

Lum

When I initially learned about the research project, I was excited! The idea of co-constructing a club with students in their school seemed wonderful. However, my own conception of a club, an inclusive community where all students who self-identified as part of the community could join, was very different from our PIs' selective approach. I found myself at an ethical impasse because I dreaded the unintentional ways we would isolate community members and the ramifications of our presence in this particular community of students and the larger school community. We needed to frame the project in a way that was transparent about who would be part of this research and why. I feared news about this new club would travel around the school and that other students who were part of the community and who, in theory, should have been able to join the club would feel excluded. Furthermore, the students chosen for the study—and therefore invited to be part of the club—unintentionally sent a message about the types of individuals we valued within this community. Lastly, the lack of transparency meant the possibility of other students from this community internalizing their exclusion as a rejection. My heart was heavy.

Errol

I often rode the subway home with twin brothers who were engaging in our study. We talked about their day-trading hobby, the ups and downs of the market that week, and their college aspirations and concerns.

One day during the session, when my job was to take low-inference notes (Bogdan & Biklen, 2007), one of the twin brothers raised his hand to explain why he stays out of public controversies. He explained it as a function of minding his own business and being polite. He commented to whoops and applause of approval, "even though I don't like gay people, I don't need to tell them to their face."

I was doubly stunned. Was it a secret that this fan-thwapping, pastel-wearing, subway buddy of his was a gay, Black man, and also sitting in the room? The brother and I had not ever talked about my homosexuality directly, but I did not consider myself closeted at the site by any means. But what was more stunning to me than an adolescent boy expressing homophobia was the coupling of that expression with approval from many in the class and the loud silences on the parts of the site gatekeeper, the experienced pedagogue running the session, and the PI in the room.

As notetaker, I was not positioned well to react in real time nor to do so without clearly rebuking the misjudgments of the other adults in the room that this behavior was okay enough to let pass. Furthermore, it had not even been a month since the whiff of misogyny from one student regarding another was rightly and heavy-handedly stamped out by the very same other adults, also in a situation wherein I was taking notes. Was this not exactly the kind of moment when our pedagogical instincts and commitments to care, responsible for shaping (not just witnessing) the civic ideas of the youth, was required? Under what circumstances and understandings of care should the one be acceptable and not the other? Yes, there were clearly and visibly many young women participating in the study. Yet is it not the invisibility of queerness that requires it to be more clearly normalized in the classroom (Sumara & Davis, 1999)?

I mentioned the seeming double standard of permitting homophobia at the site while loudly calling out misogyny in my reflective memo (Bogdan & Biklen, 2007) for the session. That reflection became the subject of a belabored and nearly one-way conversation in our team meeting. The PIs made quite clear that the silence was purposeful and that I ought to deal with my immediate and lingering affective reaction by "reconsider[ing] my positionality at the site." It was even suggested that I deal with such tensions by *deciding* to be in the closet during my research (as one PI had decided to do) so as to not have students' reactions to my sexuality get in the way of the data collection. As a kid who had been closeted in homophobic school spaces, I was both unable and unwilling to cede those spaces to bigotry. As a teacher and researcher, I saw no justification in being complicit in the creation of a homophobic space knowing that, odds are, there were queer kids in the room.

The incident did reveal to me just how bifurcated a notion of researcher positionality the heads of the team expected us, GSRs, to enact. For the sake of collecting this data to help this *population* of students, I was being asked to ignore what might be some very real needs of the students in the room. As a lifelong teacher, ignoring these needs seemed irresponsible at best and actively harmful at worst. Furthermore, a subterfuge was being demanded of me (by scholars purporting feminist ideologies of identity, no less), one that directly conflicted with my moral commitments to wielding my identities in strength as a pedagogical tool of representation that students might latch upon. I found myself then, as I continue to today, wondering "How can this be the right thing to do? How is this caring for me? How is this caring for our participants in the study?"

Shamari

Though I worked on the team at a different time than Errol, just as he recounted, one of my main roles was jotting down a few notes after each session held with the young people. I cannot remember with much clarity exactly what I was supposed to document, but I believe I was once instructed to record low-inference notes (Bogdan & Biklen, 2007). I recorded times that certain activities started, how the students seemed to feel about each activity, and how I felt "the sessions went." I often opted to exclude my personal feelings. However, after one of our sessions, I felt so bothered by what I perceived to be uncare for the students, that I included "my feelings" in my reflection. I included specific racist and homophobic examples of the ways I felt the students were being uncared for. This was not the first time I had perceived uncare. This was just the first time that I documented it in my notes. My reflection prompted a conversation in our next research meeting about jeopardizing relationships with those who granted us access to the site. It is worth mentioning that the person who I felt had mistreated the students was also the person who allowed us to work with the young people. During our team meeting, I was reminded that without this person's support, the research project would end. As I reflect on that conversation, I feel that other team members demonstrated great concern for the person who invited us into the space but did not demonstrate this same level of concern for the young people in the study.

Van Anh

I vividly remember that team meeting when Lum shared concerns about our naming the space of research as a "club." She wondered whether it would be possible to engage the young people in naming the space. Her contribution interacted directly with how we enact care with youth and the way we were taking into account (or not) the agency and the expectations that they have. After some engagement, the PIs directed us toward the next topic of discussion, and we did not return to this point of concern. In a group message among the GSRs, Lum shared, "I just get the feeling I'm doing something wrong." For weeks after this team meeting, I continued to think about what had transpired—how we moved on from this point and how we, as a team, were positioning both ourselves and the young people. It was after witnessing and listening to the stories of other GSRs on the team that I began to consistently wonder, "Why am I here?" In my role as a GSR, I felt farther and farther removed from building with the young people and one another and more and more steeped in centering "the research."

Lum

As a GSR in my first research project, I learned how naive I was about research. I started to reflect on my positionality and researcher identity, particularly how it unfolded in this project. I felt as though I was not encouraged to care for or see the participants as my brothers and sisters, but as a researcher who needed to distance myself and take an objective stance. I did not understand what this "objectivity" meant and where or when we were supposed to be objective because I saw my subjective knowledge as an asset to the collective knowledge we were bringing together as a team. I came to understand their requirement of objectivity as a request to check my epistemic knowledge at the door, which was an impossible request because "our identities are ways of making sense of our experiences. Identities are theoretical constructions that enable us to read the world in specific ways" (Mohanty, 2000, p. 43). I would have preferred a space where we, as researchers, were transparent, named, and engaged in dialogue about our respective identities and the lenses we used to make meaning and sense of what occurred on and offsite.

Shamari

During a project meeting, another team member shared that they were able to move between their various commitments depending on the space/role that they occupied. Thus, there were times that this team member could show up as an educator, researcher, or activist. And as it related to the study, they chose to put on their researcher hat and observe what was happening to the students, not interrupt it. This team member's notion of care contradicted my own. I feel a strong commitment to social justice, activism, and interruption, always. In fact, as I shared above, it is my commitment to disrupting the harm marginalized people face that led me to this work. Thus, as I move through different roles, my commitments remain the same. I do not share this as an indictment of my team member, but as an invitation to discuss the reality of team members having different notions around care, and how these differences are further complicated when there is a power dynamic.

Van Anh

Before joining the team as a GSR, I had never worked with young people in a research capacity. I am a teacher; I am a facilitator. In this way, I am who I am through my relationships with those around me. It became clear to me that the different positions we occupied on the team and within the context of the academy undergirded all of our interactions. As a GSR, I constantly second-guessed whether or not to voice my reactions or instincts because I was sitting between knowing that I was new to the role of a GSR (and, thus, wanting to position myself as a learner), wanting to be a "good" team and community member, and wanting to sustain the personal and professional relationships on the team. As an educator, I knew how I might have approached a situation to center the voices, experiences, and knowledge of young people; as a community member, I had an idea of structures that I might call upon to emphasize our interdependence. As a GSR, however, I became complicit in processes that I felt imposed our understandings and framings onto others.

Shamari

As a GSR, I felt that my beliefs and commitments were second to those of the PIs. In addition, I felt discouraged from speaking up because of these power dynamics and the fact that one of the PIs was my academic advisor. I thought about my status in my program, my funding, my ability to successfully defend my dissertation proposal in front of these folks, and as always, I thought about the young people. And it was my commitment to them and my beliefs that led me to share with the research team that I could not idly stand by while young people were, based on my notion of care, being uncared for. After a conversation around our different ideas of harm, love, and care, I was asked to move into a different role on the team so that I would not have to witness the students being "uncared for."

Lum

Our project was intentionally designed to examine students' notions of belonging, but we did not take the time to examine how these notions unfolded in our research team, which impacted the ways we related and mis/understood one another. The lack of harmony between our notions of care was not named or explored because time was not spent cultivating an environment or community within the team to have meaningful conversations about our conflicting identities, commitments, and how it impacted the ways we engaged on site with stakeholders and facilitated conversations with students. Consequently, this led to us having conflicting views and understandings that went unspoken, silently tiptoeing around the power dynamics that ensued from the lack of transparency and dialogue around our individual and collective experiences.

Van Anh

Notions of community, belonging, and care interacted with reflections of my positionality more than ever before. Who was the self that I should bring into research team meetings? Is this the same person that should work with young people? What did these selves prioritize and why? As I waded through the uncertainties of what it meant to be a GSR, I found that it was through my conversations, interactions, and communing with other GSRs on the team that I was able to make explicit who I am, where I come from, what brought me here, and what keeps me here. It was in these conversations—through Gchat, WhatsApp, Zoom, and over numerous meals—that we explicitly spoke about our commitments and values as whole people, that we shared stories from our childhood, bonded over our teaching experiences, asked one another questions about our coursework and programs, and pondered what exactly we had gotten ourselves into when decided to enter academia. On the team, I found true camaraderie and friendship with the GSRs. And I do not think I would have gotten there, if I did not feel I could trust them. I trusted the GSRs on the team because I knew them, and I knew them because they wanted to know me; they held space for me and my stories and gave me the gift of their stories. We encouraged one another and sought opportunities to step into our power. These interactions gave me the space to reflect on how much I value continuity and reciprocity within relationships of care—not as abstract "research" concepts, but as practices that we enact in our everyday lives and interactions, as values that we embody.

Conclusion

In reflecting on who we are and the ways that differing conceptualizations of care impact research partnerships, we are coming to understand that our reflections are imperfect and unfinished. By focusing on dynamics and impacts of power that arise on a research team, we see how misalignments in conceptualizations of care impact the care of the young people with whom we were working. Our experiences demonstrate that coming to a collective understanding of care among a research team is pivotal not only to the cohesion and strength of the team, but to the ways we engage in research partnerships with schools and young people. We continue to grapple with the fact that there were situations in which we felt like the youth were experiencing uncare and yet, we remained silent. Grappling with our own complicity, we have been compelled to try to identify why we felt stifled in enacting our own notions of care in the research. This process has been one way that we as individual GSRs and as a collective have seen both the complexity and the necessity of honoring our values, commitments, beliefs, and selves within research spaces. There are multiple and ongoing opportunities to act.

We offer the following suggestions to other GSRs as they consider membership on research teams so that they trust the experiences that ground them, build ongoing reflective communities, and sustain transparent research relationships:

- During initial conversations with PIs, ask:
    - What are the theoretical, epistemological, and ontological underpinnings of the research methodology? More specifically, how do these look in practice both during team meetings and during field work?
    - What structures will be in place for the research team to collaboratively discuss and work through conflict?
    - What is your stake in this work? What brought you to this project? How do you conceive ownership over the research?
- As you are making a decision to join the team, send the questions that you have over email. Doing so will ask the PIs to articulate, for the record, their responses and give you an opportunity to read, process, and evaluate their responses. You will also have the opportunity to familiarize yourself with scholars and ideas that might be referenced.
- Once you are on the team, suggest that time is devoted to an orientation both to the research and to one another. At this meeting: Ask the questions, "What brought you to this work? Why are you here?"
    - Gauge the way that different members of the team are named, invited, and recognized. This will illuminate orientations toward research, generosity, collaboration, and ownership.
- During moments when you might feel tension or confusion, ground the conversations and questions that you have within the language of the research proposals. Ask the questions: "Why?" and "How?"
    - For example, "Why this particular methodology? How is it being enacted in our fieldwork? Why does it look this particular way? How can we brainstorm additional ways this might look?"

- As you move into working with young people at research sites, consider:
  - Who is in the space and who is not? Why? Who is heard and who is not? Why? What are the different ways that young people are able to engage? Who are the gatekeepers? What are the dynamics between the young people and the adults in the space?

Research is personal. As you journey through your graduate studies, lean into your intuition with the understanding that your researcher identity is fluid and shaped by how you attune to moments of discomfort and dissonance. Reflect on what these moments tell you and ask yourself: *when I witness moments of (un)care, how will I disrupt?*

13

Pedagogical Reflections: Teaching Care in Qualitative Research Classrooms

Stephanie Masta and Ophélie Allyssa Desmet

The inclusion of adolescents[1] in qualitative research represents an important turn for the field (see Daley, 2015; Fielding, 2004; Leeson, 2014; Meloni et al., 2015; Schelbe et al., 2015; Starkey et al., 2014; Swartz, 2011). Much like the inclusion of identity-based qualitative research in the 1960s and 1970s (Denzin & Lincoln, 2008), the advent of more participatory designs since the early 2000s has encouraged adolescents' involvement in the research process (Schelbe et al., 2015). However, graduate-level courses on qualitative research do not generally discuss the nuances of conducting interpretative work with adolescents, despite classrooms often serving as the only space where novice researchers might learn about and discuss the particularities of adolescent-centered research. There is more participatory research with adolescents, but this has not translated into the incorporation of these ideas into methods classes.

Drawing from a series of pedagogical reflections, we use our positions as instructor (Stephanie) and student (Ophélie) to illustrate what a pedagogy of care looks like in a qualitative methods course. By studying instructor decisions through a pedagogy of care lens, we found that teaching care in a qualitative methods course involves focusing on relationships over research processes, providing ongoing attention and engagement to care-centered practices in the classroom, and offering support and guidance to graduate students on enacting care in their research practices. We start the chapter by defining what a pedagogy of care entails, before describing the context of this chapter, our experiences in the classroom. After outlining the context, we discuss several lessons on what it means to enact care in educational spaces. We then conclude with suggestions for those who want to enact care in their own instructional relationships.

A Pedagogy of Care

Teaching and learning care-centered adolescent research practices involve instructors and students engaging in a pedagogy of care. A pedagogy of care requires instructors to actively foster and maintain pedagogic relationships with students, while privileging trust, acceptance, diligence, and individual attentiveness (Curzon-Hobson, 2002; Docan-Morgan, T., 2011; Walker & Gleaves, 2016). Hult (1980) identified three levels of recognition in pedagogical relationships: (1) when instructors recognize and understand the student as a unique individual, (2) when instructors recognize the student as someone entitled to certain ethical rights that the instructor is obligated to respect, and (3) when instructors recognize that students have certain needs and expectations that a pedagogical service is to be delivered and has rights that protect and guarantee that these expectations are filled. Creating purposeful pedagogical relationships is essential and of great salience to students, particularly when those successful pedagogical relationships connect cognition to emotion because both influence student learning outcomes (Walker & Gleaves, 2016). Based on this, successful pedagogic relationships in qualitative methods courses occur when instructors center the instructor-student relationship, design and implement class activities that involve care, provide support and guidance to students on how to enact care in research relations (Hawk & Lyons, 2008).

Center the Instructor-Student Relationship

In all classrooms, a relationship exists between instructors and students. However, this relationship is not always at the center of pedagogical decision-making. Hence, a pedagogy of care strongly emphasizes the centering of the instructor-student relationship. This centering occurs when instructors embed care, caring, and being cared for in the classroom environment, but do so in multidimensional and empowering and not static and unitary ways (Motta & Bennett, 2018). Embedding care happens when instructors foreground care as part of the overall instructional experience and do not rely solely on their disposition to enact caring (Motta & Bennett, 2018). Instructors who center the instructor-student relationship create environments that allow for academic discomfort, where trust, openness, and reciprocity are common classroom behaviors (Walker & Gleaves, 2016). Academic discomfort is important because it allows students to wrestle with ideas or experiences that are unfamiliar to them. Care is taken seriously as a rigorously developed process that is mutual, relational, and values difference (Motta & Bennett, 2018). Centering the relationship encourages trust-building and reciprocity throughout the course (Daley, 2015).

Instructors who center the instructor-student relationship also demonstrate skills and dispositions that model care. Noddings (1984, 1992, 2012a) describes three skills that model care: listening, thinking, and believing. Listening means being attentive to the person speaking. Thinking requires taking the information shared and using it to build on what one knows about a person. Believing is listening and thinking thoroughly enough to become fascinated and absorbed by the information shared. Qualitative methods instructors can model the care they want their students to enact as researchers by engaging in these practices with their students in the classroom.

Instructors can also model care through conversations on research reflexivity, which requires researchers to pay attention to their own experiences and reflect on how those experiences inform their approach to instruction (Graham et al., 2015). Instructors who practice a pedagogy of care in their teaching generally engage in the following actions: listen to students, show empathy, support students, actively support student learning, have clear and rigorous expectations, give appropriate and meaningful feedback, and show an active concern about the lives of their students (Hawk & Lyons, 2008; Walker & Gleaves, 2016).

Design and Implement Classroom Activities Involving Care-Centered Practices

An important component of a pedagogy of care is designing and implementing classroom activities that involve care-centered practices. To provide graduate students with opportunities to practice caring skills, instructors should create a classroom climate for caring. In this classroom climate, instructors and graduate students impart knowledge and instructors encourage graduate students to develop caring skills (Noddings, 2012a). Care-centered classroom activities provide explanations of various care-centered practices and offer opportunities for students to receive feedback on their enactment of care (Alder, 2002; Swanson, 1991). One important classroom activity is guided reflection. Guided reflection involves students sharing what they learned and situating their learning within larger power structures (Glowacki et al., 2018).

Classroom environments also offer instructors and graduate students many opportunities to practice enacting care in the research process. For example, instructors and graduate students can practice the consent/assent process (Daley, 2015; Garakani, 2014). Graduate students and instructors can also practice the type of vulnerability needed in building relationships in adolescent-centered research (Daley, 2015; Swartz, 2011). Another caring action instructors and graduate students can practice is democratizing power relations, especially when the research focuses on marginalized and underrepresented voices (Karnieli-Miller et al., 2009). Instructors should allow graduate students to think through where appropriate collaboration can exist in the research process. Lastly, instructors should encourage practice in research processes that increase participant power and decrease researcher control (Karnieli-Miller et al., 2009).

Provide Support and Guidance on Enacting Care in Research

Instructors engaged with a pedagogy of care in qualitative methods courses provide support and guidance on enacting care in research. Care-centered instructors are those who interpret and translate diverse principles and motivations for caring and engage in specific practices that encompass the underpinnings of care ethics and pedagogical caring in particular contexts, such as qualitative methods courses (Hawk & Lyon, 2008). For example, instructors can use the steps of the research process (e.g., informed consent, data collection, writing up research results) to have graduate students model care in their research practices (Jardine & James, 2012; Kral et al., 2002; Krueger, 2010; Swartz, 2011). Instructors can also provide guidance on other forms of care in the research process, such as demonstrating empathy, showing active concern for participant well-being, adhering to strong ethical practice, and presenting data in non-harmful ways (Daley, 2015; Leeson, 2014; Swartz, 2011). Another form of support in a pedagogy of care is when instructors treat caring as an act of resistance. These acts of resistance might include defending students' choices and decisions, providing advice on navigating complex processes, and questioning the research process's status quo (Walker & Gleaves, 2016).

Context

In this chapter, we demonstrate what enacting a pedagogy of care looks like when teaching about adolescent-centered qualitative research. Given this, we draw from our experiences as instructor (Stephanie) and student (Ophélie) in two qualitative research methods courses: *Decolonizing Research Methodologies* and *Qualitative Data Collection and Analysis,* which occurred over a two-year time frame. Both qualitative research methods courses are advanced, requiring students to have some experience in qualitative research. Stephanie is an assistant professor of Curriculum Studies whose primary research centers on Indigenous student experiences in educational settings. Ophélie is a postdoctoral research fellow who uses mixed methods and qualitative research designs to investigate the talent development and affective needs of gifted students.[2] Foundational to Stephanie's research is using a care-centered approach in her work with adolescents. She extends her use of care to her instructional decision-making, modeling her classroom decisions on decisions she makes as a researcher. Even though many students in her courses do not work directly with adolescents, Stephanie finds it essential for students to learn what care means in the research process. Therefore, her pedagogical decisions reflect a pedagogy of care. Since Stephanie's pedagogical choices in the classroom directly influenced Ophélie's decision-making in her research process, we use our reflections on those pedagogical interactions to outline how instructors might enact a pedagogy of care in their teaching of qualitative methods courses.

Lessons Learned from Teaching Care in Qualitative Methods Courses

The process of teaching care often requires enacting care through a series of pedagogical decisions. A pedagogy of care in qualitative methods courses involves three components: centering the instructor-student relationship, creating class activities that center care, and providing support and guidance on enacting care to students engaged in the research process. This section outlines how Stephanie's pedagogical choices as an instructor and Ophélie's responses as a student represent what enacting care might look like in a university setting.

Enacting Care Means Be a Good Human First, a Good Researcher Second

A common refrain heard by students in Stephanie's classes is to "be a good human first, a good researcher second." Her goal in saying this is to reinforce the idea that people are more important than processes—or research outcomes. A pedagogy of care centers on the instructor-student relationship (Hult, 1980; Motta & Bennett, 2018), and care-centered research centers on the researcher-participant relationship (Karnieli-Miller et al., 2009). To understand what this could look like in a research environment, students need to see it practiced in the classroom environment. Many qualitative research classes focus on values such as rationality, objectivity, and neutrality (Ruck-Simmons, 2006). Still, it is essential to note that enacting care (in both educational and research settings) involves abandoning the idea that we are neutral actors. Sharing these types of situations, where instructors challenge "neutrality" of the research process, creates a sense of vulnerability also necessary in a pedagogy for care.

When discussing the importance of centering research relationships in her classroom of graduate students, Stephanie shares the following excerpt from fieldnotes from her dissertation research:

> *The other day I experienced what we would call a "learning moment" related to ideas of objectivity and "remaining neutral." After we wrapped up [what activity], Freddy [an x-year old Native student in the school where I was conducting research] paused and wanted to know if he could ask me a question. I paused and said, sure. He then went on to say, "Were things like this when you were in school?" The "this" implying racist treatment. I thought about my research training (respond with detached neutrality, but affirm) and what I wanted to do (be honest). So, I went with honesty. I shared that, "Yeah, things were like this when I was in school, which is one of the reasons I'm studying this now." He then looked at me and said, "Thank you. Because I thought I was crazy and making it up."*

Stephanie shared this to illustrate what centering a participant relationship looks like and how challenging it can be to make decisions in the moment about how best to do so (Karnieli-Miller et al., 2009). In her discussion, she highlights that researchers are often taught to be "neutral," and that affirming participants might manipulate the data. However, in the moments when participants need affirmation, doing this will not negatively affect the research. Instead it can let participants know they are valued. By being open and transparent in the classroom, instructors send the message that students can be open and transparent themselves in class—and, more importantly, in their own research spaces. Transparency and openness are keystones of a pedagogy of care and build a foundation for the other features of the approach (Froneman et al., 2016).

Stephanie also employs the "be a good human first" approach in her teaching. She consciously tries to demonstrate various skills and dispositions as an instructor that models care in the classroom space—in the hopes that students will then take up similar skills and dispositions in the field. In thinking through her experience as a student, Ophélie noted several instances when Stephanie modeled care:

> Unlike other courses (including qualitative ones), I found that the two courses I took with Stephanie were designed from a pedagogy of care meant to reflect care-centered research practices. Several little things contributed to my feeling of being cared for. Stephanie's classroom acted as a unique safe space where I felt

comfortable to be vulnerable. Her authenticity and openness created a welcoming atmosphere where I could safely explore my positionality, critically evaluate my research process, and openly reflect on my learning process. Each class started with an opening round, an opportunity to connect with other students on a personal level and a space for questions and sharing. The opening rounds served the purpose of breaking the ice and establishing rapport, as you would during interviews in a qualitative research setting. I perceived Stephanie's explicit focus on guidance and formative feedback as another act of care. For example, in *Qualitative Data Collection and Analysis*, we submitted our research journals. We documented analytical memos, twice during the semester and she gave formative feedback to challenge my thinking. The opportunity for feedback in the middle of the semester and my research work contributed to my feelings of safety and care during the course. Similarly, Stephanie's use of reflection assignments in *Decolonizing Research Methodologies* and, in particular, her formative feedback on the reflection assignments made assessments feel as if they were an extension of the classroom conversation rather than a high-stakes test of our learning. Stephanie's feedback did not include "corrections" or "valuations." Rather she gave her thoughts on what we wrote and posed questions for us to consider. This style of formative feedback allowed me to write authentic reflections and promoted a deeper engagement with the course material. Stephanie also had a wrap-up "party" as a closing event for each of the courses, through which she modeled the importance of carefully ending a caring relationship.

Stephanie's pedagogical design and the explanatory rationale for her choices—which she often shared directly with her students—created opportunities to explicitly model care, allowing students to reflect on the first-hand experiences of putting care at the center and the benefits that come from it.

Enacting Care Requires Ongoing Attention and Engagement in the Classroom

A pedagogy of care involves instructors who design and implement classroom activities focused on care-centered practices. It is not enough to tell students to treat their adolescent research participants with care; instead, instructors should provide ongoing reinforcement of how to enact care in their research interactions. To do this, Stephanie focuses on three areas: classroom arrangement, reflection assignments, and classroom discussions.

Enacting care is more than just interactions. It involves the physical spaces we inhabit. Similar to creating a comfortable space for participants in research interviews, instructors should organize their classrooms to facilitate care. Although a simple modification, Stephanie arranged the tables in a square shape, so that students face each other rather than all facing the front of the classroom in rows. Ophélie noted:

Stephanie designed the learning environment with care in mind. For example, organizing desks in a square shape created an invitation to put reflection and conversation at the center. At the start of the first class, Stephanie set expectations and explicitly centered those around care. She shared with the group why she chose this desk setup, and she introduced the idea of starting each class with an opening round as an act of care. Stephanie explained that the opening round was to give students some time to transition from whatever activity they came from to the learning activities that she had prepared for us. The opening round allowed us time to redirect our focus, while simultaneously giving us space and opportunity to share what was on our minds, however big or small, personal or professional. Therefore, the opening round helped frame the class as an open conversation about our experiences as researchers.

The opening round is a weekly question Stephanie posed to the class, designed to take up the first twenty minutes of class as students settled in for the three-hour evening session. Questions typically invited students to share something about themselves that would not be normally shared in the course of classroom conversation (e.g., "What are your thoughts on snow"). The purpose of this was two-fold: to allow students and the instructor to get to know each other to facilitate trust, which is critical to teaching and research relationships, and to demonstrate how to build rapport, a crucial element of the research relationship—particularly with adolescents. Role modeling strategies for building trust and rapport gave students ideas on how to do this in their research (Karnieli-Miller, 2009).

Another form of enacting care in the classroom involves the type of assignments instructors create for students. Stephanie used specific writing prompts that asked students to engage with the concept of care as it applied to their research. Assignments should allow students to think through (or practice) how to enact care in their research practices and provide instructors with the opportunity to provide care-centered feedback. Stephanie designed her prompts around the type of feedback she wanted to provide to the students. Care-centered feedback is essential for students to learn about care (Alder, 2002; Swanson, 1991). A pedagogy of care emphasizes student reflection as a part of building a care-centered practice (Noddings, 1984, 2012a). Ophélie shared how reflections informed her practice:

> The reflection assignments that we worked on within the *Decolonizing Research Methodologies* class were a particularly inviting tool to think through positionality and other complicated aspects of conducting educational research with adolescents (at least for me). In those written reflections and the proceeding readings and classroom conversation, I learned to question all parts of the research process. Those reflection assignments helped me dive deep into my positionality and the choices I can make as a researcher to decolonize my work. For example, I only fully realized the participant-researcher relationship's complexity when we were assigned a reading in which Mangual Figuaroa (2014) discussed an experience where she was asked to take custody of her participants' children when the participants were deported. This reading led to a vital classroom discussion in

which we explored the intensity of relationships built while conducting qualitative research studies.

The purpose of reflection is to have students think through situations that might occur in the research process prior to them occurring. While one cannot account for everything in the process, recognizing where enacting care might be necessary is important for student researchers.

Lastly, Stephanie used classroom discussions as an opportunity to share her own experiences with care in the research space. This type of expert-novice sharing allows students to ask questions and process through other scenarios they might encounter that require a care response. Stephanie shared examples of caring practices in her research with adolescents, which her students found insightful. Ophélie felt this to be useful in her learning:

> There was real power in the authentic reflection of Stephanie's experience as a researcher. This opened the conversation and led to the authentic sharing of students' experience as a researcher. I remember many times in *Qualitative Data Collection and Analysis*, where Stephanie would illustrate principles and strategies with examples of her research struggles. Through sharing experiences from her work, she taught us about following participants' lead, building trust, dealing with stakeholders, gaining access, exploring positionality, writing about difficult or negative experiences, etc. Once, Stephanie shared her dissertation and the final published manuscript that appeared in a peer-reviewed journal to illustrate how much a manuscript can transform through the review process. This was such a validating experience for me as a student. It normalized the process of revising manuscripts and taught me how to navigate the peer-review process.

Demystifying how to engage in care-centered research is an essential component in a pedagogy of care. As Ophélie noted, having someone with extensive experience in this area and willing to be vulnerable with that sharing allows students to communicate their fears and concerns in the classroom.

Enacting Care Involves Support and Guidance Inside and Outside of the Classroom

A pedagogy of care also requires providing students with support and guidance on enacting care in their research both during and after the methods classroom experience. Although qualitative methods courses cover a range of topics, they do not typically engage with care. Having an environment where students feel comfortable asking for support regarding actual practices of care is tantamount to a pedagogy of care. Ophélie noted that having the permission to ask questions in class changed how she conducted research in the field:

> I remember struggling with the intensity of the relationships I was building with my participants. I had been so focused on detached neutrality that I had not thought of my role as a caring adult for my adolescent participants. I was looking for guidance, especially as I began to make plans to leave the field. I found little to no helpful literature and received such opposite advice from people who were not experts in qualitative methods. So I brought it up in class. Stephanie engaged my question and incorporated it into class discussions and spent time with me during office hours thinking it through .... Stephanie shared the complexity of navigating a friendship in the field. She shared decisions about leaving the field and how she had thought through various consequences of her design choices. For example, she described why and how she had organized a class party at the end of her data collection to end the relationship with the high school students in her study. She also shared that she felt a deep level of gratitude for her dissertation participants and this simple acknowledgment, brought me such relief as it allowed me to feel the same way about my participants. Talking things through with her helped me explore authentic and comfortable ways to navigate the dynamic with my participants and find ways to end my research relationships with care.

Being able to learn how other researchers enact care is essential for student researchers. Therefore, it is utterly important for student researchers to have access to qualitative method experts, not only during their course work, but as they engage in their student research as well.

Suggestions for Enacting a Pedagogy of Care

Conducting adolescent-based qualitative research requires engagement in care-centered practices. However, qualitative research courses often fail to discuss the various aspects of care, let alone research with adolescents. As Stephanie and Ophélie demonstrate, there are several opportunities for instructors and graduate students to discuss care. In this section, we present suggestions for enacting a pedagogy of care in the methods classroom and applying care-centered practices in the field.

Suggestions for Enacting a Pedagogy of Care in the Classroom

When teaching, instructors should explicitly teach concepts of building relationships, ending relationships, thinking through consequences, and working with adolescents from a care-centered perspective. By making these topics explicit, instructors create opportunities for students to ask questions, address anxieties, and prepare for what they will face in the field. Through class assignments, instructors should encourage students to think through their designs with the audience in mind and challenge them to think through a study from the care-centered perspective in working with adolescents. Most methods classes involve a research proposal or study design assignment, why not add relation-building, exiting, and consequences as part of the rubric focus? Instructors should also reflect on why so few students are interested in qualitative research with adolescents. Is it because of research interest, or could it be because it is difficult and uncertain? Lastly, instructors should model, dialogue, and practice a pedagogy of care when teaching qualitative research courses. Include adolescent-based research strategies in classroom lessons. Have students read studies with adolescent participants and discuss the different methodological components within the study. Bring in guest speakers who work with adolescents to provide insight into the various challenges encountered in the field. Discuss how methods, such as observations and interviews, require care-centered skills, especially when working with adolescents. Allow students to see adolescent-based research as an important and necessary contribution to different disciplines. Providing graduate students with recurring examples of how to engage in care will inform their research practices in the field. A pedagogy of care and its various components provide an ideal framework for teaching qualitative research methods because it mirrors the central component of care one must explore when conducting qualitative research with adolescents.

Enacting Care-Centered Practice in the Field

There are several factors to consider for graduate students interested in a care-centered approach to research with adolescents. The start and end of the research process are crucial, and graduate students should select designs that place care at the center of these points. They should be intentional about the qualitative designs chosen. Thinking through these processes using an adolescent-centered lens may lessen challenges that could occur. For example, Stephanie encourages students who engage in research with adolescents to "think like a middle schooler" and consider how methodological choices affect their experiences. Graduate students should engage in dialogue and reflection by seeking feedback from all the parties involved in study design and implementation (e.g., participants, peers, instructors, advisors). Ophélie tends to ask her participants how they experienced the whole research process, why they agreed to participate, what they learned from the process, and what feedback they have for her regarding the study. She then uses this feedback to influence and shape how she designs and approaches future studies. Most importantly, graduate students should take responsibility for their role as a primary carer in their research relationship with the adolescents in their study. Through accurate reflection and understanding of their role as a researcher and carer, they can shape a research agenda centered on care both through the relationships they build and the design choices they make.

14

Establishing, Executing, and Extending Caring Community-Based Research Partnerships

Charity Lisko, Katie Woolford, and Rand Quinn

Universities—and their schools of education in particular—are reevaluating the ways faculty instructors and students engage in research, teaching, and service both in and with local communities (Benneworth, 2013; Bringle et al., 2009). These efforts are prompted in part by the desire to more effectively bridge campus-community resource gaps and research-practice divides. With the institutionalization of service learning in higher education (Lounsbury & Pollack, 2001), academic courses have increasingly provided structures for university students to work directly with K-12 schools and education organizations. Community-based participatory research (CBPR) practicums are one such forum for this work to occur. While CBPR courses have the potential to generate growth and enhance capacity across multiple stakeholders, they can also be fraught; despite careful planning and good intentions, differing collaborator backgrounds, interests, and needs can generate friction and conflict. Shifting priorities and contexts can also threaten to upend the research and the partnership altogether. These dynamics are not uncommon in conducting CBPR, and the extent to which they are overcome can depend largely on establishing and maintaining caring relationships among stakeholders (Kim & Schallert, 2011).

The philosopher Nel Noddings is among the foremost contributors to care ethics in education. For Noddings (1984), an ethic of care examines the relationship between the person giving care ("carer") and the person receiving care ("cared-for"). In caring interactions, carers are attentive: listening, observing, and setting aside (even if momentarily) their own goals and needs to prioritize those of the cared-for (Nicol et al., 2010). Noddings (2013) insists that the caring encounter also includes a response *from* the cared-for. This notion of care as deeply personal and interpersonal suggests that caring acts vary across contexts and situations, relying heavily on the carer's frame of mind and the cared-for's needs. To understand care within a school- or community-based research setting, then, researchers must consider how they demonstrate care *as well as* how schools and communities receive these acts of caring. Additionally, instructors of a CBPR course must consider whether and how students see them as caring (Alder, 2002; Kim & Schallert, 2011) as they co-construct knowledge in a shared intellectual space (Goldstein, 1999). An ethic of care, particularly among teachers and students, can also play an important role in elevating the human aspects of teaching over rules and course content (Velasquez et al., 2013).

Although research on care in education has grown in recent years, it has not adequately examined university-school-community partnerships. As CBPR courses increase in popularity, they must include intentional reflection on and analysis of their research relationships in order to avoid pitfalls, achieve reciprocity, and realize the potential for benefiting all stakeholders. By "stepping out of one's own personal frame of reference into the other's" (Noddings, 2013, p. 24), instructors and students can conceptualize *caring as a relationship* that centers community voices and responds to community needs by embedding community members in the research process.

In this chapter, we offer advice for instructors and students committed to developing caring community-based research partnerships. We draw on our respective experiences as students (Lisko, Woolford) in and instructor (Quinn) of a CBPR practicum focused on addressing local, on-the-ground issues affecting Philadelphia, its neighborhoods, and its public-school improvement efforts in partnership with community members.

Similar to many large urban districts, the School District of Philadelphia is under-resourced. In recent years, the district drastically cut programs, closed dozens of schools, endured layoffs, and borrowed hundreds of millions of dollars to meet basic operating costs. At the same time, the district serves a city with many well-resourced institutions, including the University of Pennsylvania, where our course was rostered. The city is also rich with human capital resources, including talented youth, parent, and teacher leaders, advocates, and activists. Yet, it is often difficult to create partnerships that span these various stakeholders and resources. Our practicum was designed to embed an ethic of care among university, school, and community stakeholders and to demonstrate how research can be conducted *with* rather than *on* or *in* a community (Gelmon et al., 2013; Harkavy & Hartley, 2009).

We ground our reflection within recent scholarship on CBPR and caring relationships using two partnerships from the practicum as cases to explore how relational caring may change between stakeholders and across time. Both cases illustrate how various relationships developed between instructors, students, and community stakeholders and unfolded during three phases of the partnerships: (1) *establishing* the relationship, (2) *executing* the research, and (3) *extending* the partnership beyond the semester. Our cases also offer examples of how power dynamics and shifting priorities may affect partnerships and how stakeholders can seek to re-establish caring relationships if they deteriorate during the research process. The chapter concludes with a reflection on our lessons learned for implementing and participating in a research practicum.

Community-Based Research Partnerships and Caring Relationships

A CBPR practicum provides students with structured space for civic participation and offers a grounding in the design, interpretation, and presentation of research. But it is much more ambitious in its aims. It is also a forum for community engagement that leverages multiple forms of knowledge and capacities across stakeholders—community members, university students, and instructors—to address a community issue of immediate concern. Though similar to service learning, a CBPR practicum is distinct in its emphasis on producing research products for community partners (Gelmon et al., 2013; Strand et al., 2003). Ideally, a CBPR practicum employs accepted forms of scholarship, leverages university and community resources in service of resolving pressing community challenges, and produces mutually beneficial partnerships in which stakeholders collectively determine "the issues to be addressed, the questions to be asked, the problems to be resolved, the strategies to be used, the outcomes that are considered desirable, and the indicators of success" (Bringle et al., 2009, p. 1; Gelmon et al., 2013; Miller & Hafner, 2008; Strand et al., 2003).

CBPR, service learning, and civic engagement scholars and practitioners have long understood that the relationships among stakeholders are a "defining dimension" of university-community engagement (Clayton et al., 2010). While referencing the "community" in CBPR is useful shorthand, it also carries the real possibility of masking tensions, alliances, and power differentials within participating communities (Mohan, 2001) as well as conflating community residents and community organizations (Bringle et al., 2009). To illuminate community-based research partnerships through a lens of care ethics, we leverage two frameworks, "SOFAR" and "ETT."

The SOFAR framework articulates the dyadic relationships between students, organizations in the community, faculty, administration, and residents in the community (Bringle et al., 2009). This framework unpacks commonly used phrases like "university-community," which suggests that collaborations are happening between two uniform groups. Differentiating students, administration, and faculty as three major groups within the university and classifying organizations and residents as distinct key players in the community highlights multiple opportunities for caring encounters within various research relationships. Each of these groups may have different goals, resources, roles, and power in the relationship, and as such may also have distinct patterns of communication and perceptions of care. Additional diversity may also exist within these groups (Bringle et al., 2009) and contribute to within-group dynamics of care; students, for example, may be in undergraduate or graduate programs, and some students may also be teaching assistants. Recognizing the multiple identities that exist within research relationships is an essential aspect of creating caring relationships that acknowledge and receive the full lives of participants.

The ETT framework provides a structure for investigating the complexity and dynamics of research relationships along a continuum of quality, from exploitative to transactional to transformational; it also identifies several key aspects by which to analyze research relationships, including outcomes, common goals, decision-making, and power (Clayton et al., 2010). Noddings' (2013) conceptualization of relational care aligns with the ETT continuum and offers additional language for understanding how relationship qualities may impact the carer and the cared-for. The exploitative end of the continuum reflects one-sided or unilateral relationships where the costs exceed the benefits for one or both partners, resulting in negative or even harmful outcomes. The transactional range of the continuum encompasses collaborative relationships that exhibit reciprocity and provide some mutual benefit while focusing on short-term tasks or exchanges. Some (but not necessarily all) partnerships may strive to develop transformative relationships where both partners benefit and grow, often through a longer-term, open-ended exploration of possibilities for enhancing the capacity of *both* partners as well as the partnership itself. The continuous centering of relationship quality among stakeholders throughout the stages of research supports the development and re-establishment of caring relationships as partners celebrate moments of reciprocity and transformation as well as recognize and seek to correct instances of exploitation.

Scholarship assessing CBPR and research partnerships in higher education acknowledges challenges that stakeholders encounter in building successful and caring relationships. For example, Strand and colleagues (2003) suggest that as university students participate as full partners in community-based research, they often confront questions of power and control in research relationships, including how participatory research can reshape power dynamics. In working to meet course requirements, students also encounter the challenge of balancing community needs and adhering to university academic standards (Fontaine, 2006). Despite this burgeoning literature, we have an inadequate understanding of students' roles as researchers and how students and instructors navigate both the insider-outsider and shifting carer/cared-for dynamics of research relationships with community organizations in short-term, course-driven research.

In the next section, we use an ethic of care, the SOFAR framework, and the ETT continuum to examine and reflect on the nature and quality of relationships established between stakeholders involved in the CBPR practicum. We focus on three of the SOFAR relationships: faculty-partner organizations (F-O), faculty-students (F-S), and students-partner organizations (S-O). We segment our discussion by three phases of relationship development: establishing the relationships before the semester begins, executing the relationships in order to design and conduct research, and extending the relationships beyond the semester into ongoing partnerships (see Figure 14.1). Panels A, B, and C of Figure 14.1 are adapted from Bringle et al. (2009). Arrows represent relationships between faculty, students, and partner organizations; dotted lines represent periodic relationships; and solid lines represent ongoing relationships. Relationships fall along a continuum from exploitative to transactional to transformational (Clayton et al., 2010). The three phases align to shifts in the primary university representatives participating in and maintaining the relationships with partner organizations; whereas the instructor of a CBPR practicum establishes and extends relationships with community stakeholders, students are the primary

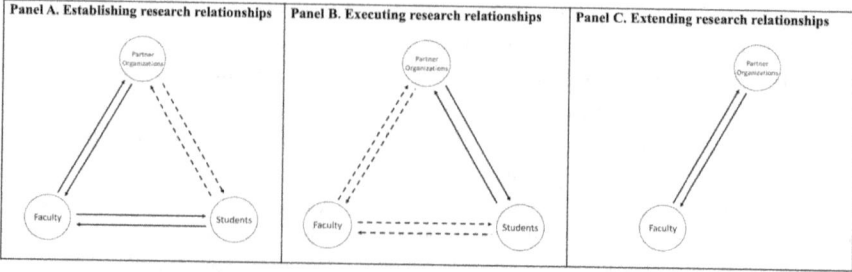

Figure 14.1 Caring community-based research partnerships

drivers in executing the research relationships. The importance of successfully navigating these phases and the transitions between them is particularly evident while executing the research relationship because it serves as a proof point for whether the relationships were properly established. The execution phase also influences the likelihood that the relationship will extend beyond the semester. As such, we devote a significant portion of the chapter to discussing relationship execution, particularly between student researchers and partner organizations.

Establishing the Research Relationships

Laying the groundwork for successful CBPR relationships requires developing early patterns of interaction centered around open communication and a common understanding of goals. The process of establishing research relationships involves balancing compromise—where power is intentionally tipped in one direction or another—with mutuality, where power and benefits are shared. This section examines the roles faculty, partner organizations, and practicum students play in establishing research relationships. To illustrate, we offer examples from our practicum experience.

Faculty-Partner Organization (F-O) Relationships

Before a research practicum begins, instructors reach out to community organizations to establish research relationships. In our practicum, the instructor (Quinn) and his teaching assistant developed partnerships with five educational organizations in Philadelphia: three public schools, an inter-congregational faith-based community organization, and an education advocacy organization representing a coalition of labor representatives and community residents. The research relationships began, appropriately, as transactional, driven by the course instructors and organization leaders. Initial conversations established a common understanding of the purpose and vision for the course, the goals and approach of each organization, and logistics including time commitments and norms for university-community collaboration. The initial commitment was short-term—just one semester—with the potential to extend the relationship if both parties expressed interest in doing so.

During this stage, instructors asked each organization's leader to identify a pressing need that would shape the project, thereby positioning the instructors as carers intent on meeting others' needs and tipping the power to define research goals toward the partner organizations. The organizational leaders' perspectives served as representative of their staff and constituents (students, parents, neighborhood residents). Instructors retained control over course logistics including the syllabus, timelines, and expectations for interim and final assignments. The final products for the course included an academic paper and a presentation to the partner organization. This dual approach to inward- and outward-facing final products reflected a desired balance between meeting the interests of the university and the stated needs of partner organizations. Overall, the instructors' approach to establishing research relationships sought to initiate a caring interaction, avoid exploitation, and lay a foundation for mutually beneficial outcomes.

Faculty-Student (F-S) Relationships

The second essential relationship established in a practicum is between the faculty and students. Predictably, the instructors also assume the role of the carer in this relationship (Alder, 2002; Kim & Schallert, 2011). Instructors initiate relationships and communicate with students through a course description, a syllabus, and early course sessions. These tools each present an opportunity to establish productive relationships while laying a foundation for future caring relations. Students respond initially by choosing to enroll and actively participate in the course.

At our practicum's first meeting, the instructors modeled their caring approach by framing their role as coaching, supporting, and facilitating student research, including periodic check-in conversations aimed at direction-setting, advice-giving, and problem-solving. Instructors also recognized students' primary responsibility as researchers by replacing in-class sessions with time for students to meet in working teams, visit school and organization sites, and conduct research activities. Finally, in framing the course, instructors used experiential anecdotes to emphasize how direct work with schools and local community organizations would require being "comfortable with uncertainty." This explicit acknowledgment established instructors in the role of experienced guides to help when students encountered uncertainty and underscored that reflection on the *experience* of the course would be valued in addition to the research products.

Student-Partner Organization (S-O) Relationships

Within the first few weeks of a practicum, instructors confront the challenge of extending the common understanding, mutual goals, and open communication established in the F-O relationship to newly formed S-O relationships. The hand-off from F-O to S-O also represents the first moment in the research relationship where the roles of the carer and cared-for are not predictably clear or consistent. As representatives from the university, students could continue to fulfill the role of carer as established by the instructors. However, a student's age, lack of research experience, or lack of local knowledge can complicate the adoption of this role. Part of the initial experience of the practicum for each student team is negotiating roles and accepting a lack of clarity within the S-O relationships.

In our practicum, instructors facilitated this transition with an information-gathering period featuring student site visits and conference calls with partner organization leaders. Leaders introduced students to the goals, mission, and culture of each organization, provided background information about their communities, and outlined their research interests. After participating in at least two information gathering sessions, students selected which partner organization's research project most interested them and formed research teams around common interests.

As may be expected at the beginning of a practicum, the relationships established between the university and our partner organizations began as transactional and were designed to complete a short-term task. Faculty, students, and partner organizations worked together to identify research outcomes that would benefit both the university and the community organizations, and to establish caring relations through receptive attention, common understanding, and mutual commitment.

Executing the Research Relationships

Once student research teams are paired with partner organizations, the S-O relationship becomes the driver for designing and conducting research projects. To reinforce this, the faculty role shifts to focus on the F-S relationship, providing support, offering advice, and encouraging reflection as students conduct research and navigate community relationships.

Student-Partner Organization (S-O) Relationships

Within the relatively short timeline of a one-semester practicum, student teams are likely to experience fluctuating highs and lows in the quality of research relationships. Student researchers may find that their relationships "move back and forth" along the ETT continuum (Clayton et al., 2010) and that stakeholders may periodically exchange caring roles with one another (Noddings, 2012).

In our practicum, the dynamics and evolution of research relationships within the execution phase varied by group along five key relationship factors: common goals, resources, power, decision-making, and outcomes (Clayton et al., 2010). To illustrate these differences, we draw on our experiences with two partner organizations. Hall High School (HHS, pseudonym) is a magnet school that draws students from across the city. HHS' research project was designed in coordination with the school principal and involved multiple groups of high school students as both participants and co-researchers. The Education Advocacy Alliance (EAA, pseudonym) is a non-profit composed of K-12 students, parents, teachers, and labor leaders who collectively advocate for citywide educational reform. EAA functioned as an intermediary between the university student research team and families in a Philadelphia neighborhood where EAA was advocating for the adoption of a community school model. As is often the case, the course focus on conducting research *with* a community was complicated by the multiple groupings of "community," and in this case, the research was conducted *with* a community organization *on behalf of* community residents (K-12 students and families) who were engaged as sources of data rather than co-researchers.

Common goals

The first objective of the S-O relationship is to establish common research goals by framing the community organization's broad interests and needs (identified in the "establishing relationships" phase) into a narrow research focus that can be reasonably tackled within the semester. Two questions regarding attention, power, and framing the research agenda arose early in our practicum as we sought to define common goals: (1) who in the community identifies the needs of the community? and (2) who in the partnership decides the final research agenda?

At HHS, the school principal expressed a need for creating an action plan to strengthen the school's culture and sense of community. The school had recently received accolades for strong academic performance, but the principal saw room for improvement in building cohesion among students beyond their academic success. Although strong culture and a sense of community are common ambitions in many schools, the research team wondered whether a strong school-based community was in fact a universal desire across stakeholders due to the school's citywide population. In CBPR, should the principal have the power to define a research agenda based on their own perspective as the organization leader, or should students and teachers craft the agenda? The research team at least partially resolved this question by inviting high school student participants to identify the school's strengths and opportunities for growth within the principal's goal of achieving a stronger school culture.

The EAA research team confronted the latter question of balancing needs between partners. While this research stage ideally features a collaborative process that tips power toward the community (Strand et al., 2003), the team found that the interests articulated by the community organization were too broad and far-reaching to tackle within a one-semester project. EAA requested support in developing a community schools initiative and wanted student researchers to conduct a feasibility study, identify missing supports, and produce an action plan for implementation. The articulated need exceeded the practicum student team's capacity, and the large scope of the work threatened to become exploitative of researchers' time and effort. After discussion with course instructors, student researchers drafted final research questions aligned to the practicum's academic expectations. Organization leaders, however, deemed these questions less helpful for making programmatic decisions. Viewed as a campus-community relationship, this interaction resulted in the students-as-carers being unable to fully displace their own needs and motives to respond to the needs of the community organization.

Resources and Power

Resources and power dynamics in research settings are often regarded as unequal, favoring the university based on the degrees, status, and experience of faculty members (Strand et al., 2003) as well as the institution's relatively vast financial resources (Harkavy & Hartley, 2009). In the context of a CBPR practicum and the S-O relationship, however, this trend may not necessarily apply. Student researchers, although representing the university, do not often bring research funding to the community partner, do not have doctorates, and (far from providing expertise) in some cases are conducting field research for the first time. This positioning may serve to balance the S-O relationship. What student researchers *can* bring to a project is time, energy, access to the university's research networks, and analytical or conceptual perspectives shaped by ongoing research (Strand et al., 2003). Partner organizations offer essential knowledge about their people, values, and experiences.

The HHS partnership deliberately included high school students in the participatory research process to recognize resources and power beyond the organization leader. The principal was notably respectful of students' capacity to enact change and expressed confidence that initiatives would be more readily adopted, as well as more sustainable, if they were driven by students rather than school staff or administration. In light of this perspective, the researchers designed focus group questions in collaboration with school leadership and included high school students in the research processes of analyzing data and identifying recommendations.

In comparison, the EAA partnership encountered more difficulty and experienced more back and forth in striving to balance resources and power. In response to the broad goals articulated by the organization, student researchers initially proposed designing a door-to-door survey that organization staff could implement later in the year. The staff, however, preferred that practicum students design and also conduct the research. Student researchers agreed to assist in conducting surveys, reflecting later that this was an attempt to rebalance power after they had unilaterally selected final research questions to pursue. Since the surveys were disconnected from the research team's academic focus, assisting with survey implementation demonstrated care by directing efforts to the community's needs rather than the researchers' interests. One example of achieving balance occurred later: the organizational staff and researchers collaborated to design data collection instruments with specific input from staff on how to approach and pose questions to local community residents. Although the student researchers did not have literature-backed language to describe these dynamics at the time, their experience demonstrated the dilemma that balance often means trading off which partner exerts power or overextends resources rather than achieving a consistent, equitable distribution of power and resources.

Decision-Making and Outcomes

Recognizing that truly equal participation in every decision of a project is "neither achievable nor always desirable" (Strand et al., 2003), identifying which partner controls which decision is another opportunity to show trust, mutual respect, and care. The intentional sharing (or transfer) of decision-making power and collaborative work toward mutually beneficial research outcomes can lead to enhanced capacity for both partners and move the relationship toward transformational growth. On the other hand, unsurprisingly, unilateral decisions can obscure or complicate outcomes and move the relationship toward exploitation of one or both partners.

The student researchers partnering with HHS sought to emphasize shared decision-making through the participatory nature of the research. Researchers first convened six focus groups of 9th graders to allow students to define, evaluate, and identify desired improvements in school culture. Participating students responded with a mixture of enthusiasm, some shyness, thoughtful observations, and as the principal had predicted, striking insights. For example, student participants expanded researchers' conceptions of school culture (initially focused on shared practices and school identity) to include interpersonal relationships through the pride they articulated in the school's diversity noting, "everyone has their own personality [...] if you are smart or socially awkward you will find your own group and feel at home."

The research team also invited a seventh group of 9th graders to comment on and interpret their peers' responses as part of the data analysis and coding process.

Student analysts contributed important insights such as the interpretation that their peers understood leadership as character and identity rather than position (students coded "being yourself" and "being driven" as essential aspects of and motivations for being a leader). This approach to data analysis demonstrated researchers' care by being receptive to and valuing youth as an important source of knowledge capable of both conceptualizing and evaluating the school's culture based on lived experiences. Involving high schoolers in the data analysis strengthened the findings of the research team, however the team also recognized that in the end it prioritized many of its own themes rather than fully adopting the participants' frame of reference. To more fully balance power, researchers could have extended the collaborative analysis session to include a conversation about the merits of the two distinct lists of themes with a goal of reaching consensus on a final list together.

The researchers also intentionally incorporated inter-relational co-construction of knowledge when presenting their findings to HHS. Student researchers presented findings directly to a group of high school student leaders, then facilitated an action-planning session to identify next steps. Involving high school students in the "so what?" and "what next?" phases of the research process reinforced the message that students, as valuable community resources, were both able and expected to take action on the research findings. One limitation of the forum, however, was the narrowed scope of participation. A common critique from communities is that after participating in research, they do not gain access to its results. In this case, the community as a larger entity was involved in the research outcome, but the individual participants were not. This may have reinforced a pattern of exploitation as students were "used" to conduct the study without direct follow-up on research findings.

Compared to the HHS partnership, the decision-making process was less balanced for the EAA group. Midway through the semester, the EAA research team experienced the impact of a core decision made unilaterally by the community organization. The research team had designed the project for a neighborhood community where EAA had established a history of support for new education initiatives. Student researchers hoped to deliver what the organization "need[ed] to act more strategically: quality information, data, and analysis" (Strand et al., 2003) by synthesizing the community's perspective on its own needs for partnerships and services. In the middle of the semester, EAA decided to shift their efforts to a new neighborhood where the organization did not have pre-existing relationships. As a result, the research team scrambled to take action that would still benefit the organization. In the end, they developed and administered a general interest survey in the new neighborhood.

After some back and forth with EAA about how to reframe outcomes given time constraints, student researchers decided independently to shift their overall focus to a case study on how EAA's leadership structure, organizing capacity, and communication practices facilitated or inhibited their goal of championing a new education initiative. Final products included recommendations for EAA and other groups interested in implementing new initiatives as well as a one-page summary of the originally proposed community school model for use by parents and community members at school meetings. During the execution phase, the mutuality of this research project substantially broke down based on two decisions that, while made for good reasons specific to individual partners, were also made without considering the other partner's frame of reference or how research outcomes would be impacted.

In the HHS case, the trajectory of the S-O research relationships could be largely characterized by care and mutuality, although after reflection, student researchers did identify decisions that could have been experienced as exploitative by the high school participants. At the school level, the project provided valuable information, data, and analysis that helped to inform a more strategic approach to the question of how to strengthen school culture. In contrast, the student team working with EAA experienced more volatility in the S-O relationship quality and struggled to achieve shared power, collaborative decision-making, and joint ownership of work products while executing the research. Although practicum instructors and students knew that flexibility would be important when working with community organizations, the magnitude and frequency of changes hindered the research relationship. Both sides experienced some level of exploitation, and the absence of clear acknowledgment of caring from either partner suggests that despite efforts from both parties to accommodate the other's needs, a caring relationship was never fully achieved (Noddings, 2012).

Faculty-Student (F-S) and Faculty-Partner Organization (F-O) Relationships

As university student teams primarily drive the execution phase of the research, instructors adopt roles that span liaison, coach, and troubleshooter. In our practicum, instructors were copied on all written communication between students and partner organizations and met with individual student teams at least twice during the semester. One tension that arose for instructors was how much and when to intervene with support. As coaches, instructors offered advice on how to focus the research, communicate effectively with organizational partners, and adjust approaches in response to challenges but tried not to intervene directly in the S-O relationships. Instructors sought to balance positive research experiences with allowing students to encounter the authentic and sometimes "messy" challenges of developing internal team processes for how to make decisions and divide work equitably. Collective struggle in these areas is a common experience in both internal and external research relationships and the instructors believed that arriving at collective solutions could build trust and efficacy for the partnership itself. Among teams that were able to establish effective relationships (for many of the reasons discussed above), this decision to emphasize coaching over intervening worked well. For teams that encountered confusion about roles and responsibilities or unforeseen circumstances, the arms-length relationship resulted in delayed resolution and frustration for all research stakeholders.

In our practicum experience, we reflected at the end of the semester as we sought to analyze and better understand the different research relationship trajectories. Since then, the lead instructor (Quinn) has incorporated readings examining research relationships into the course syllabus as well as coaching conversations, which provides students with common language and frameworks for reflection when experiencing the fluctuation and evolution of relationship dynamics.

Extending the Research Relationships

Once the semester ends, the students' relationships (S-O and F-S) conclude, narrowing the partnership to the F-O relationship between instructors and partner organization leaders. While student participation ends, the quality of the S-O relationships directly influences the prospect of extending research relationships (Clayton et al., 2010).

Faculty-Partner Organization (F-O) Relationships

Consideration of future research relationships occurred in the months following the CBPR practicum through an informal and emergent process largely driven by the lead instructor. Due to logistical complications as well as the difficulties encountered with EAA in particular, the course focused solely on partnerships with K-12 schools in following years. Fortunately, many of these school partnerships continued for several years, including HHS, which participated in each of the subsequent iterations of the practicum. In the most recent iteration of the practicum, the partnerships' focus was narrower; all research projects centered on youth voter engagement. This focus aligned with wide-scale youth voter education and registration efforts occurring across the school district and at the University of Pennsylvania. Restructuring the course by limiting both partner type and research topic improved instructors' ability to manage the course, but the lack of flexibility may have closed off potentially productive research partnerships.

In time, the lead instructor began to think about research relationships in a more comprehensive manner. Rather than developing school partnerships in service of a single course, the instructor tried to craft relationships with potential for multiple forms of research activities involving multiple levels of engagement. For practicum students, building on previously established research partnerships facilitated a deeper and more meaningful experience than starting a new project. For school partners, whether the research relationship lasted one semester or spanned several years, involvement in the practicum paved the way for *new* connections or strengthened *existing* ones—research and non-research alike—with other faculty, programs, and initiatives at the university. This ongoing, collaborative, and regenerative process has the potential to enhance capacities and build resource bases within partner schools and university classrooms. Moving forward, if the instructor and school leaders continue to revisit identities, amend goals, and pursue emergent prospects, the practicum may be seen as facilitating a move toward transformational relationships (Strand et al., 2003; Clayton et al., 2010).

Lessons Learned

The process of developing, maintaining, and in some cases attempting to reestablish a caring relationship is a joint effort influenced by the individuals engaging in the work as well as contextual factors outside of the stakeholders' control. Drawing from the literature and our lived experiences, we highlight a number of best practices and lessons learned for establishing caring research partnerships. We articulate these lessons in the context of community-based participatory research coursework, however, we hope the lessons also inform planning and reflection on broader research efforts in K-12 school settings.

Establishing Research Relationships

Faculty-Partner Organization Relationships:
- In initial outreach efforts, **faculty should solicit research topics and questions related to pressing issues faced by the partner organization.** Faculty can help partners shape these questions by communicating how a CBPR practicum differs from traditional research and service-learning, encouraging organizations to identify appropriate ways to involve community residents, and being realistic about what student researchers can accomplish within a semester.
- **Faculty should communicate openly to ensure a realistic and shared understanding of the organization's ability to support student research teams.** This includes each organization's capacity to meet with students and connect students to necessary resources (e.g., teachers, organization staff, youth, community residents, and programs or documents that may support students' work).

Faculty-Student Relationships:
- **Faculty should orient practicum students to CBPR and the importance of establishing relationships** centered around mutual respect and caring as an official part of the course.

Student-Partner Organization Relationships:
- **Practicum students and organizational partners should establish common goals** for achievable research that meets the needs of both partners and is articulated in language that is accessible and meaningful to both groups.

Executing Research Relationships

Faculty-Student Relationships:
- **Faculty and student researchers should communicate regularly** to ensure that students make sufficient progress in conducting research and to troubleshoot or address any identified obstacles as they arise.

Faculty-Partner Organization Relationships:
- **Faculty should be prepared to facilitate dialogue and manage conflict** if the relationship between a partner organization and student researchers begins to break down.

Student-Partner Organization Relationships:
- **Student researchers and partner organizations should communicate openly and identify ways to accommodate one another when obstacles arise** so that

changes are not unilateral. While this may look different depending on the type of decision that needs to be made, students can propose solutions and work with the organization to consider alternatives that still meet practicum requirements. To the extent possible, students should find ways to demonstrate care by prioritizing partner needs over personal research interests.
- **Student research teams should consider the partner's frame of reference and design final products that benefit the partner organization**; in addition to producing a formal research paper, students could consider producing policy briefs, handouts, slide decks, or other visuals that communicate information in a succinct and easy-to-understand format.
- When youth are involved in research as members of the partner organization, **university student researchers should communicate research findings to youth participants** in a relevant and digestible format.

Extending Research Relationships

Faculty-Partner Organization Relationships:
- **Faculty should debrief with organizational partners** at the conclusion of the course to learn what went well, whether the research met the needs of the partner, and what could further strengthen the relationship.

Conclusion

Research partnerships are not static; stakeholders alternate roles across research phases, internal and external factors influence decisions, and goals necessarily shift in response to changing needs and priorities. These shifts invariably shape the relationships among research partners, which in turn affect how the research unfolds and what is produced. It is therefore of paramount importance that those participating in the research remain attuned to how care is expressed and how power and decision-making are distributed as relationships are established, research is executed, and partnerships are extended beyond course-driven research. Moving beyond the rhetoric of macro-level systems and factors that need to be in place for a successful partnership, we argue that caring relationships underpin successful research. The suggestions provided here offer an opportunity for research partners to consider how to be supportive and caring throughout a research project's lifecycle.

15

Just Inquiry Rooted in Critical Care: Participatory, Intergenerational Research Tracing the Legacy of School in the Square

Samuel Finesurrey, Camille Lester,
Sherry King, Michelle Fine, and the Intergenerational
S2 Research Collective

School in the Square (S2) is a small, progressive charter school in Washington Heights, New York City, grades 6–8. The school serves 300 students, many of whom are immigrants, or the children of immigrants from the Dominican Republic living in the Bronx, Harlem and Washington Heights. In September 2019, the first graduating class of ninety-six fanned out to thirty-seven high schools across New York City's "choice" system. With a group of twelve graduates turned youth researchers, the S2 Inquiry Project was born: a longitudinal, intergenerational, participatory, and care-full project designed to accompany these young people as they would navigate high school in a city scarred by rising inequality gaps. As a five-year project, we anticipated gathering stories of struggle, as well as those of survival and triumph. We set out to collectively trace these stories within a context of gentrification, educational segregation, the aggressive policing of Black and Brown youth, the looming threat of ICE, and deportation haunting immigrant communities. Then we experienced the COVID19 pandemic, racial uprisings and on-line learning. Our research and our commitments to critical care, and each other, strengthened.

Our longitudinal study is ground in four commitments of *just inquiry*: a justice of *recognition*, enacted through culturally sustaining research practices; a justice of *relationships*, evident in deep respectful relations between educators, students, alumni, and families before and certainly during the pandemic; *a* justice of *participation*, manifest in students' strong sense of voice and agency in the Research Collective, and a justice of *re-distribution* embedded in the material and academic supports provided

---

The Intergenerational S2 Research Collective is comprised of S2 Students including Ashley Cruz, Ashley Cruz, Alondra Contreras, Ariana Peña Ramírez, Brandon Mendoza, Joel Almonte, Aidan Lam, Siarra Savinon, Noah Campbell, Jesslin Hiraldo, Lauren Santos, Samantha Bruno, Alyssa Victoria, Noel Columna, Naomi Pabon, Mya Laporte, Sheylany Paulino, and Nathan Boissier; Guttman Community College Students including Ramon Estevez, Viandry Mena, and Ariadna Villeda; S2 staff including Arnaldo Rodriguez, Evan Meyers and Sherry King, and Videographers from the Educational Video Center, Steve Goodman and Scarlett Holloway.

212   Care-Based Methodologies

to students, alumni, and families in Washington Heights, a community hit particularly hard by the pandemic. This chapter is the story of just inquiry rooted in critical care, a reflection on our first year of participatory inquiry. We explore how we crafted a multi-method participatory design, traced the journeys of youth forging diverse academic paths from middle to high school, and how we remained accountable to each other and most fundamentally to the young people and their community, before and during COVID19.

A View from the Gym: A Multigenerational Research Collective Is Born

It was a stuffy, hot, and humid day in June 2019 when approximately ninety 8th graders packed into a basement gym to meet with community college students and CUNY researchers. The graduating students were buzzing with expectation, anxious about what was to come in high school. How would their friendships and sense of community be altered? Through the introduction of this project, a multigenerational research team emerged.

First came introductions. Markers, crayons, and colored pencils covered the tables as students were asked to draw out their feelings to the prompt "As you think about your transition to high school, can you draw or write—what are you dreaming?" With this line of inquiry, we wanted to "normalize" and make visible the hopes, fears, and/or excitement these soon-to-be freshmen held about a looming transition to high school. With markers in hand, students concentrated on their papers, giggled with their friends, and whispered about their expectations of the next level. They wrestled with

Figure 15.1 *Student drawing*

making meaning of the dreams living inside of them. This first "method"—mapping—was designed to reveal our commitment to recognition, hearing from (and seeing) how young people envision their futures. We drew from Futch and Fine's (2014) methodological exploration of mapping as method. The images, statements, poetry—all hand drawn–carved space for individuals to represent complex and intersectional standpoints as you can see in Figure 15.1.

Students sketched fear of change, nervousness around making new friends, and goals centering athletic glory. So were anxieties about "God leav[ing] me alone," betrayals, tears, and wild dreams of fame (Figures 15.2 and 15.3).

Figure 15.2 *Student drawing*

Figure 15.3 *Student drawing*

After the maps were completed, we asked, "Who would like to share?" Nervous laughter, downward stares, and hugs filled the room as young people presented their work. Through their maps the students allowed us in, to hear hopes for success, fears of failure, worries of lost connections, and ties to their families. As their desires and anxieties varied, so too did their visions for the future. There were a number of self-portraits that depicted tension, nervousness, happiness, and sadness often within a single student's map. Recurring messages expressed dread of potentially losing something, someone, trust, and friendship. There were also a number of messages embedded within these maps with demanding language such as: "get your grades up," "keep grinding about your schoolwork," and "do it for your mom." And lots of basketballs.

After the mapping exercise, we asked the graduating students to write letters to themselves, as if they had just graduated from 9th grade. Honoring their funds of knowledge and their distinctive voices (Gonzalez et al., 2009), they authored letters from their future selves to their present selves. Quite a few volunteered to share. Joel stood to read his letter aloud:

Dear Joel
Congratulations! You passed 9th grade! I can't believe you also grew 7 inches and you now have facial hair. And that bullying incident wasn't as bad as you thought. So proud you are still friends with your School in the Square crew. See you soon—so proud, Bro'

Joel

At the end of this session we asked, "Would anyone like to become a paid co-researcher, over the summer and across the next five years?" A long list of names emerged. Interviews were conducted and, in the end, twelve young people were selected as youth researchers, paid for their time, committed to attending meetings, conducting oral histories, analyzing survey data, coauthoring scholarship, and participating in making a video documentary. The research collective was born, with an embryonic archive of ninety-six maps, ninety letters to self, and twelve eager student researchers.

The Human(e) Infrastructure: Creating an Intergenerational, Participatory Research Collective

In June 2019, just before we arrived in the gym, School in the Square was about to graduate their first class. Evan Meyers, founder of S2 and Sherry King, consultant, asked Michelle Fine (The Public Science Project, Graduate Center) to help them chronicle the academic, social, institutional, personal, and activist journeys of these rising 9th graders. Latinx immigrant youth and children from immigrant families were launching off to navigate high school. We agreed that the project would be student-led, intergenerational, and longitudinal, rooted in an archive of oral histories conducted over time with the alumni, through to their high school graduation. Michelle asked Guttman Community College professor Samuel Finesurrey to develop an oral history component of this research with his undergraduates, and Graduate Center doctoral student Camille Lester to work with the young people to develop and analyze a participatory survey of the graduating class. S2 extended the responsibilities and reach of Arnaldo Rodriguez, school counselor, to support alumni in their transition to high school. Twelve graduating students were selected to become youth researchers. Our team was forming.

Finesurrey was already involved in a major undergraduate-led oral history archive project and he invited three students from Guttman Community College to be paid as research mentors to the twelve S2 alumni selected as youth researchers. Ramon Estevez and Viandry Mena, both immigrants from the Dominican Republic, and Ariadna Villeda, the daughter of immigrants from El Salvador, have been instrumental in training youth researchers in oral history. By November we invited videographers Steve Goodman and Scarlett Holloway from the Educational Video Center in New York City to join, and document, the project over time. All of these people, their gifts and our collective community of knowledge and inquiry, are important to name. Together we form what Maria Elena Torre would call a participatory contact zone, an intergenerational, intercultural research collective (Torre and Ayala, 2009; Zeller-Berkman et al., 2020) dedicated to multiple methods, ground in the perspectives of youth researchers, and accountable to young people of color, their academic desires and their activist engagements (see Figure 15.4).

Organization	People	Role
School in the Square, Charter School	Evan Meyers Sherry King Arnaldo Rodriguez	Founder/CEO Educational Consultant School Counselor/Transition Counselor
Graduate Center, CUNY	Michelle Fine Camille Lester	Distinguished Professor Ph.D. Student
Guttman Community College, CUNY	Samuel Finesurrey Ramon Estevez Viandry Mena Ariadna Villeda	Professor Student Student Student
School in the Square	Ashley Cruz, Alondra Contreras, Ariana Peña Ramírez, Brandon Mendoza, Joel Almonte, Aidan Lam, Siarra Savinon, Noah Campbell, Jesslin Hiraldo, Lauren Santos, Samantha Bruno, Alyssa Victoria, Noel Columna, Naomi Pabon, Mya Laporte, Sheylany Paulino, and Nathan Boissier	Youth Researchers
Educational Video Center	Steve Goodman Scarlett Holloway	Founder Intern/Graduate EVC

Figure 15.4 *Our research collective*

Just Inquiry Rooted in Critical Care: Epistemic Commitments

Both the S2 school culture and the youth-centered participatory research design were committed to *critical care* as articulated by Renee Antrop-Gonzalez and Anthony de Jesus (2006). In their ethnographies of two Latino community-based small high schools, these writers describe loving cultures of high academic expectations, trusting interpersonal relationships between students and teachers, and a curriculum that honors the funds of knowledge that students, families, and communities brought into the schools. The S2 inquiry project builds upon this theorizing of *critical care*. We offer in this chapter the framework of *just inquiry rooted in critical care* to flesh out a culturally sustaining participatory action research project (Paris, 2012; Paris, Genishi, & Alim, 2017; Weis & Fine, 2000), theorized through critical race theory and intersectionalities (Collins, 1994; Crenshaw, 1989; Drame & Irby, 2016), and centered on the perspectives and experiences of immigrant youth of color as they traverse New York City's deeply uneven educational landscape.

This project is a braid of a very sweet, deeply relational and culturally responsive school with a youth-centered critical participatory action research project. At the heart of what we consider *just inquiry rooted in critical care*, we aspire toward four strands of justice: recognition, relationships, participation, and redistribution (see Fine, 2018; Fraser, 1995; Ginwright & Cammarota, 2002).

A justice of *recognition* has been foundational to S2 and to our research design. By recognition we mean that the school and the inquiry are structured to see, appreciate, and honor the rich cultural, linguistic, and personal "gifts" of the youth researchers, their families, and community including their home countries (see Fraser, 1995; Gonzalez et al., 2009; Paris, 2012). Students at S2 enjoy a Facing History curriculum dedicated to student inquiry into cultural, language, immigration, racial (in)justice, and rich cultural traditions and assets. With shared values, the participatory research project honors and chronicles students' (and their families') culture, history, struggle, and identities over time.

Relational justice lay at the heart of the school and the inquiry. Like the schools described by Antrop-Gonzales and de Jesus, students' relations with teachers and staff are exquisite; the soul of S2. This deep and intimate trust with dignity was most evident during COVID19, but also before. Youth researchers could (and did) turn to the counselor Mr. Rodriguez, the founder and other staff with needs, questions, confusions, pandemic-related anxieties, immigration-based struggles, and deep concerns about food, housing, and academic help. Relational justice was also woven into the research project with the inclusion of community college students from the neighborhood who have been essential to building cross-generational trust and a sense of educational possibility with the youth researchers due to proximity in age and a shared story of personal or recent familial immigration. While transcribing one of the interviews, Viandry was moved by what seemed like a younger version of her own experience: "I learned that I'm not alone. The things that I passed through, someone else is passing through the same things ... " These community college students provide the youth researchers with oral history mentoring and serve as slightly older role models, having journeyed a similar path through NYC's secondary schools just a few years earlier.

Just inquiry also involves the deep *participation* by young people engaged as co-researchers. Rooted in the belief, "No research about us without us," as a Critical Participatory Action Research project (Fine, 2018; see www.publicscienceproject.org) the S2 inquiry project centers the perspectives of the youth, with appreciation of their racial, cultural, linguistic, class, and immigration related wisdom and struggles. From the start, we wanted to ensure these youth researchers would transcend traditional understandings of themselves as "research subjects." They have become central partners in designing a project that uplifts testimonies honoring the experiences and aspirations of their peers, their kin, and NYC's immigrant communities. The project has been attentive to, and appreciative of the multiple identities, communities, and nationalities these youth claim, as well as the desires they embody, and the questions they yearn to explore.

Finally, the S2 inquiry project is rooted in a justice of material *redistribution*. In a city of extreme inequality gaps, we knew we had an obligation to consider what resources we could offer to redress the deep and multi-sector forms of inequity S2 students endure. Youth researchers (from S2 and Guttman) were paid a stipend for the training sessions, our research retreat and then additional funds per interview conducted through a grant secured by School in the Square. Youth researchers receive metro cards and food when we were meeting face to face. They are treated seriously as emergent scholars: they are given the chance to develop academic skills and experience as qualitative and quantitative researchers. Building young resumes, they present at conferences, participate in meetings with city officials, and they publish—including this chapter. The generosity, flexibility, and dedication of the school to redress inequity were, and remain, tremendous.

A final word about support. As the project was launched, we anticipated that over five years of documentation some young people might encounter difficulties in housing, confrontations with police, health issues, family concerns, and the specific obstacles facing immigrant communities. We did not want to simply document these struggles, we wanted to "be of use." In discussions between CUNY and S2, S2 founder Evan Meyers generously decided that Arnaldo Rodriguez would serve as a transition guidance counselor to the entire graduating class of 2019. Rodriguez is often the first adult to hear about the obstacles faced by graduates of S2 and their families. As he helps these high schoolers overcome the challenges they face, he also refashions their experiences of pedagogical apathy, parental anxieties, student surveillance, and school safety, among others into new topics for study.

In the chart below (Figure 15.5), we try to visualize the forms of justice that are foundational to just inquiry; delineating the epistemic commitments, illustrating some enactments, and offering up relevant citations.

	Justice of Recognition	Justice of Relationship	Justice of Participation	Justice of Material Distribution
Epistemic Justice: Knowledge Built in Recognition, Relationship, Participation, and Material Redistribution	In an intergenerational and inter-institutional research collective, all of the researchers—including the student/alumni researchers—are recognized as complex persons, rooted in cultural histories, diasporic relations, contemporary racial and gender/sexuality/disability dynamics, engaged in movements, and expressing distinct personal styles.	Students, alumni, and their families are woven into and held by a net of caring relationships in and beyond middle school.	Alumni researchers are taken seriously as core and grounding members of a multigenerational research project and as knowledge producers, paid for their labor, and recognized as authors for their contributions.	Students, alumni, and youth researchers are afforded educational opportunities, mentoring, and emotional support that more affluent students routinely access.
Illustrative Enactments: Specifics That Make The Commitment Seem Real	Interviews conducted in preferred language; serious sustained conversations with youth researchers about anonymity, confidentiality, epistemic violence, and how to name structural injustice against immigrant communities without rendering individuals vulnerable.	Alumni are invited back—and come back—for support, to "check in" on how high school is going, to consult when they want to transfer, and then when COVID19 hit, the school opened a food pantry, clothing swap, school supplies center, and support around potential evictions.	From the beginning the perspectives, questions, sampling strategies, methods, and forms of analysis were determined by the youth. No research about us, without us! We publish together, present together, and together will be conducting a professional development session by alumni for S2 educators.	Youth researchers are paid for their time, get authorship credit on publications, receive tutoring as needed and culturally responsive mental health supports even after graduation.
Citations: See full citations in reference list	Brown & Rodriguez; Fraser; Ginwright & Cammarota; Gonzalez, Moll, Amanti; Paris	Antrop-Gonzalez & De Jesus; Ayala, Cammarota, Berta-Avila, Rivera, Rodriguez & Torre	Cammarota & Fine; Fine; Kirschner & Ginwright; Torre & Ayala	Mosley, Neville, Chavez-Dueñas, Adames, Lewis, and French; Outley & Blyth; Zeller-Berkman, Legaspi-Cavin, Barreto, Tang, and Sandler

Figure 15.5 *Just inquiry: Commitments, enactments, and citations*

Building Our Collective Capacity for Oral Histories and Participatory Analysis

At our second research collective meeting, Finesurrey and his students met with the twelve youth researchers to discuss how they would gather oral histories from the full graduating class. Committed to research rooted in recognition, relationships, and participation, and joined by Latinx community college students from the same neighborhoods, Finesurrey started with a simple question as he introduced the theory, methods, and ethics of participatory oral histories: "Why is it important that the world understand your stories and those of your peers?"

This question unearthed rich insights. Then thirteen and fourteen years old, the youth researchers hoped this project would humanize the representations of their community and their generation. They understood that their participation was essential, for only they could navigate this intimate landscape with care and familiarity, gathering testimonies from former classmates. The youth researchers hoped that this work could also provide evidence for educators, researchers, and policymakers seeking equity for marginalized communities.

Grooming them to be emergent scholars, Finesurrey and the Guttman students introduced the youth researchers to common oral history practices and ethics. We explained oral histories as deep and empathic inquiries into the key moments, desires, struggles, and turning points of young lives. Together, we generated a list of common questions to create consistency across the dozens of oral histories these high schoolers would be gathering from their peers. The youth researchers then piloted preliminary interviews with one another. After giggles, erasures, "oh, no, the recorder isn't on," "can we start again?" "why am I unable to talk?" and lots of loving feedback, they decided to re-interview one another at the following August meeting.

Over Fall and Spring semesters 2019–2020, we divided up the ninety-six graduates and the youth researchers conducted four additional oral histories with S2 alumni. After every set of oral histories, we would reflect critically on the questions and our process. Some questions were changed, a few eliminated, and a number added. Again, a justice of participation was key.

Enacted through collective reflection, analysis, and revision, we analyzed the material and settled on eight central themes:

1. S2 as a Home
2. Personal Evolution at S2
3. S2's Continued Support
4. Experiencing High School
5. Safety and Surveillance in High School
6. Living Bilingual Lives
7. Ideas about Community/Identity
8. Revisioning Futures

Below, we review three of these themes to reveal how recognition, relationships, and participation infused the co-construction of powerful narratives, provoked additional questions, and unearthed new paths of inquiry.

S2 as Home: Why relationships matter. The question of "home"—especially in communities under surveillance—is often complicated and can feel invasive. And so we decided we wouldn't ask, "What do you consider home?" Nevertheless, *S2 as home* is what the graduates wanted to talk about. And so that's where the interviews drifted. We believe the relationships at School in the Square between youth interviewees and interviewers evoked the nostalgia of their middle school. One S2 graduate explained, "I would consider home School in the Square because I met a lot of people that I trust and still talk to." Another, attempting to explain the significance of their bond with the school, was proud to explain: "I feel like we built this school." Arnaldo Rodriguez appreciated the sentiment and agreed: "Students' voices—especially this first graduating class—are definitely intertwined into the school's mission … [and] the students know that."

The teachers and staff, as well as the design of the school, seem to have had a profound and lasting impact on these alumni. Referencing the S2 teachers and staff, one graduate told us: "I really feel like they're god-parents to me." The intimacy of this middle school, serving its alumni as a safe and joyful place, clearly provides a framework from which the rising 9th graders in this study felt entitled to expect strong relationships with educators and to evaluate—not always favorably—their high schools. Confirmed in the participatory survey results, S2 graduates rated their middle school as significantly more caring, filled with a sense of belonging, where "I feel respected" and "my opinions matter" than their high schools. Provoked in relationship, these reflections on the power of close staff-student relationships have been crucial in professional development, school redesign, and in helping young people select caring high schools that are "worthy" of our graduates. The data from the S2 inquiry have been fundamental as subsequent classes of graduates who are in the process of selecting appropriate high schools. They are now steered toward high schools rooted in relationship, student writing, cultural diversity, dignity, and culturally sustaining pedagogy.

Safety and Surveillance in High School: Why participation matters. With a few months of high school under their belts, we gathered for a participatory analysis session, listening carefully to the early high school experiences of each youth researcher. As we were blending the narratives gathered with the lived experiences of the student researchers, we began to hear much about safety. The S2 alum contrasted their relative sense of safety and comfort in middle school with the fear and surveillance they now confront in high school. Many of their schools are filled with members of the New York Police Department roaming the halls; many of their school openings are filled with metal detectors and scanners. The youth researchers themselves admitted new school-based fears, and they were hearing the same in interviews with peers. We decided we needed to explore these core topics of fear and safety, and pry open the seeming contradiction of feeling both safer and racially criminalized by school security measures.

Respondents detailed many disturbing experiences with police officers in schools, metal detectors, and the scanning of their fingers upon entering the building. Researchers expanded on these dynamics: "Once we get in [the school], we got to put our phones in a bag and whatever electronic devices we have in a bag. And then, after that we got searched by security, they have like metal detectors .... After they're done, they check our book bags ... " Another student described new technology being brought into their schools to surveil the students: "There would be these two scanner locations where I would go and [they] scan my finger to see that I'm present in the school." Many of the S2 graduates expressed anger at and frustration with these security procedures, arguing that they feel criminalized. And yet a few acknowledged fear in their respective high schools, ambivalent about these measures. One student explained that when arriving at school they "usually just scan my card, go through the metal detector .... It makes me feel safer."

At our January retreat, the youth researchers realized there was something missing in the questions about security in the school. In the spirit of participation, and with an interest in eliciting divergent perspectives, Finesurrey presented a quote drawn from one of their interviews and asked for responses: "I don't feel that safe ... there's a couple of gangs in the school." At first hesitantly, some of the youth researchers recounted their own fears. One responded, "I don't feel safe in the bathroom, and so I just don't go while at school." Others named staircases and bathrooms as places to stay away from. Finesurrey asked the group: "Who among you avoids going to the bathroom in your high school?" Almost one-third of the room raised their hands. The specifics of youth fears, up to that point, had not been unearthed by the original list of questions. Only after participatory discussion did the group realize that our framing of the question seemed to call for a critique of policing but did not explore students' fears. As a collective we added questions to be asked in future oral histories including, "Do any parts of your day feel unsafe?" and "Are there places or times in your school you feel unsafe?" "Where do you go when you feel unsafe?"

Living Bilingual Lives: Why recognition matters. Dedicated to a justice of recognition and cultural dignity, the project has been committed to exploring young people's sense of their heritage, nationalities, home countries, and their languages. As children, S2 graduates attended relatively homogeneous neighborhood elementary schools before attending a predominantly Latinx middle school. As they described high school, many commented on how "diverse" the schools were and more reluctantly admitted that Spanish, for instance, does not fill the hallways. The research team decided that we wanted our work to make visible the many worlds and languages that S2 alumni navigate. Realizing that most of their former S2 classmates were bilingual, with many speaking Spanish as their first language, we decided to ask about how youth move between learning in English and returning to Spanish-speaking households. So we asked, "Can you tell us about living between languages?"

Some said it was a struggle at English-only or English-dominant high schools. Some articulated a sense of intimidation and others a loss of identity: "My Spanish … [is] one part of my identity that is somewhat like going away from me just because in school it's not bilingual like everything is English and you can't always have that Spanish part in you." Another spoke of the intergenerational responsibilities, and joys, that come with bilingualism. She educates her elders and feels an obligation toward her non-English-speaking relatives: "In my English class we would have vocabulary words and I would translate them from English to Spanish, mainly for my parents so that they can understand." We had another open conversation about this quote, exploring both her care for elders and the burden of translation. In an attempt to honor their fluency in multiple languages, Finesurrey asked the youth researchers how they feel about the "superpower" of being bilingual. After a few acknowledged the gift, Rodriguez offered that in his own childhood being bilingual was a skill, but also a burden. He told the group that he was responsible for the translation of conversations and documents for his relatives and "sometimes it was tiring."

Finesurrey and Rodriguez turned to the group: "What about the rest of you?" A show of hands suggested that translation responsibilities had at some point fallen on most of the S2 alumni in the room. The youth researchers agreed to add a new question for future oral histories, "Some people say it's a burden being bilingual, others view it as a gift, and many feel it a little bit of both. What about you?" This question, the team hopes, will provide significant insight on the responsibility and wisdom held by bilingual youth living in immigrant households.

A Brief Glimpse at Participatory Survey Design and Preliminary Findings

We have collected close to 100 peer oral histories to date, but we also wanted to collect some quantitative data from the full cohort. Camille Lester worked with the S2 alumni to "popcorn" questions for a survey, again committed to a justice of recognition and participation. The survey went through multiple drafts and students were given the chance to critique, cross out, underline, circle, ask questions, pose new questions, and write in the margins what they believed was relevant. The final survey became

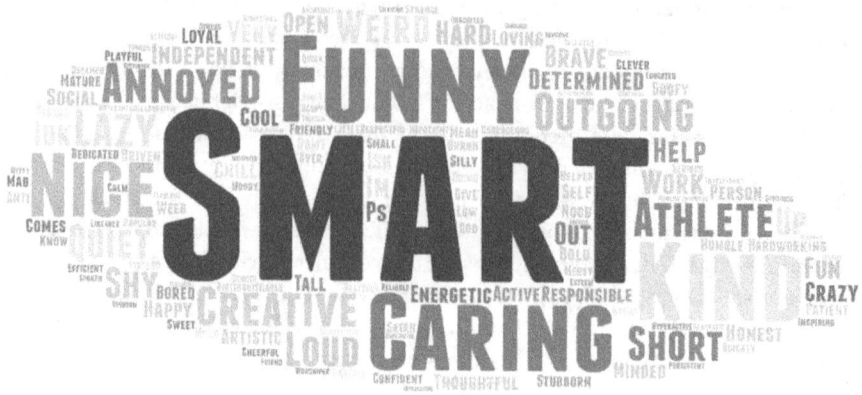

Figure 15.6 *Word cloud*

a living document of forty-six questions all related to the transition to high school, comfort, safety, and support. There were two sections, "School in the Square and Me" and "My New High School and Me." The survey was placed on Google Forms and was distributed to all S2 graduates.

A total of seventy-five School in the Square alumni completed the online survey, across a total of thirty-seven schools in New York City. Carrying forward on our commitment to a justice of recognition and participation, the survey opens with: "Please describe yourself in five words." Across the cohort, as you can see in the word cloud (Figure 15.6), the top adjectives were smart, funny, and caring.

Overall, the survey data confirmed the oral history narratives. Middle school at S2, for this inaugural graduating class, has been an experience of profound respect, comfort, risk taking, and safety, developing "voice" and confidence, knowing that "someone will catch my back," feeling "smart," "funny," and "caring." For many, although not all, high school has been a rude awakening. Lack of cultural recognition, lack of relationships, and lack of student inquiry and participation were distressing. We used time and space at our second retreat to dig more deeply into this question of being recognized, feeling safe, and experiencing a sense of belonging.

At our January 2020 retreat, after we bathed in the oral histories and the survey material, giggled and dissected the word cloud, Lester asked us all to move our chairs into a circle. The intra-/inter-generational research collective sat facing each other while grappling with the question of what does it mean to belong, to be connected? The conversation was rich and humbling, ranging from friends to family to school. We heard painful stories of feeling unsafe, being ignored in the classroom so that a teacher can "get through the material," teachers not fully engaging with the dynamic aspects of the students, disorientation with content not fully grasped, school counselors unresponsive to mental health needs, bathrooms becoming spaces to avoid and never enter, stairwells morphing into battlegrounds. We heard tensions of becoming, within deeply complicated environments. We heard voice and silencing, agency and fear, anxiety, and radical hope (Mosley et al., 2019).

Camille held space for us to deeply consider—what does it mean to feel connected and feel as if we belong, are respected, treated with dignity? We heard from the youth researchers that being seen and heard, fully, is essential for a sense of belonging. As one noted, "If I could say one thing to my teachers is to think not [in terms of their normal] expectation but [our new] reality. Not a lot of kids have it easy. You have to think about them and how to help them when they are struggling." Another student chimed in ".. my teacher doesn't try to help me. I remember this one time, the class was engaged, but I wasn't. I felt afraid to ask for help, because I felt like [the teacher] was going to judge me." Another stated, " ... My teacher always has a schedule, "you got two minutes for this," "five minutes for that," you really are not engaged in the purpose of the class, just trying to finish work ... you don't learn much. Responding to this in a hushed manner, another student stated " ... I just feel confused most of the time."

Wrapping up the conversation, a student offered: "If I could say something to my teachers, I would say interact more with my classmates to understand and know them as a person." Nourished in a middle school—and now a participatory research project—committed to recognition, relationships, and participation, there was a quiet confidence in the room, no bravado, but a sense that they know what good teaching is. Having had a taste of just inquiry and critical care at S2, they know what it means to be seen, heard, and supported; they know what it means to create knowledge, have a voice, and expect an audience.

Why Participation Matters: Building a Critical and Caring Community of Youth Scholars and Activists

To date, the bulk of our inquiry has centered on the oral histories that have been conducted and transcribed. Peers interview each other in English and Spanish about the transition into high school, are mentored by community college students with similar biographies, and they enjoy access to a transition counselor they trust. In this context where recognition, relationships, and participation are key, where labor/authorship/struggles/gifts are appreciated, the inquiry is simply richer, the narratives more complex and, we would argue, the process more just.

From September 2019 forward, we met once a month at S2. After the Fall semester of their first year in high school, in January, 2020 we held a day-long retreat at the Graduate Center to review our preliminary data and consider our next inquiry moves. Finesurrey asked: "Why does it matter that *you* are gathering the oral histories?" Joel Almonte named the benefits he and other youth derive from being the architects of this work: "It's important that we do these interviews ... it makes us feel part of the whole project, like we do matter." Siarra Saviñon, Jesslin Hiraldo, and Lauren Santos agreed that they felt "proud to be a knowledge producer." Aidan Lam added, "It feels good to be doing something productive and creative." When probed further, "What other questions should we include in the next round of interviews?" Joel Almonte added, "Where do you get your inspiration from?" Finesurrey pressed, "Why is this important, Joel? Where do you get your inspiration from?" With a soft smile the 9th grader responded, "My family. They have been through so much. I owe this to them." The question was added.

As experts on their own experiences, and those of their peers, engaging the youth as co-researchers strengthens the trustworthiness of the narratives gathered and, in more traditional terms, enhances the validity of the material. Brandon Mendoza reflected, "It's important that we do the interviews because … we can relate to [our former classmates] and they would trust us more." Alyssa Victoria agreed, "We are interviewing people who are comfortable with us." Samantha Bruno said the bonds shared by people of the same generation would prove beneficial as well: "Because I'm interviewing people around my age they would be more truthful in their answers and … more open."

Youth researcher Alyssa Victoria saw how the project could be a resource not only for herself and her peers, but also make S2 even better. Victoria hoped "the results … help improve S2 … even though it's already a good middle school." This optimism was shared by Naomi Pabon who argued that "These stories matter because people [S2 educators] … will be able to know the student's point of view." Arnaldo Rodriguez explained he is using the narratives as he counsels the next cohort of middle schoolers toward high school, considering "what really is a good option and what's not." The young people are preparing a professional development session for their educators, and we just completed a presentation of our data on pandemics and protests for the New York City Deputy Mayor for Immigrant Communities.

Our project is rooted in a justice of recognition, relationships, and participation, nested in a context dedicated to redistribution of opportunities to working class youth of color in a city of deep and vast inequities. Thus far, this inquiry has unveiled an uneven story of immigrant families navigating the NYC "choice" school system, with substantial support as needed from S2. Once COVID19 hit, online learning took hold, families grew ill, worries about rent and food spiked. Within S2 important conversations were unleashed about racial protests and culturally responsive pedagogy, food pantries and mental health, the movement for Black Lives and the distribution of winter coats for students, alumni and family members. In our first year, we have learned that relationships matter enormously, particularly for young people living in precarious circumstances, that schools must function as anchor institutions, that participatory research by youth of color builds knowledge, capacity and a radical sense of purpose, possibility and solidarity.

The Intergenerational S2 Research Collective seeks to unveil and redress cumulative harms and radical possibilities through a lens of just inquiry and critical care. Our research, like S2, takes seriously a justice of redistribution of opportunities, deep recognition, trusting relationships, and serious participation by the very young people most adversely affected by—and intimately aware of—the neoliberal reconfigurations of their education and lives in New York City. Rooted in a commitment to radical hope (Mosley et al., 2019), we ask who better than young people themselves can gather up, co-construct, and narrate thrilling and treacherous journeys through high school, through austerity, and COVID19, in a city plagued by state violence and animated by youth organizing and uprisings?

Conclusion: Caring in Contentious Times

Veena Vasudevan, Nora Gross,
Pavithra Nagarajan, and Katherine Clonan-Roy

We are living, again and always, in contentious times.

(Fine, 2018, p. 116)

When we first conceived of this book in early 2019, the United States was in the throes of a presidential administration so dark and cruel that we were afraid to imagine what would unfold in the days to come. Just as many of us feared, the Trump administration did enact policies that perpetuated systemic and structural violence against nondominant communities across the United States including, but not limited to, peoples of color, undocumented immigrants, people with dis/abilities, and LGBTQ+ communities. We were horrified as the former President himself, along with other Republican party leaders, encouraged, and reified the ugliness of white supremacy through their words and (in)actions. *Care* feels more important now, than ever, given the hate and vitriol that we continue to witness in the United States.

Just when it seemed things could not get worse, we—the editorial team and our authors—found ourselves writing and revising our chapters as a global pandemic raged, upending any remaining sense of normalcy in our lives. In the United States, the COVID-19 pandemic laid bare the persistent inequities in our social structures and systems that cater to those with wealth and privilege. We watched as youth from nondominant communities dealt with extreme loss and tragedy; financial, food, and housing insecurity; limited access to quality healthcare; and the effects of rising unemployment. The pandemic surged and shuttered schools and, subsequently, necessary social services (e.g., free-and-reduced price lunch in Title I schools) and social and emotional support for children and youth when they needed it the most. Our educational system continued to fray at the seams—students and teachers experienced a bumbling and chaotic transition to online learning including a scramble for broadband access and devices to facilitate remote learning, all while young people navigated the weight of isolation, loss, and stress alongside all the regular challenges of growing up.

Spring and summer 2020 brought with it new tragedies, in particular, the horrific killing of George Floyd, which served as a stark reminder that dehumanization of nondominant communities has grave impacts. The anti-racist uprisings—so much of it led by young people—brought hope and solidarity, but also new fears and threats of state-sanctioned violence. And so, we continue this work in contentious times, because we must.

***

The authors in our book have taught us important lessons about practicing and enacting care in a range of research contexts and with youth from many nondominant communities. What we have learned through our own studies, and in working with our authors, is that research can be an endeavor in which care is central to both our *methods* and *practices*. Methods include all of the decisions we make to frame and enact our research, from creating a research design, to data collection, to developing partnerships with schools or educational sites. Whereas the *practices* are all the ways we engage with people as a result of our research design decisions from cultivating relationships with school communities and gaining entry into various social groups, to developing relationships with youth participants, and offering support to school communities more broadly.

Care in research can be decolonizing and emancipatory by transgressing existing research paradigms in methods and practice. In research, care can shift our relationships with youth participants in transformative directions: creating new and deeper ways of knowing and opportunities for research to be responsive to youth's needs. We also learned how researchers traverse the complex landscape of emotions, intimate relationships, and how they carefully set boundaries, practice transparency, and communicate effectively about the limits of research. Finally, our authors illustrated how teaching and practicing relationality and care with graduate student researchers, within research teams, and across partner institutions are opportunities to make systemic change. Through the development of this book, we have also learned a larger lesson about another kind of care, self-care. Whether one is engaged in dissertation fieldwork or independent studies, or part of a larger research collaboration, finding moments to reflect, journal, memo, and take time for oneself becomes all the more essential when deeply ensconced in caring relationships with youth in schools.

As an editorial team, who actively grapple with many of the challenges laid out on these pages in our daily research practice, we stand firmly in our belief that the absence of care-based methods in research where children and youth from nondominant communities are the focus is fundamentally unethical and perpetuates injustice. We believe care is an essential component of school-based research because it actively supports the youth we want to learn about, with, and from; care-based methodologies acknowledge the problematic legacies that shape their lives, while actively working to improve them in small, yet purposeful, ways.

We are committed to practicing care as an essential component of school-based research endeavors because it offers the methodological tools to support the wellbeing of the youth at the center of the work: to honor youth as people, not just the data they provide; to acknowledge historical, problematic legacies in research and in schooling; and to seek to change the material conditions of youths' lives in small, but meaningful ways. These commitments attune us to thinking differently and critically about how schools engage with young people, and at the same time, about how school-based researchers engage with those same young people.

Our work must break away from the legacy of extractive and reductive research at the expense of, rather than the benefit to, the youth from whom we learn. All young people, particularly those in lower-income and/or from historically marginalized communities, deserve respect, dignity, and care. It is not just our relationship to youth participants that must change—we must also change our relationship with research itself. We must (re)consider to whom we are accountable in our research reporting and expand our responsibilities past the IRB and grant funders. Youth are our partners in this work and therefore a universal humanity and ethic of care should ground our work. There are many scholars of and in education across disciplines whose work is certainly situated, and moving further, in this direction. But there is more work to be done, and it needs to be done urgently.

***

We had a few audiences in mind when we began this writing journey. We were thinking about new scholars preparing to embark on school-based qualitative research, as well as those who are actively engaged in partnerships with school leaders, classroom educators, and for those coordinating research teams. We believe researchers can be change agents.

We encourage graduate students and early scholars to engage your academic interlocutors from your peers, to your advisors, and teachers, to center care in classroom conversations, in research work, and in training opportunities. We encourage you to speak up if you observe uncaring practices at your field sites, and advocate for youth. Further along the journey are pre-tenure scholars who work within schools but are not necessarily incentivized to care given institutional demands related to tenure and promotion. We acknowledge the very real pressures to produce research and progress in the academy, but we challenge you to root research design and decisions in care, especially when your professional advancement is made possible by young people's willingness to give their time and expertise. Finally, with regard to senior scholars, particularly those of you who lead research teams, mentor graduate students, and steer research-practice partnerships, we encourage you to spend time establishing norms, and a culture of caring, through modeling care in work with your team as well as in your relationships with school and community leaders, and youth. We also encourage you to lead for change within the academy, in the pursuit of convincing promotion and tenure committees and administrative leaders that caring in research, which often necessitates moving at a slower pace, is not only valuable but crucial if institutions want to promote equity in the communities they serve. At every level of the academy, there is vital work to be done to build structures that make care possible.

***

As for us, writing this book has been a labor of love. The four of us have seen each other through births of children, deaths of parents, graduations, many new jobs, multiple moves, breakups, and engagements. We have navigated professional frustrations and triumphs, personal hardships and joys, while continuing to come together to manifest this book. Our care for each other and for our authors and the young people in our collective work represents and encapsulates our fervent hope for a future for the academy, for schools, and for school-based research that embraces care as a necessary practice and lifts up the insights that can come from work that emanates from our shared connections and humanity.

Notes

Introduction

1. All names are pseudonyms to protect the identities of participants.
2. In this book, we use the term "youth" generally to refer to people eighteen years of age and younger. We alternatively use "children," "adolescents," "young people," or "students." These terms are not meant to be technically precise (e.g., some of the young people we met in schools were nineteen), and chapter authors may use different combinations of these and other terms.
3. We use the term "nondominant" to represent those who identify as people of color (e.g., Black, Latinx, Indigenous, Asian); people who experience poverty; people with disabilities; individuals who identify as lesbian, gay, bisexual, transgender, or queer (LGBTQ+); those from immigrant communities; resettled refugees; and people who are English learners. Moreover, children, aged 0–18, are considered "vulnerable populations" when it comes to research. Therefore, we have come to identify "youth from nondominant communities" as those individuals who are aged eighteen and younger who identify with one, or more, of the aforementioned identities.

Chapter 1

1. All school, city, and participant names are pseudonyms.
2. Relatedly, as a reciprocal act of care, teachers would also gently redirect children who were requesting my attention as I was transitioning.

Chapter 2

1. Pseudonym used for confidentiality. Names of people and places thereafter are also pseudonyms. Valentina is the feminine version of "Valentin," a name in Spanish that is known to mean strong and brave, two qualities reflected in Valentina.
2. The study examined the success of high-achieving African American and Latino male high school students.
3. By listening to the story of his grandmother and not redirecting the conversation, I was already challenging Eurocentric research practices. The protocol explicitly asked him to identify *male* role models that supported his academic success.
4. I use "Latinx" as a gender-neutral alternative to Latino, Latina, and even Latin@. I also use "Latinx" to acknowledge gender fluidity and include individuals whose gender identities fluctuate along different points of the gender spectrum.
5. "TBH," meaning to be honest. Valentina said the popular youth acronym out loud.
6. Who are you? How do your identities (i.e., race, class) influence your research approach, methodology, theory, and epistemology?

7. Who are your collaborators (or, in my case, *compañeras*)? How do you negotiate your research agenda with your collaborators?
8. What is the nature of race/class/gender, to name a few, in your study? What systemic barriers and structures shape the experiences of your collaborators?

Chapter 3

1. All names in this manuscript except those of the authors are pseudonyms.
2. A more detailed account of this process can be found at www.researchforempowerment.com.

Chapter 4

1. All names in the chapter are pseudonyms.
2. Typically, in this district, magnet schools or other "specialized" high schools require admissions exams, interviews, and satisfactory report cards to gain admittance, which limits access.
3. The school lost several students over the course of the year and gained some as well, leaving the final first year cohort at eighty-nine.
4. She used this term to describe herself in the role.
5. In this district, they had cut guidance counselors significantly the same year the school opened, so it was significant that they had a dedicated person in this role.
6. Possi was another name for the student advisory groups.

Chapter 5

1. The school and students discussed in this chapter have been anonymized. Individual names and respective school names were created by the students themselves, except for JaQuan, JaCobee, Ariah, and Zuri with whom I was unable to follow up, and Lauryn who declined to choose a pseudonym.
2. Blaze Rods and Flower Elementary Schools feed into Fun Middle School. The elementary schools host students in K–5th, with the middle school hosting students in 6th–8th grades.
3. I have striven to provide notebook transcriptions throughout this chapter as originally written, without correction. Changes were limited to names only in order to preserve anonymity and substitute pseudonyms.
4. KKL is an initialism that refers to her friend group.

Chapter 6

1. Sankofa Collegiate, as are all other names in this Chapter, is a pseudonym. Pseudonyms are used in order to protect the identity of individuals participating in this study.
2. Students were guided by a protocol that asked them to take multiple photographs that represented different parts of their identity in and out of school. Students had

the power to take pictures, and therefore, frame and define their photo responses with minimal researcher influence. These photos were then used during the interview with students as anchor-points for conversations, positioning the student as the "expert" and the researcher in a learning stance.
3. Isaiah's photo is a screenshot on his phone of the promotional movie poster for *Boyz N the Hood*. See here: https://www.npr.org/2011/07/08/137675331/boyz-n-the-hood-rings-out-20-years-later.

Chapter 8

1. The names of all people and places in this chapter are pseudonyms.
2. Because the district had experienced such an influx of Latinx families in recent years, they hired Latinx Community Liaisons, who could assist in addressing language and cultural barriers for educators, students, and families.

Chapter 9

1. Pseudonyms chosen by the participants.
2. This student group is more fully described in an article by Clonan-Roy, Gross, and Jacobs (2020).
3. Other ethnographers have noted that even when specific observations or data points cannot be included in published work at a participant's request, they can still be kept in mind to inform larger arguments (Khan, 2011).
4. Siah and Yaja were in the final weeks of their senior year and most of their classes were devoted to independent work on final projects, so each time the bell rang, they would explain to me why it was not a big deal for them to miss their next class. I felt guilty but also did not think we would get an opportunity for a conversation like this again, so I emailed their teachers an explanation for their absence.
5. "Thurl" (or "thorough") "boul" is Philadelphia slang for a truthful, solid, or upstanding peer or friend (usually a male).
6. At other moments in the conversation, both boys alluded to having initially had a crush on me which may have played a role in this jealousy.
7. By the end of this conversation, both Yaja and Siah had renewed their commitment to being part of the research, and we have discussed their consent multiple times since then (see Epilogue in chapter).

Chapter 10

1. I use the term "court-involvement" to refer to young people who are involved with the juvenile justice system, due to either a legal infraction or other circumstance (e.g., foster care).
2. Note about language use: Throughout this chapter, I use the terms "disabled youth," and "youth identified with a disability" interchangeably on purpose. My use of person-first and label-first language interchangeably comes from my lived experience in community with disabled people asserting their desire to self-identify. This comes

specifically from the ADAPT (Americans Disabled Attendant Programs Today) organization via social media sites, such as Twitter, where disabled activists often say: "please ask me if I prefer person-first or label-first language." During data collection I asked my research participants how they would like to be discussed and identified (person first or label first, or perhaps neither) and use that language.
3. By this I mean Sapphire did not use chemical treatments or add extensions to her hair. She shared with me that she preferred to wear her hair styled naturally "out" or braided.
4. The Individuals with Disabilities Education Act (IDEA, 2004) defines a low-incidence disability as "a visual or hearing impairment, or simultaneous visual and hearing impairments; a significant cognitive impairment; or any impairment for which a small number of personnel with highly specialized skills and knowledge are needed in order for children with that impairment to receive early intervention services or a free appropriate public education" (IDEA, 2019, https://sites.ed.gov/idea/statute-chapter-33/subchapter-iv/part-b/1462/c).
5. A commonly used example of the social model is that a person who uses a wheelchair is not disabled if they are in a space that they can navigate free from barriers (e.g., ramps, elevators). When the same person encounters an environment with stairs and no alternatives, they become disabled by the fact the environment has barriers for them to move freely.
6. There are far more egregious examples of the ways disabled people are cared for that are forms of abuse (cf. Piepzna-Samarashinha, 2018).

Chapter 11

1. Although we recognize the power and positioning involved in designating youth as "ELL" and "ESL," and the failure of these labels to recognize the strengths of emergent multilinguals, we use these terms because they reflect the language used commonly and consistently by school participants.
2. Our collective perspective is generated through deliberations of data, research-team discussions, and collaborative writing. Authors' first names are used to highlight individual circumstances in which James, Melanie, and Ashley acted.

Chapter 13

1. The United Nations (UN), World Health Organization (WHO), and United Nations International Children's Fund (UNICEF) define adolescent as the ages of 10–19 and youth as the ages 15–24. Given the scope of our research, we use the term "adolescent" because it accurately reflects the ages of our participants.
2. At the time this chapter was written, these were our positions. However, Stephanie is now an associate professor at Purdue University, and Ophélie is an assistant professor at Valdosta State University.

References

Foreword

Bell, L. A. (2010). *Storytelling for social justice: Connecting narrative and art in antiracist teaching*. Teachers College Press.

Ferlazzo, L. (2014, December). How does caring relate to standards? [Web blog post]. Classroom Q&A with Ferlazzo. *Edweek Magazine*. Retrieved from https://blogs.Edweek.org.teachers/classroom_qu_withlarry_ferlazzo/2014/12/.

Greene, M. (1988). *The dialectic of freedom*. Teachers College Press.

Hardy, K. (2013). Healing the hidden wounds of racial trauma. *Reclaiming Children and Youth*, 22(1), 24–8.

Howard, T. C. (2001). Telling their side of the story: African-American students' perceptions of culturally relevant teaching. *The Urban Review*, 33(2), 131–49.

Jalāl Al-dīn, Rūmī, & Barks, C. (1996). *The essential Rumi*. 1st ed. HarperCollins paperback.

Jackson, I., Sealey-Ruiz, Y., & Watson, W. (2014). Reciprocal love: Mentoring Black and Latino male through an ethos of caring. *Journal of Urban Education*, 49(4), 1–24.

Laura, C. T. (2016). Intimate Inquiry: A love-based approach to qualitative research. *Critical Questions in Education*, 7(3), 215–31.

Noddings, N. (2005b). *The challenge to care in schools: An alternative approach to education* (Second Edition). Teachers College Press.

Ohito, E. O., Watson, W., Lyiscott, J., & Sealey-Ruiz, Y. (2019). What's love got to do with it: Looking for love in urban schooling. *The Urban Review*, 51(1).

Pang, V. O. (2001). *Multicultural education: A caring-centered, reflective approach*. McGraw-Hill.

Sealey-Ruiz, Y. (2007). Wrapping the curriculum around their lives: Using a culturally responsive curriculum with African American adult women. *Adult Education Quarterly*, 58(1), 44–60.

Sealey-Ruiz, Y. (2020). *Love from the vortex and other poems*. Kaleidoscope Vibrations LLC.

Siddle Walker, V., & Tompkins, R. H. (2004). Caring in the past: The case of Southern segregated African American schools. In V. Siddle Walker & J. R. Snarey (Eds.), *Racing moral formation: African American perspectives on care and justice* (pp. 77–92). Teachers College Press.

Ware, F. (2006). Warm demander pedagogy: Culturally responsive teaching that supports a culture of achievement for African American students. *Urban Education*, 41(4), 427–56.

Watson, W., Sealey-Ruiz, Y., & Jackson, I. (2016). Daring to care: The role of culturally relevant care in mentoring Black and Latino male high school students. *Race, Ethnicity, and Education* 19(5), 980–1002.

Introduction

Antrop-González, R., & De Jesús, A. (2006). Toward a theory of "critical care" in urban small school reform: Examining structures and pedagogies of caring in two Latino community-based schools. *International Journal of Qualitative Studies in Education*, 19(4), 409–33.

Anyon, J. (1997). *Ghetto schooling: A political economy of urban educational reform.* Teachers College Press.

Behar, R. (1996). *The vulnerable observer: Anthropology that breaks your heart.* Beacon Press.

Benoot, C., & Bilsen, J. (2014). Researcher burnout: The emotional impact of doing qualitative health research on sensitive topics. *International Journal of Qualitative Methods*, 13, 487.

Bettie, J. (2003). *Women without class: Girls, race, and identity.* University of California Press.

Bettie, J. (2014). *Women without class: Girls, race, and identity.* University of California Press.

Brayboy, B. M., Gough, H. R., Leonard, B., Roehl, R. F., & Solyom, J. A. (2012). Reclaiming scholarship: Critical indigenous research methodologies. in Lapan, S. D., Quartaroli, M. T., & Riemer, F. J. (2012). *Qualitative research: An introduction to methods and designs*, 423–50. Jossey-Bass.

Carl, N. M., Kuriloff, P., Ravitch, S. M., & Reichert, M. (2018). Democratizing schools for improvement through youth participatory action research. *Journal of Ethical Educational Leadership*, 28–43.

Carspecken, L. (2018). *Love in the time of ethnography: Essays on connection as a focus and basis for research.* Lexington Books.

Clonan-Roy, K., Gross, N., & Jacobs, C. (2020). Safe rebellious places: The value of informal spaces in schools to counter the emotional silencing of youth of color. *International Journal of Qualitative Studies in Education*, 34(4), 330–52.

Creswell, J. W., & Poth, C. N. (2018). *Qualitative inquiry and research design: Choosing among five approaches* (4th ed.). Sage Publications, Inc.

Dance, L. J. (2002). *Tough fronts: The impact of street culture on schooling.* Psychology Press.

Desmond, M. (2014). Relational ethnography. *Theory and Society*, 43(5), 547–79.

Dumas, M. J. (2014). "Losing an arm": Schooling as a site of black suffering. *Race Ethnicity and Education*, 17(1), 1–29. doi:10.1080/13613324.2013.850412.

Duncan-Andrade, J. (2007). Gangstas, wankstas, and ridas: Defining, developing, and supporting effective teachers in urban schools. *International Journal of Qualitative Studies in Education*, 20(6), 617–38.

Eckert, P. (1989). *Jocks and burnouts: Social categories and identity in the high school.* Teachers College Press.

Ferguson, A. A. (2020). *Bad boys: Public schools in the making of black masculinity.* University of Michigan Press.

Fine, M. (1991). *Framing dropouts: Notes on the politics of an urban high school.* SUNY Press.

Fine, M. (2018). *Just research in contentious times: Widening the methodological imagination.* Teachers College Press.

Flores-González, N. (2002). *School kids/street kids: Identity development in Latino students.* Teachers College Press.

Freire, P. (2005). *Pedagogy of the oppressed*. 30th Anniversary Edition. Continuum.
Friesen, P., Kearns, L., Redman, B., & Caplan, A. L. (2017). Rethinking the Belmont report? *The American Journal of Bioethics*, 17(7), 15–21.
Garcia, A., Guggenheim, A., Stamatis, K., & Dalton, B. (2021). Glimmers of care: Attending to the affective everyday in ninth-grade literacy classrooms. *Reading Research Quarterly*, 56(2), 337–54.
Galletta, A. (2013). *Mastering the semi-structured interview and beyond: From research design to analysis and publication*. NYU Press.
Gillespie, K., & Lopez, P. J. (2019). *Vulnerable witness: The politics of grief in the field*. University of California Press.
González, N., Moll, L. C., & Amanti, C. (Eds.). (2006). *Funds of knowledge: Theorizing practices in households, communities, and classrooms*. Routledge.
Gray, P., & Chanoff, D. (1986). Democratic schooling: What happens to young people who have charge of their own education? *American Journal of Education*, 94(2), 182–213.
Green, K. (2014). Doing double dutch methodology: Playing with the practice of participant observer. In D. Paris & M. T. Winn (Eds.). (2014). *Humanizing research: Decolonizing qualitative inquiry with youth and communities* (pp 147–60). Sage Publications.
Gross, N., & Lo, C. (2018). Relational teaching and learning after loss: Evidence from Black adolescent male students and their teachers. *School Psychology Quarterly*, 33(3), 381.
Hays, D. G., & Singh, A. A. (2011). *Qualitative inquiry in clinical and educational settings*. Guilford Press.
Horvat, E. (2013). *The beginner's guide to doing qualitative research: How to get into the field, collect data, and write up your project*. Teachers College Press.
Khan, S. R. (2011). *Privilege: The making of an adolescent elite at St. Paul's School*. Princeton University Press.
Khan, S. R. (2012). *Privilege: The making of an adolescent elite at St. Paul's School*. Princeton University Press.
Kinloch, V., & San Pedro, T. (2014). The space between listening and storying: Foundations for projects in humanization. In D. Paris, & M. T. Winn (Eds.), *Humanizing research: Decolonizing qualitative inquiry with youth and communities* (pp 21–42). Sage Publications.
Kirkland, D. E. (2013). *A search past silence: The literacy of young Black men*. Teachers College Press.
Ladson-Billings, G. (2009). *The dreamkeepers: Successful teachers of African American children*. John Wiley & Sons.
Lareau, A. (2011). *Unequal childhoods: Class, race, and family life*. Second Edition. University of California Press.
Laura, C. T. (2016). Intimate Inquiry: A love-based approach to qualitative research. *Critical Questions in Education*, 7(3), 215–31.
Lee, S. J. (2005). *Up against whiteness: Race, school, and immigrant youth*. Teachers College Press.
Lewis, A. E. (2003). *Race in the schoolyard: Negotiating the color line in classrooms and communities*. Rutgers University Press.
Love, B. L. (2019). *We want to do more than survive: Abolitionist teaching and the pursuit of educational freedom*. Beacon Press.

Mackenzie, C., McDowell, C., & Pittaway, E. (2007). Beyond "do no harm": The challenge of constructing ethical relationships in refugee research. *Journal of Refugee studies*, 20(2), 299–319.

Madison, D. S. (2011). *Critical ethnography: Method, ethics, and performance*. Sage Publications.

McKenzie, K. B. (2009). Emotional abuse of students of color: The hidden inhumanity in our schools. *International Journal of Qualitative Studies in Education*, 22(2), 129–43. doi:10.1080/09518390801998270.

Meraji, S. M., & Demby, G. (Hosts) (2017, October-November). Raising Kings: A year of love and struggle at ron brown college prep (Special series) [Audio podcast]. In *Code Switch*. NPR. https://www.npr.org/series/557324733/a-year-at-ron-brown-high-school

Morris, E. W. (2012). *Learning the hard way: Masculinity, place, and the gender gap in education*. Rutgers University Press.

Nagarajan, P. (2018). Chutes, not ladders: The control and confinement of boys of color through school discipline. *Boyhood Studies*, 11(2), 114–30.

National Commission for the Protection of Human Subjects of Biomedical and Behavioral Research. (1979). The Belmont report: Ethical principles and guidelines for the protection of human subjects of research. Available at: http://www.hhs.gov/ohrp/regulations-and-policy/belmont-report.

Nelson, J. D. (2016). Relational teaching with black boys: Strategies for learning at a single-sex middle school for boys of color. *Teachers College Record*, 118(6), 1–30.

Noddings, N. (1984). *Caring: A feminine approach to ethics and moral education*. University of California Press.

Noddings, N. (1992). *The challenge to care in schools: An alternative approach to education*. Teachers College Press.

Noddings, N. (2005a). Identifying and responding to needs in education. *Cambridge Journal of Education*, 35(2), 147–59.

Noddings, N. (2012a). The caring relation in teaching. *Oxford Review of Education*, 38(6), 771–81.

Pacheco, M. (2009). Toward expansive learning: Examining Chicana/o and Latina/o students' political-historical knowledge. *Language Arts*, 87(1), 18–29.

Paris, D. (2011). "A friend who understand fully": Notes on humanizing research in a multiethnic youth community. *International Journal of Qualitative Studies in Education*, 24(2), 137–49.

Paris, D., & Winn, M. T. (Eds.). (2013). *Humanizing research: Decolonizing qualitative inquiry with youth and communities*. Sage Publications.

Pascoe, C. J. (2011). *Dude, you're a fag: Masculinity and sexuality in high school*. University of California Press.

Ravitch, S. M., & Carl, N. M. (2019). *Qualitative research: Bridging the conceptual, theoretical, and methodological*. Sage Publications.

Rios, V. M. (2011). *Punished: Policing the lives of Black and Latino boys*. NYU Press.

Rolón-Dow, R. (2005). Critical care: A color (full) analysis of care narratives in the schooling experiences of Puerto Rican girls. *American Educational Research Journal*, 42(1), 77–111.

Sealey-Ruiz, Y. (2016). Why Black girls' literacies matter: New literacies for a new era. *English Education*, 290–8.

Tilley, S. A., & Taylor, L. (2018). Qualitative methods and respectful praxis: Researching with youth. *The Qualitative Report*, 23(9), 2184–2204.

Tuck, E. (2009). Suspending damage: A letter to communities. *Harvard Educational Review*, 79(3), 409–28.

Tuhiwai Smith, L. (1999). *Decolonizing methodologies: Research and indigenous peoples.* Zed Books.

Valenzuela, A. (2010). *Subtractive schooling: US-Mexican youth and the politics of caring.* State University of New York Press.

Van Ausdale, D., & Feagin, J. R. (1996). Using racial and ethnic concepts: The critical case of very young children. *American Sociological Review*, 61(5), 779–93.

Vasudevan, L. (2020, February). The Practice of Partnership: Small Data and the Magic of Missteps. [Plenary]. Ethnography in Education Research Forum, Philadelphia, PA, United States.

Vasudevan, V., Gross, N., & Nagarajan, P. (2019a, March). *Researching from Liminal Spaces: The Practice of Care in School-Based Ethnography with Youth of Color* [Conference Presentation]. Eastern Sociological Society Annual Meeting, Boston, MA, United States.

Vasudevan, V., Gross, N., & Nagarajan, P. (2019b, April). *Caring and Being There: Complicating Qualitative Research with Youth of Color in School Settings* [Conference Symposium]. American Educational Research Association Annual Meeting, Toronto, Canada.

Vasudevan, V., Gross, N., Nagarajan, P., & Clonan-Roy, K. (2019, February). *Caring and Being There: Complicating Qualitative Research with Youth of Color in School Settings* [Conference Symposium]. Ethnography in Education Research Forum, Philadelphia, PA, United States.

Watson, W., Sealey-Ruiz, Y., & Jackson, I. (2016). Daring to care: The role of culturally relevant care in mentoring Black and Latino male high school students. *Race, Ethnicity, and Education* 19(5), 980–1002.

Warren, C. A. (2021). *About centering possibility in black education.* Teachers College Press.

Winkle-Wagner, R. (2018). Love in the Field: Reflections on the role of emotion in qualitative data collection. *Love in the time of ethnography: Essays on connection as a focus and basis for research,* 147–164.

Winn, M. T., & Ubiles, J. R. (2011). Worthy witnessing: Collaborative research in urban classrooms. In A. Ball & C. Tyson (Eds.), *Studying diversity in teacher education* (pp 293–306). Rowman & Littlefield.

Yosso, T. J. (2005). Whose culture has capital? A critical race theory discussion of community cultural wealth. *Race Ethnicity and Education*, 8(1), 69–91.

Chapter 1

Adler, P. A., & Adler, P. (1987). *Membership roles in field research* (Vol. 6). Sage.

Akom, A. A., Cammarota, J., & Ginwright, S. (2008). Youthtopias: Towards a new paradigm of critical youth studies. *Youth Media Reporter*, 2(4), 1–30.

Anderson, G. L. (1989). Critical ethnography in education: Origins, current status, and new directions. *Review of educational research*, 59(3), 249–70.

Baldridge, B. J. (2014). Relocating the deficit: Reimagining black youth in neoliberal times. *American Educational Research Journal*, 51(3), 440–72.

Ball, D.L. (2018). Just dreams and imperatives: The power of teaching in the struggle for public education. Presidential Address at 2018 American Educational Research Association Annual Meeting, New York, NY.

Beauboeuf-Lafontant, T. (1999). A movement against and beyond boundaries. *Teachers College Record*, 100(4), 702–23.

Behar, R. (1996). *The vulnerable observer: Anthropology that breaks your heart*. Beacon Press.

Carspecken, P. F. (1996). *Critical ethnography in educational research: A theoretical and practical guide*. Psychology Press.

Davis, N. (2017). *Hope in Those Places of Struggle: A Critical Exploration of Black Students' Agency in One Place-based and One African-centered Elementary School* (Doctoral dissertation).

Davis, N. R., Vossoughi, S., & Smith, J. F. (2020). Learning from below: A micro-ethnographic account of children's self-determination as sociopolitical and intellectual action. *Learning, Culture and Social Interaction*, 24, 100373.

Edwards, E., McArthur, S. A., & Russell-Owens, L. (2016). Relationships, being-ness, and voice: Exploring multiple dimensions of humanizing work with Black girls. *Equity & Excellence in Education*, 49(4), 428–39.

Emerson, R. M., Fretz, R. I., & Shaw, L.L. (2001). Participant observation and fieldnotes. In P. Atkinson, A. Coffey, S. Delamont, J. Lofland & L. Lofland (Eds.). *Handbook of ethnography*. Sage.

Emerson, R. M., Fretz, R. I., & Shaw, L. L. (2011). *Writing ethnographic fieldnotes*. University of Chicago Press.

Erickson, F. (1986). Qualitative methods in research on teaching. In M.C. Wittrock (Ed.), *Handbook of research on teaching* (3rd ed., pp. 119–61). New York: MacMillan.

Erickson, F. (2004). Demystifying data construction and analysis. *Anthropology & Education Quarterly*, 35(4), 486–93.

Kusenbach, M. (2003). Street phenomenology: The go-along as ethnographic research tool. *Ethnography*, 4(3), 455–85.

Ladson-Billings, G. (2013). "Stakes is high": Educating new century students. *The Journal of Negro Education*, 82(2), 105–10.

Lichterman, P. (1998). What do movements mean? The value of participant-observation. *Qualitative Sociology*, 21(4), 401–18.

Madison, D. S. (2005). Introduction to critical ethnography: Theory and method. *Critical Ethnography: Method, Ethics & Performance*, 1–16.

Neal-Jackson, A. (2018). A meta-ethnographic review of the experiences of African American girls and young women in K–12 education. *Review of Educational Research*, 88(4), 508–46.

Neal-Jackson, A. (2018). *"They Don't Want to See Us Succeed": How Micro-Interactions Produce Problematic Identities for Black Girls in US Public Secondary Schools* (Doctoral dissertation).

Noddings, N. (2002). *Educating moral people: A caring alternative to character education*. Teachers College Press.

Paris, D., & Winn, M. T. (Eds.). (2013). *Humanizing research: Decolonizing qualitative inquiry with youth and communities*. Sage Publications.

San Pedro, T., & Kinloch, V. (2017). Toward projects in humanization: Research on co-creating and sustaining dialogic relationships. *American Educational Research Journal*, 54(1_suppl), 373S–394S.

Shevalier, R., & McKenzie, B. A. (2012). Culturally responsive teaching as an ethics-and care-based approach to urban education. *Urban Education*, 47(6), 1086–1105.

Spradley, J. P. (2016). *Participant observation*. Waveland Press.

Swartz, S. (2011). "Going deep" and "giving back": Strategies for exceeding ethical expectations when researching amongst vulnerable youth. *Qualitative Research*, 11(1), 47–68.

Thomas, J. (2003). Musings on critical ethnography, meanings, and symbolic violence. *Expressions of ethnography: Novel approaches to qualitative methods*, 45–54.

Trueba, E. (1999). Critical ethnography and a Vygotskian pedagogy of hope: The empowerment of Mexican immigrant children. *International Journal of Qualitative Studies in Education*, 12(6), 591–614.

Tuck, E. (2009). Suspending damage: A letter to communities. *Harvard Educational Review*, 79(3), 409–28.

Vossoughi, S., & Zavala, M. (2020). The Interview as Pedagogical Encounter: Nurturing knowledge and relationships with youth. *Critical Youth Research in Education: Methodologies of Praxis and Care*.

Winn, M. T., & Ubiles, J. R. (2011). Worthy witnessing: Collaborative research in urban classrooms. In A. Ball & C. Tyson (Eds.), *Studying diversity in teacher education*. American Educational Research Association.

Winn, M. T. (2018). *Justice on both sides: Transforming education through restorative justice*. Harvard Education Press.

Chapter 2

Adler, P. A., & Adler, P. (1987). *Membership roles in field research* (Vol. 6). Sage.

Akom, A. A., Cammarota, J., & Ginwright, S. (2008). Youthtopias: Towards a new paradigm of critical youth studies. *Youth Media Reporter*, 2(4), 1–30.

Anderson, G. L. (1989). Critical ethnography in education: Origins, current status, and new directions. *Review of educational research*, 59(3), 249–70.

Baldridge, B. J. (2014). Relocating the deficit: Reimagining black youth in neoliberal times. *American Educational Research Journal*, 51(3), 440–72.

Ball, D.L. (2018). Just dreams and imperatives: The power of teaching in the struggle for public education. Presidential Address at 2018 American Educational Research Association Annual Meeting, New York, NY.

Beauboeuf-Lafontant, T. (1999). A movement against and beyond boundaries. *Teachers College Record*, 100(4), 702–23.

Behar, R. (1996). *The vulnerable observer: Anthropology that breaks your heart*. Beacon Press.

Calderón, D. (2016). Moving from damage-centered research through unsettling reflexivity. *Anthropology and Education Quarterly*, 47(1), 5–24.

Calderón, D., Bernal, D. D., Velez, V. N., Perez Huber, L., & Malagon, M. C. (2012). A Chicana feminist epistemology revisited: Cultivating ideas a generation later. *Harvard Educational Review*, 82(4), 513–39.

California Department of Education. (2018). Census enrollment by ethnicity: Selected years, 2017 through 2018. In EdData. Retrieved from http://www.ed-data.org/.

Cariaga, S. (2018). Towards self-recovery: Cultivating love with young women of color through pedagogies of bodymindspirit. *The Urban Review*, 51, 101–22.

Carspecken, P. F. (1996). *Critical ethnography in educational research: A theoretical and practical guide*. Psychology Press.

Cervantes-Soon, C. G. (2014). The U.S.-Mexico border-crossing Chicana researcher: Theory in the flesh and the politics of identity in critical ethnography. *Journal of Latino/Latin American Studies*, 6(2), 97–112.

Davis, N. (2017). *Hope in Those Places of Struggle: A Critical Exploration of Black Students' Agency in One Place-based and One African-centered Elementary School* (Doctoral dissertation).

Davis, N. R., Vossoughi, S., & Smith, J. F. (2020). Learning from below: A micro-ethnographic account of children's self-determination as sociopolitical and intellectual action. *Learning, Culture and Social Interaction*, 24, 100373.

Delgado, Bernal, D. (1998). Using a Chicana feminist epistemology in educational research. *Harvard Educational Review*, 68(4), 555–82.

Delgado, Bernal, D. (2020). Disrupting epistemological boundaries: Reflections on feminista methodological and pedagogical interventions. *Aztlan: A Journal of Chicano Studies*, 45(1), 155–169.

Delgado, Bernal, D., & Elenes, C. A. (2011). Chicana feminist theorizing: Methodologies, pedagogies, and practices. In R. Valencia (Ed.), *Chicano school failure and success: Past, present, future* (pp. 100–119). Routledge.

Denzin, N. K. (2003). Performing [Auto] ethnography politically. *The Review of Education, Pedagogy and Cultural Studies*, 25(3), 257–78.

Edwards, E., McArthur, S. A., & Russell-Owens, L. (2016). Relationships, being-ness, and voice: Exploring multiple dimensions of humanizing work with Black girls. *Equity & Excellence in Education*, 49(4), 428–39.

Emerson, R. M., Fretz, R. I., & Shaw, L.L. (2001). Participant observation and fieldnotes. In P. Atkinson, A. Coffey, S. Delamont, J. Lofland & L. Lofland (Eds.). *Handbook of ethnography*. Sage.

Emerson, R. M., Fretz, R. I., & Shaw, L. L. (2011). *Writing ethnographic fieldnotes*. University of Chicago Press.

Erickson, F. (1986). Qualitative methods in research on teaching. In M.C. Wittrock (Ed.), *Handbook of research on teaching* (3rd ed., pp. 119–61). New York: MacMillan.

Erickson, F. (2004). Demystifying data construction and analysis. *Anthropology & Education Quarterly*, 35(4), 486–93.

Fierros, C. O., & Delgado Bernal, D. (2016). Vamos a platicar: The contours of pláticas as Chicana Latina feminist methodology. *Chicana/Latina Studies*, 15(2), 98–121. https://thisbridgecalledcyberspace.net/FILES/3943.pdf.

Flores Carmona, J. (2014). Cutting out their tongues: Mujeres' testimonios and the Malintzin researcher. *Journal of Latino/Latin American Studies*, 6(2), 113–24.

Flores Carmona, J., Hamzeh, M., Bejarano, C., Hernandez Sanchez, M. E., & El Ashmawi, Y. P. (2018). Platicas~Testimonios: Practicing methodological borderlands for solidarity and resilience in academia. *Chicana/Latina Studies*, 18(1), 30–52.

Flores, A. I. (2016). *De Tal Palo Tal Astilla: Exploring Mexicana/Chicana mother-daughter pedagogies* [Unpublished doctoral dissertation]. Los Angeles: University of California.

Flores, J. (2016). *Caught up: Girls, surveillance, and wraparound incarceration*. University of California Press.

Garcia, N. M., & Mireles-Rios, R. (2019). "You were going to go to college": The role of Chicano fathers' involvement in Chicana daughters' college choice. *American Educational Research Journal*, 57(5), 2059–88.

Haro, B. N. (2020). *Unveiling the everyday school pushout factors of Latina students at Dolores Huerta High School: Social control, school discipline, and gender violence* [Unpublished doctoral dissertation]. University of California, Los Angeles.

Kusenbach, M. (2003). Street phenomenology: The go-along as ethnographic research tool. *Ethnography*, 4(3), 455–85.

Ladson-Billings, G. (2013). "Stakes is high": Educating new century students. *The Journal of Negro Education*, 82(2), 105–10.

Lawrence-Lightfood, S. (2005). Reflections on portraiture: A dialogue between art and science. *Qualitative Inquiry*, 11(3), 3–15.

Lichterman, P. (1998). What do movements mean? The value of participant-observation. *Qualitative Sociology*, 21(4), 401–18.

Madison, D. S. (2005). Introduction to critical ethnography: Theory and method. *Critical Ethnography: Method, Ethics & Performance*, 1–16.

Merriam, S. B. (2009). *Qualitative research: A guide to design and implementation*. John Wiley & Sons, Inc.

Morris, M. W. (2016). *Pushout: The criminalization of Black girls in schools*. The New Press.

Neal-Jackson, A. (2018). A meta-ethnographic review of the experiences of African American girls and young women in K–12 education. *Review of Educational Research*, 88(4), 508–46.

Neal-Jackson, A. (2018). *"They Don't Want to See Us Succeed": How Micro-Interactions Produce Problematic Identities for Black Girls in US Public Secondary Schools* (Doctoral dissertation).

Noddings, N. (2002). *Educating moral people: A caring alternative to character education*. Teachers College Press.

Nolan, K. (2011). *Police in the hallways: Discipline in an urban high school*. University of Minnesota Press.

Paris, D., & Winn, M. T. (Eds.). (2013). *Humanizing research: Decolonizing qualitative inquiry with youth and communities*. Sage Publications.

Prieto, L., & Villenas, S. (2012). Pedagogies from nepantla: Testimonio, Chicana/Latina feminisms and teacher education classrooms. *Equity and Excellence in Education*, 45(3), 411–29.

San Pedro, T., & Kinloch, V. (2017). Toward projects in humanization: Research on co-creating and sustaining dialogic relationships. *American Educational Research Journal*, 54(1_suppl), 373S–394S.

Shevalier, R., & McKenzie, B. A. (2012). Culturally responsive teaching as an ethics-and care-based approach to urban education. *Urban Education*, 47(6), 1086–1105.

Simmons, L. (2017). *The prison school: Educational inequality and school discipline in the Age of Mass Incarceration*. University of California Press.

Spradley, J. P. (2016). *Participant observation*. Waveland Press.

Swartz, S. (2011). "Going deep" and "giving back": Strategies for exceeding ethical expectations when researching amongst vulnerable youth. *Qualitative Research*, 11(1), 47–68.

Thomas, J. (2003). Musings on critical ethnography, meanings, and symbolic violence. *Expressions of ethnography: Novel approaches to qualitative methods*, 45–54.

Trueba, E. (1999). Critical ethnography and a Vygotskian pedagogy of hope: The empowerment of Mexican immigrant children. *International Journal of Qualitative Studies in Education*, 12(6), 591–614.

Tuck, E. (2009). Suspending damage: A letter to communities. *Harvard Educational Review*, 79(3), 409–28.

Vega, C. I. (2019). *Strolling and straddling academic boundaries: Chicana, Latina, and Indigenous motherscholars in the academy* [Unpublished doctoral dissertation]. University of California.

Vossoughi, S., & Zavala, M. (2020). The Interview as Pedagogical Encounter: Nurturing knowledge and relationships with youth. *Critical Youth Research in Education: Methodologies of Praxis and Care*.

Winn, M. T., & Ubiles, J. R. (2011). Worthy witnessing: Collaborative research in urban classrooms. In A. Ball & C. Tyson (Eds.), *Studying diversity in teacher education*. Washington, DC: American Educational Research Association.

Winn, M. T. (2018). *Justice on both sides: Transforming education through restorative justice*. Cambridge, MA: Harvard Education Press.

Chapter 3

Abma, T. A., Cook, T., Rämgård, M., Kleba, E., Harris, J., & Wallerstein, N. (2017). Social impact of participatory health research: Collaborative non-linear processes of knowledge mobilization. *Educational Action Research*, 25(4), 489–505.

Barad, K. (2007). *Meeting the universe halfway: Quantum physics and the entanglement of matter and meaning*. Duke University Press.

Boal, A. (1985). *Theatre of the oppressed*. Theatre Communications Group.

Cahill, C., Cerecer, D. A. Q., Rivarola, A. R. R., Zamudio, J. H., & Gutiérrez, L. A. (2019). "Caution, we have power": Resisting the 'school-to-sweatshop pipeline' through participatory artistic praxes and critical care. *Gender and Education*, 31(5), 576–89.

Call-Cummings, M. (2017). Establishing communicative validity: Discovering theory through practice. *Qualitative Inquiry*, 23(3), 192–200.

Call-Cummings, M., & Dennis, B. (2019). Participation as entangled self assertion. *Forum Qualitative Sozialforschung/Forum: Qualitative Social Research*, 20(2), 1–19.

Call-Cummings, M., Hauber-Özer, M., & Ross, K. (2019). Struggling with/against the unintentional reproduction of power structures in participatory research: Using reconstructive horizon analysis. *Action Research*, advance online publication.

Caraballo, L., & Soleimany, S. (2019). In the name of (pedagogical) love: A conceptual framework for transformative teaching grounded in critical youth research. *The Urban Review*, 51(1), 81–100.

Chambers, R. (2002). *Participatory workshops: A sourcebook of 21 ideas and activities*. Earthscan.

DeNicolo, C.P., Yu, M., Crowley, C.B., & Gabel, S.L. (2017). Reimagining critical care and problematizing sense of school belonging as a response to inequality for immigrants and children of immigrants. *Review of Research in Education*, 41(1), 500–30.

Dennis, B., Uttamchandani, S., Biery, S., & Blauvelt, A. (2019). LGBTQIA+ youth as multicultural educators. *Ethnography and Education*, 14(3), 360–76.

Fals-Borda, O., & Rahman, M.A. (1991). *Action and knowledge: Breaking the monopoly with participatory action-research*. Apex Press.

Fisher, M.T. (2007). *Writing in rhythm: Spoken word poetry in urban classrooms*. Teachers College Press.

Fox, M. (2019). Crossing under the highway: Youth-centered research as resistance to structural inequality. *International Journal of Qualitative Studies in Education*, 32(4), 347–61.

Freire, P. (1970). *Pedagogy of the oppressed*. Continuum.

Fuller, K. (2019). "That would be my red line": An analysis of headteachers' resistance of neoliberal education reforms. *Educational Review*, 71(1), 31–50.

Garnett, B. R., Smith, L. C., Kervick, C. T., Ballysingh, T. A., Moore, M., & Gonell, E. (2019). The emancipatory potential of transformative mixed methods designs: Informing youth participatory action research and restorative practices within a district-wide school transformation project. *International Journal of Research & Method in Education*, 42(3), 305–16.

Greene, S., Burke, K., & Mckenna, M. (2013). Forms of voice: Exploring the empowerment of youth at the intersection of art and action. *The Urban Review*, 45(3), 311–34.

Habermas, J. (1998). Remarks on legitimation through human rights. *Philosophy & Social Criticism*, 24(2-3), 157–71.

Habermas, J. (2003). *Truth and justification*. The MIT Press.

hooks, b. (1989). *Talking back: Thinking feminism, thinking black*. South End Press.

Jocson, K.M. (2008). *Youth poets: Empowering literacies in and out of the classroom*. Peter Lang Publishing.

Lather, Patti (2006). Paradigm proliferation as a good thing to think with: Teaching research in education as a wild profusion. *International Journal of Qualitative Studies in Education*, 19(1), 35–57.

Torre, M.E. (2009). Participatory action research and critical race theory: Fueling spaces for nos-otras to research. *The Urban Review*, 41(1), 106–20.

Tuck, E., & Del Vecchio, D. (2018). Representing refusals: Dilemmas in making photobased research with migrant youth. In K. Gallagher (Ed.) *The methodological dilemma revisited: Creative, critical, and collaborative approaches to qualitative research for a new era* (pp. 77–90). Routledge.

Wang, C., & Burris, M. A. (1997). Photovoice: Concept, methodology, and use for participatory needs assessment. *Health Education & Behavior*, 24(3), 369–87.

West, C. (2008). *Hope on a tightrope: Words and wisdom*. Hay House, Inc.

Chapter 4

Atkinson, P., & Hammersley, M. (1998). Ethnography and participant observation. *Strategies of qualitative inquiry* (pp. 248–61). Sage.

Brayboy, B. M., & Deyhle, D. (2000). Insider-outsider: Researchers in American Indian communities. *Theory into Practice*, 39(3), 163–9.

Creswell, J. W., & Poth, C. N. (2016). *Qualitative inquiry and research design: Choosing among five approaches*. Sage publications.

Dicks, B., Flewitt, R., Lancaster, L., & Pahl, K. (2011). Multimodality and ethnography: working at the intersection. *Qualitative Research* 11(3): 227–37.

Heath, S. B., & Street, B. V. (2008). *On ethnography: Approaches to language and literacy research. Language & literacy (NCRLL)*. Teachers College Press. 1234 Amsterdam Avenue, New York, NY 10027.

Laura, C. T. (2016). Intimate Inquiry: A love-based approach to qualitative research. *Critical Questions in Education*, 7(3), 215–31.

Noddings, N. (2002). *Educating moral people: A caring alternative to character education*. Teachers College Press.

Paris, D. (2011). "A friend who understand fully": Notes on humanizing research in a multiethnic youth community. *International Journal of Qualitative Studies in Education*, 24(2), 137–49.

Paris, D., & Winn, M. T. (Eds.). (2013). *Humanizing research: Decolonizing qualitative inquiry with youth and communities*. Sage Publications.

San Pedro, T. & Kinloch, V. (2017). Toward Projects in Humanization: Research on Co-Creating and Sustaining Dialogic Relationships. American Educational Research Journal. 54(1S). 373S–394S. doi: 10.3102/0002831216671210.

Vasudevan, L. M. (2016, April, 10). Small data, big moments: Bearing with-ness in community based research. In session Theorizing Our Lives in Critical Research

Practices: Exploring Trajectories, Relationships, and Agency Within the Social Contexts of Our Research. Presented at the Annual Meeting of the American Educational Research Association.

Vasudevan, V. (in press). *Designing their own curriculum: How youth co-constructed a dance team that opposed traditional student-school relationships.* Curriculum Inquiry.

Vossoughi, S., & Bevan, B. (2014). Making and tinkering: A review of the literature. National Research Council Committee on Out of School Time STEM, 67, 1–55.

Winn, M. T., & Ubiles, J. R. (2011). Worthy witnessing: Collaborative research in urban classrooms. In A. Ball & C. Tyson (Eds.), *Studying diversity in teacher education* (pp 293–306). Rowman & Littlefield.

Chapter 5

Abu-Lughod, L. (2008). Writing against culture. In Timothy Oakes and Patricia L. Price (Eds.), *The cultural geography reader* (pp. 62–71). Routledge.

Brown, N. E., & Young, L. (2015). Ratchet politics: Moving beyond Black women's bodies to indict institutions and structures. *Broadening the Contours in the Study of Black Politics: Political Development and Black Women.* National Political Science Review, 17(2), 45–56.

Brown, R. N. (2013). *Hear our truths: The creative potential of Black girlhood.* University of Illinois Press.

Christensen, P., & Prout, A. (2002). Working with ethical symmetry in social research with children. *Childhood*, 9(4), 477–97.

Cox, A. M. (2015). *Shapeshifters: Black girls and the choreography of citizenship.* Duke University Press.

Dyson, A. H. (1997). *Writing superheroes : Contemporary childhood, popular culture, and classroom literacy.* Teachers College Press.

Hale, J. E., & Bocknek, E. L. (2016). Applying a cultural prism to the study of play behavior of Black children. *Negro Educational Review*, 67(1–4), 77–105, 169.

Heath, S., Charles, V., Crow, G., & Wiles, R. (2007). Informed consent, gatekeepers and go-betweens: Negotiating consent in child and youth-orientated institutions. *British Educational Research Journal*, 33(3), 403–17.

hooks, b. (2004). *The will to change: men, masculinity, and love.* Washington Square Press.

hooks, b. (2006). *Outlaw culture: Resisting representations.* Routledge.

Kidd, K. (2002). Children's culture, children's studies, and the ethnographic imaginary. *Children's Literature Association Quarterly*, 27(3), 146–55.

Love, B. L. (2017). A ratchet lens: Black queer youth, agency, hip hop, and the Black ratchet imagination. *Educational Researcher*, 46(9), 539–47.

McClaurin, I. (2001). Theorizing a black feminist self in anthropology: Toward an autoethnographic approach. *Black feminist anthropology: Theory, politics, praxis, and poetics*, 49–76.

Merriam, S. B., Johnson-Bailey, J., Lee, M. Y., Kee, Y., Ntseane, G., & Muhamad, M. (2001). Power and positionality: Negotiating insider/outsider status within and across cultures. *International Journal of Lifelong Education*, 20(5), 405–16.

Quashie, K. (2012). *The sovereignty of quiet: Beyond resistance in Black culture.* Rutgers University Press.

Roberts, D. E. (1999). *Killing the black body: Race, reproduction, and the meaning of liberty.* Vintage.

Sakho, J. R. (2017). Black activist mothering: Teach me about what teaches you. *The Western Journal of Black Studies*, 41(1/2), 6–19.

Stallings, L.H. (2013). Hip Hop and the Black Ratchet Imagination. *Palimpsest: A Journal on Women, Gender, and the Black International*, 2(2), 135–9.

Willse, C. (2015). *The value of homelessness: Managing surplus life in the United States.* University of Minnesota Press.

Chapter 6

Carter, P. (2005). *Keepin' it real: School success beyond black and white.* Oxford University Press.

Clark-Ibanez, M. (2004). Framing the social world with photo-elicitation interviews. *American Behavioral Scientist*, 47(12), 1507–27.

Freire, P. (2014). Pedagogy of the oppressed. New York: Bloomsbury Publishing.

Gay, G. (2000). *Culturally responsive teaching: Theory, research and practice.* Teachers College Press.

Gay, G. (2010). *Culturally responsive teaching: Theory, research and practice.* Teachers College Press.

Gillborn, D. (2006). Critical race theory and education: Racism and anti-racism in educational theory and praxis. *Discourse (Abingdon, England)*, 27(1), 11–32.

Greenwood, D. A. (2008). A critical pedagogy of place: From gridlock to parallax. *Environmental Education Research*, 14(3), 336–48.

Harper, D. (2002). Talking about pictures: A case for photo elicitation. *Visual studies*, 17(1), 13–26.

Noddings, N. (2013). *Caring: A relational approach to ethics and moral education.* University of California Press.

Noguera, P. A. (2009). *The trouble with black boys and other reflections on race, equity, and the future of public education.* New York, NY: Jossey-Bass.

Oluo, I. (2019). *So you want to talk about race.* Hachette, UK.

Paris, D., & Winn, M. T. (Eds.). (2014). Humanizing research: Decolonizing qualitative inquiry with youth and communities. Sage.

Perry, P., & Shotwell, A. (2009). Relational understanding and white antiracist praxis. *Sociological Theory*, 27(1), 33–50.

Rolón-Dow, R. (2005). Critical care: A color (full) analysis of care narratives in the schooling experiences of Puerto Rican girls. *American Educational Research Journal*, 42(1), 77–111.

Sameshima, P. (2007). *Seeing red: A pedagogy of parallax: An epistolary bildungsroman on artful scholarly inquiry.* Cambria Press.

Solórzano, D.G., & Yosso, T.J. (2002). Critical race methodology: Counter-storytelling as an analytical framework for education research. *Qualitative Inquiry*, 8(1), 23–44.

Winn, M. T., & Ubiles, J. R. (2011). Worthy witnessing: Collaborative research in urban classrooms. In A. Ball & C. Tyson (Eds.), *Studying diversity in teacher education* (pp 293–306). Rowman & Littlefield.

Chapter 7

Annamma, S. A. (2018a). Mapping consequential geographies in the carceral state: Education journey mapping as a qualitative method with girls of color with dis/abilities. *Qualitative Inquiry*, 24(1), 20–34.

Boylorn, R. M., & Orbe, M. P. (2014). *Critical autoethnography: Intersecting cultural identities in everyday life*. Left Coast Press.

Deroo, M. R. (2018). *Pushing Past Perceptions: Critical Media Literacies of Transnational Immigrant Youth*. (Doctoral dissertation). Retrieved from ProQuest Digital Dissertations (Order No. 10839513)

Edwards, E., McArthur, S. A., & Russell-Owens, L. (2016). Relationships, being-ness, and voice: Exploring multiple dimensions of humanizing work with Black girls. *Equity & Excellence in Education*, 49(4), 428–39.

Harris Garad, B. K. (2017). *"We came together on the idea of being 'foreign'": Learning from the Educators of Immigrant and Refugee Youth* (Doctoral dissertation, The Ohio State University).

Hermann-Wilmarth, J. M., & Ryan, C. L. (2019). Reframing and reclaiming risk in queer literacy research. Research in the Teaching of English, 53(4), 390–3.

Kinloch, V. (2018). Necessary disruptions: Examining justice, engagement, and humanizing approaches to teaching and teacher education. *Teaching Works*.

Kinloch, V., & San Pedro, T. (2014). The space between listening and storying: Foundations for projects in humanization. In D. Paris, & M. T. Winn (Eds.), *Humanizing research: Decolonizing qualitative inquiry with youth and communities* (pp 21–42).

Paris, D. (2011). "A friend who understand fully": Notes on humanizing research in a multiethnic youth community. *International Journal of Qualitative Studies in Education*, 24(2), 137–49.

Paris, D., & Winn, M. T. (Eds.). (2013). *Humanizing research: Decolonizing qualitative inquiry with youth and communities*. Sage Publications.

Player, G. D. (2018). Unnormal sisterhood: Girls of color writing, reading, resisting, and being together. Unpublished dissertation, University of Pennsylvania.

San Pedro, T. J. (2013). *Understanding Youth Cultures, Stories, and Resistances in the Urban Southwest: Innovations and Implications of a Native American Literature Classroom*. Retrieved from ProQuest Dissertations (UMI 3558673).

San Pedro, T. (2018). Abby as ally: An argument for culturally disruptive pedagogy. *American Educational Research Journal*, 55(6), 1193–232.

San Pedro, T., & Kinloch, V. (2017). Toward projects in humanization: Research on co-creating and sustaining dialogic relationships. *American Educational Research Journal*, 54(1_suppl), 373S–394S.

Tobin, J., Hsueh, Y., & Karasawa, M. (2009). *Preschool in three cultures revisited: China, Japan, and the United States*. University of Chicago Press.

Wargo, J. M. (2017). "Every selfie tells a story … ": LGBTQ youth lifestreams and new media narratives as connective identity texts. *New Media & Society*, 19(4), 560–78.

Chapter 8

Abu-Lughod, L. (2002). Do muslim women really need saving? Anthropological reflections on cultural relativism and its others. *American Anthropologist*, 104(3), 783–90.

Abu-Lughod, L. (1990). Can there be a feminist ethnography. *Women and Performance*, 5(1), 111–19.

Asher, N. (2007). Made in the (Multicultural) U.S.A.: Unpacking tensions of race, culture, gender, and sexuality in education. *Educational Researcher*, 36(2), 65–73.

Banister, E., & Leadbeater, B. J. (2007). To stay or to leave?: How do mentoring groups support healthy dating relationships in high-risk girls? In B. J. R. Leadbeater & N. Way (Eds.), *Urban Girls Revisited: Building Strengths* (pp. 121–41). New York University Press.

Bettie, J. (2003). *Women without class: Girls, race, and identity*. Berkley and Los Angeles, CA: University of California Press.

Brooks, D. N. (2017). (Re) conceptualizing love: Moving towards a critical theory of love in education for social justice. *Journal of Critical Thought and Praxis*, 6 (3).

Collins, P. H. (1991). *Black feminist thought: Knowledge, consciousness, and the politics of empowerment*. Routledge.

Crenshaw, K. (1991). Mapping the margins: Intersectionality, identity politics, and violence against women of color. *Stanford Law Review*, 43(6), 1241–99.

Denner, J., & Guzman, B. L. (2006). Introduction: Latina girls transforming cultures, contexts, and selves. In J. Denner & B. L. Guzman (Eds.), *Latina girls: Voices of adolescent strength in the United States* (pp. 1–16). New York University Press.

Hansen, D. T. (2017). Bearing witness to teaching and teachers. *Journal of Curriculum Studies*, 49(1), 7–23.

hooks, b. (1990). *Yearning: Race, gender, and cultural politics*. Boston, MA: South End Press.

hooks, b. (2001). *All about love*. Harper Perennial.

hooks, b. (2002). *Communion: The female search for love*. Harper Perennial.

Laura, C. T. (2013). Intimate inquiry: Love as "data" in qualitative research. *Cultural Studies ↔ Critical Methodologies*, 13(4), 289–92.

Lewis, A. E., & Diamond, J. B. (2015). *Despite the best intentions: How racial inequality thrives in good schools*. Oxford University Press.

Nakkula, M. J., & Toshalis, E. (2006). *Understanding youth: Adolescent development for educators*. Harvard Education Press.

Pastor, J., McCormick, J., Fine, M., Andolsen, R., Friedman, N., Richardson, N., ... & Tavarez, M. (2007). Makin' homes: An urban girl thing. In B. J. R. Leadbeater & N. Way (Eds.), *Urban Girls Revisited: Building Strengths* (pp. 75–96). New York University Press.

Pipher, M. (1994). *Reviving ophelia: Saving the selves of adolescent girls*. The Berkley Publishing Group.

Rumbaut, R. G. (2004). Ages, life stages, and generational cohorts: Decomposing the immigrant first and second generations in the United States. *International Migration Review*, 38(3), 1160–205.

Stacey, J. (1988). Can there be a feminist ethnography? *Women's Studies International Forum*, 11(1), 21–7.

The state of hispanic girls. (1999). Washington, D.C.

Ward, J. V. (1996). Raising Resisters: The role of truth telling in the psychological development of African American Girls. In B. J. Ross Leadbeater & N. Way (Eds.), *Urban girls: Resisting stereotypes, creating identities* (pp. 85–99). New York University Press.

Wortham, S., Mortimer, K., & Allard, E. (2009). Mexicans as model minorities in the new latino diaspora. *Anthropology & Education Quarterly*, 40(4), 388–404.

Chapter 9

Antrop-González, R., & De Jesús, A. (2006). Toward a theory of "critical care" in urban small school reform: Examining structures and pedagogies of caring in two Latino community-based schools. *International Journal of Qualitative Studies in Education*, 19(4), 409–33.

Clonan-Roy, K., Gross, N., & Jacobs, C. (2020). Safe rebellious places: The value of informal spaces in schools to counter the emotional silencing of youth of color. *International Journal of Qualitative Studies in Education*, 34(4), 330–52.

Khan, S. R. (2011). *Privilege: The making of an adolescent elite at St. Paul's School*. Princeton University Press.

Luttrell, W. (2000). "Good enough" methods for ethnographic research. *Harvard Educational Review*, 70(4), 499–523.

Lynn, M., Bacon, J. N., Totten, T. L., & Jennings, M. (2010). Examining teachers' beliefs about African American male students in a low-performing high school in an African American school district. *Teachers College Record*, 112(1), 289–330.

McKamey, C. (2017). Learning and teaching to care for young people. *Child & Youth Services*, 38(3), 209–30.

McKenzie, K. B. (2009). Emotional abuse of students of color: The hidden inhumanity in our schools. *International Journal of Qualitative Studies in Education*, 22(2), 129–43.

Rickwood, D., Deane, F. P., Wilson, C. J., & Ciarrochi, J. (2005). Young people's help-seeking for mental health problems. *Australian E-Journal for the Advancement of Mental Health*, 4(3), 218–51.

Rolón-Dow, R. (2005). Critical care: A color (full) analysis of care narratives in the schooling experiences of Puerto Rican girls. *American Educational Research Journal*, 42(1), 77–111.

Valenzuela, A. (1999). *Subtractive schooling: U.S.-Mexican youth and the politics of caring*. State University of New York Press.

Warren, C. A., & Bonilla, C. (2018). Care and the influence of student-adult stakeholder interactions on young black men's college aspirations. *Multicultural Perspectives*, 20(1), 13–24.

Whitaker, A., Torres-Guillen, S., Morton, M., Jordan, H., Coyle, S., Mann, A., & Sun, W.-L. (2019). *Cops and No Counselors*. American Civil Liberties Union. https://www.aclu.org/issues/juvenile-justice/school-prison-pipeline/cops-and-no-counselors

Winkle-Wagner, R. (2017). Love in the field: Reflections on the role of emotion in qualitative data collection. In P. F. Carspecken, J. Clark, B. Dennis, A. Henze, P. Li, I. Skoggard, … & R. Winkle-Wagner (Eds.), *Love in the time of ethnography: Essays on connection as a focus and basis for research* (pp. 147–64). Lexington Books.

Zirkel, S., Bailey, F., Bathey, S., Hawley, R., Lewis, U., Long, D., Pollack, T., Roberts, Z., Stanback Stroud, R., & Winful, A. (2011). "Isn't that what 'those kids' need?" Urban schools and the master narrative of the "tough, urban principal." *Race Ethnicity and Education*, 14(2), 137–58. doi:10.1080/13613324.2010.519973.

Chapter 10

Algozzine, B., Morsink, C., & Algozzine, K. (1988). What's happening in self-contained classrooms? *Exceptional Children*, 55(3), 259–65.

Allan, J. (2006). Conversations across disability and difference: Teacher education seeking inclusion. In S. Danforth & S. Gabel (Eds.) *Vital questions facing disability studies in education, volume 2* (pp. 347–62). Peter Lang.

Annamma, S.A. (2018b). *The pedagogy of pathologization: Dis/abled girls of color in the school-prison nexus*. Routledge.

References

Biklen, D., & Burke, J. (2006). Presuming competence. *Equity & Excellence in Education*, 39, 166–75.

Bogdan, R., & Kugelmass, J. (1984). Case studies of mainstreaming: A symbolic interactionist approach to special schooling. In L. Barton & S. Tomlinson (Eds.), *Special education and social interests* (pp. 173–91). Routledge.

Causton-Theoharis, J., Theoharis, G., Orsati, F., & Cosier, M. (2011). Does self-contained special education deliver on its promises? A critical inquiry into research and practice. *Journal of Special Education Leadership*, 24(2), 61–78.

Connor, D. (2009). Breaking containment—the power of narrative knowing: Countering silences within traditional special education research. *International Journal of Inclusive Education*, 13(5), 449–70.

Craig, C. (2003). *Narrative inquiries of school reform: Storied lives, storied landscapes, storied metaphors*. Information Age Publishing.

Danforth, S., & Smith, T. J. (2005) *Engaging troubling students: A constructivist approach*. Corwin Press.

Davis, L. (2013). Constructing normalcy: The bell curve, the normal, and the invention of the disabled body in the nineteenth century. In L.J. Davis (Ed.) *The disability studies reader* (pp. 3–16). Routledge.

Dunn, L. (1968). Special education for the mildly retarded: Is much of it justifiable? *Exceptional Children*, 35, 5–22.

Erevelles, N. (2011). *Disability and difference in global contexts: Enabling a transformative body politic*. Palgrave Macmillan.

Ferguson, P. M., & Nusbaum, E. (2012). Disability studies: What is it and what difference does it make? *Research & Practice for Persons with Severe Disabilities*, 37(2), 70–80.

Gabel, S. (2005). Introduction: Disability studies in education. In S. Gabel (Ed.) *Disability studies in education: Readings in theory and method* (pp.1–20). Peter Lang.

Gilligan, C. (1982). *In a different voice: Psychological theory and women's development*. Harvard University Press.

Held, V. (2006). *The ethics of care: Personal, political, and global*. Oxford University Press.

Individuals with Disabilities Education Improvement Act, HR 1350, Pub. L. No. P.L. 108-446 (2004).

Kittay, E. F. (2019). *Learning from my daughter: The value and care of disabled minds*. Oxford University Press.

Kittay, E.F. (2005). At the margins of moral personhood. *Ethics* 116(1), 100–31.

Kliewer, C., Biklen, D., & Peterson, A.J. (2015). At the end of intellectual disability. *Harvard Educational Review*, 85(1), 1–28.

Noddings, N. (2003). *Caring: A feminine approach to ethics & moral education*. University of California Press.

Oliver, M., Sapey, B., & Thomas, P. (2012). *Social work with disabled people* (4th ed). Palgrave Macmillan.

Taylor, S. J. (2004). Caught in the continuum: A critical analysis of the principle of the least restrictive environment. *Research & Practice for Persons with Severe Disabilities*, 29(4), 218–30. (Reprinted from *The Journal of The Association for the Severely Handicapped*, 1988, 13(1), 41–53).

Tokunaga, T. (2016). 'We dominate the basement!': how Asian American girls construct a borderland community. *International Journal of Qualitative Studies in Education*, 29(9), 1086–99, DOI: 10.1080/09518398.2016.1201162.

Tronto, J.C. (1995). Care as a basis for radical political judgements. *Hypatia*, 10(2), 141–9.

Chapter 11

Arco-Tirado, J. L., Fernández-Martín, F. D., & Hernández-Moreno, N. (2018). Skills learning through a bilingual mentors program in higher education. *International Journal of Bilingual Education and Bilingualism*, 21(8), 1030–40.

Baldridge, B., Beck, N., Medina, J., & Reeves, M. (2017). Toward a new understanding of community-based education: The role of community-based educational spaces in disrupting inequality for minoritized youth. *Review of Research in Education*, 41(1), 381–402.

Camino, L. (2000). Youth-adult partnerships: Entering new territory in community work and research. *Applied Developmental Science*, 4(S1), 11–20.

Camino, L. (2005). Pitfalls and promising practices of youth-adult partnerships: An evaluator's reflections. *Journal of Community Psychology*, 33(1), 75–85.

Cridland-Hughes, S. (2015). Caring critical literacy: The most radical pedagogy you can offer your students. *English Journal*, 105(2), 129–32.

Espinet, I., Collins, B., & Ebe, A. (2018). "I'm a multilingual": Leveraging students' translanguaging practices to strengthen the school community. In A. M. Lazar & P. R. Schmidt (Eds.), *Schools of promise for bilingual students: Transforming literacies, learning, and lives* (pp. 118–33). Teachers College Press.

Gay, G. (2010). *Culturally responsive teaching: Theory, research and practice*. Teachers College Press.

Jones, K., & Perkins, D. (2004). Youth-adult partnerships. In C. B. Fisher & R. M. Lerner (Eds.), *Applied developmental science: An encyclopedia of research, policies, and programs* (pp. 1159–63). Sage.

Larson, R. W., Izenstark, D., Rodriguez, G., & Perry, S. C. (2016). The art of restraint: How experienced program leaders use their authority to support youth agency. *Journal of Research on Adolescence*, 26, 845–63.

Mitra, D. L. (2009). Collaborating with students: Building youth-adult partnerships in schools. *American Journal of Education*, 115, 407–36.

Mitra, D., Lewis, T., & Sanders, F. (2013). Architects, captains, and dreamers: Creating advisor roles that foster youth-adult partnerships. *Journal of Educational Change*, 14, 177–201.

Chapter 12

Achinstein, B., & Aguirre, J. (2008). Cultural match or culturally suspect: How new teachers of color negotiate sociocultural challenges in the classroom. *Teachers College Record*, 110(8), 1505–40.

Alcoff, L. (1991-1992, Winter). The problem of speaking for others. *Cultural Critique*, 20, 5–32.

Biesta, G., & Tedder, M. (2007). Agency and learning in the lifecourse: Towards an ecological perspective. *Studies in the Education of Adults*, 39(2), 132–49.

Biesta, G., Priestley, M., & Robinson, S. (2017). Talking about education: exploring the significance of teachers' talk for teacher agency. *Journal of Curriculum Studies*, 49(1), 38–54.

Bogdan, R., & Biklen, S. (2007). *Qualitative research for education: An introduction to theories and methods* (5th ed.). Allyn and Bacon.

Brayboy, B. M., & Deyhle, D. (2000). Insider-outsider: Researchers in American Indian communities. *Theory into Practice*, 39(3), 163–9.

Combahee River Collective. (2015). A Black feminist statement. In C. Moraga & G. Anzaldúa (Eds.), *This bridge called my back: Writings by radical women of color* (4th ed.) (pp. 210–18). SUNY Press.

Delgado, Bernal, D., Burciaga, R., & Flores, Carmona, J. (Eds.). (2012). Chicana/Latina testimonios: Methodologies, pedagogies, and political urgency. *Equity and Excellence in Education*, 45, 392–410.

Fine, M., & Weis, L. (1996). Writing the "wrongs" of fieldwork: Confronting our own research/writing dilemmas in urban ethnographies. *Qualitative Inquiry*, 2(3), 251–74.

Huber, L.P. (2009). Challenging racist nativist framing: Acknowledging the community cultural wealth of undocumented Chicana college students to reframe the immigration debate. *Harvard Educational Review*, 79(4), 704–29.

Kahn, P. (2016). Teaching in higher education as a collective endeavor. In B. Leibowitz, V. Bozalek & P. Kahn (Eds.), *Theorising learning to teach in higher education* (pp. 157–71). Taylor & Francis, Ltd.

Laletas, S., & Reupert, A. (2016). Exploring pre-service secondary teachers' understanding of care. *Teachers and Teaching: Theory and Practice*, 22(4), 485–503.

Lee, A. (2008). How are doctoral students supervised? Concepts of doctoral research supervision. *Studies in Higher Education*, 33(3), 267–81.

Mohanty, S.P. (2000). The epistemic status of cultural identity: On Beloved and the postcolonial condition. In P.M. Moya & M.R. Hames-García (Eds.), *Reclaiming identity: Realist theory and the predicament of postmodernism* (pp. 29–66). University of California Press.

Piepzna-Samarasinha, L.L. (2018). *Care work: Dreaming disability justice*. Arsenal Pulp Press.

Rothman, J. (1996). Reflexive dialogue as transformation. *Mediation Quarterly*, 13(4), 345–52.

Sawyer, R., & Norris, J. (2015). Duoethnography: A retrospective 10 years after. *International Review of Qualitative Research*, 8(1), 1–4.

Sedlacek, W. E., Benjamin, E., Schlosser, L. Z., & Sheu, H.-B. (2007). Mentoring in academia: Considerations for diverse populations. In T. D. Allen & L. T. Eby (Eds.), *The blackwell handbook of mentoring* (pp. 259–80). Blackwell Publishing Ltd.

Sellar, S. (2009). The responsible uncertainty of pedagogy. *Discourse: Studies in the Cultural Politics of Education*, 30(3), 347–60.

Sumara, D., & Davis, B. (1999). Interrupting heteronormativity: Toward a queer curriculum theory. *Curriculum Inquiry*, 29(2), 191–208.

Tuck, E., & Yang, K. W. (2012). Decolonization is not a metaphor. *Decolonization, Indigeneity, Education & Society*, 1(1), 1–40.

Velasquez, A., West, R. E., Graham, C., & Osguthorpe, R. (2013). Developing caring relationships in schools: A review of the research on caring and nurturing pedagogies. *Review of Education*, 1(2), 162–90.

Villenas, S. (1996). The colonizer/Colonized Chicana ethnographer: Identity, marginalization, and co-optation in the field. *Harvard Educational Review*, 66(4), 711–32.

Watson, W., Sealey-Ruiz, Y., & Jackson, I. (2014). Daring to care: the role of culturally relevant care in mentoring Black and Latino male high school students. *Race Ethnicity and Education*, 19(5), 980–1002.

Weidman, J. C., & Stein, E. L. (2003). Socialization of doctoral students to academic norms. *Research in Higher Education*, 44(6), 641–56.

Wilson, T., & Oberg, A. (2002). Side by side: Being in research autobiographically. *Educational Insights*, 7(2).

Chapter 13

Alder, N. (2002). Interpretations of the meaning of care: Creating caring relationships in urban middle school classrooms. *Urban education*, 37(2), 241–66.

Curzon-Hobson, A. (2002). A pedagogy of trust in higher education. *Teaching in Higher Education*, 7(3), 265–76.

Daley, K. (2015). The wrongs of protection: Balancing protection and participation in research with marginalized young people. *Journal of Sociology*, 51(2), 121–38.

Denzin, N. K., & Lincoln, Y. S. (2008). *The landscape of qualitative research*. Sage Publishing.

Docan-Morgan, T. (2011). "Everything changed": Relational turning point events in college-teacher student relationships from teachers' perspectives. *Journal of Communication Education*, 60(1), 25–50.

Fielding, M. (2004). Transformative approaches to student voice: Theoretical underpinnings, recalcitrant realities. *British Educational Research Journal*, 30(2), 295–311.

Froneman, K., Du Plessis, E., & Koen, M. P. (2016). Effective educator-student relationships in nursing education to strengthen nursing students' resilience. *Curationis*, 39(1), 1–9.

Garakani, T. (2014). Young people have a lot to say … with trust, time, and tools. The voices of youth in Nunavik. *Canadian Journal of Education*, 37(1), 233–57.

Glowacki-Dudka, M., Mullett, C., Griswold, W., Baize-Ward, A., Vetor-Suits, C., & Londt, S. C. (2018). Framing care for planners of education programs. *Adult Learning*, 29(2), 62–71.

Graham, A., Powell, M. A., & Taylor, N. (2015). Ethical research involving children: Encouraging reflexive engagement in research with children and young people. *Children & Society*, 29(5), 331–43.

Griffin, K. M., Lahman, M. E., & Opitz, M. F. (2016). Shoulder-to-shoulder research "with" children: Methodological and ethical considerations. *Journal of Early Childhood Research*, 14(1), 18–27.

Hawk, T. F., & Lyons, P. R. (2008). Please don't give up on me: When faculty fail to care. *Journal of Management Education*, 32(3), 316–38.

Hawk, T. F. (2017). Getting to know your students and an educational ethic of care. *Journal of Management Education*, 41(5), 669–86.

Hult, R. E. (1980). On pedagogical caring. *Educational Theory*, 29(3), 237–43.

Jardine, C. G., & James, A. (2012). Youth researching youth: Benefits, limitations, and ethical considerations within a participatory research process. *International Journal of Circumpolar Health*, 71, 1–9.

Karnieli-Miller, O., Strier, R., & Pessach, L. (2009). Power relations in qualitative research. *Qualitative Health Research*, 19(2), 279–89.

Kim, J. (2016). Youth involvement in participatory action research (PAR): Challenges and barriers. *Critical Social Work*, 17(1), 38–53.

Kral, M. J., Burkhardt, K. J., & Kidd, S. (2002). The new research agenda for a cultural psychology. *Canadian Psychology/Psychologie Canadienne*, 43(3), 154–62.

Krueger, P. (2010). It's not just a method! The epistemic and political work of young people's lifeworlds at the school-prison nexus. *Race, Ethnicity and Education*, 13(3), 383–408.

Kumsa, M. K., Chambon, A., Yan, M. C., & Maiter, S. (2015). Catching the shimmers of the social: From the limits of reflexivity to methodological creativity. *Qualitative Research*, 15(4), 419–36.

Leeson, C. (2014). Asking difficult questions: Exploring research methods with children on painful issues. *International Journal of Research and Method in Education*, 37(2), 206–22.

Mangual, Figuaroa, A. (2014). La carta de responsibilidad: The problem of departure (pp. 129–46). In D. Paris & M. T. Winn (Eds.), *Humanizing Research: Decolonizing Qualitative Inquiry with Youth and Communities*. Sage Publications.

Meloni, F., Vanthuyne, K., & Rousseau, C. (2015). Towards a relational ethics: Rethinking ethics, agency, and dependency in research with children and youth. *Anthropological Theory*, 15(1), 106–23.

Motta, S. C., & Bennett, A. (2018). Pedagogies of care, care-full epistemological practice and "other" caring subjectivities in enabling education. *Teaching in Higher Education*, 23(5), 631–46.

Noddings, N. (1984). *Caring: A feminine approach to ethics and moral education*. University of California Press.

Noddings, N. (1992). *The challenge to care in schools: An alternative approach to education*. Teachers College Press.

Noddings, N. (2010). Moral education and caring. *Theory and Research in Education*, 8(2), 145–51.

Noddings, N. (2012a). The caring relation in teaching. *Oxford Review of Education*, 38(6), 771–81.

Ruck-Simmons, M. (2006). Invisible violence and spiritual injury within post-secondary institutions: An anti-colonial interrogation and response. In G. J.S. Dei & A. Kempf (Eds.), *Anti-colonialism and education: The politics of resistance* (pp. 271–92). Sense Publishers.

Schelbe, L., Chanmugam, A., Moses, T., Saltzburg, S., Williams, L. R., & Letendre, J. (2015). Youth participation in qualitative research: Challenges and possibilities. *Qualitative Social Work*, 14(4), 504–21.

Starkey, H., Akar, B., & Jerome, L. (2014). Power, pedagogy, and participation: Ethics and pragmatics in research with young people. *Research in Comparative and International Education*, 9(4), 426–40.

Swanson, M. K. (1991). Empirical development of a middle range theory of caring. *Nursing Research*, 40(3), 161–5.

Swartz, S. (2011). "Going deep" and "giving back": Strategies for exceeding ethical expectations when researching amongst vulnerable youth. *Qualitative Research*, 11(1), 47–68.

Tilley, S. A., & Taylor, L. (2018). Qualitative methods and respectful praxis: Researching with youth. *The Qualitative Report*, 23(9), 2184–2204.

Walker, C., & Gleaves, A. (2016). Constructing the caring higher education teacher: A theoretical framework. *Teaching and Teacher Education*, 54, 66–76.

Chapter 14

Alder, N. (2002). Interpretations of the meaning of care: Creating caring relationships in urban middle school classrooms. *Urban education*, 37(2), 241–66.

Benneworth, P. (2013). *University engagement with socially excluded communities.* Springer.

Bringle, R. G., Clayton, P. H., & Price, M. F. (2009). Partnerships in service learning and civic engagement. *Partnerships: A Journal of Service Learning & Civic Engagement,* 1(1), 1–20.

Clayton, P. H., Bringle, R. G., Senor, B., Huq, J., & Morrison, M. (2010). Differentiating and assessing relationships in service-learning and civic engagement: Exploitative, transactional, or transformational. *Michigan Journal of Community Service Learning,* 16(2), 5–21.

Fontaine, S. J. (2006). Integrating community-based participatory research into the curriculum. *Journal of Higher Education Outreach and Engagement,* 11(2), 45–56.

Gelmon, S. B., Jordan, C., & Seifer, S. D. (2013). Community-engaged scholarship in the academy: An action agenda. *Change: The Magazine of Higher Learning,* 45(4), 58–66.

Goldstein, L. S. (1999). The relational zone: The role of caring relationships in the co-construction of mind. *American Educational Research Journal,* 36(3), 647–73.

Harkavy, I., & Hartley, M. (2009). University-school-community partnerships for youth development and democratic renewal. *New Directions for Youth Development,* 2009(122), 7–18.

Kim, M., & Schallert, D. L. (2011). Building caring relationships between a teacher and students in a teacher preparation program word-by-word, moment-by-moment. *Teaching and Teacher Education,* 27(7), 1059–67.

Lounsbury, M., & Pollack, S. (2001). Institutionalizing civic engagement: Shifting logics and the cultural repackaging of service-learning in US higher education. *Organization,* 8(2), 319–39.

Miller, P. M., & Hafner, M. M. (2008). Moving toward dialogical collaboration: A critical examination of a university—school—community Partnership. *Educational Administration Quarterly,* 44(1), 66–110.

Mohan, G. (2001). Beyond participation: Strategies for deeper empowerment. In B. Cooke & U. Kothari (Eds.), *Participation: The new tyranny?* (pp. 153–67). London & New York: Zed Books.

Nicol, C., Novakowski, J., Ghaleb, F., & Beairsto, S. (2010). Interweaving pedagogies of care and inquiry: Tensions, dilemmas and possibilities. *Studying Teacher Education,* 6(3), 235–44.

Noddings, N. (1984). *Caring: A feminine approach to ethics and moral education.* University of California Press.

Noddings, N. (2012). The language of care ethics. *Knowledge Quest,* 40(5), 52–7.

Noddings, N. (2013). *Caring: A relational approach to ethics and moral education.* University of California Press.

Strand, K., Marullo, S., Cutforth, N., Stoecker, R., & Donohue, P. (2003). *Community-based research and higher education.* Jossey-Bass.

Velasquez, A., West, R. E., Graham, C., & Osguthorpe, R. (2013). Developing caring relationships in schools: A review of the research on caring and nurturing pedagogies. *Review of Education,* 1(2), 162–90.

Chapter 15

Antrop-González, R., & De Jesús, A. (2006). Toward a theory of "critical care" in urban small school reform: Examining structures and pedagogies of caring in two Latino community-based schools. *International Journal of Qualitative Studies in Education*, 19(4), 409–33.

Ayala, J., Cammarota, J., Berta-Avila, M., Rivera, M., Rodriguez, L., & Torre, M.E. (Eds.). (2018). *Entre-Mundos: A Pedagogy for the Americas*. Peter Lang.

Collins, P. (1994). Shifting the center: Race, class, and feminist theorizing about motherhood. In E. N. Glenn, G. Chang, & L. N. Forcey (Eds.), *Mothering: Ideology, experience, and agency* (pp. 45–64). Routledge.

Crenshaw, K. (1989). Demarginalizing the intersection of race and sex: A black feminist critique of antidiscrimination doctrine, feminist theory and antiracist politics. *University of Chicago Legal Forum*, 1989(1), Article 8.

Drame, E.R., & Irby, D.J. (Eds.). (2016). *Black participatory research: Power, identity and the struggle for justice in education*. Palgrave Macmillan.

Fraser, N. (1995). From redistribution to recognition: Dilemmas of justice in a post-socialist age. *New Left Review*, July-August.

Futch, V., & Fine, M. (2014). Mapping as method: History and theoretical commitments. *Qualitative research in psychology*, 11(1), 42–59.

Ginwright, S., & Cammarota, J. (2002). New terrain in youth development: The promise of a social justice approach. *Social Justice*, 29(4 (90)), 82–95.

Gonzalez, N., Moll, L., & Amanti, C. (2009). *Funds of knowledge: Theorizing practices in households, communities and classrooms*. Taylor and Francis.

Mosley, D., Neville, H., Chavez-Dueñas, N., Adames, H., Lewis, J., & French, B. (2019). Radical hope in revolting times: Proposing a culturally relevant psychological framework. *Social Personality Psychology Compass*, 1–12.

Paris, D. (2012). Culturally sustaining pedagogy: A needed change in stance, terminology, and practice. *Educational researcher*, 41(3), 93–7.

Paris, J., Genishi, C., & Alim, H. (2017). *Culturally sustaining pedagogies*. Teachers College Press.

Torre, M. E., & Ayala, J. (2009). Envisioning PAR Entre-mundos. *Feminism and Psychology*, 19(3), 387–93.

Weis, L., & Fine, M. (2000). *Construction sites: excavating race, class and gender among urban youth*. Teachers College Press.

Zeller-Berkman, S., Legaspi-Cavin, M., Barreto, J., Tang, J., & Sandler, A. (2020). Better together: The promise, preconditions, and precautions of a youth-adult partnership approach to collaborative research. In G. Brion-Meisels, J.T. Fei & D.S. Vasudevan (Eds.), *At our best: Building youth-adult partnerships in out-of-school time settings* (pp. 159–78). Information Age Publishing.

Conclusion

Fine, M. (2018). *Just research in contentious times: Widening the methodological imagination*. Teachers College Press.

Index

academy, the 12, 49, 55, 144, 175, 179–80, 183, 227
   academic hierarchies 15, 36, 54, 160
   academic pressures 10, 12, 167, 227
adolescents 2, 31–44, 59–72, 89–102, 103–15, 119, 133–45, 147–58, 187, 190, 193–6
adult-youth relationships. *See* researcher participant relationships
affection 7, 91, 120, 134, 141
agency 4, 22, 24–6, 28–30, 45, 75, 77–8, 83, 86, 90, 106, 159–60, 165, 171, 175–6, 178, 180, 182, 211, 222
American schools
   caring and uncaring 3–4, 48
   sites of emotional abuse 4, 134
   students' sense of belonging 219, 222–3
   systemic inequities xviii, 2, 21, 27, 120, 211, 217, 224
anti-blackness 73–88
autonomy 4, 45, 107, 154

behavior 28, 74, 76, 90, 95, 128, 138, 140, 181, 188
bilingual education 108, 159, 161–5, 167–9, 219, 221. *See also* English language learners (ELLs)
Black boys 89–102, 133–45. *See also* Black children and youth
Black children and youth 19–30, 73–88, 89–102, 133–45
   Black joy 73–88
Black girls 19–30, 73–88, 103–15, 147–58. *See also* Black children and youth
Black Lives Matter movement xiii, 76, 105, 224
Black Ratchet Imagination (BRI) 13, 74–88. *See also* Love, Bettina
Brayboy, Brian 9, 60, 176

care-based research methodology, definition of 9–11
care and caring. *See also* ethic of care; ethics of care; pedagogy of care
   aesthetic caring 134
   authentic caring 8, 21, 35, 97, 134, 142–3
   care praxis 45, 55, 135
   caring as *being there* 3–4, 10, 12, 60, 62, 65–7, 71, 92, 106, 143, 169
   caring *for* 7, 9, 31, 43, 46, 48–55, 68, 71, 108–9, 134, 136, 142–4, 159–60, 164, 169, 175–6, 181, 222
   caring *with* 7, 12, 46, 48, 52–5, 141, 168
   caring *within* 7–8, 40, 61, 73–9, 135, 150–2, 184, 197, 199
   critical care 1–15, 211–24, 225–8 (*see also* ethnography, critical ethnography)
   culturally-responsive caring 14, 151–71 (*see also* culturally-responsive pedagogy)
   reciprocal caring 13, 70 (*see also* reciprocity)
   self-care 11, 77, 226
   transformational caring 46, 48–9
community-based participatory research (CBPR) 197–210
   practicums 197–201, 204, 208–9
consent, informed 6, 9, 143, 189
   ongoing consent 6, 9, 55, 78, 92, 104, 106, 108, 111–13, 143–4, 158, 169, 185, 187, 192–4, 200, 208
   parental consent 77–8
COVID-19 pandemic 211–12, 225
culturally-responsive pedagogy 224. *See also* care and caring; culturally-responsive caring
culture 5, 20, 25, 33, 62, 73, 75–7, 87, 134, 144, 161, 167, 202, 204–7, 216, 227

decolonization 32, 76, 87, 128, 190, 192–3, 226
dehumanizing practices xviii, 3, 8, 107, 121, 131, 147, 225
dialogic spiral 109
disability studies 14, 147, 150
    disability studies in education framework (DSE) 150–1
disabled youth 147–58
dissertation studies 2, 20–31, 59–71, 73–88, 89–102, 103–15, 119–31, 133–45, 147–58, 184, 194–5, 226
double dutch methodologies (DDM) 22. *See also* humanizing research

elementary school 22, 73–4, 77, 95, 162, 221
English language learners (ELLs) 14, 159, 161–4, 165–70
ethic of care 7–8, 45, 76, 86, 149, 197–8, 200
ethics of care 14, 31–2, 34–5, 38, 148–50
    Chicana/Latina Feminist theory 35–6 (*see also pláticas*)
    pedagogical relationships 7–8, 45
ethnography 21, 23, 31, 34, 62, 123, 129–31. *See also* fieldnotes; interviews; participant observation; photo elicitation; researcher participant relationships, play; social media
    critical ethnography 12, 20–2, 29, 31, 33–4, 41–2

fieldnotes 22–4, 29, 36, 62, 65, 85, 87, 89, 93, 95, 137–9, 142, 152, 163, 191. *See also* ethnography
field notebook 74

graduate school 1, 11–12, 61, 82, 112, 126, 128–9
graduate student researchers 14, 131, 175–85, 226
    moral and ethical commitments 175–8, 181–2, 184–5
    power dynamics 175–6, 178, 183–4

hallway conversations 66–71, 91, 93–4, 96, 99, 101–2, 134, 136–9, 221. *See also* ethnography

hanging out 1, 69–70, 137. *See also* ethnography
high school 5, 12, 14, 23, 31–2, 36, 46–7, 49–50, 52, 59–62, 64–6, 68–9, 103–5, 108, 112, 122, 133, 135, 142, 152, 161, 164, 179–80, 195, 203–7, 211–12, 214–24
honesty xvi, 5, 11, 39, 52, 120, 124, 129, 141, 176, 191
hooks, bell 55, 69, 87, 119–21, 123, 130
humanizing research 8, 19, 31, 38, 42–3, 60, 91, 103, 105–6, 110, 120, 128–9, 134. *See also* Paris, Django; Winn, Maisha

immigrants 1, 22, 33, 47, 104–6, 108, 159, 161, 211, 214–17, 221, 224–5
impression management 5, 53, 64
Indigenous children and youth 106. *See also* Native children and youth
interviews 7, 12, 22–3, 25, 27–9, 32–4, 41, 48–9, 51, 62, 81, 90, 96–7, 99, 105–6, 108, 135, 138, 142, 151–2, 162–3, 166, 168, 192, 196, 214, 216, 218–20, 223–4. *See also* ethnography
intimate inquiry 119–31, 133–4. *See also* Laura, Crystal

justice 7, 15, 19–23, 25, 27, 29, 37, 42, 45, 60–2, 91, 106–7, 120–1, 130–1, 159–62, 164, 166–9, 171, 183, 211, 216–17, 219, 221–2, 224
just inquiry 211–24

Kinloch, Valerie 8, 9, 19, 60, 70, 103–15, 120, 128. *See also* San Pedro, Timothy

Latina girls 31–44, 119–31, 159–71. *See also* Latinx children and youth
Latinx children and youth 31–44, 119–31, 159–71, 211–24
Laura, Crystal 8–9, 60–1, 70, 92, 120–2, 124, 126–30. *See also* intimate inquiry; love; witnessing
LGBTQ+ 47, 225
literacy/literacies 3, 61, 70

love 8–9, 13–14, 52, 60–1, 68–9, 73, 76, 79, 85–6, 105, 119–24, 126–31, 134, 177, 179–80, 184, 227. *See also* hooks, bell; Laura, Crystal
  and care 14, 60–1, 119–21, 123–4, 128–9, 131, 184
Love, Bettina 3, 75–6, 78, 80, 92, 120. *See also* Black Ratchet Imagination (BRI)

mandated reporting 122–3, 125–6, 128–9
meaning making 3, 20, 23, 30, 49, 110, 114
methodological guidance 29–30, 42–3, 55–6, 70–1, 86–7, 102, 113–15, 130–1, 143–4, 157–8, 169–71, 185–6, 195–6, 208–10, 223–4
middle school 11, 13, 15, 47, 64, 66, 69–70, 73–4, 81, 119, 127, 129, 196, 219–24
narratives 26, 75–7, 92, 97, 106–7, 114, 178, 219–20, 222–4
Native children and youth 191. *See also* Indigenous children and youth
neoliberalism 12, 45–6, 50, 52, 54–5, 224
Noddings, Nel 7, 9, 19, 21, 61, 92, 120, 134–5, 141, 149, 151, 188–9, 193, 197–9, 203, 207. *See also* ethic of care
nondominant communities 1–5, 89, 92, 102, 120, 225–6

parallax 91–5
Paris, Django 6, 8–9, 19, 21, 33, 38, 60, 91, 97, 103, 105–6, 108, 216. *See also* humanizing research
participant observation 20–4, 29–30, 33, 60, 108, 123–4, 151–2. *See also* ethnography
participatory research 45–56, 187–210, 211–24. *See also* community-based participatory research (CBPR); youth participatory action research (YPAR)
  participatory intergenerational research 214–23
pedagogy of care 187–96
photo elicitation 13, 90
pláticas 32–3, 36–42
play 73–4, 76–83, 87–8

positionality, researcher 4–6, 14–15, 29–30, 39, 63, 74, 78, 91–2, 101, 105, 108, 134–5, 175–6, 178, 181–2, 184, 192–4. *See also* reflexivity; researcher participant relationships
  former teacher 2, 22, 89–90, 114, 122, 165, 179–81
  identity differences 3, 5, 91–2, 101, 103–15
  insider-outsider 74, 177, 200
  least-adult identity 5
  shared positionality 3, 5, 29, 39, 91–2, 101, 177
positivist research 6, 129
power dynamics 7, 15, 27, 35, 37–8, 40, 42, 45–6, 48, 50, 52, 54, 108, 114, 120, 130, 135, 144, 169–71, 175–6, 183–4, 198, 200, 204
praxis 34–5, 42, 45–6, 48, 54–6, 86, 89, 91, 97, 135
projects in humanization 60, 107–8. *See also* humanizing research

qualitative research instruction 31–3, 187–96, 197–210. *See also* graduate school; graduate student researchers; teaching with care

racial uprisings 211. *See also* Black Lives Matter movement
  Floyd, George's killing 225
racism 3, 28, 37, 91, 101, 105, 120, 124, 179
reciprocity 11–13, 15, 33–4, 36, 50–2, 54, 73, 76, 129, 150–1, 184, 188, 198–200. *See also* researcher participant relationships
reflexivity 7, 9, 31–43, 55, 84, 152, 155, 188. *See also* positionality, researcher
research collectives 46–9, 52, 54, 211–12, 214–15, 218, 222, 224. *See also* youth participatory action research (YPAR)
research design 6, 9, 83, 108, 135, 148, 153, 158, 190, 205, 216, 226–7
researcher participant relationships. *See also* positionality, researcher; reciprocity

authentic researcher relationships 153, 157
disrupting traditional research paradigms 31–43, 59–72, 73–88, 103–15 (*see also* youth participatory action research (YPAR))
ethical considerations 6, 31–44, 119–31, 133–45
navigating multiple roles 5, 19–30, 31–44, 45–57, 59–72, 73–88, 89–102, 119–31, 133–45
sustained relationships 103–4, 111–13, 144–5
trusting relationships 60, 97, 160, 224
research teams 159–71, 175–86, 197–210, 211–24. *See also* community-based participatory research; graduate school; graduate student researchers; youth participatory action research (YPAR)
resistance xviii, 10, 45–6, 50, 55, 76, 85–6, 189
respect 9–10, 13–14, 23–6, 28–9, 45, 48, 55, 60, 65, 68, 75, 86, 91–3, 97, 101, 120, 123–4, 133, 136–7, 141, 176, 179, 188, 204–5, 209, 211, 219–20, 222–3, 227
disrespect 77–8, 94

San Pedro, Timothy 8, 9, 19, 60, 70, 103–15, 120, 128. *See also* Kinloch, Valerie
social media 2, 87, 104, 107–12, 114, 124, 135–6
student-led groups 59–71, 159–71

teaching with care 187–96, 197–210. *See also* pedagogy of care; qualitative research instruction
text messages 51, 145, 165
transparency 10, 13, 15, 49, 55, 180, 184, 191, 226

Ubiles, Joseph 8–9, 21, 68, 70, 92–3, 97

Valenzuela, Angela 3, 8, 35, 134–5
Vasudevan, Lalitha 15, 61
vulnerability 5, 9, 34, 36, 61, 75–6, 83, 87, 97–9, 189, 191
vulnerable students 4, 8–9, 65, 68, 77, 111, 119, 136, 147, 191, 194

Winn, Maisha 6, 8–9, 19, 21, 23, 33, 38, 60, 68, 70, 91–3, 97, 105, 108. *See also* humanizing research
witnessing 10, 12, 20, 60–1, 65–6, 70, 93–5, 121–30, 181–6. *See also* Laura, Crystal
affirmative witnessing 91–3

youth-adult partnerships (Y-APs) 159–71
youth-adult relationships. *See* researcher participant relationships
youth participatory action research (YPAR) 45–57, 211–24
care praxis 45–6
caring *for* each other 50–2
caring *with* a collective 52–4
co-researchers, caring of 49–50
just inquiry 211–12, 216–18, 223–4
youth researchers 51, 211, 214–21, 223. *See also* youth participatory action research (YPAR)

www.ingramcontent.com/pod-product-compliance
Lightning Source LLC
Chambersburg PA
CBHW052220300426
44115CB00011B/1761